THE SUPERNATURAL TRANSFORMATION SERIES

Volume III

The Heart Journey

The Believer's Guide to the Heart Revolution

PHIL MASON

The Heart Journey

Unless otherwise identified, all Scripture citations are from the NEW KING JAMES VERSION © 1982 Thomas Nelson inc. Used by permission.
Scripture quotations identified as (KJV) are taken from the Holy Bible, King James Version Public Domain
Scripture quotations marked (NIV) are taken from the Holy Bible, New International Version®, NIV®. Copyright © 1973, 1978, 1984 by Biblica, Inc.™ Used by permission of Zondervan. All rights reserved worldwide. www.zondervan.com
Scripture quotations marked (NLT) are taken from the Holy Bible, New Living Translation, copyright 1996. Used by permission of Tyndale House Publishers, Inc., Wheaton, Illinois 60189. All rights reserved.
Scripture quotations marked (NASB) taken from the New American Standard Bible®, Copyright © 1960, 1962, 1963, 1968, 1971, 1972, 1973, 1975, 1977, 1995 by The Lockman Foundation. Used by permission. www.Lockman.org
Scripture quotations marked (AMP) are taken from the Amplified® Bible, Copyright © 1954, 1958, 1962, 1964, 1965, 1987 by The Lockman Foundation Used by permission. www.Lockman.org
Scripture quotations identified (Moffatt) are from *The New Testament: A New Translation*, copyright © 1964 by James Moffatt, published by Harper & Row, Inc. Used by permission
Scripture quotations identified (J.B. Phillips) are from *The New Testament in Modern English,* translated by J. B. Phillips. © J. B. Phillips, 1958, 1960, 1972. Used by permission of Macmillan Publishing Co., Inc.
Scripture quotations identified as (MSG): Peterson, Eugene H. *The Message: The Bible in Contemporary Language.* Colorado Springs: NavPress, 2002, Used by permission All emphasis in Scripture quotations is the author's.
Scripture quotations marked TPT are taken from *Song of Songs* and *Letters from Heaven*: The Passion Translation Copyright © 2013. Used by permission of 5 Fold Media. LLC Syracuse NY 13039 United States of America. All rights reserved.

Cover Art; titled "Deep Waters" by Froyle Neideck. Froyle is a contemporary visual artist and Kingdom Pioneer of prophetic creativity. With 20 years professional experience, specializing in creating bold paintings of dramatic color and rich texture, she is well known for her cutting edge painting style that releases heaven through the arts. Froyle is the Creative Arts Pastor at Pour It Out Church on the Sunshine Coast, Australia, where her passion to see people walk in the fullness of God is amplified through this revival culture. Froyle is an artist and a speaker and has a powerful life message of releasing freedom and calling people into the destiny of who God has created them to be.

God wants to draw us ever closer to His heart. To be completely immersed in His presence until we are totally surrendered, in Him. 'Deep Waters' is an expression of this experience.

More paintings by Froyle Neideck can be viewed at froyleart.com

Quantum Ministries Ltd. Copyright Reserved 2018
PO Box 1627, Byron Bay, New South Wales
Australia 2481
philmason@tribebyronbay.com

The Supernatural Transformation Series

Volume I

The Knowledge of the Heart

An Introduction to the Heart Revolution

Volume II

The New Creation Miracle

The Foundation of the Heart Revolution

Volume III

The Heart Journey

The Believer's Guide to the Heart Revolution

Volume IV

The Glory of God and Supernatural Transformation

Spiritual Dynamics of the Heart revolution

About the Author

Phil Mason is married to Maria and together they have four adult children; three sons and a daughter. Phil and Maria are the spiritual directors of Tribe, Byron Bay; a spiritual community located in Byron Bay, Australia. The Tribe was pioneered by Phil and Maria in 1998. Phil and Maria are also the directors of Tribe Ministry School that is located in Byron Bay. The school equips and activates disciples of Christ in the supernatural kingdom ministry of Jesus. Phil completed his Bachelor of Theology degree at Flinders University in South Australia in 1991. In addition to training and equipping the local church, Phil and Maria travel widely throughout Australia and the nations under the banner of 'The Heart Revolution.' The Heart Revolution was birthed out of a deep passion to see the church find deeper wholeness through the healing and transformation of the heart. Their passion is to raise up a generation of mature sons and daughters who can be sent out as beloved sons, carrying the heart of the Father to the nations.

As the directors of Tribe, Byron Bay, Phil and Maria planted the church on the foundation of the Kingdom Ministry of Jesus and have sought to remain faithful to a divine mandate not to allow their church to drift away from the call to build lives collectively upon the foundation of genuine intimacy with God and with one another in community. The Tribe endeavors to be a community where everyone is committed to becoming a people of the heart. The principles and insights outlined in this book have been hammered out in the life of community. None of it is theory; it has all been comprehensively road-tested. Were it not for the 20+ years of experience in building a community of people who welcome the supernatural ministry of Jesus to the heart, Phil would not have authority to address the issues contained in this series of books.

Phil is also the director of 'Christocentric Light;' a ministry that takes teams into New Age festivals throughout Australia, releasing demonstrations of the supernatural ministry of Christ. They are now seeing thousands of miracles in the New Age marketplace. Phil is also the director of the Byron Bay Healing Room. To find out more about Phil and Maria and their ministry please visit the following websites;

www.tribebyronbay.com
www.tribeministryschool.com
www.heartrevolution.com.au
www.philmason.org
www.mariamason.org
www.tribestore.org

Contents

Acknowledgements

To my wonderful wife; Maria. You are such a great inspiration to me and you definitely play a crucial role in keeping me on my heart journey. I have learnt so much from you in the 30 years we have journeyed together. Thanks for your patience in the countless hours I have spent writing this series of books in the midst of what is already a hectic schedule of pastoring, lecturing and travelling. You have supported and encouraged me all the way to continue this journey of writing to leave a legacy of our ministry together. Thank you so much for your enduring love and prophetic wisdom. I love you!

To my four adult children; Simon, Peter, Phoebe and Toby. You guys are so amazing and I love you all so much. Without you in my life I never would have known what it means to be a father. Thanks for all the kind words you have spoken over me.

To my spiritual community; Tribe, Byron Bay. Wow! How did I end up being so blessed to be a part of such a crazy, creative bunch of wild worshippers who love the supernatural ministry of Christ? I love each and every one of you who make up this glorious community and thank you a million times over for your constant love, support and encouragement.

To Stephen and Mara Klemich. Thank you so much for all of the support and encouragement you have given in the writing of this series of books. We are so grateful to the Father for bringing you both into our lives and we are looking forward to the years of journeying together in the Kingdom of God. Thanks both of you for your generous endorsements. You're all heart!

To Ken and Linda Helser: You have both been a secret source of inspiration to Maria and I in our journey. You have such a rich spiritual legacy in your family and you exemplify a family who have fought to pursue the journey of the heart. Thanks Ken for all of your encouragement to write these books and thanks for a delightful foreword. Stay on that 18 inch journey!

Thanks also to Randy Clark, the father of the Toronto outpouring that has given rise to the Revival Alliance movement. Thanks for the very generous foreword to my book. Thanks to Wesley and Stacey Campbell. You are such kind-hearted friends. Thanks Stacey for the endorsement and those late night conversations! Thanks to Charles and Anne Stock; we love you guys so much and are grateful to you for all of your encouragement. Thanks also to Brian Simmons, Leif Hetland, Stephen and Mara Klemich and Fini De Gersigny for your very kind endorsements. Thanks to Ken Fish for proof reading the chapter on demonization. Thanks to my editorial team who have proof read my writings and for making great suggestions in how to improve these books. And finally, the biggest thanks and praise to Jesus. I hope this book glorifies you big time and advances Your kingdom by envisioning Your followers to get on board with the heart revolution. You deserve seven billion heartfelt worshippers!

Endorsements

The Heart Journey, the third volume in the Supernatural Transformation Series, is a gift to all spiritually hungry people who believe that the key to fruitfulness is the soil of the heart. After sharing a message of the heart to millions in 78 nations I finally have a blueprint that can multiply and train an army of lovers leading from their heart. Read it and let it read you. It will give you an upgrade to a love style that will transform your world! This is the gift you have been longing for. Receive it!

Leif Hetland
President - Global Mission Awareness
www.globalmissionawareness.com

Phil Mason is brilliant!! In this series of books on Supernatural Transformation, he gets to the heart of the matter. Relationships (with God and people) are all about the heart. If our hearts are wounded and jaded, every area of our lives are affected. But when we get to the deeper places of God's heart, we find freedom and healing for our own hearts. This series of books provides an exceptionally clear clarion call to experience change that is real and lasting, not superficial and transitory. I highly recommend them.

Stacey Campbell
Revival Now Ministries
Kelowna BC, Canada

Phil Mason lives and thinks outside the box! He does it with profound integrity in the context of family and creative community. The book you hold in your hand is many things. It's an antidote to superficial pop spirituality. It's a beacon on the journey to the heart of Reality. It's more a compass than a map, orienting you toward the depths of your own humanity and the Heart of the One who made all that is. If you are drawn to the mystery of authentic living; read on! Plunge into the joy of the Heart of God!

Charles Stock
Senior Pastor and River Guide
Life Center, Harrisburg,
Pennsylvania

What a journey it is to find Jesus Christ as our all and all. The Heart Journey will bring you face to face with the reality of the Healer, the Hope-Giver, the Happy God who brings us into completion and wholeness. Phil Mason has opened for us a treasure chest of understanding and revelation. I'm thankful to be his friend and to know his heart is all-out for God. You won't be disappointed as you read these life-lessons from a heart filled with passion. Read it, believe it, and pass it on!

Brian Simmons
The Passion Translation Project

Phil Mason is an Australian revivalist and an apostolic father. He has pioneered a supernatural healing community in Byron Bay and taken the gospel of power from coast to coast as his teams impact the New Age fairs with signs, wonders and miracles. This series of books will draw you into a deeper revelation of the finished work of the cross and your own supernatural role in the end time harvest.

Fini de Gersigny
Founder; Jubilee International Church

Sydney, Australia

'Speaking from the heart,' 'heartfelt,' the 'heart of the matter,' 'being bottled up' and many other familiar sayings are not just sayings any more. The realization that we need to develop people's hearts and character is upon us. We are seeing the church return to Jesus' ministry to the heart for the development and transformation of people, from the inside out. In our corporate consulting work, organizations have now adopted our 'Smart with Heart' leadership and development programs globally. Phil's books are a read and re-read series that will stretch, strengthen and lengthen your heart for bigger things.

Stephen Klemich
Founder of 'HeartStyles' and 'Achievement Concepts'
Sydney, Australia

Phil's series of books are a practical and biblically based exploration of Christ's ministry to the heart. Pursuing an understanding of the issues of the heart will bring you to a deeper intimacy with God. In seeking to recover the biblical knowledge and teaching on the heart, this series of books will lead you on a journey to reconciliation with the heart of God.

Mara Klemich Ph.D
Co-founder of 'HeartStyles' and Consulting
Psychologist Sydney, Australia

Foreword

By Dr. Randy Clark

Phil Mason's new four volume series, '**The Supernatural Transformation Series**,' boldly endeavors to deepen the work of revival and renewal in the church by taking us back to the foundational issue of the supernatural miracle of regeneration and by deepening our understanding of the experience of justification and sanctification as they relate to this miracle of regeneration. God has given us a brand new heart and this a supernatural act of heaven invading earth.

Volume I: '**The Knowledge of the Heart**,' is a strong biblical exploration of the importance the Bible places upon the heart. Phil gives us a thorough understanding of the meaning of 'heart' in the Bible and he calls the people of God to fully embrace the heart journey that Jesus intends each of His followers to recover. Jesus lives within what Phil identifies as the 'intimacy paradigm.' We are called to embrace this paradigm from the heart and allow it to revolutionize and transform our lives from the inside out. Intimacy is a journey of the heart.

Volume II: '**The New Creation Miracle**,' focuses upon the issue of conversion and the reality that God has performed the miracle of giving us a brand new heart. Phil notes, "The new creation is the cornerstone and foundation of all Paul's theology. If Paul could communicate just one thing to believers it would be the revelation of the new creation." Phil emphasizes that this new creation event is an actual new 'creation' of God; it is not just a theological fact but an experiential reality. It is a supernatural reality, not just an abstract theological reality. In fact, the new creation miracle is the focal point of heaven invading earth.

Phil engages deeply with the subject of the finished work of Christ in this book. He asserts that the distinction between the finished work in our spirit and the unfinished work in our soul is part of the subtext of the New Testament. Phil focuses on how this revelation explains the paradox that calls us sanctified, yet we must pursue sanctification; that we are cleansed but we must pursue cleansing. Phil's insights into the relationship between justification and sanctification are important in maintaining a clear biblical balance. The author also places a strong emphasis upon learning how to align ourselves with the fact of our co-crucifixion with Christ. Phil emphasizes that God cannot do this for us; that we must develop the art of coming into alignment with the finished work of regeneration through the weapon of our will.

Volume III: **'The Heart Journey'** focuses on the New Testament concept of 'entanglement.' Phil identifies seven major arenas of entanglement revealed in the New Testament: the entanglement of Satan's lies, the entanglement of sin and selfishness, the entanglement of the tree of knowledge of good and evil (meaning entanglement in the law; the mindset of external rules and regulations), the entanglement of worldly temptation, the entanglement of wounded and broken emotions, the entanglement of demonic infiltration, and the entanglement of physical biochemistry. This last sphere of entanglement explores the implications of living in a physical body that has been deeply corrupted by the fall.

Volume IV: **'The Glory of God and Supernatural Transformation,'** focuses upon the theme of deep level heart transformation explored through the lens of the ongoing supernatural Kingdom ministry of Jesus to the hearts of His people. This book places particular emphasis upon Jesus' ministry of healing the brokenhearted; a theme that has been greatly neglected by the church. In seeking to deepen our understanding of this ministry, Phil gives us five keys to healing the brokenhearted. These are; biblical revelation, the call to forgiveness and repentance, experiencing the glory of the Father's love, and discipleship. He follows up his emphasis upon healing the broken hearted with a similar emphasis upon the issue of demonization and the Christian and the biblical ministry of demolishing demonic strongholds. Phil explores the biblical relationship between brokenheartedness, demonization and the new creation.

Phil concludes the last book in his series by presenting a bold vision for the kind of supernatural freedom that Jesus intends to bring into the hearts of His people. He explores God's intention to bring many sons and daughters to glory and to fill our hearts with the glory of the Lord. This transformation from glory to glory can only be experienced as Christians receive the fullness of the Kingdom ministry of Jesus. Phil emphasizes that this deep level of heart transformation is entirely supernatural and predicated upon the church entering into the fullness of the charismatic paradigm so that we can receive all that God is seeking to pour out upon his Church. The glory of the Lord can only cover the earth as Christians are fully awakened to the supernatural ministry of Jesus and as they step into the fullness of the new creation miracle.

It is Phil's desire that this series of books will lay a strong theological foundation for training God's people in the nature of New Testament heart ministry; a supernatural ministry that calls the church to focus on deeply transforming the hearts of God's people, not just through an abstract 'positional righteousness,' but through the experiential gift of righteousness.

Not just through the experience of justification, but through the ongoing experience of the joy and freedom of sanctification. Phil also recaptures the emphasis of the early church which emphasized that the ministry of the Spirit; of being filled with the Spirit, is intended to be part of the regeneration experience.

I believe Phil Mason's new four volume series; 'The Supernatural Transformation Series,' is an important contribution to the present day theological discussion that is seeking to refocus our theology upon the Bible by letting it speak for itself; not allowing it to be interpreted through historical theological paradigms, whether they be Protestant, Roman Catholic, Orthodox, or even Pentecostal traditions. This is a read that will enlighten all of us. But more than that, it will challenge you to embrace the heart journey as you seek to live from the heart in pursuing a deeper intimacy in your relationship with God and with one another. It is time for a widespread heart revolution in the church!

Randy Clark
Global Awakening
Mechanicsburg, Pennsylvania
www.globalawakening.com

Foreword

By Ken Helser

It so happens that I was working on a book called '**Living from the Heart**' at the same time Phil was studying and putting together his early manuscripts on a book on the heart. He gave me a copy and while staying in their home I nearly did not sleep the entire night, not because of jet lag, but because I was so engrossed in his material.

I am thrilled that Phil is finally getting these messages published. Why? Because when I first announced I was working on a book about the heart, more pastors than I could count confronted me with this question: "What exactly do you mean by the heart?" They had no clue and were so confused, which got me digging. Digging deep: "Lord, what do You mean by the heart?"

Wow! That's about the same time I read Phil's material. He put it into words so simple that I got pumped and now I'm more pumped than ever! I could finally put in words what the 'heart' meant not just to me but to God! Yay Phil; thank you for digging out from the heart of God what He really means by the word 'heart!' May this series of books go all over the world, for the 'heart of the matter' is what matters most to God!

At our ministry, '*A Place for the Heart*,' we've run a school for years now called, 'The 18 Inch Journey.' It has wrecked the lives of young folks from all over the world, yet forever we are asked, "What do you mean by calling it an 18 inch journey." We always answer, "Oh, that's the distance between your head and your heart." Still, without careful digging and revelation, you cannot know what that means.

So, finally my good friend Phil Mason has poured not just his head but his whole heart into a series of books on the heart. I've read them and highly endorse him and his work, for every believer must make the '18 Inch Journey' in order to live from the Spirit and not the head... and if you are not American, that's called 'The 45.7 Centimeter Journey!'

A wise man once said, "You cannot give what you haven't got any more than you can come back from where you haven't been!" The reason I can read Phil Mason's messages on the heart and come alive from his revelation is not necessarily because he's brilliant, but because he's lived everything he's written. Nothing that Phil gives is second hand information, but the overflow of living from the heart of God! Read Phil's work and you too will understand that you are reading a man's heart who has encountered the very heart of God first hand!

Ken Helser Ministries
A Place for the Heart Sophia,
North Carolina, USA
www.aplacefortheheart.org

Introduction

Welcome to The Heart Journey; the third volume in the Supernatural Transformation series. What, you may ask, qualifies someone to write a book on the heart journey of the Christian? The answer is easy. In a single word: *failure*! Thomas Edison, the famous inventor of the light bulb fell short of his goal so many times that he lost count. He said, "I have not failed. I've just found 10,000 ways that won't work. Our greatest weakness lies in giving up. The most certain way to succeed is to try just one more time." In retrospect, Edison considered his failures to be "just as valuable to me as positive results. I can never find the thing that does the job best until I find the ones that don't."

And so it is with the heart journey. We all began the heart journey as failures but in the midst of discovering the 10,000 ways that didn't work we stumble upon the way that does and thus we take a step forward into new realms of freedom. Edison concluded, "There is always a better way!" Paul agreed, pointing to the way of love as the 'better way.' The way of love is the way of the heart. You have to admire the optimism of Thomas Edison. He said, "I am not discouraged, because every wrong attempt discarded is another step forward. Many of life's failures are people who did not realize how close they were to success when they gave up." And so it is with the heart journey. Paul repeatedly said, "We do not lose heart!" Edison echoed the tenacity of Paul who relentlessly pressed toward the goal of living a life of love from the heart.

Of course, writing a book like this can only flow out of a personal journey. I have failed far too many times to count but in my passion to keep on following Jesus I find myself getting up time and time again to come back to the tender voice of Jesus. I am daily confronted with the choice between hearing this Voice of love and hardening my heart or hearing the Voice of love and obeying from the heart. In many ways this book is the product of my personal interaction with the voice of Jesus. We all need to explore what Jesus is saying to His church in this hour? What is the Father saying to His sons and daughters? We are invited daily to rally around this tender Voice of love and to respond with all of our heart.

This third book in the series follows on the heels of the second book; *The New Creation Miracle*. It builds upon the foundation that I laid in that book so I recommend reading that book first in order to follow the concept of "line upon line; precept upon precept." I am convinced that God is seeking to transition His church into an entirely new paradigm of the heart that fully honors the glory of the new creation miracle but which also fully honors the challenging process of believers coming to terms with the sheer radicalism of the divine invitation to live from the heart in our relationship with God. As a pastor who interacts daily with believers I have come to the conclusion that none of us have done the heart journey brilliantly! In so many ways the heart journey of ever deepening intimacy with God and the supernatural transformation of the heart through grace represents the final frontier of human exploration.

Grace is heaven-invading-earth inside our hearts. Religion is earth trying to earn the blessing of heaven. Paul said, "The grace of God that brings salvation has appeared to all men!" (Titus 2:11) The outpouring of New Testament grace is something so foreign to the human heart and the way all of us as human beings have lived our lives independently of God. There are numerous complicating factors at work in the heart of every follower of Jesus that significantly hinder us from stepping into the grace paradigm and the fullness of our new creation identity. Part of the challenge is conceptual: God's "people are destroyed through a lack of [revelatory] knowledge." (Hosea 4:6) Another part of the problem is the active opposition of the evil one in continuing to blind the minds of believers to the reality of who they are in Christ and who Christ is in them. A further problem is the sheer popularity of narcissism, even within the church.

The grace paradigm deliberately makes allowance for the massive conceptual shifts to be systematically set in place within the heart as the building blocks upon which we build our new life in Christ. Our new life is built exclusively upon the foundation of revelation and faith. Even after believers have embraced these extreme conceptual shifts related to the new creation there is still a deep process of absorbing and applying these heavenly concepts and converting them into personal heart experience.

Such is the nature of the heart journey. God is so incredibly gracious with us as we come to terms with our heavenly calling and step into our new identity and our new life in Christ. As Jesus said, "The spirit indeed is willing but the flesh is weak." (Matthew 26:40)

A great battle rages around Christians embracing the radicalism of the grace paradigm and terrible confusion still abounds within the church. Paul said, "For if the trumpet makes an uncertain sound, who will prepare himself for battle?" (1 Corinthians 14:8) The prophetic call to the heart journey must become crystal clear so that we come to know exactly how God wants us to respond to what He is saying to our hearts. On the one hand, the Holy Spirit is relentlessly testifying prophetically to our regenerated human spirit that we are sons of God. Jesus is continually calling out the treasure of the new creation. But, on the other hand, God simultaneously addresses those heart issues that cause us to remain entangled in our old life. The Father disciplines every son whom He receives so that we enter into the fullness of life and holiness that is already the estate of our regenerated spirit.

It is imperative that we understand that both Jesus and the Father speak to two simultaneous realities in the heart of the New Testament believer. As we survey the New Testament it is evident that the Spirit of the Father speaks to our new identity of sonship but He also speaks to the issues of human brokenness, hardness of heart, stubbornness, sin and deception in the soul of the believer. All the rebukes, corrections and warnings spoken in the books of the New Testament are directed squarely toward born again believers who have experienced the miracle of the new birth. The very fact that the Spirit of God speaks directly to strongholds of residual selfishness indicates that these are still powerful realities that hold believers in bondage to the flesh and sometimes even to demonic power.

A survey of the writings of the Apostle Paul reveal that he also addressed two contiguous realities; the glory of the new creation revealed in the human spirit and the brokenness of the human condition revealed within the soul life of the believer. Paul never shrunk back from upholding the lofty ideal of our high calling in God as an attainable reality but he was pragmatic enough to spend most of his time dealing with the actual condition of the heart of believers who chose to persist in their selfishness.

As a case in point consider the following two passages of Paul's writings. The first is in Colossians. "For you died to this life, and your real life is hidden with Christ in God." (Colossians 3:3 NLT)

This is a true statement concerning the estate of our newly regenerated spirit because Paul recognized that our spirit is literally light years ahead of our unrenewed soul. But here is the mystery; in the next breath Paul could contrast the selflessness and sanctity of his favorite spiritual son, Timothy, who had radically taken a hold of Paul's gospel, with the rank self-centeredness of so many Christians in the very churches that Paul himself had pioneered; "I am hoping in the Lord Jesus to quickly send Timothy to you... For not even one do I have who is like-mined, one of such a character who would genuinely and with no secondary regard for himself be concerned about your circumstances. For one and all without exception are constantly seeking their own things, not the things of Christ Jesus." (Philippians 2:19-21 Wuest)

What is perhaps most alarming is that Paul was actually discussing leaders because he was contrasting Timothy with his other fellow workers in the gospel, such as Demas whose heart could not sustain the warfare that surrounded his high calling. To the Colossians Paul wrote, "Luke the beloved physician and Demas greet you." (Colossians 4:14) But later he regretfully informed Timothy that, "Demas has forsaken me, having loved this present world, and has departed for Thessalonica." (2 Timothy 4:10) But it got worse. In the next verses he says, "Only Luke is with me. At my first defense no one stood with me, but all forsook me. May it not be charged against them." (2 Timothy 4:11,16)

Remember; these are people in Paul's own churches who had sat under his glorious revelation of the new creation miracle! This is not a good report! Nevertheless, it was a pragmatic assessment of the rather ordinary condition of many first century believers who had failed to embrace the glory of Paul's revelation of the new creation. The Amplified Bible identifies this resistance as a persistent idolatry of self-deification. "So kill, deaden, deprive of power the evil desire lurking in your members: sexual vice, impurity, sensual appetites, unholy desires, and all greed and covetousness, for that is idolatry; the deifying of self instead of God!" (Colossians 3:5 AMP)

A stubbornly persistent narcissism was alive and well in Paul's own churches, rendering Paul's revelation of the glory of the new creation a tragically neglected paradigm, apparently as much in his own day as in our own. Paul urged his converts to take up their cross and to deny ungodliness, but it appears that more often than not, Christians in Paul's churches rejected the invitation to live the crucified life. He pointed to Jesus as our example: "He died for all, that those who live should live no longer for themselves but for Him who died for them and rose again." (2 Corinthians 5:15) Paul called this "the offense [or 'scandalon'] of the cross." (Galatians 5:11) The cross is the doorway to the glory of the new creation but it has to be intentionally embraced if we desire to enter into the fullness of life that Jesus came to bring us into.

The Gift of Spiritual Health

Learning to live from a radical new creation paradigm teaches us to embrace the incredible revelation that at the very core of our being we are now spiritually healthy people! Through the miracle of the new birth God has established an immovable stronghold of spiritual health in our innermost spirit that has been deeply immersed into the Holy Spirit. Apart from revelation we would never come to the realization that we are now healthy people taking a stand against the sickness of sin and emotional brokenness in our souls rather than being sick people in pursuit of spiritual health. In the Old Testament Jeremiah prophesied, "The heart is more deceitful than all else and is desperately sick; who can understand it?" (Jeremiah 17:9 NASB) This was a prophetic word delivered to the Old Testament people of God unmasking the depth of human brokenness. Their unregenerate human hearts were indeed desperately sick at the core. Their human spirit was still dead in trespasses and sins and they were in deep bondage to spiritual corruption.

But, in stark contrast, the heart of the New Testament believer is totally 'new' and it is a largely unexplored and undiscovered territory, which is why I personally think of it as a kind of 'final frontier.' God has established the beachhead of the new birth in our spirit and He has supernaturally carved out a sanctuary for Himself in the core of our being. He has established a stronghold of spiritual health, vitality and wellbeing at the center of our heart because we are in Christ. Our challenge is the wholeheartedly believe this and to learn to live out of this glorious reality of being a partaker in the divine nature of Christ. The health of our spirit flows out of the new creation miracle.

God has wrought a supernatural healing of the human spirit. Your spirit has already been comprehensively healed. We can now emphatically and truthfully say that we are healed as a present tense reality. Peter was explicitly addressing the disease of sin when he said, "He Himself bore our sins in His body on the tree, so that we might die to sin and live for righteousness; by His wounds you have been healed." (1 Peter 2:24 NIV) Another translation says, "By whose stripes you were healed." (NKJV) For born again believers, the new birth is a past tense event that has produced a new present tense reality of superabundant spiritual health and vitality at our core.

Peter was addressing the issue of sin. Many people quote this verse in reference to physical sickness but, strictly speaking, disciplined exegetes recognize that the context is actually addressing the healing of the sin condition at the core of our being. Peter affirmed Paul's revelation that our spirit is now gloriously alive because of the free gift of righteousness. (Romans 8:10) "Just as sin reigned in death, so also grace might reign through righteousness to bring eternal life through Jesus Christ our Lord." (Romans 5:21 NIV) God has supernaturally made your spirit righteous and this free gift has brought forth an explosion of new life at the core of your being. In that territory in the center of your heart you are 100% dead to sin and 100% alive to righteousness. Your spirit is no longer diseased by sin!

If our spirit has been healed and if we now have a stronghold of the supernatural life of God in our human spirit then we dishonor the work of God through the cross and the new birth if we still consider ourselves to be spiritually dead and desperately sick at our core. God wants to bring us to a place where we live in a state of constant celebration of the new creation miracle. He has indeed given us a new heart, a new nature and a whole new self, or identity to live from. We can now truthfully declare that we are healthy people who are taking a stand against sin and brokenness in our life. This is what it means to live from the new creation. Living from this new identity is the first major step on the journey of supernatural transformation. This is the breakthrough revelation many Christians need to jump-start and activate them in their supernatural heart journey.

This is the perspective that Paul fought from. He had already been made more than a conqueror through Christ. "In all these things we are more than conquerors through Him who loved us!" (Romans 8:37) "Thanks be to God, who gives us the victory through our Lord Jesus Christ." (1 Corinthians 15:57) Paul was persuaded that nothing could now separate him from the love of God in Christ. He sought to impart an entirely new vision of the heart of the believer. Working alongside the Holy Spirit, Paul relentlessly sought to unveil the miracle of the new birth so that Christians could learn how to fight from a position of strength and health so that they would experience profound supernatural change from the inside out.

The heart of the born-again Christian is now a curious mixture of things new and things old. There is not a single Christian who would deny that experientially there are still some major struggles going on inside their heart. In fact, the new birth sets in motion a new internal struggle with two diametrically opposing realities fighting for dominance. The fundamental shift that the revelation of the new birth brings is that now we approach the battle against sin, deception and emotional brokenness from an entirely different paradigm. Now we can take a stand against every enemy of the new creation from a perspective of health and victory, rather than from a perspective of defeat and sickness. This is the profound shift that the new creation miracle produces!

Paul understood that there was no other foundation for the Christian life. Without this revelation we would be left going around and around in circles for the rest of our lives. All those who are born again can now triumphantly declare that they are new creations in Christ. God has made us healthy at the core of our being and we are now seeking to activate and live from our born again spirit and allow that glorious spiritual health to permeate every part of our soul. This is the essence of the heart journey into the image of Christ and this is the new heart paradigm that God is seeking to establish in the church. God is bringing many sons to glory and we are all invited to the glorious heart journey of supernatural transformation.

The church needs a clear trumpet sound to rally us to the battle. We can only fight this battle with clear prophetic vision. If we are confused about the nature of the interior journey we will not gain the kind of supernatural traction necessary to engage in the process of being conformed to the image of the Son that God intends. "If the trumpet makes an uncertain sound, who will prepare himself for battle?" (1 Corinthians 14:8) My prayer is that this book will become that clear trumpet sound that will cut through all of the confusion and powerfully activate you to embrace with both hands and a whole heart your journey into the fullness of the glory of Christ so your life radiates the glory of the Lord to a lost and fallen world.

Phil Mason
Byron Bay, Australia
November, 2013

Chapter One

The Parable of the Human Heart

In Matthew 13 Jesus told a great parable to a large crowd about a farmer who sowed a bag of seed in a field. Little did that great multitude realize that this most famous of all of Jesus' parables, spoken by a man in a boat as the crowd gathered by the shore to listen, would eventually be heard by a couple of billion souls down through the corridors of time. The parable is simple but profound. It tells the tale of four different kinds of hearts and in broad-brush strokes it describes the various responses of the human heart to the message of the kingdom of heaven. The parable is famously known as the 'Parable of the Sower' but in truth it is really the 'Parable of the Human Heart' because the focal point is not the Sower Himself but the hearts that encounter this heavenly Voice. Jesus said,

> A farmer went out to plant some seed. As he scattered it across his field, some seeds fell on a footpath, and the birds came and ate them. Other seeds fell on shallow soil with underlying rock. The plants sprang up quickly, but they soon wilted beneath the hot sun and died because the roots had no nourishment in the shallow soil. Other seeds fell among thorns that shot up and choked out the tender blades. But some seeds fell on fertile soil and produced a crop that was thirty, sixty, and even a hundred times as much as had been planted. Anyone who is willing to hear should listen and understand! (Matthew 13:3-9 NLT)

This is one of only two parables that Jesus actually interpreted to His disciples in order to ensure they fully understood its significance. Immediately after this sermon by the shore of the sea, the disciples came to Jesus and inquired; "Why do you always tell stories when you talk to the people?" Jesus explained why He spoke in parables and then proceeded to use this particular parable of the four hearts to explain the deep spiritual truths embedded within the story. His detailed explanation served as an interpretive template for the disciples to explore all of His parables in order to mine the profound truths hidden within these simple stories. Jesus said,

> Now here is the explanation of the story I told about the farmer sowing grain: The seed that fell on the hard path represents those who hear the Good News about the Kingdom and don't understand it. Then the evil one comes and snatches the seed away from their **hearts**. The rocky soil represents those who hear the message and receive it with joy. But like young plants in such soil, their roots don't go very deep. At first they get along fine, but they wilt as soon as they have problems or are persecuted because they believe the Word. The thorny ground represents those who hear and accept the Good News, but all too quickly the message is crowded out by the cares of this life and the lure of wealth, so no crop is produced. The good soil represents the **hearts** of those who truly accept God's message and produce a huge harvest; thirty, sixty, or even a hundred times as much as had been planted. (Matthew 13:18-23 NLT)

The message of the kingdom is the gospel of Christ which offers the free gift of salvation to all who hear it and who believe. Peter likened the gospel message to a seed sown into hearts. "For you have been born again, not of perishable seed, but of imperishable, through the living and enduring word of God." (1 Peter 1:23 NIV) John similarly used the analogy of the Word of God as a seed sown into the heart. "No one who is born of God will continue to sin, because God's seed remains in him; he cannot go on sinning, because he has been born of God." (1 John 3:9 NIV) Heaven invades earth in the form of an inconspicuous little seed sown into a believing and responsive heart. Just as heaven discretely invaded earth in the cry of a tiny babe in a stable in Bethlehem, so heaven invades earth in the cry of a newborn spiritual babe who receives this glorious message from heaven. "Like *newborn babies*, crave pure spiritual milk, so that by it you may grow up in your salvation, now that you have tasted that the Lord is good." (1 Peter 2:2,3 NIV)

In another parable in Matthew 13 Jesus spoke of the potential of a tiny seed to spring into life and become a great tree that can become a safe nesting place for a multitude of birds. "The kingdom of heaven is like a mustard seed, which a man took and planted in his field. Though it is the smallest of all your seeds, yet when it grows, it is the largest of garden plants and becomes a tree, so that the birds of the air come and perch in its branches." (Matthew 13:31,32 NIV)

Pursuing the same theme Jesus immediately went on to liken this secret heavenly invasion to a small measure of yeast kneaded into a large lump of dough. "The kingdom of heaven is like yeast that a woman took and mixed into a large amount of flour until it worked all through the dough." (Matthew 13:33 NIV) As His audience understood, a tiny amount of yeast had the capacity to multiply and to thoroughly permeate a lump of dough to make it rise.

The point of all of these kingdom parables is that something as small and inconspicuous as a tiny seed or a minute measure of leaven has the potential, under the right circumstances, to go on to have a massive impact upon the person who receives the message of the kingdom. From little things, big things grow! In particular, the parable of the seed and the four kinds of hearts focuses our attention specifically upon the condition of the heart. That was the primary purpose of that parable. The idea was that whenever the seed is nurtured and adequately tended it can go on to produce anything between a 30 fold harvest all the way up to a 100 fold harvest.

The seed sown into the human heart is the message of the gospel. For those who mix this message with faith it produces the miracle of the new birth inside the heart. The seed of the new birth is sown within the soil of a human heart. So way down inside our heart of hearts we become a brand new creation. This miracle can occur with great fanfare or it can occur in the most discreet manner, to the extent that some people fail to pinpoint the exact moment the miracle occurred. From the perspective of heaven the gift of salvation is always met with great celebration. Jesus said, "There is joy in the presence of God's angels when even one sinner repents." (Luke 15:10 NLT) But here on earth the miracle can transpire without a single soul being aware of what has just happened in the realm of the Spirit. Whenever a soul is saved it resounds like thunder and lightning in the sight of the angels as heaven comes down to invade earth inside one more responsive heart.

The quality of this tiny seed sown into the human heart is beyond human comprehension. The regenerated human spirit is supernaturally baptized into, and joined to the Spirit of Christ. Christ now indwells every born again believer and His divine nature is miraculously imparted in seed form to our human spirit. Just like a natural seed, all of the attributes and defining characteristics of the mature plant are packaged within the DNA of a tiny seed. It is the same when a female human egg is joined to the male sperm; once that egg is fertilized the new life that emerges through the union of the male and female genes gives rise to an entirely new biological package where all of the attributes of that new life are already determined at the moment of conception. And so it is for those who have been born from above; we have the fullness of the nature of Christ united with our spirit so that from the very moment of the new birth we have been made partakers of the divine nature. (2 Peter 1:4) There is a special skillset required to learn how to activate and release the explosive content of the seed of the divine nature. As believers learn how to activate and live from their regenerated spirit they can potentially release the fullness of the resurrection power and nature of Jesus from within their innermost being through faith. The potential is absolutely limitless!

The seed of the new creation miracle is sown into the heart. The condition of each individual heart is as varied as the number of souls who have experienced the miracle. Everyone has their own story to tell; their own journey of brokenness and the misery that has accompanied the fall of humanity into the depths of sin and depravity. Some have strongholds of religious deception, some have strongholds of unbelief and some have strongholds of unimaginable sexual brokenness whilst others have walls of pride as formidable as the Great Wall of China. The combinations and permutations of emotional brokenness and strongholds of sin are endless. The heart of the average sinner who enters the kingdom at the moment of their conversion is still a veritable disaster area that will require a lifelong journey to restore. To draw from a crude Pauline metaphor, the pearl of salvation is deposited into a garden full of excrement. (Philippians 3:8)

Four Kinds of Hearts

Jesus taught that the seed of heaven invades the earth in a heart that is in deep trouble. The heart is the soil and the soil inevitably has its own set of distinct problems. In the first instance, "the evil one comes and snatches the seed away from their hearts." They hear the message of heavenly glory but their hearts are so hard they resemble a stony path that has been compressed by a steamroller for twenty years. The wonderful seed from heaven simply cannot penetrate a heart of stone. The birds of the air can readily snatch away this message so that it becomes nothing more than one voice in a crowded and noisy marketplace.

In the second instance the person hears the message and joyfully receives the good news resulting in the new birth. "The rocky soil represents those who hear the message and receive it with joy. But like young plants in such soil, their roots don't go very deep. At first they get along fine, but they wilt as soon as they have problems or are persecuted because they believe the Word." This second generic heart condition that Jesus described was a mixture of arable soil with a substratum of rock. There is potential for the seed to germinate and take root but the rockiness of the soil mitigates against any productivity from this kind of soil. However, in the explanation of the parable Jesus indicated that this person who heard the message received it with joy. The inbreaking of the kingdom always produces joy!

It is not as though this person didn't believe the gospel. In fact Jesus makes it clear that this person did in fact 'believe the Word.' There was a measure of faith in the equation. How many people have heard the gospel message, been swept along with the emotion of the crowd and responded initially in faith. Yet six months later, where are they? Are they in a church with hands raised praising and worshipping God? Or are they in the workplace telling their friends the story about the day they went along to church but couldn't assimilate into such a foreign culture. As soon as his friends heard he had found religion they began to mock him and the next thing he knew his back was turned on his newfound faith because he couldn't endure the rejection of his community of worldly friends. How many times has this tragedy unfolded on planet earth?

Whenever a person doesn't continue in the faith the good seed that was once sown into the heart becomes so neglected that there is no place for it anymore. They have fallen away from the faith. Jesus doesn't unpack the thorny theological question of the forfeiture of the gift of salvation in this parable but He does describe a scenario that is all too common amongst those who initially receive the gospel message with great joy. But there is an imperative to continue in the faith. After their first missionary journey Paul and Barnabas found it necessary on their homeward journey to encourage the hearts of their new converts "to continue in the faith, reminding them that they must enter into the Kingdom of God through many tribulations." (Acts 14:22 NLT) The pressures and adversities of persecution, family rejection and outright ridicule are so great that the temptation to abandon the faith sometimes reaches fever pitch. Paul says to new believers; "You must continue to believe this truth and stand in it firmly. Don't drift away from the assurance you received when you heard the Good News." (Colossians 1:23 NLT)

In the parable of the four hearts Jesus describes a condition of the human heart that is ultimately not conducive to a deepening and abiding faith. "The plants sprang up quickly, but they soon wilted beneath the hot sun and died because the roots had no nourishment in the shallow soil." A Calvinist is not going to be comfortable with the theological implications of this parable because they are committed to the idea that once saved, always saved. But there is compelling evidence throughout the New Testament that there is an exit clause from the contract. The rejection of faith (which resulted in this person returning to the world) simply means that the new birth didn't stick. Paul indicated in his discussion of Gentiles bring grafted into the olive tree and Jews being cut off from the olive tree that the issue centers around continuing in a condition of faith.

> Because of unbelief they were broken off, and you stand by faith. Do not be haughty, but fear. For if God did not spare the natural branches, He may not spare you either. Therefore, consider the goodness and severity of God: on those who fell, severity; but toward you, goodness, if you continue in His goodness. Otherwise you also will be cut off. And they also, if they do not continue in unbelief, will be grafted in, for God is able to graft them in again. (Romans 11:20-23)

Jesus described a third heart condition in the parable we are exploring. "Other seeds fell among thorns that shot up and choked out the tender blades." His explanation of this heart condition reveals that the seduction of the world lures new and immature believers back into a lifestyle that results in unfruitfulness. "The thorny ground represents those who hear and accept the Good News, but all too quickly the message is crowded out by the cares of this life and the lure of wealth, so no crop is produced." Nowhere in this description of a person with this kind of heart is there a suggestion that the person turns away from the faith. The primary issue in focus is the lack of fruitfulness. There is no crop because this person failed to nurture the seed in a way that would produce a harvest.

This new plant begins to flourish but is eventually crowded out by other weeds growing in the heart alongside the delicate plant of the new creation. The gardener neglected to pull out the weeds, (the thorns and the thistles that were growing in the heart) which were threatening to choke out the new plant. Although the life of this young plant wasn't completely destroyed so that it withered and died (like the person described by Jesus in the previous illustration), nevertheless this new plant was profoundly stunted and depleted through a state of neglect. Jesus identified two giant weeds that choked this new plant: the 'cares of this life' and the 'lure of wealth.' These are themes of worldly seduction that followers of Jesus are warned against in other places in the New Testament. These perils and pitfalls in the life of the Christian have the potential to choke out any kingdom fruitfulness in our heart. How many born again believers fall into this category? Regrettably, it is all too often the exception rather than the rule that a Christian goes on to produce a life of extraordinary kingdom fruitfulness.

The final condition of the heart described by Jesus in this parable is a heart that intentionally nurtures and cultivates the miracle of the new creation. "Some seeds fell on fertile soil and produced a crop that was thirty, sixty, and even a hundred times as much as had been planted." Clearly the purpose of contrasting this final heart condition with the three previous unfruitful hearts was to highlight the absolute necessity of creating a rich and fertile environment that would result in extreme kingdom fruitfulness. Whenever the seed of the kingdom is sown into a soil culture that is deliberately tended and cultivated to ensure maximum fruitfulness we can be certain that the seed of the new creation can grow up to full maturity.

Kingdom fruitfulness looks like the leaven of heaven leavening the entire lump of dough so that no part of the dough remains unleavened by these powerful new creation realities. Kingdom fruitfulness looks like the smallest of seeds growing up into a great tree that benefits a multitude of birds seeking safety and shelter. Kingdom fruitfulness looks like a garden with the best soil in all the land that has the potential of producing one hundred fold fruitfulness. One good seed can replicate itself well over a hundred times to produce a harvest of other lives that are similarly fruitful for the kingdom. This is the power and the glory of the new creation seed that is sown into a heart that values the seed and works with God throughout our entire life to produce a bumper harvest.

The focal point of the parable of the four hearts is the reality that this glorious seed is sown into a heart culture that has its own internal ecosystem. Each individual seed is sown into a unique personal context and the condition of people's hearts is as variable as there are people on the earth. The heart journey of the born-again believer is absolutely crucial. The new creation miracle is an explosive reality but it fails to detonate in a heart that doesn't prioritize its wellbeing. We are exhorted in the book of Proverbs to, "Keep our heart with all diligence for out of it spring the issues of life." (Proverbs 4:23) How many millions of hearts have received this precious seed but the recipient of the gift hasn't "kept their heart" by embracing the responsibility of the journey. "A little extra sleep, a little more slumber, a little folding of the hands to rest: and poverty will pounce on you like a bandit; scarcity will attack you like an armed robber!" (Proverbs 6:10,11 NLT)

The heart journey is a daily walk with Jesus in which we continually maintain and calibrate our heart each day so that we continue to seek the Lord and fix our eyes on Jesus. If we embrace the journey we will tend the garden of our heart by daily pulling out the weeds that have the potential to choke the good seed. We will water the garden with the presence of the glory of Jesus accessed through a lifestyle of worship and prayer and we will enrich the soil with a daily intake of God's word. We are responsible for the maintenance of the garden of our heart. God cannot do this for you! Nobody other than you can do this. Embracing the responsibility of a deep heart journey with God is the prerequisite for new creation fruitfulness.

The Mystery of Spiritual Growth

Every day the Father disciplines and trains us to walk in ever deepening intimacy with Him. He prunes the branches that hinder our fruitfulness by speaking to the issues of the heart that have the potential to choke the good seed of the new creation miracle. Spiritual growth springs up spontaneously as long as we embrace the call to the heart journey. Jesus told another parable about spiritual growth. The purpose of this parable was to highlight the reality that growth occurs in our lives as long as we meet the right conditions.

> The kingdom of God is like a man who casts seed upon the soil; and he goes to bed at night and gets up by day, and the seed sprouts and grows; how, he himself does not know. The soil produces crops by itself; first the blade, then the head, then the mature grain in the head. But when the crop permits, he immediately puts in the sickle, because the harvest has come. (Mark 4:26-29 NASB)

This parable unveils the mystery of spiritual growth. The farmer goes to bed at night after sowing the seed. He gets up in the morning and sees no evidence of growth. A week passes and there is still no evidence of growth. After ten days he finally sees the seedling beginning to germinate and spring up from the ground. Another few weeks pass by and he notices that the seedling is beginning to flourish. If he were to inspect the plant daily he might not discern any substantial growth. But if he were to travel away for a month he would come home to his farm and see significant growth. The same is true in our personal lives. If we monitor our heart introspectively, we fail to discern growth on a daily basis.

But if we wholeheartedly embrace our responsibility to walk out the heart journey as a daily recalibration of the soul so that we are doing all that the Lord requires of us on a daily basis, we see growth; not necessarily as a daily phenomenon but definitely in terms of the seasons of the soul. Each day we are in spiritual training, working out in the spiritual gymnasium, letting the Father love us and heal our hearts, listening to the Father as He speaks to us about what it looks like to walk in love, pulling out the little weeds of bitterness and judgmentalism as they spring up, dealing with the ungodly attitudes and motives in the hidden recesses of the heart and cleansing ourselves of the residue of wickedness that lingers from our old life.

As we keep our heart with all diligence we look back over the previous month and we see that our spiritual growth is now measurable because we have done the hard yards of a daily calibration of the heart. The purpose of this parable, which is recorded only in the gospel of Mark, is to encourage our hearts with the fact that although growth is never measured in terms of days it is definitely measurable in terms of seasons. In the life cycle of a corn plant, the end of the season of being established is followed by the season of the blossoming of the fruit. "First the blade, then the head, then the mature grain in the head." At the end of the season of the maturation of the fruit comes the season of harvest. There is a seasonal rhythm in agricultural life that echoes the seasons of our personal spiritual growth and advancement.

Our responsibility is to embrace this daily heart journey and walk with the Lord in a way that ensures that we are on a healing journey, ever moving forward in the direction of health and wholeness, never going backwards, encountering the love, the power and the glory of the Lord as we worship Him and cultivating an authentic intimacy as we deliberately keep religious pretense out of our hearts. This is what it means to break up the fallow ground of our hearts and to till the soil and cultivate the garden of the heart in a way that ensures supernatural transformation. We create the ecosystem for growth and God makes sure that the growth becomes measurable.

As Jesus taught in the parable of the four hearts, the journey begins with the miracle of the new creation deposited into our heart in seed form. As we discover that God has given us a brand new heart we begin the journey of nurturing that beautiful seed by intentionally building a heart ecosystem that gives the seed of the new creation every opportunity for maximum growth. As we embrace the heart journey we learn how to work in cooperation with the Spirit in allowing that seed to become a healthy fully developed plant so that it becomes apparent to everyone who meets us that the glory of the Lord is beginning to rise in our hearts.

This unique but extremely important parable of Jesus creates a canvas that unveils two distinct dimensions of spiritual growth. We could adopt the language of micro-heart management and macro-heart transformation. Micromanagement speaks of the imperative to recalibrate the secret life of the soul as a daily discipline, which results in transformation on a macroscopic scale. Recognizing that spiritual growth is measured in the macro scale over seasons removes the sense of anxiety that so many Christians experience when they hear the language of supernatural transformation. Our primary responsibility before God is to do the micromanagement of the daily gardening of the soul. His responsibility is to bring about the supernatural transformation that comes through the seasons of the soul. This is the glory of Jesus' parable of spiritual growth.

The language of the New Testament proclaims the supernatural formation of Christ inside of us. Paul said, "My dear children, for whom I am again in the pains of childbirth until Christ is formed in you." (Galatians 4:19 NIV) It is interesting that Paul employed the metaphor of 'travailing in childbirth' because the Greek word for 'seed' is '*sperma*.' Just as Mary carried the seed of the Messiah in her womb, so we carry the seed of Christ in our hearts through the new creation. James called this seed the 'implanted' word. "Therefore, putting aside all filthiness and all that remains of wickedness, in humility receive the word implanted, which is able to save your souls." (James 1:21 NASB) The Greek word for '*implanted*' is '*emphutos*' which actually describes something with 'germinates or sprouts' inside of us because the Word has been implanted within our hearts.

Just as this implanted seed came to maturity in Mary's womb producing the person of Jesus, so the implanted seed of Christ in our hearts through the new birth is intended by God to bring forth the measure of the stature of the fullness of Christ in our lives. As we walk out the heart journey of supernatural transformation we are systematically conformed to the image of Christ and, in the words of Peter, Christ literally rises in our hearts.

> We heard this Voice which came from heaven when we were with Him on the holy mountain. And so we have the prophetic word confirmed, which you do well to heed as a light that shines in a dark place, *until the day dawns and the Morning Star rises in your hearts.* (2 Peter 1:18,19)

All of us who desire to be supernaturally transformed inwardly into the very image of Christ would do well to learn what Jesus is teaching in His parable of spiritual growth. On a daily level there is plenty of scope for us to become anxious about the state of our hearts. We are dealing with so many factors that impinge upon the wellbeing of our soul. There is a steady flow of worldly temptations that tug upon our inner being. There are gnarly attitudes and reactions that rise up inside of us in our relationships and in the daily pressures that come upon our lives.

As the pastor of a growing local church I am interacting daily with people who sometimes give way to considerable anxiety about their personal spiritual growth. But many of these people are growing spiritually on the macro scale because they are exercising due diligence in the daily discipline of taking up their cross and passing the sentence of death upon everything that springs up inside of their hearts that doesn't look like Jesus. There are no short cuts to spiritual growth. We all have to do the 'hard yards' of the life of discipleship. The heart journey is all about becoming a disciple of Jesus so that we become like our Master.

Kenneth Wuest, in his *Expanded Translation of the New Testament* has a fascinating take on Jesus command to take up our cross. He writes: "For whoever desires to save his soul life, shall ruin it. But whoever will declare a sentence of death upon his soul life for my sake, this one shall save it." (Luke 9:24 Wuest) Paul instructed us to 'put to death' everything that doesn't look like Jesus in our hearts. This is the discipline of taking up our cross daily as

Jesus commanded. "If anyone desires to come after Me, let him deny himself, and take up his cross *daily*, and follow Me." (Luke 9:23)

This is the daily discipline of self-denial and passing the sentence of death upon our old life. As we practice this daily discipline of keeping our hearts with all diligence we create an environment in our hearts for supernatural transformation over the longer seasons of the soul. Then, when we look back over our lives retrospectively we see that we are really growing and that the image of Christ is forming in our heart and we are really beginning to look like Jesus in His life of authentic love.

The cross is central to this transformation and we cannot by-pass the establishment of the cross in the center of our heart just as it is permanently planted in the heart of Jesus. To be conformed to the image of Jesus is to be made conformable to His death. Jesus has always had the cross in His heart because to be alive to God demands that we are comprehensively dead to sin. Jesus has been eternally dead to sin and eternally alive to God. Now He invites us to be just like Him.

The life of discipleship consists in intentionally taking up our cross daily and deliberately passing the sentence of death upon our old life. As we do this the glory of the seed of the new creation is given full reign in our hearts and it permeates our entire being. Life springs forth from death. Jesus said it so well when he said, "Most assuredly, I say to you, unless a grain of wheat falls into the ground and dies, it remains alone; but if it dies, it produces much grain." (John 12:24) The cross lies at the center of the heart journey but it is consistently depicted in the Scriptures as the pathway to the fullness of life. We must die in order to truly live!

Chapter Two
Living from the Heart

God is calling every person in the entire world to live from the heart and to embark upon a deep heart journey. All of us are susceptible to living from our heads instead of our hearts. We are all far too prone to falling into the 'paralysis of analysis;' to analyze every situation intellectually instead of responding from our hearts. Living from the heart requires us to get in touch with our true feelings when we are faced with new situations in our lives. It means asking the pertinent questions of ourselves in order to probe what is really going on inside of us at a heart level. Living from the heart is the road less travelled because there is a measure of core pain inside each of us that sometimes frightens us and we don't know what to do with it. Typically, when confronted with core pain we tend to bury it and distance ourselves from it because it makes us feel powerless. But to walk as Christ calls us to walk in this life, we must get in touch with what is really going on inside of us and learn how to process our deepest pain in order to pursue genuine healing and transformation.

Learning to live from the heart is essential if we are going to learn how to walk in love. The high call to live a life of love is really a call to live from the heart. Paul said, "Therefore be imitators of God, as beloved children; and walk in love, just as Christ also loved us and gave Himself up for us, an offering and a sacrifice to God as a fragrant aroma." (Ephesians 5:1,2 NASB) Conformity to the image of Christ is impossible apart from being transformed into wholehearted lovers. We can only walk in love as Christ walked when our hearts are deeply healed and made whole. The freedom with which Christ has set us free is a deep and abiding freedom from the control of the old selfish, sinful nature so that the love of God can powerfully flow forth from our regenerated spirit. If we are still bound within our hearts by past wounding, bitterness, judgmentalism and fear we cannot be perfected in love. These are deep heart issues that we must experience freedom from in order to love sacrificially and generously as Christ loved.

So many people get stuck along the journey, so they bury the pain and try their hardest to just get on with life. But pain has a way of leaking out at the most inopportune times; usually in the context of our important relationships. Wounded and broken people often ooze their pain and end up complicating and damaging their primary relationships. Sometimes they even sabotage their relationships in order to create a safe hiding place where they no longer feel threatened or exposed. Getting 'stuck in our stuff' is a symptom of losing touch with our own hearts. When we are stuck we never seem to be able to break out of unhealthy patterns of living.

David complained to God about the heart condition of the arrogant and the ungodly. He said, "Their hearts are callous and unfeeling." (Psalms 119:70 NIV) An unfeeling heart is a dangerous thing. When someone becomes so callous that they lose touch with their own heart they become a walking time bomb! Their relationships are literally waiting to blow up! An unguarded heart that allows all sorts of issues to fester is always heading for disaster. These hidden strongholds of the heart poison our relationships and set the stage for self-sabotage. Paul also talked about those whose hearts were "past feeling." (Ephesians 4:19) In other translations we read that they have "lost all sensitivity" (NIV) or they have "become callous." (NASB) In other words, they are completely out of touch with what it means to feel the actual condition of their own heart.

Whenever people no longer live from the heart their words and their actions lack sincerity. What comes out of their mouth is no longer genuine or heartfelt, and in that broken condition they are far more likely to wound others and to cause offense. An unkept heart is a weapon in the hand of the enemy! That is why the Lord counsels us to keep our hearts with all diligence. (Proverbs 4:23) The devil loves to ride on the back of wounded believers who have lost their way in the heart journey! He's even happier with those who have never embraced the journey and who are completely stuck in their heads! This is what Paul meant when he spoke of people being 'past feeling.'

The remedy for an unkept heart is to call God's people back to living from the heart. Living this way is an art form that requires diligence and practice. It is a lost skill set that desperately needs to be recovered by every true follower of Jesus. We must be intentional about living in such a way that we remain conscious of how we are responding to the challenges of life and how we are doing in our relationships. Every situation of life arouses feelings and we have to be in touch with our true feelings if we want to live from the heart as Jesus and the Apostles prescribed.

We have to be intentional about issues of personal integrity, honesty and sincerity if we desire to live from our hearts. God is always calling us back to the heart. It is important to stay anchored to the Word of God, otherwise we have the propensity to become detached from our own heart. The prophets always called the people of God back to living from the heart. This lies at the core of true prophetic ministry.

- "So My heavenly Father also will do to you if each of you, *from his heart*, does not forgive his brother." (Matthew 18:35)
- "You desire honesty *from the heart*, so you can teach me to be wise in my inmost being." (Psalms 51:6 NLT)
- "Now that you have purified yourselves by obeying the truth so that you have sincere love for your brothers, love one another deeply, *from the heart*." (1 Peter 1:22 NIV)
- "But God be thanked that though you were slaves of sin, yet you obeyed *from the heart* that form of doctrine to which you were delivered." (Romans 6:17)
- "Work hard, but not just to please your masters when they are watching. But as bondservants of Christ, doing the will of God *from the heart*..." (Ephesians 6:6 NLT/NKJV)
- "They do not say *from the heart*, "Let us live in awe of the Lord our God." (Jeremiah 5:24 NLT)
- "They do not cry out to Me *from their hearts* but wail upon their beds. They gather together for grain and new wine but turn away from Me." (Hosea 7:14 NIV)

One of the defining characteristics of fallen human nature is the lack of inclination to live from the heart. That is not to say that the average person does not from time to time touch the true realities of the pain and brokenness that is the shared condition of all humanity. If we were entirely divorced from any kind of contact with our true feelings we would be less than human. In fact, whenever we meet people who are completely shut down emotionally we get the distinct impression that they have denied the true essence of their humanity. But in general most people find it incredibly uncomfortable to focus upon the unmanageable realities of our personal brokenness. These issues are often beyond our control and we feel powerless whenever we are forced to face those issues that lie hidden beneath the surface.

There is nothing more painful than being confronted by someone over the reality of what truly lies within, especially when we get 'busted' for bad behavior or inappropriate speech. We develop countless strategies to dodge and weave our way around these issues because we don't like the light shining into the darkened rooms of our souls. This is the primary reason that we do not live from the heart. Lost souls are, by nature, nocturnal creatures of darkness. It is a hard pill for a new believer to swallow that they have spent their entire life loving darkness rather than light. Conversion to Christ demands a new way of living and this new lifestyle centers upon learning to love the light and to live from the heart. God is relentless in calling us back to our hearts. He knows that the price tag of losing touch with our heart is impending disaster. All of the major sins that Christians become entangled in are always a reflection of a loss of contact with issues of the heart.

As we embrace the call to live from the heart God calls us to live according to the new creation. The heart of every believer contains two powerful realities. The first is the reality of the new creation and the indwelling of Christ. But the second is the reality of the unrenewed areas of the soul (our mind, will and emotions) that are still 'under construction.' Living from the heart requires us to know who we are in Christ but also to recognize those aspects of the old life that are still active in our hearts. Every believer is a new creation but God still warns us not to harden our hearts. "Today, if you will hear His voice, do not harden your hearts as in the rebellion." (Hebrews 3:15) This is a word to New Covenant believers! We may be new creations in Christ but we are still just as susceptible to hardening our hearts as anybody else on the planet!

God's prophetic call to live from the heart is one of the keys to living in the power of the new creation. A Christian who is fundamentally committed to living from their heart will continually allow the Spirit to explore the deepest rooms of their soul to unearth those issues that are still destroying their personal lives and their relationships. Only the person who is committed to living from the heart will cry out, "Search me, O God, and know my heart; try me, and know my anxieties; and see if there is any wicked way in me, and lead me in the way everlasting." (Psalms 139:23,24) David prayed a dangerous prayer! Jesus says, "All the churches shall know that I am He who searches the minds and hearts." (Revelation 2:23) When we pray "Search me, O God" we are merely coming into alignment with God who already searches the heart. God looks upon the heart and one of the signs of true conversion is when we also choose to look upon the heart.

There are a number of major satanic lies that hinder Christians from living from the heart. Perhaps the biggest lie is that the negative things that have shaped us in the past do not really matter. We often tell ourselves that certain things don't matter when the truth is, they really do! Family of origin issues, past traumas, abuse, rejection; all of these things shape our heart and influence the way we relate to others, to God and to ourselves. Telling ourselves that these things do not matter is an easy way to dismiss core pain. The problem is, when this lie becomes deeply entrenched in the heart it results in deep denial and dissociation. When someone is dissociated from their true feelings they can appear to glide through life with a Teflon coating. They convey the impression that the past doesn't matter and the hardships and the challenges of the present do not seem to matter either! This is getting to the heart of what Paul meant when he talked about being "past feeling!"

Emotionally dissociated people can talk about the wounding and the pain from their past as though they were talking objectively about someone else. It is almost as though they are outside of themselves giving a narrative of someone else's pain. Deeply dissociated people can even describe past wounds and traumas with a tone of laughter in their voice. I recall an encounter with a deeply dissociated Christian man who had just been through a painful and messy divorce. I bumped into him in a shopping center and asked him how he was going, trying my best to offer empathy and understanding. But to my amazement he chuckled about it and said he was fine and was actually feeling better now he was divorced. He had no intimate connection with his own core pain and by all appearances one might even think that there was no pain whatsoever in his life! But we all know that divorce is a very deep wound because it is almost always associated with bitterness, wounding, accusation, failure and a deep sense of loss. Solomon said, "Laughter can conceal a heavy heart; when the laughter ends, the grief remains." (Proverbs 14:13 NLT)

I have personally struggled with considerable emotional dissociation. I told myself for years that certain issues from my past did not matter. But God caught up with me and confronted me about harboring a lie in my heart. It wasn't until I renounced the lie that God began to release greater healing in my heart. Like most children I had been wounded by my parents but in my situation most of the wounds were from sins of omission rather than sins of commission. Many, many parents omit to adequately love and affirm their children because of their own brokenness and the generational brokenness they have themselves inherited. As a pastoral counsellor I listen to people pour out their life stories to me regularly. Some of these stories are horrific! Many people have suffered deep abuse and trauma. I have heard unimaginable stories of sexual and physical abuse and in comparison my personal issues appeared completely inconsequential. But sins of omission can be equally as wounding as sins of commission. It's just that sins of commission are more conspicuous!

At any given point in our personal journey God is digging deep into our hearts to get us in touch with core pain. There is something deeply significant about personal ownership of our issues. As long as we are living under the lie that the things that happened to us in our past do not matter we are not taking ownership of those issues and we are selling ourselves short of the healing that God wants to bring. The same principle applies to sin as to emotional brokenness. We have to take ownership of a particular stronghold of sin in order to find the path to freedom. The Holy Spirit convicts us of sin in our lives so we will evaluate it in the light of God's Word. When we come into agreement with God about a particular sin we are in a good position to repent, to confess it before God and to forsake it. But it is not until we take full responsibility for our sinful choices that we begin to move forward into true freedom.

We need to apply the same principle to emotional brokenness and issues of past wounding. We need to come to the point of a full and honest acknowledgement that these issues actually still exercise a measure of influence over us in the present. If we are spending all our energy trying to convince ourselves that these issues from the past do not matter we will never come into true freedom. We have to take ownership of the issue before the healing can begin. Paul talks about "bringing every thought into captivity." (2 Corinthians 10:5) We must arrest every mental process and bring it into subjection to Christ. If we need to take ownership and arrest 'every thought' why might we consider ourselves exempt from taking every emotion or every choice captive and bring those things into subjection to the Lordship of Christ? People living in the bliss of denial can tell themselves intellectually that they are free but what is really going on inside their heart? This pattern of telling ourselves that everything is OK is the very essence of religious pretense. Hiding from our own core pain will never result in healing!

Many Christians expend a lot of energy trying to convince themselves that they are not broken simply because they are new creations in Christ. The truth is we are new creations in spirit who are still dealing with issues of emotional brokenness. Our spirit has been made whole and brand new through the new creation miracle but our souls are still in desperate need of renewing. If the miracle of the new creation did it all why is God still searching our hearts and warning us against the danger of hardening our hearts? Why is God still deeply at work within us if the work is already completed? All of Paul's epistles were addressed to born again believers whose spirits had been glorified through the new creation miracle but Paul spent far more time addressing strongholds in the lives of believers than he did revealing the glory of the new creation.

"For God is working in you, giving you the desire to obey Him and the power to do what pleases Him." (Philippians 2:13 NLT) Paul taught that, "The inward man is being renewed day by day" (2 Corinthians 4:16) and that we are being transformed from one degree of glory to another. (2 Corinthians 3:18) There is plenty of work still to be done! God has a lot of unfinished business in the transformation of our lives into the very likeness of Jesus. Paul said, "Now may the God of peace Himself sanctify you entirely." In the next verse He says, "Faithful is He who calls you, and He also will bring it to pass." (1 Thessalonians 5:23,24 NASB) Paul was supremely "confident of this, that He who began a good work in you will carry it on to completion until the day of Christ Jesus." (Philippians 1:6 NIV) Much of the ongoing work of the Holy Spirit in our lives is in breaking us free from patterns of denial and emotional dissociation in order to promote deeper healing! Healing the broken places in our heart is a necessary prerequisite for us to live a life of love because unhealed Christians cannot love; they are still living in fear of further wounding and find themselves living in self-protection which is the very opposite of love.

Resisting the Holy Spirit is not just something the persecutors of Stephen engaged in. (Acts 7:51) Plenty of God's children resist the work of the Holy Spirit. Paul said, "Do not grieve the Holy Spirit of God!" (Ephesians 4:30) He also said, "Do not quench the Spirit!" (1 Thessalonians 5:19) It is important that we understand prophetically what the Spirit is seeking to do in our lives so that we can make choices to come into alignment with the purposes of God for our lives. James instructs us to "Receive with meekness the implanted word which is able to *save* your souls." (James 1:21) The Greek word for 'save' is '*sozo*' which has a much richer meaning than merely the 'salvation' of the soul. 'Sozo' means 'to heal or to make whole.' God is seeking to bring a deep transformation to our souls; to our minds, our will and our emotions. He is transitioning us from a place of brokenness into a place of glorious wholeness so that we become more and more like Jesus in this life.

Receiving the ministry of the Word and the prophetic voice of God into our hearts in a posture of humility is essential to the heart journey. Looking a little deeper at this verse in James 1:21 we see that the role of the ministry of the truth of God's Word is essential to setting us free from self deception. "Therefore, putting aside all filthiness and all that remains of wickedness, in humility receive the word implanted, which is able to save [*heal*] your souls." (NASB) Here is how I have paraphrased this passage;

> Each of you are under obligation to lay aside all moral depravity and the residual evil that contaminates and defiles your souls, and to continue to obediently receive God's word into your hearts in a posture of humility before Him, allowing it to germinate and grow inside of you in such a way that it *heals your soul* (your mind, your will and your emotions), bringing you inwardly to a place of true wholeness and health.

The healing of the soul is a significant theme in the writings of Peter and James. Peter said; "Since you have *purified your souls* in obeying the truth through the Spirit in sincere love of the brethren, love one another fervently with a pure heart." (1 Peter 1:22) I would paraphrase this passage in the following way;

> Because you have purified your souls (your mind, your will and your emotions) through your ever-deepening obedience to the truth (of God's Word) and the empowering of the Holy Spirit, it has resulted in a genuine love for your brothers and sisters that is not based in religious pretense. In light of this glorious transformation I urge you to take it to the next level by pursuing a fervent, supernatural love for everyone around you that flows through a heart and soul that has been comprehensively purified and cleansed by God.

Peter was vitally concerned with the healing and transformation of the soul of the believer. "Though you have not seen Him, you love Him, and though you do not see Him now, but believe in Him, you greatly rejoice with joy inexpressible and full of glory, obtaining as the outcome of your faith: *the salvation [sozo] of your souls*." (1 Peter 1:8,9 NASB) Peter suggests that true faith in God leads to the healing and restoration of the soul. Again, I have taken the liberty to paraphrase the text as follows;

> Even though you cannot see Jesus with your natural eyes you have put your faith and trust completely in Him and as a result your souls are being filled with a joy that is so great and so heavenly that it is far beyond your capacity to describe with words. Your soul is now literally brimming and overflowing with the fullness of divine glory because you are experientially receiving the objective of your faith in Jesus; *the deep healing and the transformation of your souls*!

Seasons of the Heart

Paul said, "Since we live by the Spirit, let us keep in step with the Spirit." (Galatians 5:25 NIV) Just as God took the Israelites on a journey from Egypt to the Promised Land, He leads each of us individually on a journey of the heart into the fullness of freedom. At any given time in our lives God is targeting a particular stronghold with the intention of pulling it down and bringing us one step closer to the free version of us. The Father disciplines His sons and daughters by addressing the issues in our lives that hinder us from moving forward into a deeper conformity to the image of His Son. He loves us just as we are but He loves us too much to leave us just the way we are!

Whenever God confronts issues in our lives He presents us with a call to deeper repentance and obedience in order to cooperate with Him in the demolition of the old life. As we just saw, the writer to the Hebrews urged his audience not to harden their hearts when God spoke to them about the actual condition of their hearts. "Today, if you will hear His voice, do not harden your hearts." (Hebrews 4:7) Whenever God speaks to us we have a choice to yield to Him and to obey or to harden our hearts and disobey. Far too many Christians get trapped in chronic disobedience and make agreements with the lies of the evil one that a certain measure of disobedience is tolerable.

God is always calling out the treasure of the new nature in us. But He also speaks to us about the areas within our heart that need to be transformed in order to establish us more fully in the new nature. Jesus did not hesitate to address strongholds of sin and deception in the church but He assured His people that His discipline and His correction was always the highest expression of His love. "As many as I love, I rebuke and chasten. Therefore be zealous and repent." (Revelation 3:19) Jesus used the word 'repent' eight times in the seven letters to the seven churches. We could imagine that there would have been some members of those seven churches who heard the word of the Lord yet who refused to repent. We could also imagine Jesus saying to some of these people "Is your heart still hardened?" (Mark 8:17)

In every season of the heart God is targeting a particular issue in our lives. It may be pride, unbelief, anxiety, rejection, fear, shame, lust, passivity, greed; the list is almost endless. God is gracious and He doesn't target so many things at once that we are made to feel inundated and demoralized by a sense of our brokenness. Usually there is one major issue that the Spirit is revealing but this can be accompanied by a string of lesser issues that are somehow linked to a major root. It is important that we learn how to articulate the various seasons that we journey through in the Spirit. Part of coming into alignment with the work of the Spirit is the ability to articulate what the Father is doing in our heart.

One of the greatest ways of sharpening ourselves in the operation of the gift of prophecy is to discern the times and the seasons of our own personal life. Our ability to zoom in on what God is doing enhances our degree of co-operation with the Spirit. This is what it means to keep in step with the Spirit. There is a rhythm of the Spirit that God seeks to synchronize our lives with. Changing from glory to glory necessitates flowing with the leading and the work of the Spirit in our hearts. Process is important! Once the Spirit initiates a healing season and we have the necessary insight to discern and articulate the season, God is able to initiate a much deeper process of transformation because our hearts are engaged in the journey. The deeper we are engaged in the process, the faster and deeper the level of healing we will experience!

Language for the Journey

We need language for the heart journey! Understanding the ways of God in the processes of change is essential. Being able to put language to the journey is even more important because the changes that God affects in your life will leave a trail for others to follow. God never runs ahead and implements deep changes in our heart without our full co-operation. He is the Master Heart Surgeon and He requires our full participation in the processes of change. If God were to hypothetically exercise His sovereignty and release a new measure of freedom into our hearts without our knowledge or understanding we would be blessed but we would be deprived of the opportunity to deepen our understanding of the ways of God. And others with whom we are journeying would be deprived of the wisdom that comes from being co-workers together with God in our own journey of transformation.

We know we are changing when we are enabled through the Spirit to articulate the nature of the change and to express the keys that were necessary in implementing the change. Remember the principle articulated by the Master: "Freely your have received; freely give!" We cannot give away what we haven't received, so our actual comprehension of the nature of the change and our ability to articulate it is one of the keys to equip the saints for the work of the ministry. Whatever we receive from God positions us to give it away. Deep heart transformation happens incrementally, leaving a trail of wisdom and understanding as we grow in our prophetic knowledge of the heart. Putting words to this inward renewal is indispensable for the enriching of the wider body of Christ. Leaders who are not journeying from the heart cannot possibly lead the people of God into any kind of significant personal transformation. For this reason the devil seeks to strike the shepherds in order to scatter the sheep.

God needs pioneers of the heart to bravely go where no man or woman has gone before. Remember, the journey of the heart is the road less travelled! God wants to raise up explorers of the heart who will explore unchartered places as forerunners in order to affect breakthrough in the life of the entire church. The deeper you go in this journey and the further God takes you off your map the greater the opportunity for the wider church to benefit from your personal spiritual odyssey. God wants to take us deep into His heart and through this journey of intimacy we will leave markers for our brothers and sisters and for the next generation. We mark these spiritual milestones on the journey with language taught to us by the Spirit so we can prophetically articulate the road map to freedom.

Whenever you feel stuck and you cannot break through a particular stronghold there is always wisdom for the journey. It is not as though God is confused or perplexed by your personal giants. He always knows the way forward and He is ever present to show us the way. The 'word of wisdom' gift is part of our equipping for the fight. God delights in dropping a 'word in season' into your heart that acts as a key to unlock a door into a new dimension of freedom. He says, "See, I have set before you an open door, and no one can shut it!" (Revelation 3:8) Jesus describes Himself as "He who opens and no one shuts, and shuts and no one opens." (Revelation 3:7) For every impossibility faced by man there is an open door in heaven and Jesus longs to take us through that door into freedom.

Paul said, "We have not received the spirit of the world but the Spirit who is from God, that we may understand what God has freely given us. This is what we speak, not in words taught us by human wisdom but in words taught by the Spirit, expressing spiritual truths in spiritual words." (1 Corinthians 2:12,13 NIV) These Spirit-inspired words are the language of the heart that bring new depths of insight into the ways of God in personal transformation. God has promised to "Restore to the peoples a pure language that they all may call on the name of the Lord, to serve Him with one accord." (Zephaniah 3:9) As you continue to journey through this book it will provide you with a clear language for the journey. In fact, that is what this book is all about. It is a road map for the journey of the heart!

One of the most important things to keep in mind as we walk with the Spirit of God in our journey of supernatural transformation is to lock on to the vision of the 'free version of you.' The Spirit is always revealing who we are in Christ and who it is that we are becoming. Whenever God reveals a stronghold or a blockage in our deepening journey of intimacy with Him we must remember that this is merely a vestige of the old life that stands as a threshold for us to cross so we can walk in the power of the new creation. We need to have a clear delineation in our thought life between that which is old and that which is new. Our new identity in Christ is inextricably tied to who we are as a new creation and as a beloved son or daughter. Our identity cannot be anchored to anything that constituted our old life. We may have issues and we may have strongholds but these no longer constitute our core identity. God supernaturally establishes our new identity in the midst of the ruins of our old life with all of its complexities and He systematically ushers us into the freedom of who we have now become in Jesus through the new birth. God is continually revealing the 'free version of you' and seeking to anchor your identity in who you are as a new creation.

The heart journey must remain focused upon the new heart that God has placed inside of us otherwise we will get lost along the journey and end up believing lies about our true identity. There are so many core identity issues that were rooted in our old life that we are in constant danger of falling into a distorted view of ourselves as the Holy Spirit seeks to reveal and expose the strongholds of the old life. We are also vulnerable to the accusations of the evil one who seeks to keep our core identity anchored to our old life. Jesus continually addressed strongholds of the old life in His letters to the seven churches but He always spoke in a manner that communicated the truth that the evil ways of the old life are fundamentally beneath the dignity of who we now are in Christ.

Whenever God's people become entangled in the old life He calls them to remembrance. The new birth seats us together with Christ in heavenly places, so Jesus said, "Remember the height from which you have fallen! Repent and do the things you did at first. If you do not repent, I will come to you and remove your lampstand from its place." (Revelation 2:5 NIV) "Remember, therefore, what you have received and heard; obey it, and repent." (Revelation 3:3 NIV) The entire vibe of Jesus' letters to the churches is a call to restoration. "Be watchful, and strengthen the things which remain, that are ready to die, for I have not found your works perfect before God." (Revelation 3:2) "You have persevered and have patience, and have labored for My name's sake and have not become weary. Nevertheless, I have this against you, that you have left your first love." (Revelation 2:3,4)

Whenever we as the people of God lose, forsake or forfeit something that is our birthright as sons and daughters God calls us back to the place He set us in when He first redeemed us and seated us together with His Son. No matter how far we roam from the reality of who we are in Christ, the Father is faithful to discipline us and call us to stand again in the reality of the new creation. We cannot embark upon this heart journey without the firm foundation of the revelation of the finished work of Christ and the finished work of the new birth inside our human spirit. Paul celebrated the reality that "your spirit is alive because you have been made right with God." (Romans 8:10 NLT) Without this foundation we are destined to slide back into an Old Covenant model of change where we are continually seeking to get right with God through our good works.

God always calls His New Covenant sons and daughters back to who they truly are in Christ. He prophesies to us afresh the revelation of the free version of who we are in Him. All of His corrections and rebukes are spoken in a redemptive context that calls out the treasure of the new creation whilst still pointing out areas where we are living under the influence of the old life. "We have this treasure in earthen vessels that the excellence of the power may be of God and not of us." (2 Corinthians 4:7) God always calls out the treasure even whilst He is revealing the things that rob us of enjoying the treasure! The New Covenant model of transformation is from the inside out whereas the Old Covenant model is from the outside in. Under the Old Covenant the people called upon the Lord who was in heaven and who was external to them to come down to deliver them. It was an earth to heaven paradigm. But under the New Covenant, which is a heaven to earth paradigm, God calls us back to what He has already done in us through the miracle of the new creation. This past tense miracle is the foundation of our transformation.

Celebrating the Process

Many Christians are looking for the magic pill that will catapult them into the fullness of their new life in Christ without accepting the biblical process of change. Embracing the heart journey means celebrating the process of change and not trying to circumvent the ways of God in the supernatural transformation of the heart. There will always be those teachers who try to negate the process by offering the magic pill and there will always be those who gather to themselves teachers who offer the magic pill. Regrettably, there is a big market for magic Christian pills that offer instant transformation without the required process.

I believe we are called to celebrate the process of transformation. It is only through the process that God teaches us His ways. If we reject the process we simultaneously reject the training that only comes through the process. There are those who celebrate the process and those who loathe the process and do everything they can to leapfrog the process through taking the magic pill. I have learnt so much through Graham Cooke who has been a dear friend and a wonderful mentor in my life. One of the things I love about Graham's ministry is his exuberant celebration of the process. He is one of the greatest teachers on the actual process of supernatural transformation. Because he has embraced the process he has become an authority on the ways of God in personal transformation. He writes;

Every change involves a letting go of one thing to reach out for what is next. It is death by instalments – the slow death of our mindsets, our attitudes, perceptions and paradigms. As we submit to each process, our appreciation of the journey grows and our faith increases. Transition is a process; it is a series of steps and stages that take us from one realm to another. Transition involves crisis. Crisis leads us to process, through which our road map will deliver us to a new place of promise if we faithfully complete this leg of the journey.[1]

It is only as we wholeheartedly embrace the process of the heart journey that we come to appreciate everything that God imparts through the journey. God has taught me to love the journey even though it is full of painful lessons. Our wisdom only grows when we embrace God's way of transformation. Magic pill theology is so seductive but given the choice between the magic pill or the divine process of heart transformation I would now willingly choose the process because that is how God imparts the wisdom and the knowledge of the heart. As we journey through the slow and arduous process of change from the inside out we grow in our capacity to minister meaningfully into the lives of those around us.

Magic pill proponents cannot guide you on this heart journey because they refuse to celebrate the journey. They are always looking for the quick fix theology that eliminates the systematic process of deep heart change. My prayer is that this book will deeply stir you to embrace the heart journey with all that is within you and to challenge yourself to stay on the journey! As you read this book why not purpose in your heart that you will come into alignment with God in celebrating the journey as much as God Himself celebrates it. Then you won't short change yourself in receiving the full impartation of the prophetic knowledge of the heart.

Chapter Three

An Apostolic Paradigm of the Heart

In order to properly define the nature of the heart journey we need to search for an all-encompassing paradigm that will accommodate all of the unique dimensions of the journey of supernatural transformation that we are invited to participate in. Discovering this biblical paradigm will position us to identify the key indicators that will help us to determine if we are really making personal progress in our heart journey with God or if we are merely treading water, or worse; if we are actually losing ground. Every journey needs a compass so we have a clear sense of direction and purpose.

As we survey the expansive vision of the New Testament there is one conceptual paradigm that stands head and shoulders above the others. This is the paradigm of the spiritual journey from being an orphan to becoming a son. Jesus set the compass for the journey when He said, "I will not leave you orphans; I will come to you." (John 14:18) Jesus comes to us as the Beloved Son to adopt us into a living relationship with His Father so that we become beloved sons.

An orphan doesn't know that he or she belongs or that they are loved, whereas a son is experientially secure in the love of their father and has a deep sense of 'home.' Before we experienced salvation we were unloved orphans searching for a sense of belonging and seeking love in all the wrong places. But as soon as we were miraculously born again into the family of God we were invited to experience what Henry Nouwen calls 'The life of the beloved.' This is the glory of our salvation; we can now experience the same love of our Father that Jesus has eternally enjoyed.

The orphan/sonship paradigm, more than any other, moves us in the direction of developing a set of key indicators to measure personal spiritual growth and healing in our hearts. This paradigm honors the reality that the new creation miracle has placed us squarely in the midst of the eternal relationship between the Father and the Son. The prophetic unveiling of our sonship through the Spirit continuously draws out our new identity that has been supernaturally bestowed upon us by our heavenly Father. Paul taught that "You have not received a spirit of slavery leading to fear again, but you have received a spirit of adoption as sons by which we cry out, "Abba! Father!" The Spirit Himself testifies with our spirit that we are children of God." (Romans 8:15,16 NASB)

Because we have received what Paul calls 'a spirit of adoption' or a 'spirit of sonship' (NKJV) our spirit has been gloriously adopted into the Father's family and the Holy Spirit is continuously testifying with our newly adopted spirit that we belong to the Father and that we are now His beloved sons. "When the fullness of the time had come, God sent forth His Son....that we might receive the adoption as sons." (Galatians 4:4,5) We are no longer orphans! We do not have an orphan spirit anymore but a gloriously adopted spirit. Our progressive conformity to the image of the 'Son' is built upon the solid foundation of something that God has already done in the regenerated human spirit. When we are first born again we have a newly adopted spirit but our soul has not yet been transformed into the image of the Son. Our new spirit is light years ahead of our unrenewed soul. That is why we find it so hard to keep up with who we have supernaturally become in Christ.

Paul taught that God has already glorified the spirit of His adopted sons and daughters. He declared that those "whom He justified, these He also glorified." (Romans 8:30) Justification is the act of making us righteous. Righteousness is the noun but justification is the verb. Through the free gift of righteousness we become the righteousness of God in our spirit so that we are righteous, just as Jesus is righteous in the sight of the Father. We now have absolute right standing before our Heavenly Father. Through the act of justification God imparts His glory to our regenerated human spirit. "And having given them right standing, He gave them His glory." (NLT) Jesus said to the Father, "The glory which You gave Me I have given them." (John 17:22) The Amplified Bible says, "Those whom He called, He also justified (made righteous, putting them into right standing with Himself). And those whom He justified, He also glorified [raising them to a heavenly dignity and condition or state of being]." (Romans 8:30 AMP)

The adopted sons and daughters can now enter into the high privilege of living from an already glorified spirit. One third of our being is already complete and already glorified! Jesus revealed that the Son comes in the glory of the Father.

"For He received from God the Father honor and glory when such a voice came to Him from the Excellent Glory: "This is My beloved Son, in whom I am well pleased." (2 Peter 1:17) In the same way, as adopted sons we now come *in the glory of the Father* because the Father is proud to speak this same word 'beloved' over us. Paul said, "He called you by our gospel for the obtaining of the glory of our Lord Jesus Christ." (2 Thessalonians 2:14) There is so much glory resting upon the message of sonship and upon the theme of our adoption!

Paul taught that all those who have believed in Christ have now been gloriously adopted by the Father. God the Father foreknew those who would believe so "He chose us in Him [the Beloved Son] before the foundation of the world, that we should be holy and without blame before Him in love, having predestined us to adoption as sons by Jesus Christ to Himself, according to the good pleasure of His will, to the praise of the glory of His grace, by which He made us accepted in the Beloved [Son]." (Ephesians 1:4-6) We have been predestined to adoption as sons! But this is just the first step in the glorious journey. "Those whom He foreknew, He also predestined to be conformed to the image of His Son, that He might be the firstborn among many brethren." (Romans 8:29) We are predestined to adoption but in addition we are predestined to be conformed to the fullness of the image of the Beloved Son. This is an experiential journey of glorious supernatural transformation.

God is deeply committed to supernaturally transforming us into the very image of His Son in this life. This is the heart journey from living like an orphan to living in the glorious freedom of the sons and daughters of God. Paul deliberately couched this profound revelation in epic terms because it unveils the glory of the ultimate purpose of God the Father. "The creation waits in eager expectation for the sons of God to be revealed." (Romans 8:19 NIV) There is a cosmic anticipation of the emergence of glorious sons and daughters. "We know that the whole creation has been groaning as in the pains of childbirth right up to the present time." (Romans 8:22 NIV)

The appearance of a new heaven and a new earth when Christ returns will be the final consummation of the new creation that commenced at the cross when Jesus cried out "It is finished!" At this moment "The creation itself will be liberated from its bondage to decay and brought into the glorious freedom of the children of God." (Romans 8:21 NIV) The miracle that has taken place inside our hearts makes us the heralds of a brand-new creation so that our present journey into glorious freedom trumpets the liberation of this creation from the tyranny of sin and death.

What an epic theme this is! Paul used language that intentionally stirs our hearts into a sense of the enormity of what we have been swept up into through our conversion to Christ. From heaven's perspective the travail of creation itself is in eager anticipation of the adopted sons and daughters rising up into a tangible expression of the freedom of sonship. God is bringing many sons and daughters to glory and the whole creation is on tippy toes in eager anticipation. As a true spiritual father Paul himself was swept into this supernatural sense of travail. "My little children, for whom I travail in birth again until Christ is formed in you." (Galatians 4:19)

Paul said, "Even we ourselves groan within ourselves!" (Romans 8:23) "Likewise the Spirit also helps in our weaknesses. For we do not know what we should pray for as we ought, but the Spirit Himself makes intercession for us with groanings which cannot be uttered." (Romans 8:26) A woman giving birth cries out as the baby is about to 'crown' and emerge from her womb. Paul invoked this confronting imagery to describe the anguish of the Spirit and his own personal anguish for the sons of God to be manifest upon the earth as a prophetic sign of the dawn of the new creation. This is where all the action is for those who believe in Christ. We have already been adopted but we are now being conformed to who we have already become in our adopted spirit. For us as believers, continuing to live like an orphan powerfully contradicts who we have become in the essence of our spirit and there is subsequently an imperative for us to step into the free version of ourselves. Our heart journey is powerfully significant in the sight of heaven!

The Father's project is infinitely greater than we could ever comprehend. How tragic it is from heaven's perspective that so many believers get gloriously saved but never go on to fully comprehend what it is that the Father is really seeking! Jesus is the "Firstborn among many brethren." The Father has given birth to a new family that constitutes an entirely new creation. He has filled our human spirit with His own glory but it is such a tragedy that so few believers go on in their journey to shine like stars in the universe. A son learns what it means to live from a glorified spirit and to let their light so shine that they become walking embassies of heaven; shining with the glory of heavenly sonship.

In order for the real heart journey to begin we must come to terms with what it means to still live, think and behave like an orphan in our heart in relation to our Father and our brothers and sisters in Christ. The Father disciplines His sons and daughters because of His love. His discipline comes as He reveals the many ways in which we still live and think like orphans even though we now live inside the King's palace. The unveiling of the old orphan heart with its attendant mindsets and behaviors represents the first step in beginning to identify the depth of our brokenness. Because we have always lived like orphans we are deeply wounded and broken. There is an orphan wound in the heart of every single human being that the Father longs to heal.

But even when the Father is unveiling the depth of the orphan wound within our soul He is simultaneously revealing what it means to be a son as He speaks prophetically to our adopted spirit. We are caught in the crossfire of heaven and earth! The revelation of the old orphan heart goes right to the heart of defining the essence of our fallen condition. In the same way, the heart of sonship defines the essence of human wholeness. Learning to live within the paradigm of orphans becoming sons ensures that we stay on track with the Holy Spirit's unveiling of the heart of the Father. It also ensures that we stay focused upon the healing of all of the broken places in our heart as we are transformed by the Father's love. Jesus came to heal the brokenhearted, which is another way of describing the healing of the old orphan heart by bringing us into the full glory and freedom of our sonship.

Jesus manifested the fullness of the heart of sonship and He lived as a Son who shone with the glory of His Father. At any point along our spiritual journey as a follower of Christ we find ourselves somewhere between the two extremes of manifesting the heart of an orphan and manifesting the heart of a son. It is in the crucible of our earthly relationships that the old orphan heart is unveiled and that is always an extremely painful process. Jesus Himself is the compass for the heart journey. As we keep our eyes fixed on Him we behold the attributes and characteristics of sonship so that the Father can chisel away whatever doesn't look like Jesus.

Because Jesus is the pattern son we must continually behold the glory of His sonship. The key indicators of spiritual wholeness are all revealed in the person of the Son. Paul taught that it is in beholding the glory of the Son that we are conformed to the same image. "But we all, with unveiled face, beholding as in a mirror the glory of the Lord, are being transformed into the same image from glory to glory, just as by the Spirit of the Lord." (2 Corinthians 3:18) Because Jesus Himself is the template of the wholeness of sonship we can derive the following key indicators of our own conformity to the image of true sonship:

1. Jesus continuously valued the heart journey with His Father and with His brothers and sisters on earth. Jesus was not exempt from the mandate to "keep your heart with all diligence." He had to diligently maintain the garden of His heart so that the weeds of temptation could not take root. He fought the good fight of faith perfectly because He maintained His heart and continually upheld the value of the heart journey. This is a primary virtue of a son. An orphan is careless about his or her heart condition and places minimal value on the mandate of keeping his or her heart. There can be no progress on the heart journey if we neglect the value of becoming a person who lives from the heart.

2. Jesus maintained a life of intimate first love for His Father in heaven. He walked in continuous fellowship with the Father. Intimacy was a non-negotiable core value for Jesus; He lived and breathed a life of deep intimacy and everything He said and did invited others around Him into this core value. A true son values intimacy with the Father and with his brothers and sisters. An orphan is a stranger to intimacy and is more accustomed to isolation and the secret life of separation and darkness. John said, "That which we have seen and heard we declare to you, that you also may have fellowship with us; and truly our fellowship is with the Father and with His Son Jesus Christ." (1 John 1:3) "If we say that we have fellowship with Him, and walk in darkness, we lie and do not practice the truth. But if we walk in the light as He is in the light, we have fellowship with one another, and the blood of Jesus Christ His Son cleanses us from all sin." (1 John 1:6,7)

3. Jesus valued people and walked continuously in love, living for others in order to empower them into their destiny in the Father. "Having loved His own who were in the world, He loved them to the end." (John 13:1) Jesus modelled a life of deep sacrificial love for human beings. He poured Himself into people because they were His greatest treasure. He sold everything in order to purchase His greatest treasure. An orphan is drowning in a sea of self-centeredness and doesn't see other people the way the Father sees them. People are a nuisance to someone living as an orphan. Relationships become dispensable. The last thing on an orphan's mind is the empowerment of others; they are in pure survival mode where only the fittest and the strongest survive.

An orphan views other people as competition and they are vulnerable to falling into rivalry and competitiveness in their quest to survive. It is not hard for an orphan to tread underfoot another person in order to ensure their own survival.

4. Jesus was emotionally engaged with everyone He came in contact with. Because His heart was so alive to perfect love He was able to connect deeply with people and to engage their hearts and draw them into intimacy. Jesus' heart pulsated with the love of the Father and this made Him deeply engaged with human beings. He lived a life of deep attachment to people and valued community far above solitude. An orphan is emotionally detached from other people. He or she is a stranger to attachment because orphans, by the very nature of the term, have never had attachment and emotional engagement expressed toward them. Orphans are emotionally dissociated and suffer an attachment disorder, often failing to bond deeply with anyone because emotional bonding has never been a part of their own personal experience. As a result an orphan will often appear detached, relationally aloof, distant and difficult to really connect with. This makes someone with an orphan heart a stranger to intimacy who will often leave behind them a trail of broken relationships and wounded hearts.

5. Jesus could feel the heart of His Father and He could feel the hearts of those around Him. As the ultimate prophet He was also the ultimate prophetic 'feeler.' Jesus could acutely discern the atmosphere that others carried. The way we carry our heart actually creates an atmosphere that prophetic feelers are quick to pick up on. If someone is emotionally present a feeler can feel the engagement of his or her heart. If they are emotionally disengaged a feeler can also feel their disengagement. John recorded that "Jesus did not trust Himself to them, because He knew all men. *He could read men's hearts.*" (John 2:24,25 AMP) "He knew them inside and out: He didn't need any help in seeing right through them." (MSG) An orphan is incapable of feeling the heart of the Father and of feeling the hearts of others. An orphan moves through life hoping that others will not notice their lack of engagement and their lack of presence.

The Epic Theme of Sonship

God is a Father to the fatherless. He always draws the solitary into family. He will never leave us as orphans but He will always comes to us and invites us into the wholeness of love. The heart journey is a healing journey that draws us out of our isolation and invites us to make love for God and for people the highest core value of our existence. God the Father sent forth His Son so that we might receive the adoption as sons and journey experientially into the life of the beloved. All of this is contained and expressed in the revelation of the New Covenant and this epic theme becomes the paradigm that best suits the glory of the heart journey because it encompasses the highest virtues that God is seeking to build into our hearts. As we embrace this journey we will reflect and shine the glory of sonship to a world that from heaven's perspective is one giant orphanage of lost sons and daughters searching for home.

As we begin our walk with the Lord we don't even realize the extent to which we are manifesting an orphan heart. But this journey can be significantly accelerated by introducing this kind of language to believers. If this is not the language of the Christian community that we have been a part of, then these concepts may not have registered in our hearts. Whenever the orphan to son paradigm is not a part of our language we unintentionally create environments where believers can potentially live for many years without ever coming to terms with the reality of the old orphan heart and that is always a great tragedy because it robs the sons and daughters of God of their true inheritance.

Over my three decades as a Christian I have been a part of many churches where the revelation of what it means to live and behave as an orphan hasn't even registered as an issue amongst many Christians. The Holy Spirit is continually seeking to unveil to us the heart of the Son in His relationship to the Father but if we fail to connect the dots we can behold Jesus as the Beloved Son without allowing it to stir up the necessary implications for our own heart. By far, the most effective way of revealing the old orphan heart with its attendant behaviors and mindsets is by revealing and teaching upon the true heart of sonship. This brings the epic theme of orphans becoming sons into the light so that it can promote the kind of transformation that our heavenly Father desires.

The development of the heart of a son is the most important issue in the personal spiritual development of every single Christian. If this epic theme is not elevated to its rightful place in the life and language of the church, Christians will be deprived of the opportunity to really embrace their personal transformation into the image of the Son. Conformity to the image of the Son is the essence of our journey of supernatural transformation. Christian history is a testament to the propensity of believers to be side tracked into bunny trails that keep us focused upon everything except the ultimate purpose of our existence. John 17 is particularly powerful in helping us to focus upon what really motivates the heart of Jesus and the Father. All of us would do well to make it the framework of our personal prayer life.

I would like to propose the idea that the revelation of the orphan heart and the revelation of the heart of true sonship creates an indispensable framework for mapping the heart journey of the believer. Everything Jesus did to reveal the heart of His Father in heaven and to unveil His own heart of Sonship in the context of the loving heart of His Father leads us inexorably to the unveiling of the orphan heart of humanity. But Jesus promised that He would not leave us as orphans. He promised that He would come to live on the inside of us and to reveal the true heart of sonship within us so that we could journey out of our old orphan heart. This is what it means to be conformed to the image of the Son and this is what is burning in the Father's heart. This is why the Holy Spirit is actively working to unveil the glory of sonship in the heart of every single believer. He is continuously testifying with our regenerated spirit and calling out the treasure.

But we must exercise care because it is entirely possible to engage these ideas conceptually without taking any real ground in our actual heart journey into love. The concepts are extremely powerful. In fact, they are so powerful that we are in danger of finding such exhilaration from the concepts alone that they can substitute for the real experiential journey of having our hearts transformed by the Father's love. Such is the danger of entertaining the loftiest concepts in the universe. These themes are so deep and profound that we can mistake our revelation of them for the actual experience of becoming the Beloved. As we gaze into the nature of the intimacy between the Father and the Son we can be so powerfully stimulated intellectually that we end up settling for less than the experience of actually being loved in the same way that the Son has been eternally loved by the Father. Jesus said to His Father; "I have declared to them Your name, and will declare it, that the love with which You loved Me may be in them, and I in them." (John 17:26) The mission of Jesus has not been fulfilled until He has loved the old orphan heart out of us.

The heart journey from being a true spiritual orphan to becoming a genuinely beloved son is the greatest journey of all human existence. It is the epic theme that transcends all other themes. The Father is bringing many sons to glory! He is taking broken lives characterized by orphan thinking (which results in orphan behavior) and transforming them into true sons and daughters who can shine the glory of sonship to a world populated by billions of orphans crying out for their Father!

Tragically, the church throughout history has more often than not resembled an orphanage rather than a family of deeply fulfilled sons and daughters who are fully secure in the love of their heavenly Father. Religion has hijacked the sons and daughters into an aberrant expression of Christianity that denies the essence of our true inner identity. The Heart Revolution pioneered by Jesus 2,000 years ago is still seeking this transformation from orphans to sons and from sons to heirs. It is a courageous journey and it is the road less travelled. We are living in a time when millions of redeemed sons and daughters are crying out for an authentic spirituality and are grieved by the substitution of a lifeless religion.

The orphan to son paradigm is the definitive apostolic paradigm of the heart. This is the paradigm that Jesus, the Beloved Son brought from heaven to earth. "God so loved the world that *He sent* His Son!" The Father sent forth His Son because only a Son can reveal the Father. Everything about sonship prophetically declares the reality of fatherhood and everything about fatherhood prophetically declares the reality of sonship. Jesus said to the orphanage of humanity; "I will come to you!" His mission was to come to the orphans to miraculously absorb them through the new birth into the same dimension of divine union with the Father that He Himself has eternally enjoyed.

The apostolic mission of Jesus is not complete until the love with which the Father loved the Son is experientially established within the hearts of the adopted sons and daughters. Salvation is not the goal, it is merely the gateway of access into the love of the Father. Once this love has been experientially restored to the human heart He can then say to us, "As the Father has sent Me, I also send you." (John 20:21) The apostolic paradigm is all about 'sending.' An apostle is a 'sent one.' Jesus told a parable about the wicked vinedressers who had commandeered the vineyard; a metaphor for the nation of Israel.

> A certain man planted a vineyard, leased it to vinedressers, and went into a far country for a long time. Now at vintage-time he sent a servant to the vinedressers, that they might give him some of the fruit

of the vineyard. But the vinedressers beat him and sent him away empty- handed. Again he sent another servant; and they beat him also, treated him shamefully, and sent him away empty- handed. And again he sent a third; and they wounded him also and cast him out. Then the owner of the vineyard said, 'What shall I do? *I will send my beloved son.* Probably they will respect him when they see him." But when the vinedressers saw him, they reasoned among themselves, saying, "This is the heir. Come, let us kill him, that the inheritance may be ours." So they cast him out of the vineyard and killed him. Therefore what will the owner of the vineyard do to them? He will come and destroy those vinedressers and give the vineyard to others. (Luke 20:9-16)

The Father speaks over humanity in their lost and broken state and says, "I will send My Beloved Son!" God has now spoken through His Son. "In the past God spoke to our forefathers through the prophets at many times and in various ways, but in these last days *He has spoken to us by His Son.* The Son is the radiance of God's glory and the exact representation of His being, sustaining all things by His powerful word." (Hebrews 1:1-3 NIV) The Apostle John said, "To all who received Him, to those who believed in His name, He gave the right to become the sons of God; children born not of natural descent, nor of human decision or a husband's will, but born of God." (John 1:12,13)

Both Paul and John were sent forth by the Father. They became apostolic fathers because they had fully embraced the apostolic paradigm of the heart. Both of these glory-filled sons made this paradigm the core of their preaching ministry in order to raise up a generation of beloved sons and daughters who would enter into the fullness of the joy of the life of the beloved. They understood that it was the glory of the Father to send forth a company of beloved sons and daughters into the world, whose sonship would prophesy of the love of the Father, just as Jesus' Sonship revealed the glory of His Father. "We have seen His glory, the glory of the One and Only, who came from the Father, full of grace and truth." (John 1:14 NIV)

Paul focused upon the glory of our adoption and John focused upon living in the love of the Father. "Behold what manner of love the Father has lavished upon us, that we should be called the sons of God." (1 John 3:1) There is nothing more prophetic on the face of the earth than orphans becoming beloved sons and daughters. This is the heartbeat of apostolic/prophetic ministry. Jesus, the ultimate prophet, prophesied of the glory and love of the Father. The deepest essence of His prophetic ministry was to reveal the love of His Father and to bring adopted sons and daughters into the rich experience of the Father's love. Whenever 'prophetic ministry' is dislocated from the revelation of sonship it becomes a *bastardized* message. The writer of Hebrews described Christians who reject the loving discipline of the Father as "bastards and not sons." (Hebrews 12:8 KJV)

God is again seeking to restore the fullness of true prophetic and apostolic ministry where He speaks through His beloved sons and daughters to this orphan generation. God speaks powerfully through His true sons. The essence of human brokenness is defined in the word 'orphan;' but the essence of human wholeness is defines in the word 'son.'

Chapter Four

The Context of the Heart Journey

"A word fitly spoken is like apples of gold in settings of silver."

(Proverbs 25:11)

Gold and silver always appear together in Scripture as the two most highly precious metals. In fact, these two words appear together 168 times in the Bible.[2] According to the Lord, gold is designed to appear in settings of silver. Gold shines most brightly in the context of silver. These two precious metals were made for each other. The extraordinary value of these metals serves as a metaphor for the riches of God Himself. "Yes, the Almighty will be your gold and your precious silver." (Job 22:25) The Father and the Son are our precious gold and silver.

The gold speaks metaphorically of the heart of Christ and the silver speaks metaphorically of the heart of the Father. The heart of Christ, the Son, has been eternally *set* in the context of the heart of His Father. Jesus said, "Believe me when I say that I am *in* the Father." (John 14:11 NIV) Christ is the apple of gold in the setting of silver. He is the apple of His Father's eye. "Keep me as the apple of Your eye; Hide me under the shadow of Your wings." (Psalms 17:8) Jesus is the 'Beloved' Son of the Father. "For he who touches you touches the apple of His eye." (Zechariah 2:8) As the incarnate Word, Christ is the apple of gold in the setting of silver. In the Song of Songs we also discover that the Bridegroom is likened by His bride to an apple tree whose fruit is sweet. "Like an apple tree among the trees of the woods, so is my Beloved among the sons. I sat down in His shade with great delight and His fruit was sweet to my taste." (Song of Songs 2:3)

But the life of Christ was further adorned with the precious stones of the relationships He built on earth. These are the "friends of the Bridegroom."

(Matthew 9:15) The life of Jesus on earth was also set in the context of the sons and daughters He was bringing to glory. He was the firstborn among many brethren. The redemption of mankind is a family story; God sets the solitary in families. He is a relational God and His gift of redemption is all about the restoration of relationships.

Jesus is not ashamed to call us brethren because we have been given equal standing before the Father alongside Him. We are His jewels. "They shall be Mine," says the Lord of hosts, "On the day that I make them My jewels." (Malachi 3:17) Zechariah said, "They will sparkle in His land like jewels in a crown." (Zechariah 9:16) John said, "Then I looked, and behold, a white cloud, and on the cloud sat One like the Son of Man, having on His head a golden crown." (Revelation 14:14) I believe that we are the jewels set in the golden crown of Christ. Jesus' life is adorned with the jewels of the many sons and daughters He presents to His Father through His redemptive work on the cross.

As a consequence of the atonement Christ now lives in the hearts of His brethren. The Spirit of Sonship has been poured into our heart and we are now in Christ and He is in us. Because Christ is in the Father, the Father has now also become the context of our lives. Our heart, indwelt by Christ now becomes that apple of gold in the setting of silver; we are in the Son and we are also in the Father. Paul spoke of gold, silver and precious stones as the only viable building material for the lives of the saints. He juxtaposed the gold, the silver and the precious stones against the consumable materials of wood, hay and straw that cannot endure the fire of God.

> Now if anyone builds on this foundation with gold, silver, precious stones, wood, hay, straw, each one's work will become clear; for the Day will declare it, because it will be revealed by fire; and the fire will test each one's work, of what sort it is. (1 Corinthians 3:12)

The relationships of love that we cultivate with the Father and with His beloved sons and daughters are the only building materials that will abide forever. Whatever is not built on the foundation of intimate relationship will be burned up. There is a temptation to substitute love with knowledge as the building material of the kingdom. But Paul pointed out to the Corinthians that "Knowledge puffs up, but love edifies." (1 Corinthians 8:1) Our relationships built upon the foundation of the supernatural love of God are the only things that we will carry with us into eternity. "Love will last forever, but prophecy and speaking in unknown languages and special knowledge will all disappear. There are three things that will endure – faith, hope, and love – and the greatest of these is love." (1 Corinthians 13:8,13 NLT) To Paul, knowledge was nothing but wood, hay and straw whereas love is represented by gold, silver and precious stones.

In the same way that the golden crown of Christ has now been adorned with the jewels of the companionship of many brethren, so our lives are adorned with the precious stones of relationship in community. We are the living stones that make up the temple. The Apostles were the twelve foundation stones of the New Jerusalem and each of the Apostles were symbolized as precious stones. (Revelation 21:14-21) But even though the Apostles are worthy of double honor for the sake of their great work in founding the church, each of us who are in Christ are equally God's precious stones. Building with gold, silver and precious stones mean building with relationships of love that will last forever. 41 times we are told in the NIV Bible; "His love endures forever!"

Building with Love

There are two ways that Christians can set out to build their personal lives. As we have already seen, Paul contrasted the building of the temple with the materials of gold, silver and precious stones with those who built with wood, hay and straw; all materials that would eventually be consumed by fire. Paul entered into a dispute with the incipient Gnostics in the church in Corinth because they were drifting into the error of replacing love with knowledge. This was a common problem in Greek culture, which elevated wisdom and knowledge above love and relationships in community. As a result, those who exalted knowledge began to exalt themselves over their brethren and began pulling away from them in pride.

Love always moves our heart to deepen our relational bonds with one another but superior knowledge carries with it the temptation to exalt ourselves over anyone who doesn't have the same level of superior wisdom and knowledge that we enjoy. Paul responded to this dangerous spiritual trajectory by juxtaposing knowledge against love and it is hard not to imagine that he was thinking of the exaltation of knowledge as the wood, hay and stubble that would one day be burned up in the fire. "Where there is knowledge, it will pass away." (1 Corinthians 13:8 NIV)

Some of the Greek believers in the Corinthian church were seeking knowledge as an end in itself. They boasted that they possessed knowledge and they were proud of their superior philosophical wisdom and knowledge; sufficient to exalt themselves over their brothers and sisters in Christ! Paul unhesitatingly confronted those who were attempting to alter the foundation of the kingdom from love to knowledge. He contrasted the power of one loving father with the knowledge of thousands of knowledge-based instructors. "For though you might have ten thousand instructors in Christ, yet you do not have many fathers; for in Christ Jesus I have begotten you through the gospel." (1 Corinthians 4:15)

Love is the only building material with which we can build the holy temple. According to Paul, the body of Christ, the mystical temple, "grows and **builds itself up in love**, as each part does its work." (Ephesians 4:16 NIV) Paul described the church as a temple that was being built by God as a glorious habitation of the Spirit. "Now, therefore, you are no longer strangers and foreigners, but fellow citizens with the saints and members of the household of God, having been built on the foundation of the apostles and prophets, Jesus Christ Himself being the chief corner stone, in whom the whole building, being joined together, grows into a holy temple in the Lord, in whom you also are being built together for a dwelling place of God in the Spirit." (Ephesians 2:19-22)

Love is the only building material that lasts into eternity. Everything else passes away. Paul specifically cautioned against building the temple on a faulty foundation. "According to the grace of God which was given to me, as a wise master builder I have laid the foundation, and another builds on it. But let each one take heed how he builds on it. For no other foundation can anyone lay than that which is laid, which is Jesus Christ." (1 Corinthians 3:10,11) Jesus is the foundation and the foundation is a person. God is love! For God the building of this temple is entirely personal. Straight after Paul gave this warning he proceeded in the next verse to contrast the building material of gold, silver and precious stones with the building material of wood, hay and stubble.

If these are the only enduring building materials with which we can build then we need to understand that it is through the development of an intimate love relationship with God and with our brothers and sisters in Christ that we build the holy temple. Jesus said that the greatest command is to love the Lord with all our hearts and to love our neighbor as ourselves. This commandment of love carries over from the Old Testament into the new. Without love we are nothing! (1 Corinthians 13:1-3) If love is the building material then we must get on the same page with Jesus and invest ourselves into ever deepening relationships of love.

This is how Paul built the temple. He poured himself into others and built a strong foundation for spiritual growth. And this I pray, that your love may abound still more and more…" (Philippians 1:9) "And may the Lord make you increase and abound in love to one another and to all, just as we do to you." (1 Thessalonians 3:12) Needless to say, the foundation of love reveals the reality that this is a journey of the heart. We are to love the Lord with all our heart. Paul said, "Now the purpose of the commandment is love from a pure heart." (1 Timothy 1:5) Peter instructed us to "love one another fervently with a pure heart." (1 Peter 1:22) The call to walk in love as Christ loved us is the most heart searching and heart challenging call we will ever face. This new commandment to love tests the strongest of hearts.

The context of the heart journey is relationship and community. We are invited into the intimate fellowship or community of the Father, Son and Holy Spirit and we are invited into fellowship with the saints and to build community here on earth that reflects the atmosphere of heaven on earth. If we are not pursuing relationships from the heart we are not even in the main game. Building relationships of love is what Paul had in mind when he called us to build the temple with gold, silver and precious stones. The Father and the Son are the gold and the silver and our brothers and sisters in Christ are the precious stones or jewels.

We cannot grow in love unless we are rightly related to the Godhead and to the body of Christ. Jesus built relationships with His disciples that were deeply set in the Father. Because we are 'in Christ' we also become the 'apple of His eye.' We too become those apples of gold in settings of silver. We have been permanently 'set' in the costly silver of the Father heart of God and our lives are adorned with the precious stones of the saints. This means that the two-fold context of the heart journey of growing in love is the Secret Place of the Most High God and the mystical body of Christ or 'community.'

We cannot navigate the heart journey without engaging with God in the Secret Place and engaging with our brothers and sisters in community. If the devil can rip a believer out of intimate engagement with the Father in the Secret Place and out of intimate spiritual community he has sabotaged their spiritual walk and doomed them to live in the outer court of theological knowledge. We can only do this heart journey by coming into the Secret Place where God searches our hearts and minds. In the same way, we can only do this heart journey in the context of accountable relationships with brothers and sisters who can speak the truth in love into our heart. We cannot say to our brethren "I have no need of you" (1 Corinthians 12:21) anymore than we can say to God, "I have no need of You."

The authors of the New Testament deliberately left no room for us to wiggle our way out of an ever-deepening fellowship with the saints. Like Paul, John also confronted a crisis in the church where Greek influenced believers were walking away from their brethren. As with the situation in Corinth, these Christians were exalting themselves over their brothers and sisters because they believed they had superior spiritual knowledge. There was no fundamental difference between this crisis and the one Paul confronted in Corinth. John was addressing the aftermath of a blow up in the church where a group of gnostic believers deliberately "went out from us." The 'us' in this instance was the apostolic community of faith.

"They went out from us, but they were not of us; for if they had been of us, they would have continued with us; but they went out that they might be made manifest, that none of them were of us." (1 John 2:19) John had to draw a clear line in the sand because these gnostic believers were exchanging the apostolic foundation of love, sonship and brotherhood for the Greek foundation of knowledge. John went as far as saying that "anyone who does not love his brother" is not a child of God! (1 John 3:10) "If someone says, "I love God," and hates his brother, he is a liar; for he who does not love his brother whom he has seen, how can he love God whom he has not seen?" (1 John 4:20)

John emphasized again and again in his first epistle the need to obey Jesus' commandment to love one another. He deliberately linked love for God with love for the brethren, arguing that any claim to love God that was not deeply anchored in love for the fellowship of the saints was a deception. "We know that we have passed from death to life, because we love the brethren. He who does not love his brother abides in death. Whoever hates his brother is a murderer, and you know that no murderer has eternal life abiding in him. By this we know love, because He laid down His life for us. And we also ought to lay down our lives for the brethren." (1 John 3:14:16) John left no room to wiggle our way out of building community.

Solomon also carried a vision for family as a necessary consequence of faith in God. "A man who isolates himself seeks his own desire; he rages against all wise judgment." (Proverbs 18:1) "A *recluse* is self-indulgent, snarling at every sound principle of conduct." (NLT) There is only one setting for growth in love and that setting is community. Isolating ourselves emotionally or geographically from our brethren is tantamount to raging against all sound biblical wisdom. No one can embark upon the heart journey of love apart from real authentic Christian community.

In the same way no one can embark on the heart journey of love without coming into the Secret Place of the Most High God and engaging our heart with the very heart of God. It is in the secret place of intimate prayer, worship and fellowship with God that He reveals our heart and convicts us of the deepest motives and attitudes that eat away at true spiritual growth in love. This is very confronting but it is the truth that sets us free. The devil works overtime to rip believers out of their intimate engagement with God on a daily basis where the Lord searches the hearts and minds. In like manner, he works overtime to destroy our core relationships to draw us into a place of isolation from the hearts of our brothers and sisters.

The powers of darkness are deeply aware that the only context of the heart journey is the Secret Place and spiritual community. These are the two areas of our lives that are relentlessly under attack because if the evil one can pull us out of these two unique spiritual environments he knows that it will short circuit the heart journey by pulling us out of our hearts and back into our heads where all we have is theological knowledge instead of intimate heart engagement. We must counter this attack with a passionate intentionality to engage our hearts with the Father by spending time in His presence and engaging our hearts with our brethren in intimate fellowship where we are sharing what we are walking through within our hearts and where we open up our lives to receive deep heart ministry by receiving God's love through our brethren.

Spiritual community is intended to be the safest place on earth. It is a beautiful gift to us from the Father to provide an environment of accountability and loving care for our personal spiritual wellbeing. But sadly, so many Christians do not experience the blessing of true spiritual community. The writer of Hebrews said, "Let us not give up meeting together, as some are in the habit of doing, but let us encourage one another." (Hebrews 10:25 NIV) This is not just talking about going to church on Sunday but it refers to walking in the light and having fellowship and intimate relationship with one another.

Whenever a follower of Jesus isolates him or herself from loving, accountable relationships in community they are effectively forsaking the heart journey of growing in love. There is no heart journey without deepening heart relationships with fellow believers who have access to our hearts. And there is no heart journey without actively pursuing relationship with God through prayer and worship in the Secret Place. As basic as these two realities are to the Christian life it is amazing how many Christians check out of the two primary things that Jesus set in place for the heart journey to be powerfully activated in our lives. Jesus came to pioneer a heart revolution by getting every person on page with Him in His call to live from the heart. We are called to love God with all of our heart and to love our brothers and sisters with a whole heart. The heart journey is the divine call to love and to be loved. Jesus said that this would be the defining characteristic of all of His disciples. "By this all will know that you are My disciples; if you have love for one another." (John 13:35)

Chapter Five

The Promised Land of the Heart

"Blessed is the man whose strength is in You; whose heart is set on pilgrimage." (Psalms 84:5)

"Are you on your heart journey?" That is the language I am hearing more and more amongst a new generation of believers as they ask the question if we are really journeying with our Heavenly Father and our brothers and sisters *from the heart* or if we are struck in a cerebral Christianity that excuses us from doing the 'hard yards' of deep level heart transformation. There is a heart journey to which all New Testament believers are called. God calls us out of the world with the intention of bringing us into the fullness of our inheritance. Getting saved is not an end in itself; it is a means unto a much greater end; namely the transformation of our hearts so the glory of the Lord may be revealed through the church.

This was the pattern for the children of Israel as God brought them out of Egypt with the express purpose of bringing them into the Land that He promised their father, Abraham. "We were slaves of Pharaoh in Egypt, and the Lord brought us out of Egypt with a mighty hand… He *brought us out* from there, that He might *bring us in*, to give us the land of which He swore to our fathers." (Deuteronomy 6:21,23) Israel's pilgrimage was out of Egypt, through the wilderness and ultimately into the Promised Land. "I have also established My covenant with them, to give them the land of Canaan, *the land of their pilgrimage*, in which they were strangers." (Exodus 6:4) This was the great pilgrimage or journey of the people of God out of Egypt, the house of bondage, into Canaan, the house of glorious freedom and divine inheritance.

The writer of Hebrews tells us that there are promises set before the Christian just as there were promises laid up for the Old Testament people of God. We have a better covenant built upon better promises. (Hebrews 8:6) We have the promise of a "better country; that is a heavenly one," (Hebrews 11:16) and this verse clearly reveals that the new 'Promised Land' of the believer is not an earthly strip of geography but a heavenly land with a heavenly city. Our pilgrimage is a pilgrimage of the heart as we embrace the challenge of the heart journey to take possession of everything that God has promised His New Covenant sons and daughters. Our hearts ought to be set on pilgrimage as we rise up to take possession of all that God has for us to lay hold of. We dare not settle in the wilderness.

The Old Testament conquest of the Promised Land is a powerful prophetic type of the personal conquest of our own hearts. Once we are born again we have a vast invisible territory to conquer and to bring under the dominion of the kingdom of heaven. In 1 Corinthians Paul asserted that the Old Testament narrative of Israel's conquest of Canaan speaks powerfully to us as New Testament believers with a destiny to be overcomers. "Now all these things happened to them as examples, and they were written for our admonition, upon whom the ends of the ages have come." (1 Corinthians 10:11) Paul taught explicitly that everything that happened to Israel in their corporate heart journey out of Egypt and into the Promised Land was a prophetic instruction to Christians concerning their own heart journey of partaking in the righteousness and the glory of Christ.

God had a clear prophetic destiny for His people. The ultimate purpose of His call upon Israel to take the Promised Land was to reveal the glory of the Lord within the Land. When Israel rebelled against the Lord and refused to enter the Promised Land the Lord said; "But truly, as I live, all the earth shall be filled with the glory of the Lord." (Numbers 14:21) In other words, God's agenda was to reveal His glory throughout the entire earth through a faithful remnant that He intended to establish in the Land. This promise was ultimately fulfilled by Jesus who was the true seed of Abraham who stood with His feet planted firmly in the Promised Land as He opened up the hope of glory to Israel and subsequently to all the Gentiles. The glory of the Lord was revealed by Jesus for all mankind to see and it shone forth from Israel's Promised Land as a beacon of light in a dark and fallen world. "The people who walked in darkness have seen a great light; those who dwelt in the land of the shadow of death; upon them a light has shined." (Isaiah 9:2)

Six Prophetic Lessons for the Heart

In 1 Corinthians 10 Paul draws out six valuable lessons for New Testament Christians from the history of Israel. He deliberately linked the exodus and conquest narrative to a number of significant heart issues faced by contemporary Christians. This becomes a template for our reading of the whole of the Old Testament as it is interpreted through the lens of the heart journey of New Testament Christians. Paul boldly asserted that the entire story is prophetic for us as New Testament believers. St. Augustine famously said, "the New is in the Old concealed and the Old is in the New revealed!"

> Moreover, brethren, I do not want you to be unaware that all our fathers were under the cloud, all passed through the sea, all were baptized into Moses in the cloud and in the sea, all ate the same spiritual food, and all drank the same spiritual drink. For they drank of that spiritual Rock that followed them, and that Rock was Christ. But with most of them God was not well pleased, for their bodies were scattered in the wilderness. Now these things became our examples, to the intent that we should not lust after evil things as they also lusted. And do not become idolaters as were some of them. As it is written, "The people sat down to eat and drink, and rose up to play." Nor let us commit sexual immorality, as some of them did, and in one day twenty-three thousand fell; nor let us tempt Christ, as some of them also tempted, and were destroyed by serpents; nor complain, as some of them also complained, and were destroyed by the destroyer. Now all these things happened to them as examples, and they were written for our admonition, upon whom the ends of the ages have come. (1 Corinthians 10:1-11)

Paul reminded the Christians in Corinth; "God was not pleased with most of them." (1 Corinthians 10:5 NIV) He drew a direct parallel between God's displeasure toward the unfaithful conduct His Old Covenant people and the unrighteous conduct and unbelief of Christians who were similarly arousing the displeasure of the Lord. There is a great paradox here because; through the miracle of regeneration and the free gift of righteousness there is one sense in which God is as pleased with us as His sons and daughters as He is with His only beloved Son. Yet, when His children walk in rebellion and unbelief it clearly arouses His displeasure toward our conduct. We are called to fully please the Lord in all things. The author of Hebrews tells us; "Without faith it is impossible to please Him." (Hebrews 11:6) Persistence in sin and unbelief doesn't please our Father.

Paul specifically prayed; "For this reason, since the day we heard about you, we have not stopped praying for you and asking God to fill you with the knowledge of His will through all spiritual wisdom and understanding. And we pray this in order that you may live a life worthy of the Lord and may please Him in every way." (Colossians 1:9,10 NIV) The NKJV says, "That you may walk worthy of the Lord; *fully pleasing Him*." The New Testament clearly articulates the things that please and displease the Lord. "Now the just shall live by faith; but if anyone draws back, My soul has no pleasure in him." (Hebrews 10:38) Paul's purpose in writing 1 Corinthians 10 was to draw a clear parallel between the immoral and idolatrous conduct of the Corinthians and the immorality and idolatry of the Israelites as they journeyed through the wilderness.

Paul writes; "These things occurred as examples to keep us from setting our hearts on evil things as they did." (1 Corinthians 10:6 NIV) Christians can just as easily set their hearts upon evil things as Israel did and end up displeasing the Lord. Paul continued; "Do not be idolaters, as some of them were." (1 Corinthians 10:7 NIV) Christians can be just as idolatrous as historic Israel was and such idolatry amongst New Testament believers is extremely displeasing to the Lord. Paul also warned; "We should not commit sexual immorality, as some of them did." (1 Corinthians 10:8 NIV) In the same way, Christians can also give themselves over to sexual immorality, which is extremely displeasing to the Lord.

Paul identified another parallel between the rebellion of Israel and the rebellion of New Covenant believers. "We should not test the Lord, as some of them did and were destroyed by serpents." (1 Corinthians 10:9 NIV) Here, Paul is referencing an incident in Israel's history where they put God to the test and it was extremely displeasing to Him.

> Then they journeyed from Mount Hor by the way of the Red Sea, to go around the land of Edom; and the soul of the people became very discouraged on the way. And the people spoke against God and against Moses: "Why have you brought us up out of Egypt to die in the wilderness? For there is no food and no water, and our soul loathes this worthless bread." So the Lord sent fiery serpents among the people, and they bit the people; and many of the people of Israel died. (Numbers 21:4-6)

Putting the Lord to the test stirs up the displeasure of the Lord. Jesus said to the devil; "It is written: "Do not put the Lord your God to the test." (Matthew 4:7, Exodus 17:2) "The people of Israel argued with Moses and tested the Lord by saying, "Is the Lord going to take care of us or not?" (Exodus 17:7) Testing God in this way is a blatant expression of unbelief and rebellion that denies the revelation of God's power and His glory.

> But they continued to sin against Him, rebelling in the desert against the Most High. They willfully put God to the test by demanding the food they craved. They spoke against God, saying, "Can God spread a table in the desert?" When he struck the rock, water gushed out, and streams flowed abundantly. "But can He also give us food? Can he supply meat for his people?" When the Lord heard them, He was very angry; his fire broke out against Jacob, and his wrath rose against Israel for they did not believe in God or trust in his deliverance." (Psalm 78:17-22)

The children of Israel 'tested the Lord' by grumbling and complaining against the Lord and calling into question the goodness of His nature when He had so clearly revealed His glory in so many tangible ways.

> All these men who have seen My glory and the signs which I did in Egypt and in the wilderness, and have put Me to the test now these ten times, and have not heeded My voice; they certainly shall not see the land of which I swore to their fathers, nor shall any of those who rejected Me see it. (Numbers 14:22,23)

If the children of Israel had not seen any tangible demonstrations of His glory and His power they could be forgiven for wondering why God had led His people out of Egypt and into a harsh and barren wilderness. But His relentless provision of manna, fire by night and cloud by day robbed the Israelites of any basis to test the Lord with their constant accusations against His goodness. Every time it was recorded that Israel tested the Lord it was set against the backdrop of God's display of His mighty power and glory.

> How often they rebelled against Him in the desert and grieved Him in the wasteland! Again and again they put God to the test; they vexed the Holy One of Israel. They did not remember His power - the day He redeemed them from the oppressor, the day He displayed His miraculous signs in Egypt. (Psalm 78:40-43)

They soon forgot what He had done and did not wait for His counsel. In the desert they gave in to their craving; in the wasteland they put God to the test. And He gave them their request but sent leanness into their soul. (Psalms 106:14)

The New Testament parallel is immediately apparent. The Corinthians lived in the midst of signs and wonders and an outpouring of the glory of God through the ministry of Paul. He engaged in "demonstrations of the Spirit and of power" amongst them. Indeed, the Corinthian church was founded on mighty signs and wonders. Testing the Lord or 'putting God to the test' occurs when we have seen the glory of the Lord revealed but we speak and behave as though God is not good or that He doesn't care for us. "We should not test the Lord, as some of them did and were destroyed by serpents." (1 Corinthians 10:9 NIV) Of course, this parallel was not a mistake. If the Corinthians were to persist in their complaining and grumbling against Paul as the Lord's anointed they were literally opening themselves up to the demonic realm and risking the possibility of also being destroyed by serpents (or demons).

In fact, Paul's next comment was; "We should not complain, as some of them also complained, and were destroyed [*apollumi*] by the Destroyer." (1 Corinthians 10:10) Grumbling and complaining displeases the Lord because it is rooted in unbelief and it denies the history of the revelation of God's glory to His people. Paul taught specifically that Christians can be destroyed by the evil one if they choose to give themselves over to a pattern of relentless negativity. There is an explicit reference to the evil one embedded in this warning that should alert us to the danger of demonic infiltration into our soul that can come as Christians traffic in spiritual darkness. Paul warned the Corinthians that they too could end up shipwrecked and destroyed by the Destroyer. Of course he was warning them about the devil. "His name in Hebrew is Abaddon, and in Greek, Apollyon – the Destroyer." (Revelation 9:11) Paul gave a clear prophetic warning to Christians that this could happen to them just as it happened to the children of Israel if they also fell into complaining and grumbling against the Lord and His anointed apostolic leaders.

Paul had only just warned Christians in the previous verse about the danger of being 'destroyed by serpents.' He no doubt had one particular serpent in mind. In his second epistle he warned the Corinthians about the Serpent's capacity to beguile and deceive believers.

> But I am afraid that just as Eve was deceived by the serpent's cunning, your minds may somehow be led astray from your sincere and pure devotion to Christ. For if someone comes to you and preaches a Jesus other than the Jesus we preached, or if you receive a different spirit from the one you received, or a different gospel from the one you accepted, you put up with it easily enough. (2 Corinthians 11:3,4 NIV)

Some within the Corinthian church had made themselves vulnerable to the infiltration of the serpent and His cunning lies. They had been infiltrated by 'a different spirit' (in contrast to the Holy Spirit) and were effectively demonized through their eventual rejection of the Pauline gospel of grace. Thus we can see how Paul is employing the narrative of the pilgrimage of the Old Testament people of God and transforming it into a prophetic parallel of the heart journey of believers who also have to journey through all sorts of trials and tribulations that echo the afflictions and trials of the Israelites in the wilderness and in Canaan.

But Paul is not merely infusing these ancient narratives with prophetic content. On the contrary, he asserts that all of these things happened to them as a deliberate type and shadow of things to come, suggesting that God orchestrated and designed the exodus/conquest paradigm as a narrative that would be uniquely instructive to the church of Christ to describe the journey of the heart in laying hold of the fullness of God's prophetic destiny and purpose for His New Covenant people 'upon whom the ends of the ages have come.' That is an extraordinary thought that staggers our minds if it is indeed true. I would suggest that there are far too many profound prophetic 'coincidences' for it all to be some kind of accident of history.

Hebrews and the Heart Journey Template

Just like Paul, the author of Hebrews employs the exact same Old Testament paradigm of the exodus/conquest and draws out profound heart lessons for New Testament believers. We see this most clearly in Hebrews chapter 3 and 4.

> And Moses indeed was faithful in all his house as a servant, for a testimony of those things which would be spoken afterward, but Christ as a Son over His own house, whose house we are if we hold fast the confidence and the rejoicing of the hope firm to the end.

Therefore, as the Holy Spirit says: "Today, if you will hear His voice, do not harden your hearts as in the rebellion in the day of trial in the wilderness, where your fathers tested Me, tried Me and saw My works forty years. Therefore I was angry with that generation and said, "They always go astray in their heart and they have not known My ways. So I swore in My wrath, "They shall not enter My rest." Beware, brethren, lest there be in any of you an evil heart of unbelief in departing from the living God; but exhort one another daily, while it is called "Today," lest any of you be hardened through the deceitfulness of sin. For we have become partakers of Christ if we hold the beginning of our confidence steadfast to the end, while it is said: "Today, if you will hear His voice, do not harden your hearts as in the rebellion." For who, having heard, rebelled? Indeed, was it not all who came out of Egypt, led by Moses? Now with whom was He angry forty years? Was it not with those who sinned, whose corpses fell in the wilderness? And to whom did He swear that they would not enter His rest, but to those who did not obey? So we see that they could not enter in because of unbelief. Therefore, since a promise remains of entering His rest, let us fear lest any of you seem to have come short of it. For indeed the gospel was preached to us as well as to them; but the word which they heard did not profit them, not being mixed with faith in those who heard it. For we who have believed do enter that rest, as He has said: "So I swore in My wrath, "They shall not enter My rest," although the works were finished from the foundation of the world. For He has spoken in a certain place of the seventh day in this way: "And God rested on the seventh day from all His works;" and again in this place: "They shall not enter My rest." Since therefore it remains that some must enter it, and those to whom it was first preached did not enter because of disobedience, again He designates a certain day, saying in David, "Today," after such a long time, as it has been said: "Today, if you will hear His voice, do not harden your hearts." For if Joshua had given them rest, then He would not afterward have spoken of another day. There remains therefore a rest for the people of God. For he who has entered His rest has himself also ceased from his works as God did from His. Let us therefore be diligent to enter that rest, lest anyone fall according to the same example of disobedience. (Hebrews 3:5-4:11)

The recurring theme of this extended passage was the admonition to New Testament believers not to fall into the same pattern of rebellion and hardness of heart that the children of Israel exhibited when God called them to enter the rest of the Promised Land. These are themes that Paul similarly developed in 1 Corinthians 10, except his focus was exclusively upon the exodus/wilderness narrative.

Entering God's Rest

This concept; "They shall not enter My rest," comes from a passage in Psalm 95:7-11 where the writer rehearses the failure of Israel to obey God on their heart pilgrimage to go in to possess the Promised Land. The writer of Hebrews asserts that there is a place of rest for New Testament Christians where they find a place of rest from all their enemies. Moses spoke of a time "when you cross over the Jordan and dwell in the land which the Lord your God is giving you to inherit, and *He gives you rest* from all your enemies round about so that you dwell in safety." (Deuteronomy 12:10)

God Himself promised there would be a time "when the Lord your God has given you rest from your enemies all around." (Deuteronomy 25:19) This season of rest from all of their enemies came toward the end of Joshua's life. "The Lord gave them rest all around, according to all that He had sworn to their fathers. And not a man of all their enemies stood against them; the Lord delivered all their enemies into their hand." (Joshua 21:44) Israel could only enter this place of victorious rest in the battle if they fully obeyed the Lord and refused to harden their hearts. In fact, God promised to fight all their enemies on their behalf as long as they fully obeyed Him.

Like Paul, the writer of Hebrews draws out a number of major heart lessons for New Testament believers if they are to enter this place of obtaining all of the promises of the New Covenant through faith and patience.

1. Do not harden your heart.

2. Do not go astray in your heart.

3. Do not allow an evil heart of unbelief to rise up.

4. Do not disobey when you hear God's voice.

God requires the full assurance of faith on this supernatural heart journey as we press forward to lay hold of the New Covenant Promised Land of living in the glory of Christ in the New Jerusalem. Our eyes are no longer on a strip of geography in the Middle East. They are set upon a *"better, heavenly"* inheritance, and the writer of Hebrews confidently asserts that this spiritual Promised Land is a mystical reality that we entered into through the new birth.

> These all died in faith, not having received the promises, but having seen them afar off, were assured of them, embraced them and confessed that they were *strangers and pilgrims on the earth.* For those who say such things declare plainly that they seek a homeland. And truly if they had called to mind that country from which they had come out, they would have had opportunity to return. But now they desire a better, that is, *a heavenly country.* Therefore God is not ashamed to be called their God, for *He has prepared a city for them.* (Hebrews 11:13-16)

The writer of Hebrews goes on to describe the New Jerusalem as our heavenly Promised Land. This is intentionally juxtaposed against the old Jerusalem, the beloved capital and crown jewel of the Old Covenant Promised Land. "But you *have come* to Mount Zion and to the city of the living God, the heavenly Jerusalem, to an innumerable company of angels..." (Hebrews 12:22) Our spiritual heart pilgrimage is to live in the glory of the heavenly Jerusalem. We are now focused upon "A better covenant, which was established on better promises." (Hebrews 8:6) Ours is a better 'spiritual' Promised Land. John saw a vision of the New Jerusalem and it was filled with the radiance of the glory of God.

> And he carried me away in the Spirit to a mountain great and high, and showed me the Holy City, Jerusalem, coming down out of heaven from God. It shone with the glory of God, and its brilliance was like that of a very precious jewel, like a jasper, clear as crystal. (Revelation 21:10,11 NIV)

The Promised Land as a Type of the Heart

As I read these revelations in Paul and in the book of Hebrews there appears to be a New Testament imperative that each of us who believe in Christ ought to adopt the paradigm of a radical new *heart pilgrimage* to live in the fullness of a new Promised Land with a better city. Equipped with this upgraded prophetic perspective we can come to the narrative of the journey of Israel as they sought to take possession of Canaan and view it as a glorious prophetic vision of the New Testament heart journey of the followers of Christ. Indeed, these Old Testament narratives are dripping with prophetic significance for us. They are filled with stunning parallels. I would suggest that we could actually merge the two admonitions of 1 Corinthians 10 and Hebrews 4 together into a synthesis:

> Now all these things happened to them as examples, and they were written for our admonition, upon whom the ends of the ages have come. Let us therefore be diligent to enter that rest, lest anyone fall according to the same example of disobedience. (1 Corinthians 10:11 and Hebrews 4:11)

The entire narrative of the exodus, the wilderness and the conquest of Canaan is a *type* and a *shadow*. The Greek word Paul used for '*examples*' was *tupos*, from which we derive the English word 'type.' The word means a 'resemblance' or a 'pattern.' Paul even regarded all of the Old Testament festivals and Sabbaths as nothing more than prophetic 'shadows.' This would suggest that the entire Old Testament narrative of the pilgrimage of Israel was also "a *shadow* of things to come, but the substance is of Christ." (Colossians 2:17) Equipped with this prophetic interpretation of Israel's journey we can come to the narrative of the conquest of Canaan as both a 'type' and a 'shadow' of the heart journey of the New Testament people of God as we journey into rest from all of our enemies and as we aggressively seek to lay hold of our inheritance of the glory of Christ.

The Old Testament is full of prophetic types. None of these are accidental. They are prophetic pictures designed by God as a deeper layer of prophetic significance embedded within His written Word. Every prophetic type corresponds to a New Testament 'antitype.' An antitype is a person or a thing that is intentionally represented or foreshadowed by a type or shadow. We discover that the Greek word '*antitupon*' is used to highlight the way a prophetic type is fulfilled in the New Testament. "For Christ has entered into heaven itself to appear now before God as our Advocate. He did not go into the earthly place of worship, for that was merely a copy [*antitupon*] of the real Temple in heaven." (Hebrews 9:24 NLT) So we see that the earthly Holy of Holies in the tabernacle of Moses was a type and the true Holy of Holies in heaven is the antitype. This unique prophetic paradigm is reflected throughout the Old and New Testaments, prompting St. Augustine to say; "The New is in the Old concealed; whilst the Old is in the New revealed."

God Planted His Son, Israel in the Promised Land

God described the whole nation of Israel as His son. "Israel is My son; My firstborn." (Exodus 4:22) "When Israel was a child, I loved him and out of Egypt I called My son." (Hosea 11:1) God called His son out of slavery and into sonship. Paul highlighted the prophetic significance of this theme when he said, "For you did not receive a spirit that makes you a slave again to fear, but you received the *Spirit of sonship.* And by Him we cry, "Abba, Father." (Romans 8:15 NIV) Concerning Israel, Paul said; "Theirs is the adoption as sons; theirs the divine glory, the covenants, the receiving of the law, the temple worship and the promises." (Romans 9:4) In calling them 'His people' God adopted Abraham's descendants as His very own. Paul's theology of the 'Spirit of adoption' is built upon the prophetic precursor of God's adoption of Israel as His son. The difference of course between the Old Testament concept of adoption and that of the New was that under the Old Covenant it was a visitation culture: God came *upon* His chosen people. But in the New Covenant it is a habitation culture where God comes to dwell within the hearts of His people.

We don't see very much evidence at all in the Old Testament of the Father/son paradigm between Yahweh and His people. But we do get occasional glimpses into the kind of relationship between God and His people that anticipated the future expression of the Father/son paradigm of the New Testament. "You deserted the Rock who *fathered* you; you forgot the God who gave you birth. The Lord saw this and drew back, provoked to anger by his own *sons and daughters*." (Deuteronomy 32:18,19) "Is this the way you repay the Lord, O foolish and unwise people? Is He not your *Father*, your Creator, who made you and formed you?" (Deuteronomy 32:6)

In calling Israel His adopted son, God gave a clear prophetic precursor of the Father/son relationship unveiled in the New Covenant. Most of the time God's corporate son behaved much more like an orphan than a son. The children of Israel came out of Egypt living and thinking like slaves and not like sons. The narrative of Israel's profound brokenness is the tale of a corporate orphan community that never embraced the paradigm of God as a loving Father. They came out of Egypt as slaves and never got free of the slave mentality as a people. They lived under a spirit of slavery in spite of God's appeal to them as a loving Father.

God called His son out of Egypt and then brought him into the land of Canaan, eventually naming this new nation 'Israel.' God called His son into a land still to be conquered. To the Father, Israel was the hope of glory sown as a seed into the Promised Land. "I bring My righteousness near, it shall not be far off; My salvation shall not linger. And I will place salvation in Zion, for *Israel My glory.*" (Isaiah 46:13) "You are My Servant, Israel, in whom I will show My glory." (Isaiah 49:3 NASB) "I will yet bring an heir to you, O inhabitant of Mareshah; *the glory of Israel shall come* to Adullam." (Micah 1:15) Of course, Mareshah and Adullam were Canaanite cities in the Promised Land.

Israel was planted like a seed in the midst of a hostile environment. This is unquestionably a prophetic type of the new creation seed of sonship planted as God's hope of glory in the center of the human heart. But there is an old orphan heart that still remains to be subdued and conquered by the Spirit of sonship. God has given us a brand new identity of sonship within our spirit. "The Spirit Himself testifies with our spirit that we are God's children." (Romans 8:16 NIV) This is the beginning of the conquest of the new Canaan; the human heart. This new identity in our spirit is now at war with an old identity within our soul. The unrenewed regions of the heart are heavily populated with old orphan strongholds and the giants still taunt and condemn us with lies that seek to hold us in bondage to our old orphan identity.

God Gave His Son an Inheritance

God says prophetically to Canaan; "I will yet bring an heir to you!" Israel, God's son had been made an heir because he had been declared a son. Straight after God calls us sons He declares that we are also heirs. "Now if we are children, then we are heirs; heirs of God and co-heirs with Christ." (Romans 8:17 NIV) In the Old Testament the Promised Land was continually described as the *inheritance* of the people of God.

> When you come into the land of Canaan, this is the land that shall fall to you as an *inheritance*; the land of Canaan to its boundaries. (Numbers 34:2)

> For the Lord will greatly bless you in the land which the Lord your God is giving you to possess as an *inheritance*. (Deuteronomy 15:4)

After the death of Moses the servant of the Lord, it came to pass that the Lord spoke to Joshua the son of Nun, Moses' assistant, saying: "Moses My servant is dead. Now therefore, arise, go over this Jordan, you and all this people, to the land which I am giving to them; the children of Israel. Every place that the sole of your foot will tread upon I have given you, as I said to Moses. No man shall be able to stand before you all the days of your life; as I was with Moses, so I will be with you. I will not leave you nor forsake you. Be strong and of good courage, for to this people you shall divide *as an inheritance the land* which I swore to their fathers to give them. Only be strong and very courageous. (Joshua 1:1-7)

The children of Israel carried this vision of inheritance in their hearts as they entered the Promised Land. Moses was taken to a mountaintop to view the Promised Land from afar even though the Lord didn't allow him to ever enter the Land. Paul prayed continually that the saints would have a mountaintop revelatory vision of the inheritance of the saints.

Therefore I also, after I heard of your faith in the Lord Jesus and your love for all the saints, do not cease to give thanks for you, making mention of you in my prayers: that the God of our Lord Jesus Christ, *the Father of glory*, may give to you the spirit of wisdom and revelation in the knowledge of Him, the eyes of your heart being enlightened; that you may know what is the hope of His calling, what are *the riches of the glory of His inheritance* in the saints. (Ephesians 1:15-18)

The inheritance of the saints is the riches of the glory of God revealed in the person of Christ who now lives inside of all who have been made new creations. "To them God willed to make known what are *the riches of the glory* of this mystery among the Gentiles: which is Christ in you, *the hope of glory.*" (Colossians 1:27) The glory of God is a storehouse of unlimited resources for the saints. "God who takes care of me will supply all your needs from *His glorious riches*, which have been given to us in Christ Jesus." (Philippians 4:19 NLT) These glorious riches provide all things to us that we need for life and godliness. "I pray that out of *His glorious riches* he may strengthen you with power through his Spirit in your inner being." (Ephesians 3:16)

The new inheritance of the saints has become the riches of the glory of God! This is Paul's manifesto. He was powerfully committed to raising up a generation who would rise up to take a hold of their full inheritance and press in to live in a land filled with the glory of God's power and love. Each step of the interior journey of the heart now brings us closer and closer to living in the fullness of God's glory as we learn how to overcome all of our enemies and establish the glory of God's kingdom within our own personal lives.

The Hope of the Glory

There is a hope that has been set before us both personally and corporately. We dare not merely tread water until Christ returns, wallowing in our sin and brokenness. "We who have fled to take hold of the hope offered to us may be greatly encouraged. We have this hope as an anchor for the soul, firm and secure. It enters the inner sanctuary behind the curtain, where Jesus, who went before us, has entered on our behalf." (Hebrews 6:18-20 NIV) There is a place reserved for us in the Spirit that is filled with great glory and every spiritual blessing in the heavenly places in Christ. "*This hope* we have as an anchor of the soul, both sure and steadfast, and which enters the Presence behind the veil, where the forerunner has entered for us, even Jesus." (NKJV) This glorious hope is centered upon "Christ in you, the hope of glory." (Colossians 1:27) All Christians ought to have a confident expectation of being transformed from glory to glory. "Therefore, having been justified by faith, we have peace with God through our Lord Jesus Christ, through whom also we have access by faith into this grace in which we stand, and rejoice in *hope of the glory of God*." (Romans 5:1,2) God has ordained that we lay hold of the hope of the glory of Christ in our heart as our spiritual inheritance.

> Therefore, brethren, having boldness to enter the Holiest by the blood of Jesus, by a new and living way which He consecrated for us, through the veil, that is, His flesh, and having a High Priest over the house of God, let us draw near with a true heart in full assurance of faith, having our hearts sprinkled from an evil conscience and our bodies washed with pure water. Let us hold fast the confession of *our hope* without wavering, for He who promised is faithful. (Hebrews 10:19-23)

Israel had a great hope because God had promised them a vast region of land as their inheritance. But we have a better hope because we have been promised a glorious place in the Spirit to occupy and possess. We have been given a better country to live in. The book of Hebrews is all about believers entering into our new inheritance that has been promised us by God. The anonymous author of Hebrews writes to Jewish believers, seeking to shift their focus away from the inheritance of a piece of land to a glorious heavenly inheritance. "For this reason Christ is the mediator of a New Covenant, that those who are called may receive *the promise of the eternal inheritance.*" (Hebrews 9:15) The Promised Land of Canaan was a temporal inheritance until the true, eternal inheritance came in Christ. The ancient land of Canaan now serves as nothing more that a prophetic type and shadow of a better country.

The writer of Hebrews tells us the story of Abraham and the promise of Isaac. Then he says, "And so, after he had patiently endured, he *obtained* the promise." (Hebrews 6:15) The New Testament parallel of course is the obtaining of a greater promise. "He called you by our gospel, *for the obtaining of the glory* of our Lord Jesus Christ." (2 Thessalonians 2:14) "We do not want you to become lazy, but to imitate those who through faith and patience *inherit what has been promised.*" (Hebrews 6:12) "Therefore do not cast away your confidence, which has great reward. For you have need of endurance, so that after you have done the will of God, you may *receive the promise.*" (Hebrews 10:35,36) Each of us now have an infinitely greater hope and inheritance that the Old Testament people of God. Paul taught that our inheritance was to obtain the glory of God!

> For this reason, since the day we heard about you, we have not stopped praying for you and asking God to fill you with the knowledge of His will through all spiritual wisdom and understanding. And we pray this in order that you may live a life worthy of the Lord and may please Him in every way: bearing fruit in every good work, growing in the knowledge of God, being strengthened with all power according to his glorious might so that you may have great endurance and patience, and joyfully giving thanks to the Father, who has qualified you *to share in the inheritance of the saints* in the kingdom of light. (Colossians 1:9-12)

The Leadership of Yeshua

Another interesting parallel between the life of Israel, the corporate son and the life of the New Testament people of God is the leadership of Joshua. Israel entered the land under the leadership of Joshua or Yeshua in Hebrew. Joshua was formerly called Hoshea from birth but curiously, Hoshea underwent a prophetic name change to Yeshua on the eve of the twelve spies being sent into Canaan to spy out the land. "And Moses called Hoshea the son of Nun; Joshua." (Numbers 13:16) This was done because Joshua was clearly a prophetic type of Christ. Now, Jesus leads us in the conquest of our own hearts, which becomes His Promised Land. The Father has promised the Son a great company of brothers and sisters.

Under the prophetic leadership of Yeshua 'Israel the son' underwent a baptism and a circumcision of the heart as the first prophetic act upon entering the land. Israel miraculously passed through the waters of baptism. God parted the waters of the Jordan just as He supernaturally parted the Red Sea. They were all baptized in the Red Sea into Moses but they were all baptized into Yeshua in the Jordan as they crossed over into the Promised Land. Jesus Himself was baptized in the Jordan where the Father prophetically called Him His beloved Son. Our hearts are circumcised through baptism into Christ at the very moment the Father adopts us as His sons and daughters and declares us His beloved. Paul deliberately identified baptism into Christ with 'circumcision of the heart.'

> When you came to Christ, you were 'circumcised,' but not by a physical procedure. It was a spiritual procedure – the cutting away of your sinful nature. For you were buried with Christ when you were baptized. And with him you were raised to a new life because you trusted the mighty power of God, who raised Christ from the dead. You were dead because of your sins and because your sinful nature was not yet cut away. Then God made you alive with Christ. He forgave all our sins. (Colossians 2:11-13 NLT)

We are supernaturally placed into the Promised Land through baptism and through spiritual circumcision according to the pattern of the children of Israel as they entered the land that God had promised to them as an inheritance. These are remarkable parallels!

Learning to Exercise Kingdom Authority

Immediately upon entering the Land, Israel the son was challenged to exercise authority and to subdue Canaan. The land of Canaan becomes a glorious prophetic type of the heart of the believer. Once God's corporate son was planted within the borders of the Promised Land they were challenged to stand in the authority of sonship and exercise dominion and rule through subduing the land. Through the free gift of righteousness we have been given a scepter of authority. "A scepter of righteousness is the scepter of Your kingdom." (Hebrews 1:8) God places this scepter of righteousness in the hands of His children. The authority of the kingdom is given in its fullness to God's sons and daughters and they are given a brand new core identity of sonship. But Israel could only win their outer battles as they won the interior battle of standing in their identity as a son in relation to their Father. When they lived under the authority of their Father they could rule as a son. Whenever they rebelled against their heavenly Father their enemies prevailed over them. And so it is for us as sons and daughters under the loving authority of our Heavenly Father. Because we are in the Beloved Son the same authority that the Father gave Jesus has been given to us.

> The Lord says to my Lord: "Sit at My right hand until I make Your enemies a footstool for Your feet." The Lord will stretch forth Your strong scepter from Zion, saying, "Rule in the midst of Your enemies." (Psalm 110:1,2 NASB)

Israel under Joshua was called to take a courageous stand in battle. "Have I not commanded you? Be strong and of good courage; do not be afraid, nor be dismayed, for the Lord your God is with you wherever you go." (Joshua 1:9) The prophetic picture of Israel, the Son planted in a hostile land is a picture of the seed of sonship through the new creation planted in the heart. Our new heart is a heart of sonship. But it is only as we stand in the free gift of righteousness and sonship that we can rule over our own heart and overcome all our interior enemies. Israel, the son's prophetic destiny was conquest; to rule in the midst of their enemies and drive every enemy out of the Land. In the context of great adversity Jesus said to His disciples, "By your patience possess your souls." (Luke 21:19) Our soul, with all of its unrenewed frontiers and strongholds is the new Promised Land we are called to possess. The conquest of Canaan was a lifelong journey of warfare and battle, first to conquer and then to maintain and defend the ground that had been won.

God raised up Joshua and Caleb to lead because they were of a different spirit: they didn't see giants; they saw grasshoppers. They carried a vision of God as a mighty warrior who would fight on behalf of Israel because the battle belonged to the Lord. They had won their interior battles and were qualified to lead a company of warriors in fighting their outward battles. Because they knew the heart of the Lord they could lead with vision and continually call the children of Israel back to the revelation of Yahweh as the conquering King. They couldn't establish the kingdom in the Promised Land unless the kingdom had first been established in their personal lives.

Kingdom authority is all about the exercise of spiritual dominion and rulership. "Your kingdom is an everlasting kingdom and Your dominion endures throughout all generations." (Psalms 145:13) "Rule in the midst of Your enemies!" (Psalms 110:2) "You will rule over many nations but none will rule over you." (Deuteronomy 15:6 NIV) "Those who captured Israel will be captured, and Israel will rule over its enemies." (Isaiah 14:2 NLT) All the kings of Israel were evaluated by whether they exercised kingdom authority and rule of the nation of Israel by driving out the inhabitants of the Land and casting down the high places.

Israel, God's son, was called to exercise headship over all of their enemies. "The Lord will make you the head and not the tail; you shall be above only, and not be beneath, if you heed the commandments of the Lord your God, which I command you today, and are careful to observe them." (Deuteronomy 28:13) If the Israelites didn't exercise spiritual dominion within the Land their enemies would exercise dominion in the Land. The narrative of Joshua and Judges explains the ebb and flow of Israel's rulership over their enemies. "For at that time the Philistines *had dominion over* Israel." (Judges 14:4) But later, as Israel was restored to a place of obedience to Yahweh they were empowered to overthrow their enemies. "So the Philistines *were subdued* and did not invade Israelite territory again." (1 Samuel 7:13 NIV)

Living within the Land was always a question of who would exercise dominion. Nehemiah gave this commentary on the ebb and flow of Israel's authority. "After they had rest they again did evil before You. Therefore You left them in the hand of their enemies *so that they had dominion over them*; Yet when they returned and cried out to You, You heard from heaven and many times You delivered them according to Your mercies." (Nehemiah 9:28) The real golden age of Israel's conquest came under the reign of Solomon because King David, his father had paved the way for a nationwide exercise of dominion. "For he [Solomon] *had dominion* over all the region on this side of the River from Tiphsah even to Gaza, namely over all the kings on this side of the River; and he had peace on every side all around him." (1 Kings 4:24)

The spiritual implications of Israel's fluctuating fortunes within Canaan for our personal heart journey is quite plain to see. There is a strong theme of warfare that surrounds our individual heart journey of conquest. God has laid the supernatural foundation through our baptism into Christ and the supernatural circumcision of our hearts. He has established a stronghold of His glory in the center of our heart but we must fight for our inheritance because our enemies are fighting against us in order to withstand us entering into our inheritance. We must fight because the enemy has brought the fight to us. If we didn't have a belligerent enemy we could easily march in to possess the fullness of our inheritance. But we must fight because we have an adversary, the devil who doesn't want to see a single Christian take possession of the inheritance of the riches of the glory of Christ. Israel's enemies within Canaan are a prophetic type of the powers of darkness that actively resist us possessing all that the Lord has given us as heirs of the kingdom.

Israel, the Son was given a vast territory with huge regions to conquer. The crossing over of Israel into the Land established a beachhead within the borders of Canaan and the establishment of this beachhead sent tremors of fear through the heart of Israel's enemies. The children of Israel were given by inheritance a vast geographical region of the Middle East to occupy and possess. And so we see that for us as New Covenant believers the vast territory of our human heart must also be subdued just as the Promised Land had to be subdued.

"So Joshua conquered all the land: the mountain country and the South and the lowland and the wilderness slopes, and all their kings; he left none remaining. And Joshua conquered them from Kadesh Barnea as far as Gaza, and all the country of Goshen, even as far as Gibeon. All these kings and their land Joshua took at one time, because the Lord God of Israel fought for Israel." (Joshua 10:40-42) We were born for conquest. "In all these things we are *more than conquerors* through Him who loved us." (Romans 8:37) "For everyone born of God overcomes the world. This is the victory that has overcome the world, even our faith. Who is it that overcomes the world? Only he who believes that Jesus is the Son of God." (1 John 5:4,5 NIV) "But thanks be to God, who gives us the victory through our Lord Jesus Christ." (1 Corinthians 15:57)

As we survey the vast interior of our own hearts we see all the regions that are still to be conquered. Sometimes it can be discouraging because our hearts can be easily overwhelmed by the vastness of the assignment. But God has promised to fight for us with His supernatural power. Whenever we come into alignment with our assignment, trusting the grace of God to strengthen our hearts to prevail against every single enemy, God steps in and supernaturally vanquishes all of our interior enemies.

Violent Conquest

Israel was given a divine mandate to occupy the land and to violently expel its inhabitants. There was a strong dimension of warfare that accompanied the occupation of the Land. If we are honest we may admit that the violence that the nation of Israel exercised against their enemies within the Land is highly offensive to our moral and ethical sensibilities. But there is a greater picture here. As Paul revealed, all of the things that happened to Israel were a prophetic type that speaks to us upon whom the ends of the age have come. The entire picture of the conquest of Canaan through warfare and bloodshed is a prophetic picture of our violent battle against principalities and powers that actively resist our full occupation of the inheritance of the glory. Jesus said, "The kingdom of heaven suffers violence, and the violent take it by force." (Matthew 11:12)

God used the violence of Israel's warfare with the inhabitants of Canaan to teach them the nature of war. "These are the nations the Lord left to test all those Israelites who had not experienced any of the wars in Canaan (he did this only *to teach warfare* to the descendants of the Israelites who had not had previous battle experience): the five rulers of the Philistines, all the Canaanites, the Sidonians, and the Hivites living in the Lebanon mountains from Mount Baal Hermon to Lebo Hamath. They were left to test the Israelites to see whether they would obey the Lord's commands, which He had given their forefathers through Moses." (Judges 3;1-4 NIV) The prophetic antitype of this call to total war is the imperative for followers of Christ to understand the violent nature of our interior battle. We are commissioned to become warriors of the heart who engage the issues in our own heart that would overcome us if we refuse to step on to the battlefield and to fight.

The ungodly nations the Israelites were commanded to dispossess were highly demonic cultures that practiced blood sacrifices to demonic beings and false gods. The land was heavily infested with demons, altars, satanic rituals and high places of idol worship. These ungodly nations even practiced child sacrifice. God raised up Israel as an instrument of judgment against these depraved, ungodly nations that were given over to child sacrifice and comprehensively evil occult practices. It was not at all uncommon in the Old Testament for the Lord to raise up a nation as an instrument of judgment against an ungodly nation. Even Babylon was raised up by God to overthrow Israel once their cup of iniquity was full.

We are mandated to violently overthrow all of our spiritual enemies. In the book of Daniel, Daniel saw the powers of darkness "making war against the saints, and prevailing against them until the Ancient of Days came and a judgment was made in favor of the saints of the Most High and the time came for the saints to possess the kingdom." (Daniel 7:21,22) Even in the book of Revelation we see that the 'beast' "was given power to make war against the saints and to conquer them." "Woe to the inhabitants of the earth and the sea! For the devil has come down to you, having great wrath, because he knows that he has a short time." (Revelation 12:12) "And the dragon was enraged with the woman, and he went to make war with the rest of her offspring, who keep the commandments of God and have the testimony of Jesus Christ." (Revelation 12:17) Just like Israel, if we do not rise up as warriors of the heart we will be conquered by our invisible enemies. We must overcome or be overcome!

Israel's mandate was to exercise kingdom authority in driving out all unrighteousness and to establish righteousness and justice throughout the land. "Therefore understand today that the Lord your God is He who goes over before you as a consuming fire. He will destroy them and bring them down before you; so you shall *drive them out* and destroy them quickly, as the Lord has said to you." (Deuteronomy 9:3) "Every place on which the sole of your foot treads shall be yours: from the wilderness and Lebanon, from the river, the River Euphrates, even to the Western Sea, shall be your territory." (Deuteronomy 11:24)

God reaffirmed this promise to Joshua on the eve of the conquest. "Every place that the sole of your foot will tread upon I have given you!" (Joshua 1:3) "Happy are you, O Israel! Who is like you, a people saved by the Lord, the shield of your help and the sword of your majesty! Your enemies shall submit to you and you shall tread down their high places." (Deuteronomy 33:29) But even once a section of land had been occupied it was still re-contested by the enemy. Many times the enemies of Israel rose up and overthrew the Israelites and regained dominion over vast tracts of land that had previously been occupied. This ebb and flow of dominion reflects out own wrestling match with principalities and powers. Sometimes we prevail against our enemies but sometimes, as in any wrestling match, our adversary can prevail against us.

Whenever we make small compromises in our heart we can find ourselves out-maneuvered by the schemes of the evil one. We have to adopt a zero tolerance policy towards all of our invisible enemies because whatever we tolerate will ultimately dominate. This is how it was for ancient Israel in the land of Canaan and this is how it is for us in the warfare between the kingdom of God and the kingdom of darkness. God told Israel to have a zero tolerance policy in Canaan and not to compromise even in the slightest way or the enemy would have a basis to prevail against them.

> When the Lord your God brings you into the land which you go to possess, and has cast out many nations before you, the Hittites and the Girgashites and the Amorites and the Canaanites and the Perizzites and the Hivites and the Jebusites, seven nations greater and mightier than you and when the Lord your God delivers them over to you, you shall conquer them and utterly destroy them. You shall make no covenant with them nor show mercy to them. Nor shall you make marriages with them. You shall not give your daughter to their son, nor take their daughter for your son. For they will turn your sons away from following Me. But thus you shall deal with them: you shall destroy their altars, and break down their sacred pillars, and cut down their wooden images, and burn their carved images with fire. For you are a holy people to the Lord your God; the Lord your God has chosen you to be a people for Himself, a special treasure above all the peoples on the face of the earth. (Deuteronomy 7:1-6)

Little by Little

God revealed that this would be a systematic process of conquest just as our heart journey is a process. We are engaged in a war of attrition against both our interior and our exterior enemies. The Lord said to Israel; "I will not drive them out from before you in one year. *Little by little* I will drive them out from before you, until you have increased, and you inherit the land." (Exodus 23:30) This admonition was echoed in the book of Deuteronomy on the eve of the conquest. This principle of attrition speaks so powerfully to us concerning our heart journey of systematically overcoming all of our interior and exterior enemies.

> If you should say in your heart, "These nations are greater than I; how can I dispossess them?" you shall not be afraid of them, but you shall remember well what the Lord your God did to Pharaoh and to all Egypt: the great trials which your eyes saw, the signs and the wonders, the mighty hand and the outstretched arm, by which the Lord your God brought you out. So shall the Lord your God do to all the peoples of whom you are afraid. Moreover the Lord your God will send the hornet among them until those who are left, who hide themselves from you, are destroyed. You shall not be terrified of them; for the Lord your God, the great and awesome God, is among you. And the Lord your God will drive out those nations before you *little by little*; you will be unable to destroy them at once. But the Lord your God will deliver them over to you, and will inflict defeat upon them until they are destroyed. (Deuteronomy 7:17-23)

Israel was mandated to utterly destroy their enemies and take no prisoners! God instructed the Israelites to both 'drive out' and 'destroy' the inhabitants of the land. This included the men, the women and the children. "Therefore understand today that the Lord your God is He who goes over before you as a consuming fire. He will destroy them and bring them down before you; so you shall *drive them out* and *destroy them quickly*, as the Lord has said to you." (Deuteronomy 9:3) The mandate was to 'dispossess' the pagan worshippers from the Land and establish the worship of Yahweh throughout the Land. "You shall *dispossess* the inhabitants of the land and dwell in it, for I have given you the land to possess." (Numbers 33:53) The cup of iniquity was filled and it was time in God's schedule for judgment against the seven nations of Canaan. "It is because of the wickedness of these nations that the Lord is driving them out from before you." (Deuteronomy 9:4)

God used Israel as His instrument of judgment against those nations and He instructed Israel to utterly wipe them out as a demonically infested, reprobate culture. "For every abomination to the Lord which He hates they have done to their gods; for they burn even their sons and daughters in the fire to their gods." (Deuteronomy 12:31) "You shall utterly destroy all the places where the nations which you shall dispossess served their gods, on the high mountains and on the hills and under every green tree. And you shall destroy their altars, break their sacred pillars, and burn their wooden images with fire; you shall cut down the carved images of their gods and destroy their names from that place." (Deuteronomy 12:2,3)

God Himself fought alongside Israel to establish them in their own land. "Moreover the Lord your God will send the hornet among them until those who are left, who hide themselves from you, are destroyed." (Deuteronomy 7:20) All the Lord required of Israel was a heart of obedience and He promised to fight for Israel. We see a great example of this in the book of Joshua where the Lord descended and fought against their adversaries.

> Joshua ascended from Gilgal, he and all the people of war with him, and all the mighty men of valor. And the Lord said to Joshua, "Do not fear them, for I have delivered them into your hand; not a man of them shall stand before you." Joshua therefore came upon them suddenly, having marched all night from Gilgal. So the Lord routed them before Israel, killed them with a great slaughter at Gibeon, chased them along the road that goes to Beth Horon, and struck them down as far as Azekah and Makkedah. And it happened, as they fled before Israel and were on the descent of Beth Horon, that the Lord cast down large hailstones from heaven on them as far as Azekah, and they died. There were more who died from the hailstones than the children of Israel killed with the sword. (Joshua 10:7-11)

Take No Prisoners

The prerequisite for total victory over all of their enemies was full obedience. This was the lesson the Lord sought to teach Israel over and over again once they entered the Promised Land. When they walked in full obedience the Lord would fight for them. Whenever they compromised with the inhabitants of the Land their enemies would prevail ruthlessly against them. Their call to full obedience to all of God's commands is a powerful reminder to us on our journey of the heart to live in the fullness of all that God has promised us. Any compromise with the enemy would be fatal.

There is one story that particularly illustrates this principle of zero tolerance. The Lord said to King Saul; "I will punish Amalek for what he did to Israel, how he ambushed him on the way when he came up from Egypt. Now go and attack Amalek, and utterly destroy all that they have, and do not spare them." (1 Samuel 15:2,3) "Saul attacked the Amalekites. He also took Agag king of the Amalekites alive, and utterly destroyed all the people with the edge of the sword. But Saul and the people spared Agag and the best of the sheep, the oxen, the fatlings, the lambs, and all that was good, and were unwilling to utterly destroy them." (1 Samuel 15:7-9) Saul was powerfully rebuked by the Lord for not wiping out the Amalekites and it was this event that cost him his Kingship over Israel.

Jesus called for an uncompromising ruthlessness in our heart journey. He said, "If your hand or foot causes you to sin, cut it off and cast it from you. It is better for you to enter into life lame or maimed, rather than having two hands or two feet, to be cast into the everlasting fire. And if your eye causes you to sin, pluck it out and cast it from you. It is better for you to enter into life with one eye, rather than having two eyes, to be cast into hell fire." (Matthew 18:8,9) Of course, the cutting off of our hand or the plucking out of our eye is highly metaphorical, but this is a call to a level of spiritual violence that literally takes no prisoners.

God's absolutely uncompromising approach to the treatment of the members of these ungodly nations is a prophetic picture of the folly of Christians making even the smallest compromises with darkness. "But if you do not drive out the inhabitants of the land from before you, then it shall be that those whom you let remain shall be irritants in your eyes and thorns in your sides, and they shall harass you in the land where you dwell." (Numbers 33:55) The concept of total annihilation makes us extremely uncomfortable. But what if it is ultimately intended to be a prophetic picture of the ruthless and uncompromising stance that we must take within our own hearts in relation to sin if we truly want to be free?

Israel's seemingly small compromises led to their captivity and bondage. Whenever Israel compromised they made room for the enemy to prevail. Whenever Israel failed to exercise authority to establish righteousness in the Land they left a void for the enemy to fill. Often they compromised sexually with the fertility cults. Sometimes they even married foreign wives against the expressed will of God. They made ungodly covenants and agreements with the enemy. They committed spiritual adultery by worshipping and serving other gods. Many times Christians set up and serve idols in their hearts. Christians are just as vulnerable to idolatry as their spiritual ancestors. "Now all these things happened to them as examples, and they were written for our admonition, upon whom the ends of the ages have come. (1 Corinthians 10:11)

Surrounded by Enemies

Within the Promised Land Israel was confronted by seven enemy nations, enemy armies, walled cities, mighty strongholds, mountain fortresses and giants. In the Promised Land there were numerous enemy strongholds to be overthrown. And so it is in our heart journey. "For the weapons of our warfare are not carnal but mighty in God for pulling down strongholds." (2 Corinthians 10:4) Israel was confronted by the presence of seven nations greater and mightier than them. These formidable nations exercised sovereignty over various geographical regions of Canaan. They were massive unconquered territories that would take considerable time, wisdom and courage to overthrow. They represent seven arenas of epic battle. We are at war with the lies of the devil, with sin and selfishness, with religion, with the seduction of the world, with demonic infiltration, with our own emotional brokenness and with the desires of our physical body.

Within these seven nations were numerous enemy cities and encampments. These represent major strongholds of the enemy as they were walled cities that were built to withstand attacks. Cities such as Jericho, Ai, Gibeon and Hebron required divine strategies in order to see them overthrown. Some of these cities were built as mountain fortresses. For example the Jebusites lived in a city that wasn't overthrown until King David began his rule as king. These elevated, walled cities represent major issues in our heart that must be systematically overthrown. They are representative of unbelief, hardness of heart, fear, rejection, idolatry, rebellion and witchcraft, just to name a few of the major issues that Christians face in their own heart journey.

Beyond the walled cities were the mountains of Canaan. Like the cities, these mountains represent significant strongholds of the human heart that need to be conquered spiritually. Jesus said, "You will say to this mountain: "Be removed!" (Mark 11:23) We are called to be mountain takers who conquer and scale the heights. God's intention is that the mountains be *'brought low.'* "The voice of one crying in the wilderness: "Prepare the way of the Lord; make straight in the desert a highway for our God. Every valley shall be exalted and *every mountain and hill brought low*; the crooked places shall be made straight and the rough places smooth; the glory of the Lord shall be revealed and all flesh shall see it together; for the mouth of the Lord has spoken." (Isaiah 40:3-5) "This is the word of the Lord to Zerubbabel: "Not by might nor by power, but by My Spirit," says the Lord of hosts. "Who are you, O great mountain? Before Zerubbabel you shall become a plain!" (Zechariah 4:6,7)

Taking the mountains is always highly strategic in any battle because the mountains in the Promised Land were places of prophetic vision. The mountains and hills were also places of worship and devotion. The high places of Canaan were legendary. They were always associated with idolatry, with the building of altars and a place of sacrifice to false gods. They are clearly a prophetic picture of the idols we have exalted in our hearts. Israel was instructed to overthrow and tear down the high places of idolatry and replace the worship of the gods of the Canaanites with the worship of Yahweh. Once these high places were conquered they became the places that the Israelites presented offerings to Yahweh.

Israel also faced formidable armies and garrisons of the enemy who actively opposed Israel's conquest. The narrative of taking the Promised Land was littered with stories of great battles where thousands of soldiers lay slain on the mountains and the plains of Canaan. This becomes a powerful picture of what Paul called "the spiritual hosts of wickedness in heavenly places." (Ephesians 6:12) These are the enemy foot soldiers; the hordes of hell that march against the city of God. Paul's advice as we face this barrage of evil spirits is: "Therefore take up the whole armor of God, that you may be able to withstand in the evil day, and having done all, to stand." (Ephesians 6:13) The heroes of the faith stand as an inspiration to us. The writer of Hebrews says that it was through their faith in God that they "conquered kingdoms, administered justice, and gained what was promised.... who escaped the edge of the sword; whose weakness was turned to strength; and who became powerful in battle and *routed foreign armies*." (Hebrews 11:33,34 NIV)

The conquest of Canaan was also hindered by the presence of enemy strongholds. These strongholds were usually located in mountainous regions that were inaccessible and unassailable. Again, they are a prophetic picture of personal strongholds in the heart of every believer. Paul adopted this metaphor when he spoke specifically of 'pulling down strongholds' of the mind and 'bringing every thought into captivity to the obedience of Christ.' (2 Corinthians 10:4,5) The follower of Jesus has to contend with strongholds of the mind, strongholds of the will and strongholds of the emotions in their heart journey of supernatural transformation. Paul's use of this language further endorses the view that even after we are born again we face formidable strongholds within our own heart that must be systematically overthrown and pulled down.

Intimidated by Giants

There were also giants in the land that needed to be conquered. There is considerable biblical evidence that a remnant of giants lived in the land of Canaan. The twelve spies encountered these giants and ten of the spies who returned were greatly intimidated by these inhabitants of the land. They were variously identified as the 'Anakim,' the 'Rephaim,' the 'Zamzummin' and the 'Emim.' "The Emim lived there formerly, a people as great, numerous, and tall as the Anakim. Like the Anakim, they are also regarded as Rephaim, but the Moabites call them Emim." (Deuteronomy 2:10,11 NASB) These unusually tall people dwelt in the land of Ammon, east of the Jordan; "a land of giants [Rephaim]; giants formerly dwelt there. But the Ammonites call them Zamzummim; a people as great and numerous and tall as the Anakim."(Deuteronomy 2:20,21)

However, the Anakim also dwelt in the mountains of Canaan. Their presence represented a double challenge to the Israelites; it was one thing to face giants but it was another that they dwelt in mountain strongholds. "At that time Joshua came and cut off the Anakim from the mountains: from Hebron, from Debir, from Anab, from all the mountains of Judah, and from all the mountains of Israel; Joshua utterly destroyed them with their cities. None of the Anakim were left in the land of the children of Israel; they remained only in Gaza, in Gath, and in Ashdod." (Joshua 11:21,22) Under Joshua the children of Israel had became an army of mountain takers and giant killers. The giants were overthrown and the only stronghold that remained of the Anakim were eventually overthrown by King David. "Then Goliath, a Philistine champion from Gath, came out of the Philistine ranks to face the forces of Israel. He was a giant of a man, measuring over nine feet tall!" (1 Samuel 17:4 NLT) The last of these giants, including the brother of Goliath and his four sons were finally overthrown under David's reign. (1 Samuel 21:19-22)

These giants had intimidated and taunted Israel. This was a prophetic picture of ruling spirits who intimidate and taunt the people of God. Joshua and Caleb saw them as grasshoppers and this qualified them to lead the children of Israel into the Promised Land because they were fearless in the face of formidable enemies. Their conquest of the giants and David's conquest of Goliath became the ultimate archetype of spiritual bravery and courage which speaks of overcoming seemingly insurmountable obstacles. Ray Hughes says, "There's a giant standing between you and your destiny!" Each of us face our giants. They are inward strongholds that are often fueled by fear and intimidation from the powers of darkness who seek to convince us that these inner struggles are impossible to conquer. But we were born to be giant slayers who are destined to be overcomers and more than conquerors.

There were seven nations mightier and stronger than the Israelites that needed to be systematically conquered and dispossessed. There were walled cities, mountain strongholds, high places, enemy armies and giants. All of these enemies speak of the challenges that lay before each of us in our heart journey if we are to go on to fill the Promised Land of our hearts with the glory of the Lord. Under Joshua, Israel was fueled by a vision to exercise conquest and to inherit a land that already belonged fully to them because it already belonged to the Lord. God promised to vanquish all of their enemies if they were obedient to step into the battle as an act of obedient faith in the promises of God. The whole thing was a divine set up to reveal the glory of the Lord.

Israel's Failure

Israel's failures in the Land speak prophetically of the failings of our own hearts in our journey into freedom and wholeness. The narrative of the conquest of Canaan was a mixture of failures intermingled with great victories. Sometimes Israel prevailed over their enemies but other times their enemies prevailed over them and Israel was severely oppressed. After the conquest under the strong leadership of Joshua the Israelites began to flounder in the Land and the enemies that had not been driven out of the Land rose up to oppress Israel. In the following passage of Scripture from the book of Judges we see this ebb and flow of failure and success.

> So the people served the Lord all the days of Joshua and all the days of the elders who outlived Joshua, who had seen all the great works of the Lord which He had done for Israel. Now Joshua the son of Nun, the servant of the Lord, died when he was one hundred and ten years old. And they buried him within the border of his inheritance at Timnath Heres, in the mountains of Ephraim, on the north side of Mount Gaash. When all that generation had been gathered to their fathers, another generation arose after them who did not know the

Lord nor the work which He had done for Israel. Then the children of Israel did evil in the sight of the Lord, and served the Baals; and they forsook the Lord God of their fathers, who had brought them out of the land of Egypt; and they followed other gods from among the gods of the people who were all around them, and they bowed down to them; and they provoked the Lord to anger. They forsook the Lord and served Baal and the Ashtoreths. And the anger of the Lord was hot against Israel. So He delivered them into the hands of plunderers who plundered them; and He sold them into the hands of their enemies all around, so that they could no longer stand before their enemies. Wherever they went out, the hand of the Lord was against them for calamity, as the Lord had said, and as the Lord had sworn to them. And they were greatly distressed. Nevertheless, the Lord raised up judges who delivered them out of the hand of those who plundered them. Yet they would not listen to their judges, but they played the harlot with other gods, and bowed down to them. They turned quickly from the way in which their fathers walked, in obeying the commandments of the Lord; they did not do so. And when the Lord raised up judges for them, the Lord was with the judge and delivered them out of the hand of their enemies all the days of the judge; for the Lord was moved to pity by their groaning because of *those who oppressed them and harassed them*. And it came to pass, when the judge was dead, that they reverted and behaved more corruptly than their fathers, by following other gods, to serve them and bow down to them. They did not cease from their own doings nor from their stubborn way. Then the anger of the Lord was hot against Israel; and He said, "Because this nation has transgressed My covenant which I commanded their fathers, and has not heeded My voice, I also will no longer drive out before them any of the nations which Joshua left when he died so that through them I may test Israel, whether they will keep the ways of the Lord, to walk in them as their fathers kept them, or not." Therefore the Lord left those nations, without driving them out immediately; nor did He deliver them into the hand of Joshua. Now these are the nations which the Lord left, that He might test Israel by them, that is, all who had not known any of the wars in Canaan (this was only so that the generations of the children of Israel might be taught to know war, at least those who had not formerly known it), namely, five lords of the Philistines, all the Canaanites, the Sidonians, and the Hivites who dwelt in Mount Lebanon, from Mount Baal Hermon to the entrance of Hamath. And they were left, that He might test Israel by them, to know whether they would obey the commandments of the Lord, which He had commanded their fathers by the hand of Moses. Thus the children of Israel dwelt among the Canaanites, the Hittites, the Amorites, the Perizzites, the Hivites, and the Jebusites. And they took their daughters to be their wives, and gave their daughters to their sons; and they served their gods. So the children of Israel did evil in the sight of the Lord. They forgot the LORD their God, and served the Baals and Asherahs. Therefore the anger of the Lord was hot against Israel, and He sold them into the hand of Cushan-Rishathaim king of Mesopotamia; and the children of Israel served Cushan-Rishathaim eight years. When the children of Israel cried out to the Lord, the Lord raised up a deliverer for the children of Israel, who delivered them: Othniel the son of Kenaz, Caleb's younger brother. The Spirit of the Lord came upon him, and he judged Israel. He went out to war, and the Lord delivered Cushan-Rishathaim king of Mesopotamia into his hand; and his hand prevailed over Cushan-Rishathaim. So the land had rest for forty years. Then Othniel the son of Kenaz died. And the children of Israel again did evil in the sight of the Lord. So the Lord strengthened Eglon king of Moab against Israel, because they had done evil in the sight of the Lord. Then he gathered to himself the people of Ammon and Amalek, went and defeated Israel, and took possession of the City of Palms. So the children of Israel served Eglon king of Moab eighteen years. But when the children of Israel cried out to the Lord, the Lord raised up a deliverer for them: Ehud the son of Gera, the Benjamite, a left-handed man. (Judges 2:7-3:15)

God uses the failure of the people of God to teach us obedience. After Joshua, Israel turned their hearts away from the Lord and served other idols. Therefore the Lord gave them over to their oppressors and they endured seasons of great defeat, harsh oppression and harassment. Because of Israel's disobedience the Lord allowed their enemies to persist in the Land in order to test their hearts. "But as we have been approved by God to be entrusted with the gospel, even so we speak, not as pleasing men, but God who tests our hearts." (1 Thessalonians 2:4) The test is always about our full obedience to the Lord.

"For to this end I also wrote, that I might put you to the test, whether you are obedient in all things." (2 Corinthians 2:9)

God allows the ongoing struggle with our flesh to teach us the nature of spiritual warfare and its relationship to our interior battles. The powers of darkness capitalize upon those remaining strongholds of disobedience and brokenness within our heart in order to hold us in bondage and captivity. God allowed some of Israel's enemies to persist in the land in order to *"Teach warfare* to the descendants of the Israelites who had not had previous battle experience." (Judges 3:2 NIV) Israel was taught obedience by the presence of their oppressors. God used Israel's enemies to test their hearts. "And you shall remember that the Lord your God led you all the way these forty years in the wilderness, to humble you and test you, *to know what was in your heart*, whether you would keep His commandments or not." (Deuteronomy 8:2) When Israel walked in obedience they prevailed; when they walked in disobedience they suffered defeat and oppression.

When Israel rebelled against Yahweh they provoked Him to anger. They continually had to learn the harsh lesson that their rebellion strengthened the hand of their enemies. In the same way God allows the devil to remain in order to test our hearts. Whenever we walk in disobedience we strengthen the hand of the enemy in our life. The evil one actually energizes the hearts of the disobedient. (Ephesians 2:2) This is meant to be the rude awakening that turns our hearts to full obedience to the Lord.

Rebellion and Demonization

Israel's disobedience and moral failures led to them into fellowshipping with demons. Turning to other gods always opens the heart of the believer to demons. "They made Him jealous with their foreign gods and angered him with their detestable idols. They sacrificed to demons, which are not God – gods they had not known, gods that recently appeared, gods your fathers did not fear. You deserted the Rock, who fathered you; you forgot the God who gave you birth." (Deuteronomy 32:16-18) The narrative of Israel compromising with demons speaks prophetically to New Testament believers. "You turned to God from idols to serve the living and true God." (1 Thessalonians 1:9) "Little children, keep yourselves from idols." (1 John 5:21) Worshipping and serving idols leads Christians into fellowship with demons.

The things which the Gentiles sacrifice they sacrifice to demons and
not to God, and I do not want you to have fellowship with demons.
You cannot [simultaneously] drink the cup of the Lord and the cup of
demons; you cannot [simultaneously] partake of the Lord's table and
of the table of demons. (1 Corinthians 10:20,21)

Paul explicitly warned Christians that if they walk according to the example of
Israel's rebellion and disobedience they will also end up fellowshipping with
demons. Paul's conclusion and stark warning to Christians was; "Therefore,
my beloved, flee from idolatry." (1 Corinthians 10:14) Jesus similarly warned
that disobedient Christians would be handed over to the tormentors. (Matthew
18:34) Paul warned New Covenant believers of the danger of being "destroyed
by the Destroyer" if they compromised with the demonic realm. Moses
prophesied that the time would come when Israel would compromise in the
Land and would be devoured by the devourer.

The Lord said to Moses: "Behold, you will rest with your fathers;
and this people will rise and play the harlot with the gods of the
foreigners of the land, where they go to be among them, and they
will forsake Me and break My covenant which I have made with
them. Then My anger shall be aroused against them in that day, and I
will forsake them, and I will hide My face from them, and *they shall
be devoured.* And many evils and troubles shall befall them, so that
they will say in that day, "Have not these evils come upon us because
our God is not among us?" And I will surely hide My face in that day
because of all the evil which they have done, in that they have turned
to other gods. (Deuteronomy 31:16-18)

Peter must have had this passage of Scripture in mind when he said, "Be sober,
be vigilant; because your adversary the devil walks about like a roaring lion,
seeking whom he may *devour*." (1 Peter 5:8) The devil is called the
'devourer.' The Lord promised; "I will rebuke the *devourer* for your sakes so
that he will not destroy the fruit of your ground, nor shall the vine fail to bear
fruit for you in the field," says the Lord of hosts." (Malachi 3:11) Both Paul
and Peter warned us of the danger of being devoured by the destroyer if we do
not learn from Israel's failures.

The parallels between Israel and the New Testament church are striking and
somewhat foreboding. All of the things that happened to Israel are a deliberate

prophetic type of the heart journey of the New Covenant people of God. The entire narrative of Israel's pilgrimage through the wilderness and the Promise Land is prophetically instructive to our own hearts. The types and antitypes are too powerful to ignore so it is not surprising that Paul, under the instruction and inspiration of the Holy Spirit should draw out a number of powerful prophetic lessons from the successes and failures of Israel. He gives us a prophetic paradigm in 1 Corinthians 10 that gives us license to further explore the types and antitypes that are concealed in the Old Testament. Paul only draws out a handful of lessons but he sets us up to explore a vast region of prophetic significance for us in the journey of our hearts out of chronic disobedience and into a life of obedience that results in incredible freedom and wholeness if only we can take to heart the plethora of profound spiritual lessons that are ingeniously concealed in the narratives of Israel's sojourn.

Little by little we advance in our heart journey until our hearts are filled with the glory of the Lord and every aspect of our lives shine with the radiance of our sonship. Just like Jesus, our spirit is now filled with glory but unlike Jesus, our soul must be comprehensively restored and renewed. Our heart journey is a deep restoration of our souls as we are fully and comprehensively delivered from the defilement of sin, of demons and of our deep brokenness that has corrupted and wounded our souls. Our destination is glory. "All have sinned and fallen short of the glory of God" (Romans 3:23) but "He called you by our gospel for the obtaining of the glory of our Lord Jesus Christ." (2 Thessalonians 2:14) Our new Promised Land is a heart set free and made whole in a way that comprehensively manifests our new nature of sonship. We must learn to conquer the mountain of 'me!' David prophetically described this supernatural restoration of our souls in a way that still speaks so powerfully to us as New Covenant believers:

> The Lord is my shepherd; I shall not want. He makes me to lie down in green pastures; He leads me beside the still waters. He *restores my soul*; He leads me in the paths of righteousness for His name's sake. Yea, though I walk through the valley of the shadow of death, I will fear no evil; for You are with me; Your rod and Your staff, they comfort me. You prepare a table before me in the presence of my enemies; You anoint my head with oil; my cup runs over. Surely goodness and mercy shall follow me all the days of my life and I will dwell in the house of the Lord forever. (Psalm 23:1-6)

Chapter Six

Entangled in the Father and the Son

The heart journey that we have been invited into is a supernatural journey from start to finish that radically transcends all natural or earthly transformational modalities. It is comprehensively built upon a 'heaven to earth' paradigm and has nothing to do with the earthly aspirations of religion to build a tower to reach heaven. (Genesis 11:4) Religion is always predicated upon earth reaching out to heaven. The real heart journey that our Father invites us into begins with a miraculous new birth and it consists in both the unveiling of our new identity of sonship and the systematic violent conquest of everything within our heart that exalts itself above this new reality.

My decades of personal experience as a follower of Jesus and as a pastor and counselor has taught me that most Christians do not really live from a radical new creation paradigm. What is intended by God to be the launch pad of a supernatural life has somehow been reduced to a final destination in the hope that before a Christian dies they might finally come to grips with who they really are in Christ. Our life is indeed "hidden with Christ in God." (Colossians 3:3) The Greek word Paul used for 'hidden' is '*kruptos,*' which means something that is concealed. The miracle of the new birth is deeply hidden and indiscoverable to our five earthly senses because it is invisible. Try looking for your 'spirit' and see if you can locate it physically. In the same way, try to locate the Holy Spirit. He is a nonlocal being who dwells outside of the dimensions of space and time. Paul taught that your human spirit is now gloriously embedded 'in the Holy Spirit.'

Through the new birth we have been given the privilege of mystically sharing in the life of the Father and the Son through the presence of the Holy Spirit. Jesus described His own life as being deeply entangled in the life of His Father. "Believe Me when I say that I am in the Father and the Father is in Me." (John 14:11 NIV) "Even though you do not believe Me, believe the miracles, that you may know and understand that the Father is in Me, and I in the Father." (John 10:38 NIV) "Don't you believe that I am in the Father, and that the Father is in Me? The words I say to you are not just My own. Rather, it is the Father, living in Me, who is doing His work." (John 14:10 NIV)

Early church theologians called this phenomenon '*perichoresis*.' Perichoresis is made up of two Greek words: '*peri*' which means 'around' and '*chorein*' which means 'to contain." The word literally means to 'contain around.' Theologians describe this state of existence as a 'mutual indwelling' where each individual retains his or her unique identity. It describes the mutual inter-penetration and indwelling of the Father, the Son and the Holy Spirit. Perichoresis is therefore an attribute of the Trinity. Theologians describe God as existing in three persons yet being mystically one.

The ancient Hebrew 'Shema Yisrael' declared: "Hear O Israel; the Lord our God; the Lord is *one*." (Deuteronomy 6:4) But curiously, the Hebrew word for 'one' is '*echad,*' which means one in a plurality such as 'one' cluster of grapes. The three persons of the Triune Godhead dwell in one another in a sweet society of mutual love and affection. The Father, the Son and the Holy Spirit are all one! Perichoresis is expressed in intimate fellowship. The Father loves the Son and the Son Loves the Father. Jesus described God as "The Father who dwells in Me!" (John 14:10)

The great mystery at the heart of our universe is that humanity has been invited into this divine relationship. We are invited into this state of divine perichoresis! Jesus proclaimed, "On that day you will realize that I am in my Father, and you are in me, and I am in you." (John 14:20) He takes the language that was originally reserved exclusively to describe the nature of His unique relationship with the Father and He transfers it to all who are part of the new creation. This is a staggering reality. It is a feast for the heart that transcends knowledge and understanding.

Jesus prayed, "Holy Father, protect them by the power of Your name – the name You gave Me – so that they may be one as We are one." (John 17:11 NIV) "My prayer is not for them alone. I pray also for those who will believe in Me through their message, that all of them may be one, Father, just as You are in me and I am in You. May they also be in Us so that the world may believe that You have sent Me." (John 17:20,21 NIV) Perichoresis is the language of mutual indwelling that constitutes the spiritual blessedness of all who have been mystically united with the Father and the Son. "That Christ may *dwell* in your hearts through faith." (Ephesians 3:17)

Living from a Glorified Spirit

According to the New Testament, glory is the family trait; it is the shared attribute of the saints living in divine perichoresis in Christ. From heaven's perspective, the church in Jesus Christ has, in one sense, already been glorified spiritually. According to Paul, our spirit, in mystical union with the Spirit of Christ, has been glorified as a consequence of our perfect justification. Paul said, those "whom He justified, these He also glorified." (Romans 8:30) Justification is the divine act of making a believer perfectly righteous in the sight of God. But Paul extends this idea beyond the 'imputation' of righteousness when he said that we who believe have actually become the righteousness of God in Christ. (2 Corinthians 5:21) Righteousness has not only been legally *imputed* to us; it has also been experientially *imparted* to us!

This free gift of sparkling perfect righteousness gives us absolute right standing before God. The NLT says, "And having given them right standing, He gave them His glory." The Amplified Bible says, "Those whom He called, He also justified (acquitted, made righteous, putting them into right standing with Himself). And those whom He justified, He also glorified; raising them to a heavenly dignity and condition or state of being." Both the act of justification and the act of glorification are in the aorist tense, meaning that they are both a past tense finished work in our spirit. Our justification has resulted in our spiritual glorification because God has imparted the glory of His righteousness to our human spirit.

Paul said, "Your spirit is alive because of righteousness." (Romans 8:10 NIV) God imparted His glory to our human spirit at the moment of the new birth. Jesus said, "I have given them the glory You gave Me so they may be one as We are one." (John 17:22 NLT) The glorification of our spirit has already taken place! It is an astonishing and almost inconceivable reality that we who believe in Christ now have a glorified spirit! One third of our entire being has already been brought to completion! We are now mystically joined to the Lord to such an extent that Paul says we have become 'one spirit.' "He who is joined to the Lord is **one spirit** with Him." (1 Corinthians 6:17) Our spirit is deeply and fully immersed in "the Father of glory,' in Christ the "King of glory" and in "the Spirit of glory.'

There are a number of Pauline verses that clearly reveal that God has already imparted His glory to our regenerated spirit. "Therefore, since we have been made right in God's sight by faith, we have peace with God because of what Jesus Christ our Lord has done for us. Because of our faith, Christ has brought us into this place of highest privilege where we now stand and we confidently and joyfully look forward to sharing God's glory." (Romans 5;1,2 NLT) The Amplified Bible indicates that this is not merely a future hope of sharing God's glory when our bodies are finally glorified. Rather, "Let us rejoice and exult in our hope of experiencing and enjoying the glory of God." (Romans 5:2 AMP) Paul points to a present experience of this glorious hope when he said (just 3 verses later) that our "hope does not disappoint us because God has poured out His love into our hearts by the Holy Spirit, whom He has given us." (Romans 5:5 NIV)

The present outpouring of the glorious love of the Father results in the present and immediate experience and enjoyment of the glory of God. This is a perfect and glorious love that never disappoints. Christ in us, in mystical union with our spirit becomes our confident expectation of glory. "For it has pleased God to tell His people that the riches and glory of Christ are for you Gentiles, too. For this is the secret: Christ lives in you, and this is your assurance that you will share in His glory." (Colossians 1:27 NLT) The writer of Hebrews insists that we have already come to "the spirits of righteous men made perfect." (Hebrews 12:23 NIV)

We have been perfected in oneness and glory in the Father and the Son and now we are confident of His glory being revealed from within our spirit through the miracle of the new creation. This is what Jesus could see when He said, "The glory which You gave Me I have given them, that they may be one just as We are one: I in them, and You in Me; that they may be made perfect in one, and that the world may know that You have sent Me, and have loved them as You have loved Me." (John 17:22,23)

Paul's theology of the new creation radically stretches the borders of our imagination. There can be no doubt that Paul believed that all those who have received Christ have stepped immediately into an inheritance of the riches of the glory of God in their regenerated spirit. He said "He called you by our gospel for the obtaining of the glory of our Lord Jesus Christ."   (2 Thessalonians 2:14) All who have responded to this glorious gospel have already obtained an inheritance that is beyond our wildest dreams. Radical new creation theology is an invitation to step into a dimension of glorious provision through the infinite supply of God's glorious Spirit joined supernaturally to our spirit. Peter was in agreement with Paul. He said, "As we know Jesus better, His divine power gives us everything we need for living a godly life. He has called us to receive His own glory and goodness!" (2 Peter 1:3 NLT)

Whilst our spirit is already one with God and already glorified as a past tense miracle, our soul is being glorified in the present from one degree of glory to the next but only when believers consciously choose to submit to the heart journey of being conformed to the image of the Son. Upon the foundation of this mystical perichoresis Jesus prayed, "I in them and you in Me. May they be brought to complete unity to let the world know that You sent Me and have loved them even as You have loved Me." (John 17:23 NIV) This is the journey of the glorification of the soul in which we are conformed, in our mind, will and emotions to the image of the glorified Christ. Jesus is coming back for a glorious church! The Father declared prophetically through Isaiah that "I shall glorify My glorious house." (Isaiah 60:7 NASB)

Perichoresis and Quantum Entanglement

There is a strange new phenomenon that has been discovered at the quantum level of nature. Scientists have discovered a curious phenomenon called 'quantum entanglement.' I explore this theme in much greater detail in my book *'Quantum Glory'* but I want to introduce you to this phenomenon of nature at a quantum scale because it speaks prophetically concerning our divine perichoresis with the Father, the Son and the Holy Spirit. So many aspects of nature speak prophetically of great spiritual truths. When I first grasped this concept it sent me into a state of theological and experiential ecstasy!

Let me describe this phenomenon. Two photons that were once one photon, which are split using a beam splitter, remain strangely 'entangled' with one another even if they both hypothetically travel to the opposite ends of the universe. How do we know this is true? Every photon has an attribute called 'spin.' There are only two options with spin; either up or down. Somehow, scientists are able to 'nudge' a photon so that its spin can be reversed. When this is done to a photon that is already in an 'entangled' relationship with its twin photon it was discovered that the interference of the spin of the first photon had an instantaneous impact on its entangled partner no matter where that partner photon was in the universe! If one photon is nudged it immediately reverses the spin of its entangled partner.

Albert Einstein described this troubling phenomenon as "spooky action at a distance." Other scientists have called it an invisible 'ghost link' between quantum particles. Quantum physicists have all been shocked by the discovery of this phenomenon. The consistency of this phenomenon in quantum experiments points to the existence of another layer of reality that exists in what is now universally accepted as an additional dimension of our universe. The standard understanding of the universe is that matter exists in three spatial dimensions. Through Einstein's breakthroughs in the field of relativity in the first half of the 20th century, time came to be regarded as a fourth dimension so that it is now universally accepted that we live in a four-dimensional space-time continuum.

Physicists have coined a new term to describe the discovery of this extra dimensional entanglement of quantum particles. Scientists appear to have stumbled upon what they now call a new 'non-local' dimension within our universe that is non-locatable in space or time. This discovery has turned conventional concepts of physics upside down. In the physical world everything is locatable. We depend upon everything being found in its correct location; our keys, our wallet, our toothbrush etc. To describe a layer of reality as being fundamentally 'non-local' in nature really means that it is spatially non-locatable. Scientists once dogmatically insisted that the only ultimate reality in our universe was physical reality and that there was nothing that existed outside of physical space. The shock of quantum non-locality has jarred physicists out of this conventional understanding of the universe. A quantum physicist named John Stewart Bell devised a mathematical proof that irrefutably proved once and for all that we live in a physical universe that continually intersects with a non-local universe. This discovery has actually become a significant key to understand the entire quantum world.

What is quite remarkable about this discovery is that scientists have now attained incontrovertible evidence of the existence of at least one extra dimension. Biblical theology, built upon the premise of the existence of God and the spirit world, has always insisted that there are dimensions outside of time and space. Quantum physics and quantum entanglement in particular have now proven the existence of extra dimensions where communication occurs *instantaneously*, even theoretically from one end of the universe to another. There is no time delay in the interaction between two entangled photons. We are not talking about the transfer of information at the speed of light. Instead quantum entanglement posits an instantaneous, superluminal transfer of information because the two entangled particles are effectively joined in another non-local dimension outside of space and time.

Entangled with One Another

All of this has profound implications both scientifically and theologically. Quantum entanglement is now an established feature of our universe that points prophetically to a spiritual entanglement that also transcends space and time. Many times, natural things speak prophetically of spiritual things. This is the whole basis of the parables and the types and symbols of the Bible, most of which are rooted in nature. New Testament theology asserts a spiritual entanglement between Christ and His bride, but also between brothers and sisters in Christ. The supernaturally renewed human spirit has the ability to traverse space and time and to be mystically entangled with God and with one another in Christ in the realm of heaven. "So we, being many, are one body in Christ, and individually members of one another." (Romans 12:5)

Paul unveils a deep mystical union of perichoresis when he says, "For as the body is one and has many members, but all the members of that one body, being many, are one body, so also is Christ." (1 Corinthians 12:12) He implies that Christ is now unveiled as a many membered body! Our Father seeks to "gather together in one all things in Christ, both which are in heaven and which are on earth; in Him." (Ephesians 1:10) We who have faith in Christ are now living in a deep mystical union with one another through becoming partakers in the life of the Spirit and the divine nature. This is infinitely deeper than attending merely the same church. It is a union of spirit not only with God but also with one another. This means that our identity as sons and daughters is now inseparably linked to our corporate identity as the bride or body of Christ.

Paul alluded to this unique property of the human spirit a number of times in his epistles when he asserted that he was present 'in spirit' even though he was not present physically. On one occasion he gave instructions to the leaders in Corinth to action the excommunication of an unrepentant brother who was deeply entangled in an ungodly relationship with his stepmother. He said, "In the name of our Lord Jesus Christ, when you are gathered together, ***along with my spirit***, with the power of our Lord Jesus Christ, deliver such a one to Satan for the destruction of the flesh that his spirit may be saved in the day of the Lord Jesus." (1 Corinthians 5:4)

Paul was in another city when he wrote this command but he revealed that he was in some way mystically joined to his brethren in Corinth through the new creation. If Paul only said this once we might dismiss it as a strange anomaly or a metaphor of unity in the Spirit but he confirmed his prophetic insight into a deeper level of mystical entanglement when he said to the saints in Colossae; "For though I am absent in the flesh, yet *I am with you in spirit*, rejoicing to see your good order and the steadfastness of your faith in Christ." (Colossians 2:5) This was presumably not just something which Paul had attained that was exclusive to him but rather a reality that pointed to a deep mystical union in the spiritual realm that is true for all of us who are in Christ. Had Paul so developed and trained his spirit that he could see what was happening in another location? We will never know this side of heaven but it certainly is a tantalizing thought. Bilocation is certainly strongly implied throughout the New Testament.

Entangled Particles of Light

Jesus Himself gives us further compelling evidence of a kind of spiritual entanglement which quantum entanglement, as a natural phenomenon, prophetically points to and illustrates. In nature, photons are the very substance of light. In fact, light is made up of these mysterious quantum particles that carry energy. Concerning Himself, Jesus said "I am the light of the world!" (John 8:12) But He also said to His followers; "You are the light of the world." (Matthew 5:14)

This is not just a nice metaphor meaning that we are secondarily an expression of light in the world because Christ is in us as the primary source of spiritual light. Paul said that we have now become light through the new creation. "For you were once darkness, but now *you are light* in the Lord." (Ephesians 5:8) Your new spirit has become light because He is light. John said, "Because as He is, so are we in this world." (John 4:17) Jesus is the heavenly man and therefore we have become heavenly. "As was the man of dust, so also are those who are made of dust; and as is the heavenly Man, so also are those who *are heavenly*. And as we have borne the image of the man of dust, we shall also bear the image of the heavenly Man." (1 Corinthians 15:48,49)

Christ is the light of the world and therefore we have become the light of the world because of the miracle of the new creation. That is why Paul said, "We now shine like stars in the universe!" (Philippians 2:15 NIV) The Father is called the "Father of lights!" (James 1:17) But guess what! We are those lights!!! Jesus said, "Let your light so shine..." (Matthew 5:16) "Arise, shine! For *your* light has come!" (Isaiah 60:1) We are deeply entangled in the Father and the Son through the presence of the Holy Spirit. We are like entangled partners of light that shine across the universe. We shine because Jesus shines! Quantum entanglement merely points prophetically to a shared reality amongst those who have been made partakers of the divine nature. God's glory has been imparted to our spirit through mystical union with God's own Spirit because glory is the unique family trait of all those who have entered into the new creation.

Through the miracle of the new creation God has, in a nanosecond, supernaturally disentangled the human spirit from sin and darkness. He has severed the cords of death, He has cleansed our spirit from any demonic infiltration and He has rendered our spirit comprehensively righteous to the extent that we could not be any more righteous before God even in a million years time. Christ's own righteousness has been imparted to our spirit through the new birth. Our spirit has, according to Hebrews, been comprehensively perfected in the sight of God. All who are in Christ have now come "to the spirits of righteous men made perfect." (Hebrews 12:23 NIV) This state of perfection suggests absolute completion to the extent that it cannot be improved upon. He has, in our spirit, made all things new!

The Entanglements of the Soul

However, to extend the metaphor of quantum entanglement the writers of the New Testament reveal that there is still a lingering entanglement with darkness in the soul of the believer that hinders us from enjoying the full experience of our mystical entanglement in the Father and the Son. The state of our soul is far from perfection or completion. When we are first born again our soul is still deeply broken and profoundly entangled in sin, darkness and sometimes even in demonic bondage even though our spirit is now glorified and permanently entangled in the Father and the Son. Our spirit is now in exactly the same state of perfect righteousness and purity as the spirit of Jesus was when He walked upon the earth. However, experientially, our soul is deeply entangled in the world and in darkness.

It is only as we intentionally embrace the heart journey of supernatural transformation that we begin to escape the entanglements of the world so that we enter into the glorious freedom that is the inheritance of the saints. To the extent that we experientially escape the entanglement of everything that now constitutes our 'old' life, to that same extent we enter into the pure bliss and enjoyment of what belongs to us by birthright as new creations in Christ. Every time God breaks the nexus of various dimensions of our soul to spiritual darkness we are emancipated into the experiential freedom of our glorious perichoresis with God.

Our transformational journey is predicated upon the inherent glory of our sonship. No other foundation can be laid other than the glorification of the human spirit in Christ. We are now in the Beloved Son and the Beloved Son is in us. We are now in the Father and the Father is in us. All that is true of Jesus in relation to His Father is transferred to us as sons and daughters! Sonship is the ultimate purpose at the heart of the cosmos. There is no higher purpose in God. That is why our conformity to the image of the Son is what lies at the very white hot center of God's prophetic purpose for our life here on earth. But tragically so many Christians do not embrace the heart journey of supernatural transformation and never enter into the joy and glorious freedom of their sonship.

> For those God foreknew He also **predestined** to be conformed to the likeness of His Son, that He might be the firstborn among many brothers. And those He predestined, He also called; those He called, He also justified; those He justified, He also glorified. (Romans 8:29,30)

Our destiny [or, our *pre-determined destination*] is to comprehensively escape every single entanglement of darkness so that we step into the supreme glory of our sonship. We are confronted in the New Testament by two different dimensions of entanglement. Paul explicitly identified various aspects of the believer's ongoing entanglement in sin and in the spiritual darkness of this world. But he also boldly declared the believer's mystical union and entanglement in Christ. On three occasions Paul said,

- "Brethren, the grace of our Lord Jesus Christ be with your spirit. Amen" (Galatians 6:18)

- "The Lord Jesus Christ be with your spirit. Grace be with you. Amen." (2 Timothy 4:22)
- "The grace of our Lord Jesus Christ be with your spirit. Amen." (Philemon 1:25)

This is our entanglement in the gracious life of Christ. Jesus held forth the vision of our whole body being full of light but sadly many Christians remain experientially full of darkness in their soul because of their continued entanglement in sin. "The lamp of the body is the eye. If therefore your eye is good, your whole body will be full of light. But if your eye is bad, your whole body will be full of darkness. If therefore the light that is in you is darkness, how great is that darkness!" (Matthew 6:22,23) It is a great enigma that although we are entangled with God in our human spirit we are often still entangled in darkness in our soul. The powers of darkness clearly have points of legal access to the soul of the believer who makes choices for darkness against light.

The Seven Entanglements of the Heart

Paul, Peter and the writer of Hebrews all used the explicit language of *'entanglement'* to describe the believer's ongoing bondage to sin, brokenness and darkness in the unrenewed regions of our soul. The New Testament teaches the principle that any form of 'entanglement' causes a person to be overcome and brought into bondage and a snare. Referring to our entanglement in sin and worldliness, Peter used a phrase in which he described Christians who "are again *entangled in it and overcome*." (2 Peter 2:20 NIV) The goal of every Christian ought to be to escape every form of entanglement in spiritual darkness and to disentangle our lives from the snares, or traps of the devil. There are seven major arenas of entanglement for the believer. Our heart journey consists largely in disentangling ourselves from these entanglements of darkness in order to enter into the fullness of the blessed experience of our divine entanglement with Christ. In the following seven chapters we will explore each of these seven arenas of entanglement and the keys to escaping them.

Chapter Seven

Entangled in Satan's Lies

All Christians, no matter how mature or how young they are in the Lord are vulnerable to the entanglement of demonic deception. To illustrate this I would like to begin this chapter by telling a true story that happened a few centuries ago. A small documented revival broke out in a village in the mountains to the east of Ankara in Turkey when a traveling revivalist and his two companions passed through the village. In all probability this region, steeped in pagan religion, had never before heard the true gospel of the grace of God. A few hundred people came to the Lord in a sovereign move of God that was extremely unusual, as Christianity had never taken root in Turkey. To this day 99% of people in that nation identify themselves as Muslims and less than 1% identify themselves as Christians.

Amongst the population of this village there was a virulent expression of occultism where a secretive group engaged in an unusually dark expression of witchcraft that had been passed down for generations. The leader of this coven was a particularly evil warlock who was rumored to be a Satanist. He had considerable magical powers and many of the villagers were so impressed by his witchcraft that they came to believe that he had received these powers from God. Many villagers were under his hypnotic control. It was well known that he had the ability to cast horrifically evil spells upon people who opposed him. Rumors were circulating that he had the power to put death curses upon people that caused people to die within a very short period. He had a group of devoted disciples who gathered around him to learn how to cast these evil spells that resulted in sudden disease, madness and even death.

This warlock deeply despised the Christians because it was well known that they were praying fervently for him and his followers to leave the village. He was particularly obsessed with destroying the church because a handful of his followers had converted to Christianity and had begun exposing what he had been doing in his secret occult rituals. So he sent infiltrators into the church masquerading as new converts and through this secretive strategy the warlock began compiling a list of all of the Christians, their names, addresses and private details about their lives. As his anger increased he began casting especially evil spells upon them. Some of the Christians became violently ill and a number of them even died. They began fighting amongst themselves. Many of them became so disoriented spiritually that they began to fall away from the Lord. His witchcraft was so powerful that the small church began to crumble and diminish. Then, the guy who triggered the small revival a few years earlier heard about what was taking place in the village but he was so busy leading a revival in another city that all he could do was write a letter to them and say; "Oh, foolish Galatians! Who has cast an evil spell on you?" (Galatians 3:1 NLT)

These bewitching spells were generated by the devil himself but his sinister agenda was ably assisted by a group of false Christians who had secretly infiltrated the churches. "Some false brothers had infiltrated our ranks to spy on the freedom we have in Christ Jesus and to make us slaves." (Galatians 2:4 NIV) These 'messengers of Satan' were a continual thorn in Paul's side. Everywhere Paul travelled, he established his new converts in the gospel of grace but this company of false apostles who transformed themselves into 'messengers of light' continually sought to infiltrate Paul's churches, bringing these new converts back under the law. (See 2 Corinthians 11:13-15, 12:7) The result of this heavy witchcraft assignment in the spirit realm was a number of Christians became so powerfully deceived and bamboozled that they had begun falling away from Jesus. "I am astonished that you are so quickly deserting the One who called you!" (Galatians 1:6 NIV) The 'warlock,' of Galatia of course, is the devil who targets Christians in order to assail them with a stream of deception and gross distortion. Whilst the devil is capable of powerful witchcraft it seems his power is effectively multiplied when people on earth choose to partner with his evil schemes.

Our Warfare with the Deceiver

John identified the devil as the deceiver of the entire earth. "The great dragon was cast out, that serpent of old, called the Devil and Satan, who deceives the whole world." (Revelation 12:9) Since he was humiliated and 'cast out' (John 12:31) through the work of the cross the devil is absolutely enraged. "Woe to the inhabitants of the earth and the sea! For the devil has come down to you, having great wrath, because he knows that he has a short time." (Revelation

12:12) The target of his rage is exclusively focused upon the church, described in Revelation 12 as the 'woman.' "So the serpent spewed water out of his mouth like a flood after the woman that he might cause her to be carried away by the flood." (Revelation 12:15) Satan is the "father of lies" and there is such a malevolent stream of carefully crafted deception sent against the church, that few Christians have historically escaped every single aspect of entanglement in his powerful spells.

We only need to ask the following question to realize how prevalent the deception of the evil one is: what would a Christian look like who was living in 100% freedom from all satanic deception? What level of revelation would such a Christian be walking in that it could be said of them that they are completely free of even the slightest trace of deception or spiritual disorientation. Of course, only Jesus fits this description. Even Paul, with his unsurpassed degree of divine revelation still claimed to know only 'in part.'

"Now, our knowledge is partial and incomplete, and even the gift of prophecy reveals only part of the whole picture! But when full understanding comes, these partial things will become useless. Now we see things imperfectly as in a cloudy mirror, but then we will see everything with perfect clarity. All that I know now is partial and incomplete, but then I will know everything completely, just as God now knows me completely." (1 Corinthians 13:9,10,12 NLT) Paul also said, "If anyone thinks that he knows anything, he knows nothing yet as he ought to know!" (1 Corinthians 8:2) The truth is that our partial knowledge and revelation still leaves considerable room for a degree of earthly distortion and plenty of room for upgrades as we transition from the depths of the carnal mind to the soaring heights of the fullness of the mind of Christ.

For a Christian to walk completely free of any trace of deception or distortion he or she would have to walk in the full measure of the mind of Christ who is the only person who has ever walked the earth in perfect freedom from the lies and witchcraft of the evil one. The issue is not whether we are deceived by the devil or not; the issue is the level to which we are deceived. The annoying thing about deception is that we don't realize how deceived we have been until we finally come out from under the devil's evil spells. All of us are on the journey of escaping the deception of the evil one and we are all transitioning from a state of complete blindness into the glory of God's marvelous light. Every single revelation brings us one step closer to complete freedom from deception. Jesus said, "You shall know the truth, and the truth shall make you free!" (John 8:32)

The ministry of the Spirit is to reveal the truth of God that sets us free. That is why He is called the 'Spirit of Truth.' But there is a counter 'ministry' and that is a sinister and malevolent ministry of well-crafted lies and deliberate deceit that intentionally targets Christians. Regrettably the deceiver scans the hearts and minds of all Christians in order to craft specific lies that are strategically designed to lock believers into a state of deception and distortion. All Christians suffer from these evil witchcraft assignments and the truth is that we are all in and out of various states of mild delusion and disorientation. Sometimes these demonic assignments can come upon us suddenly and violently. Of course, the more revelation a Christian has and obediently walks in, the more freedom he or she will experience from these demonic assignments.

God brilliantly and cleverly uses these assignments to establish us in the truth but being established in truth is predicated upon a life of radical obedience to God and that is where so many Christians get tripped up. If the enemy can trap us in a lifestyle of chronic disobedience he has free and regular access to the heart and the mind and he can energize our thought life through the infiltration of lying spirits. Down through the ages there has been a long history of Christians who have suffered various degrees of deception, distortion and disorientation in their minds because of the devil's relentless ministry of targeted lies. We are living in a full-scale war zone and we are always being scanned and targeted. Coming fully under the Lordship of Jesus is the only way to be free of all deception.

It is the work of the devil to keep Christians from entering into a deep heart engagement with the truth of God's Word. God intends to usher the obedient heart into a profound truth encounter and to keep His sons and daughters in a place of obediently gazing upon the person of Christ who described Himself as "*the* Truth." (John 14:6) Truth is embodied in a person and therefore the truth is something, or more precisely, 'someone' that we encounter in our hearts. The Greek word for 'truth' is '*aletheia*.' When Christ said He was 'the Truth' He was in effect saying He was the personification of absolute, capital 'R' Reality!

If we can behold and comprehend Him we are gazing into the very face of ultimate Reality. When the author of Hebrews commanded us to 'fix our eyes on Jesus' he was inviting us into a lifestyle of sustained truth encounter. The eyes and face of Jesus reflect ultimate reality. Because the devil is the 'father of lies' he seeks, above all things, to hinder believers from obediently beholding the glory of God in the face of Jesus Christ. He doesn't really care how much theological knowledge a Christian has. He is only threatened when a Christian purposes to walk in the truth in a sustained manner through a life of obedient devotion to the person of Christ.

Walking in the Truth

The Apostle John said, "It has given me great joy to find some of your children walking in the truth, just as the Father commanded us." (2 John 4 NIV) Walking in truth is a heartfelt apprehension of capital 'R' Reality held within a heart of obedience to God and His Word. It is equivalent to walking in the light, walking in the Spirit, abiding in God's love or abiding in God's word. Jesus said, "If you abide in My word then you are My disciples and you shall know the truth and the truth will make you free." (John 8:31,21) Walking in the truth is an expression of receiving the truth of God's word into our hearts and holding it in an attitude of reverent obedience and love for God.

Many Christians mistake their intellectual knowledge or their memory of biblical truths for actually "walking in truth." For many believers the truth is a memory, perhaps even a recent memory of biblical truth recently observed instead of a heart apprehension of absolute Reality revealed in the person of Jesus who is the personification and embodiment of the Truth. Walking in truth is a deep heart engagement of obedience and devotion. God is seeking those who tremble at His word. "Behold, You desire truth in the inward parts and in the hidden part You will make me to know wisdom." (Psalms 51:6) This is much more than an intellectual comprehension of revelatory truths. It is a place of living in a continual encounter with the very person of Jesus who is the truth.

There is something so powerful in a life of genuine obedience to the truth. Jesus said, "If anyone is willing to *do* His will *he will know* of the teaching; whether it is of God or whether I speak from Myself." (John 7:17 NASB) The only person who comes into a living understanding and an intimate knowledge of the Truth is the one who hears God's word and really obeys it. Paul said,

"For with the heart one believes." (Romans 10:10) Faith is always a matter of the heart. "For indeed the gospel was preached to us as well as to them; but the word which they heard did not profit them, not being mixed with faith in those who heard it." (Hebrews 4:2) The gospel message is of no effect unless it leads to what Paul called the "obedience of faith." (Romans 16:26) When it is held and deeply valued by an obedient heart, by a doer of the word rather than a hearer only, the true believer enters into a living truth encounter. Truth is something to be encountered in the heart rather than considered in the mind. A. W. Tozer explained this when he said;

> The essence of my belief is that there is a difference, a vast difference between fact and truth. Truth in the Scriptures is more than a fact. A fact may be detached, impersonal, cold and totally disassociated from life. Truth, on the other hand is warm, living and spiritual. A theological fact may be held in the mind for a lifetime without its having any positive effect upon the moral character; but truth is creative, saving, transforming and it always changes the one who receives it into a humbler and holier man. Theological facts are like the altar of Elijah on Mount Carmel before the fire came; correct, properly laid out but altogether cold. When the heart makes the ultimate surrender, the fire falls and true facts are transmuted into spiritual truth that transforms, enlightens and sanctifies. The church or the individual that is Bible taught without being Spirit-taught has simply failed to see that truth lies deeper than the theological statement of it. We only possess what we experience![3]

The devil doesn't mind when a Christian merely dabbles in the word of God without devoting him or herself to a life of radical obedience to the Lordship of Christ. But he trembles whenever a true disciple purposes in his or her heart to actually live a life of radical obedience to the Word. There is a perverse sense in which the devil actually finds great delight when a Christian reads the Word of God with no real heart intention to obey it or to live according to it. The certain outcome is that this person who reads God's word without obeying it from the heart will end up more religious and hence more deceived. Disobedient Christians are sitting ducks for spiritual deception.

For me personally, one of the most vividly memorable scenes from *The Lord of the Rings* movie trilogy was when Frodo accidentally stumbled into Shelob's lair. Shelob, the gigantic spider, (the arachnophobe's ultimate nightmare), entrapped Frodo and begun to spin him relentlessly in a web after having stung him with a hideously toxic venom. What a prophetic picture of the poison of the devil's lies and his capacity to spin a web of deceit around the soul of the disobedient believer. The devil can only penetrate our heart with the poison of his lies when we are not fully walking in the truth. The Spirit of Truth continuously exposes every lie of the evil one for those who have ears to hear but if we forsake that place of humble teachability because we refuse to walk in obedience we place ourselves in a position of considerable vulnerability to the entanglements of the devil's lies.

Four Primary Spheres of Deception

The devil feeds us a continual stream of lies about four specific spheres of human relationship. He lies to us about the character of God through which he seeks to poison our relationship of trust in God, he lies to us about himself, minimizing the significance of his subtle lies and distortions of the truth. He lies to us about ourselves, convincing us that we aren't who the Scriptures declare that we are and, fourthly, he lies to us about those whom we are in relationship with in order to isolate us in mistrust and suspicion of our brethren.

The devil is a liar by nature. "When he lies, he speaks his native language, for he is a liar and the father of lies." (John 8:44 NIV) Fundamentally, his lies are **_relational lies_** that are strategically designed to isolate us and to cut us off from God and from our brothers and sisters in Christ. Isolation is never a good idea. In fact, it is a spirit of deception that drives human beings into isolation. In our isolation from God we are even greater victims of deception. In our isolation from one another in the body of Christ we are vulnerable to the disorientation that comes through our foolish independence. A fool isolates himself but a wise man immerses himself in accountable relationships. "A man who isolates himself seeks his own desire; he rages against all wise judgment." (Proverbs 18:1) Such isolation and independence is pure foolishness in heaven's eyes.

Lies About God

The primary issue surrounding our deception in relation to God concerns our perception of the nature and character of God. The devil works overtime to deceive us about what God is really like. As a case in point, the depiction of

God as an angry taskmaster, so common in many historical religious traditions, is guaranteed to make people want to hide from such a vindictive and punitive God. The truth, of course, is that God is the ultimate Lover of our souls who loves us with an infinite and perfect love. The Bible is a seamless revelation of the person and works of God. A. W. Tozer, in his famous volume, *The Knowledge of the Holy*, writes;

> All of God's acts are consistent with all of His attributes. No attribute contradicts the other, but all harmonize and blend into each other in the infinite abyss of the Godhead. All that God does agrees with all that God is and being and doing are one in Him. The familiar picture of God as often torn between His justice and His mercy is altogether false to the facts. To think of God as inclining first toward one and then toward another of His attributes is to imagine a God who is unsure of Himself, frustrated and emotionally unstable, which of course is to say that the one of whom we are thinking is not the true God at all but a weak, mental reflection of Him badly out of focus.
>
> God being who He is, cannot cease to be what He is, and being what He is, He cannot act out of character with Himself. I think it might be demonstrated that almost every heresy that has afflicted the church through the years has arisen from believing about God things that are not true, or from overemphasizing certain true things so as to obscure other things equally true. To magnify any attribute to the exclusion of another is to head straight for one of the dismal swamps of theology; and yet we are all constantly tempted to do just that. For instance, the Bible teaches that God is love; some have interpreted this in such a way as virtually to deny that He is just, which the Bible also teaches. Others press the Biblical doctrine of God's goodness so far that it is made to contradict His holiness. Or they make His compassion cancel out His truth. Still others understand the sovereignty of God in a way that destroys or at least greatly diminishes His goodness and love. We can hold a correct view of truth only by daring to believe everything God has said about Himself.[4]

So much has been written on the nature, the character and the attributes of God. Tozer's book, *The Knowledge of the Holy* is as good an introduction as you will ever find on the subject of who God is in His divine nature. This present volume is not the place to explore this subject in any detail other than to say that every believer in God ought to invest time in exploring the nature and character of God in His word and in books such as *The Knowledge of the Holy*, which was powerfully formative in my early walk with Jesus. The better we know God the less likely we are to fall victim to the devil's barrage of lies concerning the nature of God.

If we really know the God of the Bible and Jesus through whom He has revealed Himself we will be spared considerable deception in this life. We should all join Paul in the cry of his heart when he said, "That I may know Him…" (Philippians 3:10) In the *Preface* to *The Knowledge of the Holy*, Tozer notes that, "The low view of God entertained almost universally among Christians is the cause of a hundred lesser evils everywhere among us."[5] Having a clear apprehension of the nature and character of God is the starting point for building a worldview that is healthy and reflective of absolute Reality. The knowledge of God is the foundation for our very lives. If this foundation is destroyed or compromised it will create a ripple effect, triggering a cascading descent into error and distortion throughout every part of our lives as believers.

Lies About the Devil

The devil entices believers into independent thinking and he doesn't have to try very hard. If the root of an independent spirit isn't addressed and brought under the power of the cross a person will likely trust his or her own judgment above the wise teachers and counselors that God places around us. Jesus said, "I am sending you prophets and wise men and teachers." (Matthew 23:34 NIV) We can embrace the safety of a multitude of counselors as King David did by surrounding himself with prophets and trusted advisors or we can exalt our own understanding by assuming that we are always right, thus pushing away the wise counsellors whom God has provided to help us see our blind spots and who can bring another layer of objectivity into our life. "There is a way that seems right to a man, but in the end it leads to death." (Proverbs 14:12 NIV)

A Christian who consistently minimizes the significance of the spiritual warfare that surrounds the lives of all who have been supernaturally planted in Christ sets him or herself up for considerable deception. As a trainer and equipper I have taught on the reality of spiritual warfare for over three decades. In early 1980, a few months into the beginning of my walk with

Christ, I was privileged to sit under Dean Sherman, a veteran YWAM teacher who has devoted his life to awakening young Christians to the reality of the warfare that we are living in.

In a three-day seminar, both Dean Sherman and Winkie Pratney unpacked the spiritual dynamics of the cost of walking in independence from Christ and our brethren in the body of Christ. They unmasked the devil's strategy to trap the believer in a place of independence where they do not listen to wise counsel and refuse to submit themselves to a wider body of believers who can support them in their spiritual journey. They established the biblical link between the root of independence and spiritual deception. I consider myself blessed to have heard such powerfully revelatory teaching so early in my walk with Christ. That seminar set me on a course of seriously considering the spiritual warfare dimension in my own life and in my friends in terms of the devil's power to blind believers.

Ever since that time I have trained Christians to appreciate the significance of the reality of spiritual warfare. Paul urged believers to consider the fact that we are daily wrestling with principalities, powers and the rulers of the darkness of this world. He pleaded with Christians not to be ignorant of the devil's schemes and devices. (2 Corinthians 2:11) Peter believed that there was a real devil that roamed around like a predatory lion seeking whom he may devour. (1 Peter 5:8) I continually meet Christians who have what I consider to be a significantly deficient regard or understanding of the true nature of spiritual warfare. I have met missionaries and church planters who have sought to go into demonically energized locations to establish a work for God who haven't had a developed understanding of the nature of the battle they were entering into. It wasn't good.

A low view of spiritual warfare and a reticence to give the subject the attention it deserves can be traced back to the devil himself who entices Christians to underestimate the intensity of the warfare in the name of avoiding unpalatable thoughts and topics of discussion. Some Christians try to ignore this dimension of our lives in the name of not giving the devil the headlines. Perhaps they are in reaction to those demon obsessed Christians who give the devil too much attention to the point of being drawn into an unhealthy fascination with what Jesus called "the deep things of Satan." (Revelation 2:24) If we want to know what a balanced and healthy approach to this subject looks like we need to consider the approach of both Jesus and Paul in exposing the works of the evil one when appropriate without becoming obsessed with a demon hiding around every corner.

Satan always seeks to minimize the importance of spiritual warfare amongst Christians. He is the architect of the culture within the church that finds it 'uncool' or unpalatable to focus upon these realities. The net effect of this unhealthy trend within the church is the very thing Paul urged believers to overcome: a widespread ignorance of the devil's schemes and devices. The truth is, we are thrust into full-scale war as Christians and we need to be comprehensively equipped with all the weapons of our warfare. We have to engage in hand-to-hand combat with the devil and with principalities and powers because these malevolent spirit beings bring the battle to us. We are forced to contend because we have a very active adversary who viciously contends against us to keep us locked down in a state of passivity concerning the warfare and to hold us in deep deception concerning the nature of the battle.

Lies About Ourselves

Satan's flood of deception deliberately and strategically targets believers' perception of themselves. Ever since the miraculous new birth we have a brand new core identity of sonship as part of the new creation package. Simply put; born again Christians do not know themselves until they receive divine revelation into their true core identity. Paul challenged the Corinthians to see themselves from heaven's perspective because they were behaving in a manner that revealed the reality that they were deceived concerning their true spiritual identity. He said, "Examine yourselves as to whether you are in the faith. Test yourselves. *Do you not know yourselves*, that Jesus Christ is in you?" (2 Corinthians 13:5) Paul probed them with the reality that perhaps they didn't really know themselves at all. They were sons of heaven behaving as sons of earth.

In the same epistle Paul said, "Therefore, from now on, we regard no one according to the flesh." (2 Corinthians 5:16) In the very next verse Paul made a prophetic declaration over the Corinthians as he called out the treasure of their new core identity. "Therefore, if anyone is in Christ, he is a new creation; old things have passed away; behold, all things have become new." (2 Corinthians 5:17) The truth is, "You are not in the flesh but in the Spirit, if indeed the Spirit of God dwells in you." (Romans 8:9) According to Paul the

Christian life begun "in the Spirit." (Galatians 3:3) We are no longer defined by the flesh or by our old carnal nature. Yet, how many Christians still define themselves according to their old nature instead of their new nature?

One of the primary strategies of the evil one is to blind us to the miracle of the new creation so we get locked into a perception of ourselves that is inconsistent with our new core identity as sons and daughters of an infinitely loving heavenly Father. "The Spirit Himself testifies with our spirit that we are God's children." (Romans 8:16 NIV) This is the glorious truth of who we are in Christ. This new identity as beloved sons has the power to usher in massive supernatural transformation. It is of little surprise that the devil counters this single revelatory truth with all his might in order to hold us into a distorted perception of ourselves. God has a perfect perception of us that He is eager to share with each of us. If we truly desire to overcome the evil one we must invest ourselves into cultivating a revelatory self-perception so that with ever-increasing clarity we grow in seeing ourselves from heaven's perfect perspective. The Holy Spirit preaches the new creation until we believe it with all of our heart.

None of us have perfected this heavenly self-perception. Paul insisted that we all see in part and that this partial knowledge will only be brought to absolute completion when the perfect comes at the end of the age. In the meantime we are invited into never-ending upgrades as we position ourselves under the ministry of the Spirit of truth who is continuously unveiling who we really are in Christ. The new creation truth that we have become the righteousness of God in Christ and that our old sinful nature has been 'cut away' in order to make us partakers of Christ's own divine nature is the only thing that will deliver us from living under a continuous stream of satanic accusation and condemnation.

"Therefore, there is now no condemnation for those who are in Christ Jesus." (Romans 8:1) This is not a relative statement but an absolute statement if only we can see ourselves through heaven's eyes. Because we have been justified freely by His grace we have been made perfectly righteous in Christ and everything that is true of Christ in His spirit when He walked on earth is true of our spirit as a consequence of our glorious redemption in Christ. "Because as He is, so are we in this world." (1 John 4:17) "He who does what is right is righteous, just as He is righteous." (1 John 3:7) Our justification through faith in His blood gives us perfect standing in the presence of God. "Who dares accuse us whom God has chosen for His own? Will God? No! He is the one who has given us right standing with Himself. Who then will condemn us?" (Romans 8:33,34 NLT) There is absolutely no grounds for condemnation or accusation for those who have been made perfectly right with God. As John declared; we overcome the accuser of the brethren through the blood of the Lamb. (Revelation 12:10) We have received a perfect salvation in our glorified spirit!

Lies About Others

A perennial temptation for all of us is to align ourselves with this spirit of accusation that continually streams forth from hell. Christians who fall victim to the propaganda of hell inadvertently find themselves calling out the old nature in one another instead of calling out the treasure of the new creation. Satan's ministry of accusation never stops. John wanted us to know that the Accuser accuses the brethren "day and night." (Revelation 12:10) That means we have to fend off, not only the accuser's accusations against us personally but also his accusation of others that he whispers in our ear. To the extent that we fall into the devil's trap of aligning ourselves with this ministry of faultfinding and accusation, to that same extent we bind our brothers and sisters to their old identity with our judgments. If you call out the beast it might rise up to bite and devour you.

If we consider just how much back-biting, judging, criticizing and condemning goes on within the hearts of believers toward their brothers and sisters in Christ we can appreciate the problem the church has been facing over the past 2,000 years. Is it any wonder the church has been catastrophically divided? There is only one way of escape from this relentless satanic barrage of lies; we must see our brothers and sisters through Jesus' eyes. We must come to a place of elevated vision where we see the glory of the new creation in the heart of every single believer. We need to understand by revelation that the new heart God has given our brethren is of infinite worth in defining that person from heaven's perspective. Our responsibility is to prophetically call out the treasure of the glory of the new creation.

This is a very real battle for every single Christian that has ever walked the planet. Every day, we get to see the brokenness in the hearts of those who we are walking in relationship with. Husbands see their wives' brokenness and wives see their husbands' brokenness. Fathers and mothers see their children's brokenness and children see the brokenness of their parents. The more we get to intimately know the people that we are journeying with the more we see the broken places in their heart. Church members begin to see their leader's brokenness and leaders see the broken places in the hearts of folks in their churches. With this deepening knowledge of one another's hearts comes a unique temptation from the evil one.

In response, we can either move in the new heart of love and mercy that the Father has placed within us, which, in reality is His heart of love flowing through us, or we can align ourselves with the evil one's heart of accusation and faultfinding. The way these scenarios usually play out in our home life and in our church life is, more often than not, shaped by our broken responses to other people's brokenness. In our immaturity and susceptibility to blame shift and to judge one another the enemy quickly jumps on our backs, bringing considerable distortion through the pain that arises because of the brokenness and then he entices us to step onto the merry-go-round of faultfinding and judgment. For many Christians this becomes their permanent address and they simply cannot get off the merry-go-round because they have bought into the lie that their accusation is fully justified because of the perceived failure of others to walk in the love they ought to be walking in.

If we don't have a revelatory vision of the glory of the new creation in the heart of every single believer that we are in relationship with, we will descend into the lower vision of perceived failure and disappointment in others. This lower vision has its own internal logic and can be justified because the perceived failure of others and their personal brokenness is often very real. But if our vision of heavenly realities is waxing dim, even to the point of completely losing sight of the glory of the new creation miracle in others, we can live our lives in such a way that we define others according to their flesh and we can call out their brokenness instead of calling out the treasure of the new creation.

A husband and wife who descend into the abyss of faultfinding and dragging one another down are actually doing the devil's work. Paul warns about falling into the devil's trap and doing his will. Whenever Christians descend into this abyss of condemning and accusing their brethren the only way of escape is "that they may come to their senses and escape the snare of the devil, having been taken captive by him to do his will." (2 Timothy 2:26) The only thing that can bring them to their senses is a fresh infusion of new creation glory so they can be lifted up to a great high mountain and see the New Jerusalem afresh and recognize that its citizens are a brand new company of heavenly sons and daughters who are now seated in heavenly places.

In all of the snares of the devil and in all of his attempts to set a trap through carefully constructed lies and deception, it is the power of the prophetic to lift us up out of the fog-filled valleys and to place our feet upon a great high mountain where our panoramic vision is restored. God is always calling us to 'Come up here' so we see the New Jerusalem in all her glory as a bride prepared for her Husband. As redeemed sons and daughters, we are all citizens of heaven; we are all of an entirely new creation and a new order of human beings who are fashioned after the Heavenly Man, Jesus. Whatever we do to the least of these, His brethren, we do to Him. Our treatment of our brothers and sisters in Christ becomes our treatment of Jesus. Saul of Tarsus persecuted the church and Jesus tapped him on the shoulder and said, "Saul, Saul, why are you persecuting Me?" (Acts 9:4)

Through the mystical union of the new birth the Father and His people are now one! "For he who touches you touches the apple of His eye." (Zechariah 2:8) Paul taught that Christ is now a many membered body. "For as the body is one and has many members, but all the members of that one body, being many, are one body, so also is Christ." (1 Corinthians 12:12) The church is literally the 'body of Christ.' This is not a theological metaphor. Paul revealed the reason some Corinthian believers were sick and some had died. "For if you eat the bread or drink the cup unworthily, ***not honoring the body of Christ***, you are eating and drinking God's judgment upon yourself. That is why many of you are weak and sick and some have even died." (1 Corinthians 11:29,30 NLT)

The Power of Community

Prophetic Christians living in the power of true prophetic community are far less susceptible to the lies of the evil one. The prophetic always begets a greater increase of the prophetic. "In Your light we see light." (Psalms 36:9) "To those who use well what they are given, even more will be given, and they will have an abundance." (Matthew 25:29 NLT) In Christian community, when we are rightly related to one another in the bonds of love and the gift of supernatural unity through the Spirit, we build a fortress of defense against all of the lies of the evil one. God has prepared a place of protection against the flood of deception. John saw a startling vision on the Isle of Patmos that revealed that God had prepared a special place of protection from all of the lies of the devil.

> When the dragon saw that he had been hurled to the earth, he pursued the woman who had given birth to the male child. The woman was given the two wings of a great eagle, so that she might fly to the place prepared for her... where she would be taken care of... out of the serpent's reach. Then from his mouth the serpent spewed water like a river, to overtake the woman and sweep her away with the torrent. But the earth helped the woman by opening its mouth and swallowing the river that the dragon had spewed out of his mouth. (Revelation 12:13-16 NIV)

This prophetic vision is extremely helpful in understanding the big picture of the great spiritual battle that rages around us and even inside of us. God has prepared a place of protection for us from all of the lies of the evil one. The anointing of the Spirit of Truth dwells within us. John said, "But you have an anointing from the Holy One, and you know all things." (1 John 2:20) John could only say this on the basis of the new creation truth that we now possess the 'mind of Christ.' He also said, "I am writing these things to you about those who are trying to lead you astray. As for you, the anointing you received from Him remains in you, and you do not need anyone to teach you. But as His anointing teaches you about all things and as that anointing is real, not counterfeit – just as it has taught you, remain in Him." (1 John 2:26,27 NIV)

The Holy Spirit of Truth dwells within every single believer. So why are so many Christians languishing under such a heavy blanket of deception? It all comes back to the condition of the heart. The safest place on earth from the deluge of satanic lies and the distortion of the truth is in a prophetic community of radically obedient disciples who love God with all of their heart, where truth and love are celebrated together and where people learn to tremble beneath the sheer glory of the word of God. In order to avail ourselves of this place of glorious protection we have to overcome some preliminary hurdles of isolation and independence but if we can overcome these initial barriers and can find our place under godly leadership in a healthy expression of community we can enter a safe place where we can truly know the truth and the truth can set us free.

Prophetic community nurtures the mind of Christ in the safety of a multitude of counsellors. It is only in this spiritual environment that we "overcome the evil one" (1 John 2:14) and get to see Satan crushed beneath the feet of the church. (Romans 16:20) There is no individualistic solution to overcoming the lies of the evil one. There is only a corporate solution because as soon as we believe we can overcome the devil in isolation from one another we are automatically deceived. If you are reading this and you genuinely desire to come out from every trace of the devil's lies and deception I urge you to recognize that prophetic community is God's remedy to the flood of deception engulfing the church and the world. We cannot 'walk in the truth' as we discussed earlier in this chapter without immersing ourselves into the family of God on earth. This is a vital part of our full obedience to Christ.

God is raising up apostolic safe houses that carry the Father's heart. Under the glory of apostolic, prophetic government there is a place of incredible strength where the sons and daughters can flourish in realms of unimaginable safety and freedom. "God sets the solitary in families." (Psalms 68:6) In the graphic horror of Frodo being poisoned and entangled in Shelob's web it was Samwise Gamgee, his loving companion, who fought Shelob, driving him into retreat and rescuing Frodo from this horrific attack. "Two are better than one. If one person falls, the other can reach out and help. But people who are alone when they fall are in real trouble." (Ecclesiastes 4:9,10 NLT) If you are an isolated Christian dislocated from prophetic community I urge you to rethink your strategy to overcome and immerse yourself into a company of people who love the truth and who love one another. This is God's ordained pathway to escape the entanglement of an ever-increasing barrage of witchcraft and evil spells that issue from the invisible warlock who despises the church, knowing that his time is short. We are all personally responsible to disentangle ourselves from every web of deception through the power and the wisdom of Christ who dwells within us, ever leading us by His Spirit into all truth.

Chapter Eight

Entangled in Sin and Selfishness

"Therefore, since we have so great a cloud of witnesses surrounding us, let us also lay aside every encumbrance and *the sin which so easily entangles us*, and let us run with endurance the race that is set before us."
(Hebrews 12:1 NASB)

The Bible is, among many things, a compendium of the knowledge of sin. Because of the fall of our original parents in the Garden the authors of Scripture, under the inspiration of the Holy Spirit, have made the unveiling of the fallen nature a major priority in both the Old and New Testaments. Jesus Himself made this a high priority. As we piece together the revelatory threads that complete this tapestry of the fallen human condition we come to see that the unveiling of the nature of sin and of human selfishness is of great importance to God. Without the biblical exposé of sin in all of its sinfulness people might be left to think that their situation is not perilous, especially when left to their own understanding. God wants us to see sin from heaven's perspective. Paul taught that, "All have sinned and fallen short of the glory of God." (Romans 3:23) The depth of sin is juxtaposed against the height of glory that was Adam and Eve's original estate.

Without the knowledge of sin, who would be conscious of their need of a Savior? And without an understanding of our desperate need for a Savior who will call upon the name of the Lord in order to be saved? The Bible drives home the reality of sin in a way that offends us. It is hard for us to hear about the utter depravity of the sin condition. It is a most unpleasant subject. It jars against all false notions of intrinsic human goodness. There is a natural propensity of all human beings to deny the depth of their brokenness. There is also considerable warfare surrounding the unveiling of the old sinful nature. I could feel the indignation and wrath of the evil one as I wrote this chapter on the nature of sin. The devil would much prefer that Christians persist in a shallow understanding of sin so that they don't come into agreement with God about the horror of the sin condition. As you read through this chapter I guarantee that you will be tempted to skip over it but I urge you to persevere. The exposé of sin is not about wallowing in the Old Testament; it is as much a part of the revelation of the New Testament as it is of the Old. There are things that God wants us to see about the reality of sin so we all need to exercise great patience as the Holy Spirit teaches us about the insidious nature of sin.

Paul unveiled a deep revelation on the reality of human sinfulness, especially in the book of Romans where he explains the spiritual mechanics of our deliverance from the power of sin through the atonement of Christ. We all come to Christ with an extremely limited and shallow knowledge of the insidious nature the sin. The earliest phase of our introduction to Christ usually entails a mere entry-level understanding that something is fundamentally wrong with us and that we really need help. If asked to define what Paul identified as the 'flesh' most new believers would draw a complete blank! As far as an ability to articulate the essence of the human condition most new believers do not have a clear or comprehensive understanding of the true nature of sin or the depths of our selfishness. It is only as we begin to read the Bible that we embark on a journey of discovery as the Scriptures reveal the true depths of the fallen human condition. Outside of Christ, every single human being lives under the dominion of sin because they are all descendants of Adam. Paul declared that the "wages of sin is death," (Romans 6:23) therefore "in Adam all die!" (1 Corinthians 15:22) Apart from Christ we are dead in our trespasses and sins.

A shallow view of sin and selfishness is the chief cause of believers becoming trapped in a life of disobedience and compromise. We don't have to be in the church for very long to realize that many Christians wink at their disobedience and have learnt to embrace compromise with sin as a lifestyle. But if we take our directives from heaven we cannot justify a life of continuing in sin. The grace of the gospel is more than sufficient to empower believers to life a life of radical obedience to God, free from the compromise of worldliness. Part of the remedy for this compromised spiritual condition is in cultivating a radically biblical view of the depravity of sin. True repentance is coming into full agreement with God concerning the exceeding sinfulness of sin.

Our New Relationship to Sin

A major part of our heart journey is in disentangling ourselves from sin. The greatest catalyst to set us on a path to genuine freedom from the power of sin is to understand the power of the gospel through which our relationship to sin has been fundamentally changed through the supernatural activity of God. If we truly desire to disentangle ourselves from the snare of sin we have to see what God has done in our heart of hearts through the regeneration of our spirit. The new birth is the beginning of the deconstruction of the edifice of sin in the human heart as God establishes a heavenly beachhead in the human spirit. The revelation that our spirit is already comprehensively dead to sin and alive to God is the heavenly launch pad to a life of freedom from the power of sin. To the extent that we live and abide in that finished work of Christ in our spirit we are empowered to live within the Holy of Holies. Jesus commands us to "Abide in My love." (John 15:9) John confidently proclaimed that, "Whoever abides in Him does not sin." (1 John 3:6) Our goal is to walk continually in God's love and escape the corruption of sin.

But in spite of the stronghold of righteousness that has been established within the human spirit every born again believers has to deal with the ongoing issue of sin in the human heart and all its subtle entanglements. In that sense Christians still stand in solidarity with the sinful condition of the whole of humanity. "All have sinned and fallen short of the glory of God!" (Romans 3:23) Paul expressed this solidarity with a sinful world that had rejected and crucified Christ. Ironically, he did this as the foremost advocate of the new creation! Late in his ministry he wrote in his first epistle to Timothy; "Here is a trustworthy saying that deserves full acceptance: Christ Jesus came into the world to save sinners – *of whom I am the worst*. But for that very reason I was shown mercy so that in me, *the worst of sinners*, Christ Jesus might display His unlimited patience as an example for those who would believe on Him and receive eternal life." (1 Timothy 1:15,16 NIV)

It is strange to hear Paul use this kind of language in his expression of solidarity with the community of sin because Paul was the chief custodian of the theology of the new creation miracle through which God delivers us from the penalty of sin through the new birth. This is a strange paradox. It was Paul who, under the inspiration of the Spirit, introduced the concept of the believer being dead to sin in Christ. Romans 6 was Paul's theological epiphany: the boldest statement in human history of the glory of our new existence in Christ.

Even though Paul could still identify with the world of sin, in this outrageous prophetic declaration Paul establishes our ultimate solidarity with Jesus in His death to sin through the cross and in His resurrection to a life of being gloriously alive to God. It is this solidarity with the death and resurrection of Christ that triumphs over our solidarity with a sinful world. Paul confidently declares that if we are in Christ our relationship to sin has fundamentally changed at the very core of our being. This prophetic revelation is the launch pad to a life of victory over sin.

> Shall we continue in sin that grace may abound? Certainly not! How shall we who died to sin live any longer in it? Or do you not know that as many of us as were baptized into Christ Jesus were baptized into His death? Therefore we were buried with Him through baptism into death, that just as Christ was raised from the dead by the glory of the Father, even so we also should walk in newness of life. For if we have been united together in the likeness of His death, certainly we also shall be in the likeness of His resurrection, knowing this, that our old man was crucified with Him, that the body of sin might be done away with, that we should no longer be slaves of sin. For he who has died has been freed from sin. Now if we died with Christ, we believe that we shall also live with Him, knowing that Christ, having been raised from the dead, dies no more. Death no longer has dominion over Him. For the death that He died, He died to sin once for all; but the life that He lives, He lives to God. Likewise you also, reckon yourselves to be dead indeed to sin, but alive to God in Christ Jesus our Lord. (Romans 6:1-11)

The focal point of this miraculous transformation in the heart is the human spirit. Paul proclaimed that the heart of every single believer in Christ has been supernaturally circumcised.

> When you came to Christ, you were 'circumcised,' but not by a physical procedure. It was a spiritual procedure – the cutting away of your sinful nature. For you were buried with Christ when you were baptized. And with Him you were raised to a new life because you trusted the mighty power of God who raised Christ from the dead. You were dead because of your sins and because your sinful nature was not yet cut away. Then God made you alive with Christ. He forgave all our sins. He cancelled the record that contained the

charges against us. He took it and destroyed it by nailing it to Christ's
cross. (Colossians 2:11-14 NLT)

Your old sinful nature was literally cut away by the 'Surgeon's scalpel' so that
your spirit was comprehensively delivered, once and for all from the presence
and power of sin and made gloriously alive through the impartation of the very
righteousness of Christ to your human spirit. Subsequently, your spirit is now
100% dead to sin and 100% alive to God. Your spirit is now just as righteous
as Christ Himself and through the impartation of His divine nature of perfect
righteousness and perfect love you now enjoy perfect standing before the
Father in the core of your being. Your human spirit has been brought to a state
of glorious completion in Christ. God has established an unshakeable
stronghold of His righteousness in our spirit and He has carved out a sanctuary
for His glory to abide in our spirit. The regenerated spirit of believers has
become the new Holy of Holies.

However, even though we are new creations in Christ, the Holy Spirit still
reveals strongholds of sin in the soul of the believer. If you have any doubts
about this I recommend you examine the way in which Jesus addressed the
seven churches in Revelation 2 and 3. The work God has done in your spirit is
a finished work whereas the work He is doing in your soul is far from finished.
"Being confident of this, that he who began a good work in you will carry it on
to completion until the day of Christ Jesus." (Philippians 1:6 NIV) One of the
great dangers for us as followers of Christ is that as God reveals sin in our
hearts we might lose sight of the fact that we are new creations in Christ. This
is an issue of core identity. From heaven's perspective God now relates to us
according to our new identity as sons and as saints. He no longer relates to us
as sinners in the ultimate sense because our spirit is comprehensively dead to
sin. But God does acknowledge the presence of sin in the heart of the believer
and He calls us out from under the power of sin to live a victorious life free
from the entanglement of sin.

If we are indeed dead to sin through our spiritual baptism into Christ then why
do we need to think about sin if it is something we are comprehensively dead
to? We could justifiably ask the question: if we are new creations in Christ and
God has made us truly 'dead to sin and alive to God' in Christ, then why do
we need to have a comprehensive knowledge of the flesh? Surely if we spend
too much time focusing upon the flesh won't we end up missing the reality of
the new creation? This is a legitimate concern and I will seek to give a clear

answer to this issue. I think the answer lies in the fundamental dichotomy of the condition of the spirit and the soul. The moment of your salvation the living and active Word of God separated soul from spirit like a razor sharp surgeon's scalpel, forever making a line of demarcation between the finished work of God in the regenerated spirit and the unfinished work of God in the human soul. The Holy of Holies of your spirit man is now gloriously free from the very presence of sin whereas your soul is still potentially defiled by sin. A cursory reading of the New Testament makes it crystal clear that even those under Paul's glorious apostolic ministry still had a challenging time disentangling their souls from the defilement of sin.

We come to Christ with at best an extremely sketchy knowledge of our broken condition. Paul said, "We don't yet see things clearly. We're squinting in a fog, peering through a mist." (1 Corinthians 13:12 MSG) But God deems it important for each of us to understand what the Scriptures call the exceeding sinfulness of sin. Through the lens of the Word of God sin becomes "exceedingly sinful." (Romans 7:13) This is not to say that the revelation of the sinfulness of sin actually exceeds the reality of the condition. On the contrary, we grasp the exceeding sinfulness of sin when we apprehend just how diabolical sin is and what it cost God to redeem us through the atonement of Christ as we come to realize that His blood was shed in order to redeem each of us from the penalty and the power of sin. Paul labored so that believers would have an accurate comprehension of the diabolical nature of sin and the depths of brokenness and depravity that sin has wrought in the human race. This is a significant theme in the New Testament. Paul never shied away from exposing sin in the fullness of its utter depravity.

Every believer in Christ needs an encounter with God where they realize by the Spirit of revelation that it was their sin that led to Christ dying for them personally on the cross. God seeks to bring every one of us to the place of recognizing that Jesus died for us personally! One factor that has contributed to the proliferation of so many compromising, lukewarm churches in the world today has been a shallow and superficial understanding of the sinfulness of sin. I would argue that God wants His New Covenant people to enter into a comprehensively biblical understanding of the exceeding sinfulness of sin. He wants us to see it the way He sees it from heaven. This is an intrinsic element in the development of a thoroughly biblical worldview. It is as though we need to see sin in all of its ugliness to fully apprehend the surpassing glory and holiness of God. That is why Paul deliberately juxtaposed sin against the backdrop of the glory of God. "All have sinned and fallen short of the glory of God." (Romans 3:23)

But there is a problem in saying that New Covenant believers need to be thoroughly immersed in a biblical revelation of sin. Sin no longer constitutes the true inner identity of born again believers. We are no longer identified as sinners but as saints and as sons and daughters of God. Nevertheless God still seeks to unveil the sinful nature to His children so that they grow in a comprehensive knowledge of their enemy. Christians have three major enemies: the world, the flesh and the devil and all three of these enemies are implacably hostile toward God. We will be in a state of warfare with these enemies until our death or until Christ returns. It is absolutely imperative that we know our enemy! God reveals the exceeding sinfulness of sin to His children so they have a thorough knowledge of what it is they have been delivered from through the new birth and what it is they are now being delivered from through the purifying and sanctifying work of the Holy Spirit. This is the paradox of sanctification that I discussed in Chapter Six of '*The New Creation Miracle*,' which is Volume Two in my series on Supernatural Transformation. If you haven't read that book or that chapter in particular I strongly recommend you to read it, as it is foundational to the heart journey of every believer in Christ.

The Interior Conflict

As we grow as Christians we ought to be growing in a parallel understanding of who we are as new creations and in a deeper revelation of the absolute depravity of our old sinful nature. As we mature in Christ the new creation miracle appears more and more glorious just as the depths of sin and selfishness appear more and more diabolical and destructive. It is regrettable but true that all Christians experience an ongoing struggle with the old sin nature. Temptation is a fact of life for the believer in the midst of this present evil world. The writer of Hebrews said, "But recall the former days in which, after you were illuminated, you endured a great struggle..." (Hebrews 10:32) He said, "In your struggle against sin, you have not yet resisted to the point of shedding your blood." (Hebrews 12:4 NIV) "Therefore, since we are surrounded by such a great cloud of witnesses, let us throw off everything that hinders and *the sin that so easily entangles*, and let us run with perseverance the race marked out for us." (Hebrews 12:1) All New Testament authors acknowledge this ongoing struggle against the insidious nature of sin.

Paul described himself as a 'boxer' (1 Corinthians 9:26) and as a 'fighter.' (1 Timothy 6:12) He referenced this intense inner conflict in Galatians. "For the desires of the flesh are opposed to the Holy Spirit and the desires of the Spirit are opposed to the flesh (godless human nature); for these are antagonistic to each other – continually withstanding and in conflict with each other!" (Galatians 5:17 AMP) He affirmed that all believers experience an ongoing interior battle against fleshly lusts. Both Peter and James confirmed this new inward battle that commenced the day the Holy Spirit invaded our hearts. Peter said, "I warn you to keep away from evil desires because they fight against your very souls." (1 Peter 2:11 NLT) Another translation calls them "fleshly lusts which wage war against the soul." (NASB) James called this interior warfare; "the whole army of evil desires at war within you." (James 4:1 NLT)

In this chapter we want to unpack a detailed revelation of our old sinful nature so that we can be equipped to fight the good fight against worldly and fleshly lusts. It is not who we are any more in terms of our new core identity in Christ but it certainly affects each of us because God is still in the process of experientially delivering us from our entanglement with sin, selfishness and all of its dark consequences. It is as if God were pleading with each of His sons and daughters, saying, "Know your enemy!" The Holy Spirit is now training us as saints to live a life of righteousness and true holiness.

As long as we live in this mortal body we will be vulnerable to the sin nature. The essence of the flesh is the old self-centered self. The flesh is always just one selfish choice away. Paul says that believers now have two ways of walking. Before we were born again we only had one way of walking and that was called 'walking in the flesh.' We lived under the power of sin and we had never tasted even the slightest freedom from the power of sin. But now the grace of God has been abundantly poured out on us and we have been gloriously empowered to say 'No' to ungodliness. Now, because the Spirit dwells in us we have the option to either 'walk in the Spirit' or to 'walk in the flesh.' We walk in the flesh whenever we make choices that are selfish and we walk in the Spirit whenever we yield in our hearts to the Lordship of Christ and choose to make Christ the center of our lives instead of ourselves. We are now called to a life of radical obedience to walk in love instead of sin. The life of being an overcomer consists in learning the art of walking in the Spirit, abiding in Christ, abiding in His Word and abiding in His love. These are all different ways of expressing the same reality of walking in newness of life with Christ at the center of our lives.

With this in mind God unveils the sinful self-centered old nature in order to show us what it is that He has called us to put to death. We are dead to sin once for all in our spirit man and this new reality now empowers us to go into our 'inner room' and commune with a holy God from the first day of our new life in Christ. As we have already seen, your spirit is a sanctuary that has been comprehensively cleansed and set apart to God and your spirit has been fully immersed into Christ and the Holy Spirit. Nevertheless there is a lifetime of learning to deny ourselves and to put to death in the soul realm (the mind, will and emotions) the nature of the flesh. Jesus Himself walked in daily self-denial. If He was not exempt from this obligation then neither are we! John Wesley asked believers the poignant question; "Who will you deny? Yourself or the Lord?" At any moment of our lives we are either denying one or the other.

This is where we make the biblical distinction between soul and spirit by acknowledging that there is a part of us that has been made dead to sin, as a once and for all finished work and another part of us (our souls) where we are learning how to deny ourselves and to apply the power of the cross to every vestige of that which is now considered 'old' and passing away. This is an unfinished work in our lives and it requires a life of full cooperation in bringing everything under the power of the cross of Christ. The issue of obedience to God is central to this process. The spirit has been comprehensively renewed but the soul is still being renewed. The latter half of Romans 6 unpacks the role of our obedient choices in activating the power of the new creation and walking in righteousness and true holiness.

> Therefore do not let sin reign in your mortal body so that you obey its evil desires. Do not offer the parts of your body to sin, as instruments of wickedness, but rather offer yourselves to God, as those who have been brought from death to life; and offer the parts of your body to him as instruments of righteousness. For sin shall not be your master, because you are not under law, but under grace. What then? Shall we sin because we are not under law but under grace? By no means! Don't you know that when you offer yourselves to someone to obey him as slaves, you are slaves to the one whom you obey – whether you are slaves to sin, which leads to death, or to obedience, which leads to righteousness? But thanks be to God that, though you used to be slaves to sin, **you obeyed from the heart** the form of teaching to which you were entrusted. You have been set free from sin and have

become slaves to righteousness. I put this in human terms because you are weak in your natural selves. Just as you used to offer the parts of your body in slavery to impurity and to ever-increasing wickedness, so now offer them in slavery to righteousness leading to holiness. (Romans 6:12-18 NIV)

What is the 'Flesh?'

How we define the 'flesh' is essential in moving toward a biblical view of the internal struggle that we all experience the moment God established the beachhead of His Spirit inside of us. You may have just noticed that the Amplified Bible translated the flesh as the 'godless human nature.' The NIV translates Paul's term 'in the flesh' as "controlled by the sinful nature." (Romans 7:5) The NLT translates it as "controlled by our old nature." The Amplified Bible says "Walk and live habitually in the Holy Spirit – responsive to and controlled and guided by the Spirit; then you will certainly not gratify the cravings and desires of the flesh – of human nature without God." (Galatians 5:16 AMP) So we have three definitions of the flesh: our sinful nature, our old nature and human nature without God.

Kenneth Wuest adds an extra nuance to his description of the flesh. He says, "The *evil nature* constantly has a strong desire to suppress the Spirit and the Spirit has a strong desire to suppress the evil nature." (Galatians 5:17 Wuest) The Message Bible also defines the flesh as "godless human nature." Another interesting term used by Paul is our 'old man.' He says, "Our old man was crucified with Him." (Romans 6:6) The Message calls this "our old unrenewed self" whereas the NLT calls it our "old sinful selves" and the NIV calls it "our old self." My old self was the old 'me' before the new birth where my old, evil, sinful human nature was entrenched at the center of my being, unchallenged by the presence of the Spirit of holiness. The flesh is therefore a sinful and selfish state of existence that is fundamentally defiant to God and His righteousness.

Paul clearly taught that this 'old, sinful and selfish nature' is still a present reality in the life of every follower of Christ and that it is our responsibility to bring it under the rule and reign of the power of the cross and to put it to death. Paul was addressing born again Christians when he said, "Do not be deceived, God is not mocked; for whatever a man sows, that he will also reap. For *he who sows to his flesh* will of the flesh reap corruption, but he who sows to the

Spirit will of the Spirit reap everlasting life." (Galatians 6:7,8) Paul recognized that believers who began their walk with God in the power of the Holy Spirit could easily end up in the flesh. "Are you so foolish? Having begun in the Spirit, are you now being made perfect by the flesh?" (Galatians 3:3)

The 'old nature' of the believer is therefore identical to the present nature of fallen man. It is one and the same. Therefore, the generic biblical unveiling of the sinful nature of fallen humanity is equally applicable to the unveiling of this exact same 'old nature' in the believer. The only difference is that the believer has died to the old nature through his new life in Christ. That is why it is now called 'old!' The challenge is to live out this reality that we are indeed dead to everything that constitutes the old nature. If we reject the reality of the new creation we automatically default back to the old self with its passions and desires. Paul said, "For the law of the Spirit of life in Christ Jesus has made me free from the law of sin and death." (Romans 8:2) Watchman Nee, the author of *The Normal Christian Life* likened the law of the Spirit to the law of aerodynamics and the law of sin and death to the law of gravity. As long as the law of aerodynamics with its principle of thrust and lift is in operation it defies the law of gravity. But as soon as the engine is switched off, a 350 ton jet is immediately subject again to the law of gravity. A horrible thought to all of us who regularly fly!

Paul's exhortations to put off the old and to put on the new; to "put to death the deeds of the body" (Romans 8:13) and to "put to death the sinful, earthly things lurking within you" (Colossians 3:5 NLT) takes on much greater significance as we discover the unfolding revelation of the nature of the flesh in all of its depravity and learn how to apply the power of the cross to our old man. The Message Bible says, "So kill the evil desire lurking in your members...the deifying of self!" (Colossians 3:5 MSG) This is the most compelling reason why God continues to unveil the sinful nature within our hearts. He will not do *for us* that which He has purposed to do *through us* as our hearts are systematically transformed from glory to glory. This is a journey that cannot be sidestepped, circumvented or avoided. Step by step He walks us through the journey of deep heart transformation, always looking for our complete cooperation in the sanctification of our entire heart. With this in mind we can explore the generic unveiling of the sinful nature throughout the entire Bible knowing that it has universal applicability to every living being, including those who are new creations in Christ because it is a revelation of that which we now regard as 'old' or 'passing away' within our hearts. We *must* know our enemy!

As we explore the biblical revelation of fallen human nature remember we are examining who we once were. You have a new sinless nature and you are a partaker of the divine nature at the core of your being so this is NOT who you now are as a born again believer. This is no longer your identity. But for the purposes of this chapter we will examine the nature of fallen man, which is identical to that which the Bible identifies as your 'old' nature or your 'old man.' We need to explore the revelation of the sin nature as a reality that has 'passed away' otherwise we are not honoring the miracle of the new creation. "Therefore, if anyone is in Christ, he is a new creation; *old things have passed away*; behold, all things have become new." (2 Corinthians 5:17) If we explore this old nature as a description of 'who we are' we will end up completely condemned. But Paul said, "Therefore, there is now no condemnation for those who are in Christ Jesus." (Romans 8:1) The reason we are no longer condemned is because we are new creations in Christ!

I cannot stress this enough! As you read through this chapter rejoice that this is what Jesus has already delivered you from in your spirit. Read it through the lens of the new creation miracle and see yourself as God now sees you! There may be moments when you come under the conviction of the Holy Spirit as you recognize certain old traits that are still an issue for you. But even if the Spirit shows you areas of your old life that still exercise an influence within your heart, rejoice, because this is no longer your true identity. There may be areas that you still need to repent of. Repentance and confession is clearly still an imperative for born again believers. If God reveals in us areas of entanglement with sin, we repent before God, we confess our sins and turn away from them so that sin no longer exercises dominion over us. "If we confess our sins, He is faithful and just to forgive us our sins and to cleanse us from all unrighteousness." (1 John 1:9)

Unveiling the Flesh

Jesus is the "Lamb of God who came to take away the sins of the world." (John 1:29) His goal was to reveal the depths of human sinfulness in order to promote full repentance and cleansing at the deepest level of our hearts. Without this repentance there could be no salvation. Jesus actually went deeper than the law. The law revealed the presence of sin in the world but

Jesus took the unveiling of the sinful nature to new depths by internalising the reality of sin. Because the Old Testament revelation was incomplete it did not convey the full picture. We see a good example of this deeper unveiling of the reality of sin in the Sermon on the Mount. Jesus said, "You have heard that it was said to those of old, 'You shall not commit adultery.' But I say to you that whoever looks at a woman to lust for her has already committed adultery with her *in his heart*." (Matthew 5:27,28)

Jesus employed the same principle with the commandment about murder. "You have heard that it was said to the people long ago, 'Do not murder, and anyone who murders will be subject to judgment.' But I tell you that anyone who is angry with his brother will be subject to judgment." (Matthew 5:21,22 NIV) In effect, Jesus said, "The law said this, but I'm saying this!" John developed this same idea in his first epistle. The law said, "Do not murder," but John said, "Anyone who hates his brother is a murderer." (1 John 3:15 NIV) This principle permeates the New Testament. God deepens the revelation of sin beyond outward acts to heart attitudes and motives.

When the Old Testament prophets confronted the reality of sin, God was looking for more than a superficial response. He was not looking merely for the cessation of certain outward behaviors. He was seeking a profound inward change of heart. The Pharisees thought that by cleaning the outside of the cup they were pleasing God. They did not murder nor did they commit adultery. They did not steal nor did they practice idolatry. But did they entertain greed in their hearts? Did they hate their neighbor? Did they wrestle inwardly with lust, pride, anger and selfishness? Jesus confronted this shallow view of sin when He said, "You clean the outside of the cup and dish, but inside they are full of greed and self-indulgence. On the outside you appear to people as righteous but on the inside you are full of hypocrisy and wickedness." (Matthew 23:25,28 NIV) This superficial concept of sin has been perpetuated by many within the church who have failed to grasp the teachings of Christ concerning the absolute depravity of the sin nature. Larry Crabb describes this as an "iceberg view of sin." He writes:

Perhaps the major error of Evangelical churches today involves a deficient and shallow understanding of sin. Many pastors preach an "iceberg view" of sin. All they worry about is what is visible above the water line. Like a naïve sea captain steering his vessel around the tip of the iceberg with no awareness that there is a mountain of ice beneath the surface that could wreck his ship, Christian teachers and disciplers are too often satisfied when their people turn from church-defined sins of misbehavior. A great mass of sinful beliefs and misdirected motives is never dealt with under this approach. The result is external conformity that masquerades as spiritual health.[6]

Jesus intentionally headed off this false concept of sin by focusing on the invisible condition of the heart. Followers of Christ, above all people on the face of the earth, ought to understand that sin does not consist merely in the outward deeds that people do. Neither is repentance merely the cleaning of the outside of the cup. How could so many Christians throughout history possibly miss this revelation when Jesus spelt it out in such black and white terms? Whenever the church descends into a popular religious culture that measures righteousness by outward conformity we become satisfied if our people merely abstain from certain external thing such as heavy drinking, gambling and sex before marriage. The problem lies in this shallow level of satisfaction that, at least visibly, Christians appear to be better people than those who do not have Christ in their lives because they do not openly practice visible sin.

Paul called believers 'saints' but he called himself the 'worst of sinners.' He claimed that we are dead to sin in Christ but he also acknowledged that in the life of our soul we still struggle against sin and the temptation to sin. He proclaimed a unique solidarity with Christ in His death to sin and in His resurrection to newness of life but he also proclaimed a sense of solidarity with the whole of humanity in their entanglement in sin. Paul spent a considerable amount of his time seeking to help Christians to disentangle themselves from the tentacles of this evil master. So much of the content of his epistles focused on the journey of extricating believers from the entangling power of sin.

We naïvely flatter ourselves with the thought that we are not like the heathen who do not believe in God. Remember Jesus' famous portrayal of the heart of the religious man? "The Pharisee stood up and prayed about himself: "God, I thank you that I am not like other men – robbers, evildoers, adulterers – or even like this tax collector. I fast twice a week and give a tenth of all I get." (Luke 18:11,12 NIV) There is a little Pharisee inside every one of us who takes pride in our religious attainment by exalting ourselves above those who do not believe in God. Agreement with God's standards of righteousness and morality does not necessarily constitute the conformity of the heart to this inward standard of righteousness. This was the great error of the

Pharisees who agreed with God's word but who had not done the deep heart journey of cleansing the inside of the cup.

If we were to compare ourselves with those around us who recklessly plunge themselves into all manner of sins we could take pride in the degree to which we have changed outwardly. Peter said, "Your former friends are very surprised when you no longer join them in the wicked things they do." (1 Peter 4:4 NLT) Whenever anyone abstains from drunkenness, blasphemy, swearing and fornication the world sits up and takes notice. What's wrong with this person and why don't they join us in the party? External abstinence from sinful practices is indeed a substantial improvement upon our former condition and there is a strong temptation to rest in a certain level of spiritual attainment. But who are we called to compare ourselves with? If we measure ourselves by local standards there will always be someone we can exalt ourselves over. There are always people that we can compare ourselves with and thus convince ourselves that we are not like other men. Paul addressed this issue of those who compared themselves with others. He said that whenever people "measure themselves by themselves and compare themselves with themselves, they are without understanding." (2 Corinthians 10:12 NASB)

Jesus Personified Righteousness

There is only one person in the entire universe with whom we ought to make a comparison and that is Jesus. God Himself makes the comparison in order to reveal the presence of sin in the human heart. He said, "Be holy, because I am holy." (1 Peter 1:16 NIV) Jesus said, "Be perfect, therefore, as your heavenly Father is perfect." (Matthew 5:48 NIV) Jesus said, "I have set you an example that you should do as I have done for you." (John 13:15 NIV) We are called to follow in the footsteps of Christ and to walk as He walked. We are called to be conformed to the image of Jesus Christ. He is the standard by which we ought to compare ourselves. Whenever we lower the standard we will always find someone with whom we can compare our level of spirituality and in our own distorted thinking we will find grounds to exalt ourselves over others. The truth is that "all have sinned and fallen short of the glory of God." (Romans 3:23) The glory of God has been revealed in the sinless perfection of the heart of Jesus and when we meditate upon what some have described as the 'immaculate heart' of Christ we are deeply confronted by our need for deeper transformation as we contemplate the depths of our selfishness in the light of Jesus' heart of extraordinary love.

When God gave the Ten Commandments, He revealed an ethical standard of righteousness by which we could understand the exceeding sinfulness of sin. As Paul said in Romans 7, the law was good. "The law is holy, and the commandment is holy, righteous and good. Did that which is good, then, become death to me? By no means! But in order that sin might be recognized as sin, it produced death in me through what was good, so that through the commandment sin might become utterly sinful." (Romans 7:12,13 NIV) The law was 'good' but Christ is better! In the person of Christ the world witnessed the personal incarnation of the purity, righteousness and holiness of God. Christ put a personal face on the righteousness of God! It was one thing to understand the ethics of the law but it was an entirely different thing to encounter someone who embodied and even exceeded the righteousness of the law. Jesus said, "Do not think that I came to destroy the Law or the Prophets. I did not come to destroy but to fulfil." (Matthew 5:17) The law produced death but Christ came that we might have life in abundance. The contrast between the ministry of the Old Covenant and that of the New Covenant is that the law was, in Paul's words, the "ministry of death" whilst the ministry of Christ was the ministry of life. "For the letter kills, but the Spirit gives life." (2 Corinthians 3:6)

God found fault with the covenant of law but with His one and only Son He was "well pleased." "If the first covenant had been faultless, there would have been no need for a second covenant to replace it. But God himself found fault with the old one." (Hebrews 8:7,8 NLT) The Father was well pleased to present His Son to the world because his Son was the personal representation of the purity and righteousness of the heart of God. The world desperately needed to see the purity of God with a human face. What did a pure heart look like? Look no further than the sinless Lamb of God who embodied and revealed the purity of the divine nature and who called His people to purity of heart. "Blessed are the pure in heart, for they shall see God." (Matthew 5:8)

Jesus is God's revelation of the pure heart and by both His words and His very presence He revealed the impurity of the human heart. Jesus did not hesitate to highlight the depravity of the heart. In fact, this revelation of the impurity of the human heart was central to His teaching and preaching as we have already seen in the previous quotes from the Sermon on the Mount. Jesus was the ultimate revelation of a life free from selfishness. He was comprehensively selfless in that He lived for love. He embodied the love of God to such an extent that an examination of the lifestyle and the heart of Jesus revealed what an unselfish person really looks like. The law concerned itself with adherence to a rigorous code of outward conformity whereas Jesus concerned Himself with the real condition of the human heart.

Sin is revealed in our relationships to God and our neighbor. The heart of sin is deeply set upon self-will and is fundamentally opposed to the will of God. Jesus shocks us with the revelation of personal evil. Because He had a comprehensive understanding of human nature He made blanket statements about the evil orientation of the human heart. In the most matter of fact way, Jesus could say, "If you then, *being evil*, know how to give good gifts to your children, how much more will your Father who is in heaven give good things to those who ask Him!" (Matthew 7:11) What an affront to our personal dignity! The Pharisees prided themselves on their own righteousness and goodness but Jesus said to them, "Brood of vipers! How can you, *being evil*, speak good things? For out of the abundance of the heart the mouth speaks." (Matthew 12:24) Jesus revealed that, "the evil man brings evil things out of the evil stored up in him." (Matthew 12:35 NIV) Imagine how greatly this must have offended the Pharisees who had convinced themselves that they were righteous!

The very presence of Jesus somehow brought human evil into the light. In the same way demons manifested in His presence, so too, sinful men manifested in His presence. Jesus the prophet never afforded men the luxury of leaving evil concealed in their hearts. He drew it out and exposed it to the light. As the 'Light of the World' He exposed personal evil and brought into the light that which was done in secret. He revealed the fact that "men loved darkness instead of light because their deeds were evil. Everyone who does evil hates the light, and will not come into the light for fear that his deeds will be exposed." (John 3:19,20 NIV) They may not come to the light but the light had come to them and the light of Christ actively exposed the evil that was concealed within. The light has shone into the darkness and the world will never be the same!

Jesus is "The true light that gives light to every man." (John 1:9 NIV) According to John, Jesus "gives light to everyone. The light shines through the darkness, and the darkness can never extinguish it." (John 1:4,5 NLT) The evil heart of man, offended by the intensity of the light, sought desperately to extinguish this light. His enemies thought they had succeeded until Christ rose again from the dead. But the light shines on and God has forever established a benchmark of purity. The burden of sinful man is now to actively extinguish the light. Every single day of their lives people now choose either to embrace the light or turn away from it and seek to quench it.

Sinful man is continually confronted by the reality of the light. Every time he sees a church or a Christian message on a billboard he rejects the light. Every time a Christian advertisement appears on his television he rejects the light. Every time he reads or writes the date he must push from his mind the fact that time is measured by the coming of the light. Every Easter and every Christmas he must expel from his thought life the reality of the birth and death of Christ. Sinful man is confronted by Christ daily because God has gone on the offensive. He has declared war against the darkness by sending forth the Light!

 Sin is no longer measured merely by the law of Moses. It is measured by our response to the reality of Christ, the light of the world. Jesus said it was the role of the Holy Spirit to convict the world of sin. "When He comes, He will convict the world of guilt in regard to sin and righteousness and judgment: *in regard to sin, because men do not believe in Me.*" (John 16,8,9 NIV) The NLT says, "The world's sin is unbelief in me." The coming of Christ has forever redefined the very nature of sin. Jesus urges us to believe in the light. "While you have the light, believe in the light, that you may become sons of light." (John 12:36) Christ has exposed the darkness and the evil heart of fallen man and humanity must now choose between darkness and light. Jesus uncovered the truth that mankind loved darkness rather than light. Similarly, Paul revealed that fallen men and women love themselves, love money, pleasure, in fact, everything except God.

> But realize this, that in the last days difficult times will come. For men will be lovers of self, lovers of money, boastful, arrogant, revilers, disobedient to parents, ungrateful, unholy, unloving, irreconcilable, malicious gossips, without self-control, brutal, haters of good, treacherous, reckless, conceited, lovers of pleasure rather than lovers of God." (2 Timothy 3:1-4 NASB)

The Flesh Hates God

There is a natural antipathy in the fallen human heart toward righteousness, holiness and goodness. It is not that fallen humans, by nature, merely do not like God or that they prefer darkness to light. It is that they hate God, they hate that which is good, and they hate everything to do with righteousness. This is the flesh unveiled. In Romans 1 Paul literally cataloged the condition of the fallen heart. At the core of this unflattering description he described fallen humanity as "haters of God."

> Even as they did not like to retain God in their knowledge, God gave them over to a debased mind, to do those things which are not fitting; being filled with all unrighteousness, sexual immorality, wickedness, covetousness, maliciousness; full of envy, murder, strife, deceit, evil-mindedness; they are whisperers, backbiters, **haters of God**, violent, proud, boasters, inventors of evil things, disobedient to parents, undiscerning, untrustworthy, unloving, unforgiving, unmerciful." (Romans 1:28-30)

Richard Lovelace, in his book, *'Dynamics of Spiritual Life'* describes this intense enmity of the flesh toward God.

> Although most human beings give the appearance at times of being confused seekers of the truth with a naïve respect for God...the reality is that unless they are moved by the Spirit they have a natural distaste for the real God, an uncontrollable desire to break His laws and a constant tendency to sit in judgment on Him when they notice Him at all. They are at moral enmity with the God revealed in the Bible. Since His purposes cross theirs at every juncture, they really hate Him more than any finite object, and this is clearly displayed in their treatment of His Son. They are largely unconscious of this enmity. It is usually repressed through their unbelief...[7]

Paul's description of the human condition in Romans chapter 1 deeply offends the human mind; we tend to recoil from this shocking truth. Most people are so deeply committed to maintaining the appearance of righteousness and goodness that the true condition of the heart lies buried beneath layer upon layer of denial. According to the Bible, any appearance of personal goodness is nothing but religious pretense. Asaph, the Psalmist wrote, "The haters of the Lord would pretend submission to Him." (Psalms 81:15) At the conclusion of his unflattering description of the sinful heart in 2 Timothy 3, Paul said that these same people, "have a form of godliness but deny its power." (2 Timothy 3:5) This 'form,' or 'appearance' of godliness is nothing more than the well trained rehearsal of actors on the stage of life who are deeply committed to appearing to be something that they are not. "Though they pretend to be kind, their hearts are full of all kinds of evil." (Proverbs 25:26 NLT) We are surrounded by the myth of inherent human goodness but Jesus emphatically said, "No one is good but One, that is, God." (Matthew 19:17) This revelation runs through the Scriptures like a seamless garment.

David penned one of the most indicting passages of Scripture concerning the universality of human sin. "They are corrupt and have done abominable iniquity; there is none who does good. God looks down from heaven upon the children of men, to see if there are any who understand, who seek God. Every one of them has turned aside; they have together become corrupt; there is none who does good, no, not one." (Psalm 53:1-3) Paul quoted this passage in Romans chapter 1. Because fallen people are all sympathetic toward evil they often don't even wince when people blaspheme the name of Christ even though blasphemy is the very essence of human evil. Though most people do not consider themselves to be evil, neither do they commit themselves to be completely free of evil in their hearts. Fallen people are largely ambivalent toward evil; they know it's wrong but they tolerate it because of its universality. John White discusses this human ambivalence toward evil in his book, 'Changing on The Inside.'

> Evil is part of the reality of who we are. It exists in all of us because we – the entire human race – have chosen to run our lives our own way. If we believe we have evil under control, then we have never seriously tried to be rid of it. Most of us do not pursue evil, but neither do we commit ourselves to leading model lives. We aim at "passing grades" – whatever society tolerates and whatever else we can get away with. Any serious commitment to live a truly good life can cause us serious problems, for then we are confronted with the sobering reality of evil within us. Not all of us discover this, because we do not seriously aim high. We never discover what I would call the *beast in the basement*, – a beast that lurks in all of us, although we are but rarely aware of its existence. Most of us, of course, never 'side with evil' in its more blatant forms. We are 'nice' people, and as such we are blind to the virulence of evil in all of us.[8]

Because, in our natural fallen state, we were completely devoid of revelation, we did not see the condition of our own hearts as God saw it, therefore we were able to wink at the presence of evil. God sees the beast in the basement while humanity pursues blissful ignorance. "The Lord saw that the wickedness of man was great in the earth, and that every intent of the thoughts of his heart was only evil continually." (Genesis 6:5) By and large, humanity is unmoved by the presence of evil because of their secret solidarity with evil. The core of this solidarity is the universal commitment to a life of independence from God. From God's perspective, "each one follows the dictates of his own evil heart, so that no one listens to Me." (Jeremiah 16:12) Evil thrives unchecked in the heart that refuses to acknowledge the Lord. The whole of humanity is like King Rehoboam of whom we read in 2nd Chronicles, "He did evil, because he did not prepare his heart to seek the Lord." (2 Chronicles 12:14) It is only as we set our hearts to follow God and to turn from all evil that we even begin to discover the beast that lurks inside our hearts. This is what Paul called 'the flesh' and it is our own worst enemy because this godless, evil nature wars against the Spirit! Someone once said; we have met the enemy and it is us!

As a devout Jew, Paul discovered the beast in the basement only when he purposed to follow righteousness. "For the good that I want, I do not do, but I practice the very evil that I do not want. But if I am doing the very thing I do not want, I am no longer the one doing it, but sin which dwells in me. I find then the principle that evil is present in me, the one who wants to do good." (Romans 7:19-21 NASB) As we have already seen, sin is more than the outward deeds that people commit. It is part of who we are as a consequence of the fall. "A person is not a sinner because he sins, he sins because he is a sinner."[9] Richard Lovelace brilliantly describes the nature of sin.

> The structure of sin in the human personality is far more complicated than the isolated acts and thoughts of deliberate disobedience. In its biblical definition, sin cannot be limited to isolated instances or patterns of wrongdoing; it is something more akin to the psychological term *complex*: an organic network of compulsive attitudes, beliefs and behavior deeply rooted in an alienation from God. Sin originated in the darkening of the human mind and heart as man turned from the truth about God to embrace a lie about Him and consequently a whole universe of lies about His creation. Sinful thoughts, words and deeds flow forth from this darkened heart automatically and compulsively, as water from a polluted fountain. The human heart is now a reservoir of unconscious disordered motivation and response, of which unrenewed persons are unaware if left to themselves, for "the heart is deceitful above all things, and desperate-

ly corrupt; who can understand it" (Jeremiah 17:9) The mechanism by which this unconscious reservoir of darkness is formed is identified in Romans 1:18-23 as repression of traumatic material, chiefly the truth about God and our condition."[10]

Now I told you that this revelation of sin is not an easy pill to swallow. As we survey the biblical unveiling of human sinfulness all of us find something within us rising up in our own self-righteous defense. We want to shrug this description off and say that it describes only the lowest of sinners, those who end up in jail or those who perpetrate evil crimes. But this is the biblical description of a condition called the flesh and that flesh is in every single human being. It is a universal condition and it is characterized by the hatred of God and His righteousness. We are called to come into agreement with God in seeing sin, not through our jaded eyes that have become accustomed to the darkness and the culture of blasphemy, but through the eyes of the Lord who sees sin from the perspective of heaven that is filled with purity and holiness. God sees sin as exceedingly sinful and He loves righteousness and hates iniquity. He shares His divine perspective on sin so that we will come into full agreement with Him and repent of our apathy concerning sin.

The Promised Land

The book of Hebrews calls New Testament believers to enter the Promised Land. For us in the New Covenant this is not a strip of geography in the Middle East but the fullness of life in Christ. We live in the Promised Land when we live in the power of the new creation. It is only as we seek to overthrow the enemies of our own soul that we come face to face with the beast in the basement. We thought we were fairly OK until we actually sought to enter the Promised Land. Suddenly we found ourselves encompassed about by innumerable giants; each one intimidating us like Goliath intimidated the army of Israel with his taunts and mockery. We feel like grasshoppers in the sight of these giants and our hearts are discouraged by the prospects of the battle. It's at this point that many Christians turn back and cower in unbelief. The writer to the Hebrews said concerning the children of Israel that they "entered not in because of unbelief." (Hebrews 4:6 KJV) It takes genuine courage and faith in God to face off the giants and overcome them one by one.

Many Christians have turned to Christ but have been paralyzed by fear and intimidation simply by glimpsing the enemies of their soul. When God

God begins to unveil the sinful heart with its innumerable host of ungodly attitudes, intentions, motives and desires we are confronted by our own unbelief. The vast majority of believers throughout the history of the church have failed to enter the Promised Land of the unselfish heart of Jesus because of unbelief. They are trapped in a state of spiritual limbo. They don't want to go back to the world because they know it is a place of darkness and evil but neither do they have the heart for the battle that lies ahead of them if they are to enter the land. This is the spiritual address of many Christians and it is a tragedy of immense proportions because they remain trapped in a place of unbelief and disobedience their entire Christian lives. This is why the book of Hebrews is such a significant New Testament book. It outlines the place of rest for the Christian and then challenges us to press into this dimension of glorious freedom. Faith is the victory that overcomes the world and it is by faith that we subdue our enemies one by one.

The first giants that God confronts in our heart are the giants of unbelief, rebellion and disobedience for unless these giants are confronted and overcome we will not stand a chance of entering the Promised Land. It is not just that the people of God sometimes do not have the stomach for the fight; it is often a case of outright disobedience and rebellion against the voice of God. The enemies of our own soul are also the enemies of God. If we will not withstand evil in our own souls neither are we willing to withstand the issues in our own lives that rob us from intimate fellowship with God. Hebrews warns us against having an evil heart of unbelief in departing from the living God. Our battle against evil is a fight to the finish. If we don't take a stand against personal evil it will rule our lives and we will spend our entire lives in rebellion against God. Whatever we tolerate will ultimately dominate!

The Lord calls us to break every agreement with the powers of darkness and to align ourselves exclusively with the truth of His word. If we do not actively resist evil in our own lives we are in rebellion against God and we will never enter the Promised Land of life in Christ. God relentlessly confronts the evil heart of unbelief until we bow the knee to the Lordship of Christ in repentance. God's promise is the enjoyment of a new heart and an entirely new life in His Son and we dare not shrink back from the promise for if we shrink back from the light we are running straight into the arms of the darkness.

> Therefore, since a promise remains of entering His rest, let us fear lest any of you seem to have come short of it. For indeed the gospel

preached to us as well as to them; but the word which they heard did not profit them, not being mixed with faith in those who heard it. For we who have believed do enter that rest...Since therefore it remains that some must enter it, and those to whom it was first preached did not enter because of disobedience, again He designates a certain day, saying in David, "Today," after such a long time, as it has been said: "Today, if you will hear His voice, Do not harden your hearts." For if Joshua had given them rest, then He would not afterward have spoken of another day. There remains therefore a rest for the people of God. For he who has entered His rest has himself also ceased from his works as God did from His. Let us therefore be diligent to enter that rest, lest anyone fall according to the same example of disobedience. For the word of God is living and powerful, and sharper than any two-edged sword, piercing even to the division of soul and spirit, and of joints and marrow, and is a discerner of the thoughts and intents of the heart. And there is no creature hidden from His sight, but all things are naked and open to the eyes of Him to whom we must give account. (Hebrews 4:1-13)

Now, if we carefully follow the thought of the writer of this amazing book we will see where he is taking us. First of all he makes it clear that there is a place in the realm of the Spirit that God intends for us to enter, just as there was a geographical place in the Old Testament called the Promised Land. This spiritual destination is only entered by faith. If we are still under the power of an evil heart of unbelief we will never enter this place of spiritual rest. But if we will respond to the voice of God in faith and obedience He will shatter the power of unbelief and hardness of heart and will lead us by the hand into the Promised Land. Then the writer to the Hebrews confronts us with the reality that the word and the voice of God exposes and unveils the hidden thoughts, attitudes, motives and intentions of the human heart. Do you see the connection? It may help to read the above passage again to capture the flow of thought.

If we will embark on this spiritual odyssey God will be faithful to reveal the giants one by one and to teach our hearts to fight the good fight of faith. He has promised us victory over every single enemy of our soul and He will not rest until we have conquered every single one! With each individual victory our hearts are strengthened with the revelation of God's amazing power and love. The warrior heart of Jesus rises up within us and we get a taste for the battle. Before long we are unstoppable. We gladly confront every single giant because every time we do, we get a fresh glimpse of our wonderful warrior King. One level of faith is the springboard for the next level of faith. We journey from "faith to faith." (Romans 1:17) We are called to confront and overcome the giants and to become giant-slayers! "By faith the walls of Jericho fell down after they were encircled for seven days." (Hebrews 11:30) By faith David confronted Goliath armed with just a few smooth stones.

David was one of the mightiest warriors in the Old Testament but it was his own son Solomon who made the point that "He who is slow to anger is better than the mighty, and he who rules his spirit than he who takes a city." (Proverbs 16:32) The warriors of Israel may well have overcome the giants in Canaan but they may never have overcome the giants in their own heart. David's mighty men were undoubtedly inspired by his prowess as a warrior-king but even David failed to conquer his own lust. Overcoming the giants of the soul takes courage. The mature reflections of the Psalmist exemplify this life of the spiritual warrior.

> O Lord, you have searched me and you know me. You know when I sit and when I rise; you perceive my thoughts from afar. You discern my going out and my lying down; you are familiar with all my ways. Before a word is on my tongue you know it completely, O Lord. You hem me in – behind and before; you have laid your hand upon me. Such knowledge is too wonderful for me, too lofty for me to attain. If I say, "Surely the darkness will hide me and the light become night around me," even the darkness will not be dark to you; the night will shine like the day, for darkness is as light to you. Search me, O God, and know my heart; test me and know my anxious thoughts. See if there is any offensive way in me, and lead me in the way everlasting." (Psalm 139:1-6,11,12,23,24 NIV)

True Repentance

This prayer of David took tremendous courage but David had a heart for the fight. He had been overtaken by his own lust and had fallen back into the darkness but he got up again and re-entered the battle. There is no braver prayer than to ask God to search our hearts for when we pray this prayer we can be sure that God will initiate a process of inner transformation that will result in tremendous freedom, though the process may be extremely uncomfortable and humbling. Repentance is good medicine for the soul and the deeper our repentance the deeper the level of transformation that we will experience. Superficial repentance results in superficial change. Zero repentance results in zero change.

God is interested in getting to the roots of the sin nature because every sinful thought, word or deed has deep roots that need to be uprooted by the Spirit of God. Jesus said, "Every plant that my heavenly Father has not planted will be pulled up by the roots." (Matthew 15:13 NIV) God is calling us to move beyond our iceberg view of sin and to recognize that beneath the surface there are deep roots that lock us tightly into patterns of sin. These roots must be exposed and addressed if we are to experience deep level supernatural transformation.

Ownership of the issues and true heart repentance are the prerequisites for God to speak His word of cleansing. If we will own and confess our sins He will cleanse us of all unrighteousness. Then He will prophesy over us, saying, "Now ye are clean through the word which I have spoken unto you." (John 15:3 KJV) The leper had to acknowledge that he had leprosy before he could ask for cleansing. "A man with leprosy came to him and begged him on his knees, "If you are willing, you can make me clean." Filled with compassion, Jesus reached out his hand and touched the man. "I am willing," he said. "Be clean!" Immediately the leprosy left him and he was cured." (Mark 1:40-42 NIV) Jesus longs to cleanse His church with "the washing of water by the word," (Ephesians 5:26) but He waits for us to come into the light so that our deeds may be exposed. Repentance lies at the very heart of spiritual transformation, as Larry Crabb observes.

> Every "personal problem" (any problem in living not directly traceable to some organic malfunction) has its ultimate roots in a broken relationship with God and a commitment to a higher priority than knowing God. If that is true, then counselling should be designed to repair the fractured relationship with God by promoting the sort of repentance that leads to a deep enjoyment of God and an honest commitment to serve Him. But most theories of counselling try to effect change without ever dealing with matters of repentance and obedience. And the few theories that do address these matters reduce repentance to a simple decision to conform one's behavior to biblical standards. Deep repentance that concerns itself with the

subtle, perverse loyalties of a deceitful heart is rarely involved in most approaches to counseling.[11]

Deep level heart repentance lay at the core of the ministry of Christ. The first word recorded on the lips of Christ in the Gospel of Mark was the call to "repent!" (Mark 1:15) Jesus had no time for superficial repentance. He insisted on repentance at the deepest level of our being. A shallow view of sin produces a shallow repentance and one that falls seriously short of true biblical repentance. Jesus went after the deep roots of rebellion against God, hatred of the light, spiritual pride, idolatry, lust, greed, anger, judgmentalism, unforgiveness and narcissism. The heart of prophetic ministry is deeply confrontational. It confronts man at the deepest possible level and radically interferes with his whole orientation in life. Repentance is a profoundly radical concept, which opens the door to profound change. It is the recognition that there is no true life outside of God and that our stubborn declaration of independence has led only to death. "There is a way that seems right to a man, but in the end it leads to death." (Proverbs 14:12 NIV)

Within the fallen heart of man lurks a multitude of dark and sinful motives and attitudes. These are the factors that control and direct our outward behavior and God actively seeks to confront and interrupt these processes deep within our being. In our fallen state our heart is literally flooded by what God calls "the multitude of your iniquities." (Jeremiah 30:14) Before God begins to invade a person's life their heart is a veritable wellspring of ungodly attitudes and motives that are diametrically opposed to God and His ways. The heart is a deep reservoir of evil intentions and desires that reject God at every turn. When God begins to unveil the heart of man we are literally astonished at the height, the width and the depth of the depravity of the human heart. As we take each step closer to God we have to come face to face with the beast in the basement. As David grew in revelation he was literally astonished by the enormity of human depravity and what he described as the "multitude of their transgressions." (Psalm 5:10) It isn't that people merely have a few 'personal problems.' Viewed through the lens of divine revelation the heart of the sinner is fundamentally broken. David found the progressive unveiling of his own heart equally as shocking. Earlier in his walk with the Lord he may have been aware of the occasional bout of anxiety but as the unveiling of his heart increased he came to discover what he described as "the multitude of my anxieties within me." (Psalm 94:19)

Mourning the condition of both our own heart and the hearts of others is an indicator of our level of revelation and repentance. Solomon had tremendous depth of insight into the true condition of the heart. He concluded that, "The heart of the wise is in the house of mourning, but the heart of fools is in the house of pleasure." (Ecclesiastes 7:4 NIV) As Solomon grew in his understanding of the heart it intensified his own sense of sorrow. "In much wisdom there is much grief, and increasing knowledge results in increasing pain." (Ecclesiastes 1:18 NNAS) Nobody wants to live in perpetual pain except prophets who are willing to feel the pain in the Father's heart over His lost sons and daughters. Jesus said, "Blessed are those who mourn, for they shall be comforted." (Matthew 5:4) The Lord said to Ezekiel, "Walk through the streets of Jerusalem and put a mark on the foreheads of all those who weep and sigh because of the sins they see around them." (Ezekiel 9:4 NLT) Righteous Lot was a man set apart because he "was distressed by the filthy lives of lawless men." (2 Peter 2:7 NIV) When Isaiah experienced a prophetic revelation of the holiness of God he said, "Woe is me, for I am undone! Because I am a man of unclean lips, and I dwell in the midst of a people of unclean lips; for my eyes have seen the King, The Lord of hosts." (Isaiah 6:5)

God's perception of the human heart is so radically different to our own. We are often so occupied with excusing ourselves and blame shifting that we fail to see things as God sees them. But the very nature of divine revelation is coming to see things as God sees them. Watchman Nee said, "When God opens our eyes that we may know the intent of our heart and the deepest thought within us in the measure that He Himself knows us – this is revelation. As we are naked and laid bare before Him, so are we before ourselves as we receive revelation. This is revelation; for us to be allowed to see what our Lord sees."[12] There are only two kinds of people, those who can see and those who cannot. Paul had experienced a high level of spiritual revelation and he knew that if others couldn't see what he could see, God would have to show it to them. "All of us who are mature should take such a view of things. And if on some point you think differently, that too God will make clear to you." (Philippians 3:15 NIV)

Jesus could see into the human heart and He had no illusions about the seriousness of its condition. He said, "The evil man brings evil things out of the evil stored up in his heart. For out of the *abundance* of the heart his mouth speaks." (Luke 6:45) The most people are generally willing to acknowledge is that they have a few 'issues' or 'problems' in their life which occasionally get out of control. But Jesus viewed the fallen heart as a fountain of uncleanness and iniquity. The Greek word for '*abundance*' (as in, 'the *abundance* of the heart') is '*perisseuma*' and according to Colin Brown, it means, "exceeding the usual number or size; extraordinary, abundant, profuse, superfluous."[13] The *Strong's Concordance* describes it as a "surplus or super-abundance." This is not flattering if we are committed to diminishing the significance of our personal sin issues. The occultist would say that he 'dabbles' in witchcraft or sorcery but God describes it as, "the multitude of your sorceries," and "the great abundance of your enchantments." (Isaiah 47:9) Paul spoke of those who "always heap up their sins to the limit." (1 Thessalonians 2:16 NIV) Human beings relentlessly play down the seriousness of their situation. Whenever we yield to sin it always moves in and takes over. "Therefore," James said, "Lay aside all filthiness and *overflow* of wickedness." (James 1:21) James used the same word '*perisseuma*' for the '*overflow*' of wickedness. Christians are called to put it all to death and not to allow even a trace of the leaven of wickedness to remain in their hearts.

Sin and Selfishness

If the divine appraisal of the human heart is accurate then even 'nice' people have hearts that are literally festering with ungodly sinful attitudes, intentions and motives. Our capacity to pretend to be free of these influences is in itself part of the whole complex of unrighteousness that controls the heart. God is focused upon the attitudes, the purposes, the intentions and the motives of the heart because these are the governing principles that dictate our thoughts, our words and our deeds. If we are to come into agreement with the mind of Christ we must begin to think about these deeper issues and to allow God to expose them in order to promote deep level repentance. When we think of repentance we automatically think of the obvious outward things that we shouldn't do such as stealing, swearing or drunkenness, but we must have our minds renewed in order to focus upon the subtle strategies of the heart to pursue our own selfish purposes. In the words of C.S. Lewis in his famous poem; '*As the Ruin Falls*,' he came to this confession:

All this is flashy rhetoric about loving You,
I've never had a selfless thought since I was born.
I am mercenary and self-seeking through and through,
I want God, you, all friends merely to serve my turn.

The ruin falls only when we discover the deepest root of the flesh and that is our self-centered independent existence apart from God. Jesus taught the necessity of a radical self-denial that searches out and repents of our deep commitment to self. "If anyone desires to come after Me, let him **deny himself**, and take up his cross daily, and follow Me." (Luke 9:23) Theologians rightly defined sin as expressed in selfishness,[14] suggesting that most expressions of the self-life are essentially sinful. But we ought to exercise caution in making sin exclusively defined by selfishness alone. There is an appropriate expression of self- interest for the Christian that is not in itself sinful. The law said, "Love your neighbor as *yourself*." (Matthew 19:19) This would suggest that there is an appropriate expression of self-love just as there is an appropriate form of self-respect and personal dignity.

Paul put the whole matter in perspective in Philippians. "Do nothing from *selfishness* or empty conceit, but with humility of mind regard one another as more important than yourselves; do not merely look out for your own *personal interests*, but also for the interests of others." (Philippians 2:3,4 NASB) It is only natural to look after our own interests and ourselves. Jesus doesn't want us to deny ourselves to the point of becoming everybody's doormat. We need to have clearly defined boundaries to guard against being abused or exploited. Jesus looked after Himself by taking time out to rest and recuperate from His busy ministry schedule. Paul said, "After all, no one ever hated his own body, but he feeds and cares for it." (Ephesians 5:29) There is a healthy expression of self-interest but in general we define 'selfishness' as the opposite of love.

When Jesus spoke of denying ourselves, He certainly did not mean that we should hate ourselves. He simply meant that we should not exalt, serve or worship ourselves or to think of ourselves more highly than we ought. (Romans 12:3) The issue is self-centeredness and the idolatry of self. In our narcissistic culture people are literally encouraged to worship themselves. In turning from God we end up worshiping and serving the creature rather than Creator. (Romans 1:25) We are to have no other gods before Him but the heart of the old sin nature is to exalt ourselves as God. When we turn away from the Living God we become our own 'god' and our will becomes absolute. "Therefore hear this now, you who are given to pleasures, who dwell securely, who say in your heart, "I am, and there is no one else besides me..." (Isaiah 47:8) This kind of narcissistic self-love is the very essence of sin. Paul said, "But realize this, that in the last days difficult times will come. For men will be ***lovers of self***...lovers of pleasure rather than lovers of God..." (2 Timothy 3:1,2,4 NASB)

There are numerous secret sins of the self-life that many externally focused Christians have never even considered. The Bible describes humanity as "self-willed,"[15] "self-seeking,"[16] "self-satisfied,"[17] "self-exalting,"[18] "self-opinionated,"[19] "self-conceited,"[20] "self-obsessed,"[21] "self-focused,"[22] "self-loving,"[23] "self-absorbed,"[24] "self-centered,"[25] "self-serving," [26]"self-confident,"[27] "self-promoting,"[28] "self-deceivers,"[29] full of "self-indulgence,"[30]"self-gratification,"[31] "selfish ambition,"[32] and "self-importance."[33] Larry Crabb, who specializes in explaining many of these subtle strategies of the heart, highlights one key stronghold of the self-life that controls much of our behavior. He discusses the reality of the inevitable pain and brokenness that emerges from our relationships and our 'below the water line' strategies to avoid this pain.

> We are simply not aware of all that we are doing in our deceitful hearts. And we don't want to be aware of what we really believe and the direction we in fact are moving. We don't want to feel the relational pain that threatens to destroy us. But our pain and the strategies we use to run from pain must be faced. Pain can drive us to the Lord. Wrong strategies should be met with repentance. As relational beings we devise strategies for responding to life that will keep the pain out of awareness...Our strategies essentially consist of interpersonal styles of relating that help us to achieve what we want; a level of distance from others that ensures invulnerability to further hurt. Beneath every method of relating can be found a commitment to self-interest; a determination to protect oneself from more relational pain. Yet most of us are not aware of the self-protective motivations beneath our relational strategies. Why not? In Proverbs 20:5 the purposes of man's heart are said to be like deep waters. In shallow water you can see to the bottom. In deep water you can't! Part of the self-deception we practice is the denial of what our motives really are to the point where we simply do not see them. Repentance involves much harder work than apologizing for losing our temper and promising never to do it again. Sin hidden from view needs to be surgically removed like a tumor. Relational pain needs to be exposed in order to understand the protective purposes of wrong strategies.[34]

When we begin to think in terms of the self-centered strategies, motives and attitudes of the heart we are getting closer to the roots of the old sin nature and we are moving toward a realm of deep level heart transformation as we repent of the very things that motivate us to do the things we do. Paul said, "For what I am doing, I do not understand. For what I will to do, that I do not practice; but what I hate, that I do." (Romans 7:15) As God sheds light on the hidden motives of the heart we begin to understand why we do some of the crazy things that we do. Every act has an underlying motive and these motives are deeply rooted in sinful attitudes and responses. Jesus systematically addressed and dealt with these deep level sin issues in his public teaching ministry. He was answering questions that his audience were not even asking but His teachings were an investment into people's futures. As we walk through life the Holy Spirit takes the words of Jesus and applies them to the situations of life that we find ourselves in. Then we discover the radical applicability of the teachings of Christ to the issues of life that touch us most deeply. An excellent example of this is the issue of judgmentalism. Jesus said,

> Do not judge, or you too will be judged. For in the same way you judge others, you will be judged, and with the measure you use, it will be measured to you. Why do you look at the speck of sawdust in your brother's eye and pay no attention to the plank in your own eye? How can you say to your brother, 'Let me take the speck out of your eye,' when all the time there is a plank in your own eye? You hypocrite, first take the plank out of your own eye, and then you will see clearly to remove the speck from your brother's eye. (Matthew 7:1-5 NIV)

The issue of judgmentalism is so close to home that it's really not funny! Human beings, the whole world over are tarred with the same brush. Jesus could speak these words with all confidence because judgmentalism is an attitude that cuts right to the heart of the human condition. We want mercy for ourselves but judgment for others. The very things we condemn others for, we do ourselves (or at least we have done ourselves in the past or will possibly do in the future). We are preoccupied with excusing ourselves for the things we have done wrong. We are all highly skilled personal defense attorneys. We are practiced at excusing our own actions and when we are caught in the act we plead for mercy and understanding. But then in the next breath we will stand in accusation of someone else who does the very same thing to us. This is one of the strange universal quirks of human nature, which powerfully validates the divine inspiration of the Word of God. We can be certain that the

Scriptures are not human in origin on the basis of this single fact alone. We are so deeply dedicated to covering up our Pharisaical hearts that no mere mortal would ever speak the words that Jesus spoke!

Jesus told the penetrating story of the man who was shown mercy for a huge debt that he owed but who immediately turned around and began to throttle the person who owed him a tiny debt. (Matthew 18:23-35) The Scriptures consistently expose this hidden motive of the heart. How can we persist in our lack of mercy when Jesus spoke so powerfully to this very issue? How can we allow attitudes of superiority and judgmentalism to flourish in our hearts when they have been exposed as evil? How can we point the finger at others when our hearts are exactly the same as those whom we condemn? The Pharisees were taught this lesson in a most humiliating way when they flung the woman caught in adultery at the feet of Jesus. Jesus said, "If any one of you is without sin, let him be the first to throw a stone at her." (John 8:7 NIV) Jesus spoke just a few words that cut so deeply to the heart that one by one the Pharisees dropped their stones and walked away humiliated. Which of the Pharisees had never committed adultery in their hearts? Which of the Pharisees had never looked upon a woman to lust after her in his heart?

So we draw to a close our chapter on the entanglement of sin and selfishness. Remember, if you are born again; this is no longer your identity or your true inner nature. It has been purged from your spirit and you are a glorious new creation. But we stand in solidarity with fallen humanity insomuch as we are all 'tarred with the same brush.' Sin still touches our hearts even though we are now followers of Jesus. The thing we share in common with fallen humanity is that we still wrestle with an old nature that is identical in kind to their present fallen nature. But as new creations we must face and learn to subdue everything that constitutes this 'old man' through the power of the cross. Everything that is true of our new life in our spirit must now become true of the formerly darkened regions of the soul as we put to death what God has already put to death on the cross and experientially enter into the fullness of life that God seeks to extend to every aspect of our mind, our will and our emotions.

We must never forget that the old man has been already crucified with Christ so we are not talking about some kind of self-mortification process that is driven by human effort. Putting to death the reality of sin in our members is nothing more than an actualization of a reality that took place 2000 years ago when you died to sin with Christ on the cross. When He died; you died with Him. Paul said, for "we judge thus: that if One died for all, then all died; and He died for all, that those who live should live no longer for themselves, but for Him who died for them and rose again." (2 Corinthians 5:14,15) In other words we must no longer be selfish! Whenever Paul experienced the inner conflict between the flesh and the Spirit and the rising up of the sinful, selfish old man he simply made this prophetic declaration: "I have been crucified with Christ; it is no longer I who lives, but Christ lives in me." (Galatians 2:20) He reminded himself that, "Those who are Christ's have crucified the flesh with its passions and desires." (Galatians 5:24)

Every moment of our lives we activate by faith the reality that we are now dead to sin and alive to God in Christ. This is who we are in Him! Overcoming our entanglement with sin is a major aspect of the heart journey to which we are called. Each of us are called to step onto the battlefield and violently overthrow every aspect of our old life that still seeks to reign in our mortal body. We must never forget that we now live a radically grace-empowered life and the grace of God actively teaches us to say 'No' to all ungodliness and worldly lusts. (Titus 2:12 NIV) Jesus said, "Go and sin no more!" (John 8:11) He commanded us to "Be perfect, just as your Father in heaven is perfect." (Matthew 5:48) We must never lower the standard of our pursuit of a sin free existence and we must guard against secret agreements to wink at disobedience. "What shall we say then? Shall we continue in sin that grace may abound? God forbid!" (Romans 6:1,2) It is only when we are armed with this mindset that we are positioned to overcome the sin that so easily entangles us.

Chapter Nine

Entangled in Worldly Temptation

"For if, after they have escaped the defilements of the world by the knowledge of the Lord and Savior Jesus Christ, they are again entangled in them and are overcome, the last state has become worse for them than the first." **(2 Peter 2:20 NASB)**

The new birth has comprehensively changed our relationship to the world. In a moment, through the supernatural action of God we are changed in our spirit and delivered from this present evil world. Jesus said, "My kingdom is not of this world." (John 18:36) All those who have entered His kingdom and are now 'in Christ' are, from heaven's perspective, no longer *of* this world. We belong to the kingdom of the Father! Suddenly this world is no longer our home to the extent that it has actually become hostile toward those who are in Christ just as it was hostile toward Jesus Himself. "If the world hates you, keep in mind that it hated Me first. If you belonged to the world, it would love you as its own. As it is, you do not belong to the world, but I have chosen you out of the world. That is why the world hates you." (John 15:18,19 NIV) We now belong to the Father as adopted sons and daughters.

But even though we are now in Christ and in His kingdom and we are not of the world anymore, if you are anything like me you now find the world a strange place because you suddenly find, as a follower of Jesus that the world is relentlessly pulling upon us, calling us back to our old worldly lifestyle. It is as though 'the world' is an active spiritual force much like the force of gravity that continually exerts an effect upon us. There is a very real reason why the world exercises such a strong pull upon our souls and we have to see the truth about the real nature of the world, because if we don't see the world through Jesus' eyes we are at risk of being lulled into a false sense of reality concerning the threat that the world actually represents toward those who are now in Christ.

The World and the Evil One

Jesus prayed to His Father on behalf of His disciples that they would be protected from the world. "I have given them Your word; and the world has hated them because they are not of the world, just as I am not of the world. I do not pray that You should take them out of the world, but that You should keep them from the evil one. They are not of the world, just as I am not of the world." (John 17:14-16) So, Christians are now 'in the world' but they are not 'of the world.' From a New Testament perspective, this present evil world is comprehensively energized by the devil and by the demonic realm. John said, "We know that we are of God, and that the whole world lies in the power of the evil one." (1 John 5:19) Three times in the Gospel of John, Jesus called the devil "the prince of this world." (John 12:31, 14:30 and 16:11 NIV)

In like manner, Paul also called the devil the prince of this world. "You once walked according to the course of this world, according to the prince of the power of the air, the spirit who now works in the sons of disobedience." (Ephesians 2:2) Paul even called the devil the small 'g' god of this world. "Satan, the **god** of this evil world, has blinded the minds of those who don't believe, so they are unable to see the glorious light of the Good News that is shining upon them." (2 Corinthians 4:4 NLT) Because of the presence of sin and rebellion in the world, the entire world is conceived in terms of demonic power. When Paul talked about the '*spirit*' than now **works** in the sons of disobedience he used the Greek word '*energeo.*' He asserted that all who walk in disobedience, Christian or non-Christian, live in a dimension where this demonic energy has the capacity to energize people in their sin and disobedience. Sin and rebellion are the works of the evil one.

There is considerable evidence in the New Testament that 'the world' is revealed as an environment that is highly energized by evil spirits and under the direct influence and control of the devil and his power. According to John, Babylon, this present world system, "has become a dwelling place of demons, a prison for every foul spirit, and a cage for every unclean and hated bird." (Revelation 18:2) In Paul's language, there is an evil 'spirit' that energizes the world of sin and darkness. "Now we have received, not **the spirit of the world**, but the Spirit who is from God, that we might know the things that have been freely given to us by God." (1 Corinthians 2:12) John said something quite similar. He said, "The Spirit who lives in you is greater than *the spirit* who lives in the world." (1 John 4:4) Jesus revealed a deep antithetical reality between the Spirit of truth and the spirit that energizes this world with lies. He described the Holy Spirit as "the Spirit of truth, whom the world cannot receive, because it neither sees Him nor knows Him." (John 14:17) Because the entire world lies in the power of the evil one there is now a profound enmity between the world and the people of God. There is also a deep enmity between the words that we speak as those who are not of this world and the words that are spoken by those who are of this world.

John said, "The world does not know us, because it did not know Him." (1 John 3:1) As apostolic ambassadors of heaven John could say, "We are from God; he who knows God listens to us; he who is not from God does not listen to us. By this we know the spirit of truth and the spirit of error." (1 John 4:6 NASB) John urged spiritual discernment in recognizing the source of every so-called prophetic utterance. "Beloved, do not believe every spirit, but test the spirits, whether they are of God; because many false prophets have gone out into the world." (1 John 4:1)

Those who do not speak according to the sound words of Jesus are under the power of the evil one. "This is the spirit of the Antichrist, which you have heard was coming, and is now already in the world." (1 John 4:3) Many people choke on the absolute black and white nature of Scripture but Jesus made it very clear that these spiritual realities were explicitly black or white. On some matters there are simply no grey areas.

Jesus and the authors of the New Testament deliberately unmasked the demonic activity of the devil and the powers of darkness that operate within this present world. The world is never depicted as a benign or safe place for believers. It is profoundly hostile. James said, "Do you not know that friendship with the world is enmity with God? Whoever therefore wants to be a friend of the world makes himself an enemy of God." (James 4:4) Whenever Christians lose sight of the supernatural realities that energize this evil world they can be lulled into thinking that the world is really quite a safe place. If a follower of Christ loses touch with the revelatory perspective of New Testament theology they can readily be deceived into living according to the world in such a way that they become entangled in worldly deception.

Whenever a Christian is seduced back under the world they end up walking "according to the course of this world." (Ephesians 2:2)

We cannot afford to lose sight of the fact that because we are 'in Christ' we are no longer of this present evil world. Paul said, "the world has been crucified to me, and I to the world." (Galatians 6:14) Because we have been born from above we are now actually dead to sin and dead to the world in Christ. We cannot afford to walk any longer according to the ways of this world. "As for you, you were dead in your transgressions and sins, in which you used to live when you followed the ways of this world and of the ruler of the kingdom of the air, the spirit who is now at work in those who are disobedient." (Ephesians 2:1,2 NIV) But now, because God has performed such a great miracle within your resurrected spirit you are compelled to recognize that, "you have died with Christ to the elementary principles of the world." (Colossians 2:20 NASB)

Now, we are solemnly obligated to live according to our new identity as sons and daughters and to come out from the world and every demonic spiritual influence that permeates the world. Because we are not of the world by nature we must experientially choose to come out of the world. "Therefore, 'come out from among them and be separate,' says the Lord. 'Do not touch what is unclean and I will receive you. I will be a Father to you and you shall be My sons and daughters, says the Lord Almighty.'" (2 Corinthians 6:17) An angel carried John away in the Spirit and unveiled Babylon to him as "a dwelling place of demons, a prison for every foul spirit, and a cage for every unclean and hated bird." (Revelation 18:2) Just two verses later, as John was beholding the utter depravity of Babylon he heard a voice saying, "Come out of her My people, lest you share in her sins, and lest you receive of her plagues. For her sins have reached to heaven and God has remembered her iniquities." (Revelation 18:4,5)

Because we are spiritually dead to the world we must actively come out of the world and refuse to touch that which is unclean. Paul exercised the same principle in dealing with the world as he employed in dealing with sin. He taught that because we are now 'dead to sin' in Christ we must actively 'put to death' everything that constituted our old sinful life. In like manner because we are 'dead to the world' in Christ we must actively 'come out' of the world and set ourselves apart completely to God. We have a responsibility to come out of the world. If we 'touch the unclean thing' we automatically become defiled by the demonic spirits that are in the world. Straight after Paul warned against touching that which is unclean he said, "Therefore, having these promises, beloved, let us cleanse ourselves from all defilement of flesh and spirit, perfecting holiness in the fear of God." (2 Corinthians 7:1 NASB)

The defilement of the world comes through the presence of worldly lusts within the human heart working in tandem with the defilement of 'spirit,' which speaks of the defiling 'spirit that is in the world.' Paul sought to train the Corinthian believers to recognize the presence of this demonic spirit whenever they crossed the line by stepping outside of the revelation and power of the Holy Spirit. The Corinthians were entertaining false apostolic leaders who were teaching a false gospel. Those who placed themselves under these false teachers were immediately defiled by 'another spirit.' Paul rebuked them for putting up with this garbage. "For if someone comes to you and preaches a Jesus other than the Jesus we preached, or if you receive a different spirit from the one you received, or a different gospel from the one you accepted, you put up with it easily enough." (2 Corinthians 11:4 NIV) From Paul's perspective, anything of the world outside of the glorious person of Jesus Christ is a source of vile spiritual defilement from which we must cleanse ourselves through the power of the Holy Spirit.

The Lust of the Eyes

> Do not love the world or the things in the world. If anyone loves the world, the love of the Father is not in him. For all that is in the world; the lust of the flesh, the lust of the eyes, and the pride of life; is not of the Father but is of the world. And the world is passing away, and the lust of it; but he who does the will of God abides forever. (1 John 2:15-17)

Lust within the human heart is identified as the primary source of corruption and defilement in the world. Peter said that God had "given to us exceedingly great and precious promises, that through these you may be partakers of the divine nature, having escaped *the corruption that is in the world through lust*." (2 Peter 1:4) Paul said that whoever "sows to his flesh will of the flesh reap corruption." (Galatians 6:8) The devil and his cohort of evil spirits energize this present evil world but that dimension of supernatural evil cannot defile a person unless they set their desires upon the world. James unveiled the actual mechanics of this process. "Each one is tempted when he is carried away and enticed by his own lust. Then when lust has conceived, it gives birth to sin; and when sin is accomplished, it brings forth death." (James 1:14,15 NASB) This is the progression. The world tempts us to partake of its sins and if it arouses lust, or evil desire within the heart and we reach out to partake of the world we are immediately seduced and defiled by the world and all of its evil influences.

Paul used the term 'worldly lusts.' "For the grace of God that brings salvation has appeared to all men, teaching us that, denying ungodliness and **worldly lusts**, we should live soberly, righteously, and godly in the present age." (Titus 2:11,12) The reason these desires are identified as 'worldly lusts' is because the world exercises a strong seductive force upon the human heart. The devil sets the snare using the bait of the world and he leverages the brokenness inside the human heart in order to seduce people to take the bait and fall into his trap. There would be no 'evil world' except for the wrong choices to reach out and partake of the temptations of the devil. This was the original sin in the Garden of Eden. Looking back at the narrative of the fall we should take note that the eyes played a crucial role in the undoing of Adam and Eve.

> Now the serpent was more crafty than any of the wild animals the Lord God had made. He said to the woman, "Did God really say, 'You must not eat from any tree in the garden?'" The woman said to the serpent, "We may eat fruit from the trees in the garden but God did say, "You must not eat fruit from the tree that is in the middle of the garden, and you must not touch it, or you will die." "You will not surely die," the serpent said to the woman. "For God knows that when you eat of it **your eyes** will be opened, and you will be like God, knowing good and evil." When the woman **saw** that the fruit of the tree was good for food and **pleasing to the eye**, and also desirable for gaining wisdom, she took some and ate it. She also gave some to her husband, who was with her, and he ate it. Then **the eyes** of both of them were opened, and they realized they were naked. (Genesis 3:1-7 NIV)

The world of sin is built upon the foundation of human sensuality. That is why John talked about 'the lust of the eyes.' The whole mechanism of the human temptation to sin revolves around sensory stimuli that entice us to partake of that which has been forbidden by God. This was the original sin in the Garden and it is the principle that the serpent has used ever since. We 'see' something that is appealing to the sensory realm and we foolishly reach out for it and partake of it. Unless a Christian actively resists temptation and the seductive power of the world they will fall for it over and over again because it is always based upon the fact that the world is pleasing to the eye. The pornography industry thrives on this single principle. It deliberately plays upon the vulnerability of human sexuality to reach out for instant gratification. If the world can touch that place within us where we foolishly set our desire upon the lusts of the eyes we immediately fall victim to the devil's power of seduction.

The word 'harlot' that is used in relation to Babylon [the whore of Babylon] is the Greek word *'porne.'* From heaven's perspective, the porn industry is much broader that mere pornography. Everything that the devil displays before our eyes that exercises any seductive power becomes part of the serpent's global porn industry. Even Jesus was subjected to every form of seductive temptation. "The devil took Him up on an exceedingly high mountain and showed Him all the kingdoms of the world and their glory. And he said to Him, "All these things I will give You if You will fall down and worship me." (Matthew 4:8,9) The evil one always plays upon latent lustful desire to lure and entice people to indulge in sin. "Whoever *looks* at a woman to lust for her has already committed adultery with her in his heart." (Matthew 5:28) The prophets traditionally invoked the language of adultery to expose the dynamics of sin and temptation in the hearts of God's people. "Adulterers and adulteresses! Do you not know that friendship with the world is enmity with God?" (James 4:4) We need to see that the entire system of this world is one giant strip tease designed to entice us to set our affections upon the things of this world instead of upon Christ.

Lust and Desire

The concept of human lust is such an important theme in Scripture. One of the primary characteristics that define us as human beings is an intense hunger and thirst that never seems to be satisfied. Remember the famous song by the Rolling Stones titled, "I can't get no satisfaction..." The words of this song epitomize the cry of the human heart to find that place of deep inner fulfilment. People are driven to try to satisfy the longings of the soul in a multitude of different ways. While the list is endless there are a number of typical things that people everywhere turn to in order to try to fill up the hollow core within their souls; drugs, alcohol, partying, sexual encounters, food, entertainment, wealth, power, fame etc. Whatever it is that people give themselves to, the reality is that the next day the deep dissatisfaction returns to gnaw at their soul once again. The temporary 'high' leaves us even more dissatisfied the morning after. If one thing does not bring satisfaction we simply keep on trying another and another in the hope that we will finally find that thing that will fill the void. Every form of addictive behavior has its origin in the relentless drive to satisfy the emptiness that eats away at us in our innermost being.

The Bible describes this driving quest of the soul for satisfaction as 'lust, desire or intense longing.' '*Epithumia*' is the Greek word that is most often translated into these English words. Interestingly, '*epithumia*' is used in the New Testament in both a good, neutral and evil sense. For example Paul used '*epithumia*' to describe his 'intense desire' to see his brethren in Thessalonica. (1 Thessalonians 2:7) He also used the word to describe his desire to depart and to be with Christ. (Philippians 1:23) Yet, on the other hand he frequently used '*epithumia*' to describe "the passions and desires of our evil nature." (Ephesians 2:3 NIV) The fact that this Greek word is used alternatively in both a good sense and in an evil sense indicates that 'desire' or 'intense longing' is intrinsic to our identity as image bearers. When we walk in the flesh these desires are channeled in the direction of sin, hence the term, the lusts of the flesh. But in contrast Paul alluded to the desires of the Spirit. "But I say, walk by the Spirit, and you will not carry out the desire of the flesh. For the flesh sets its desire against the Spirit, and the Spirit against the flesh; for these are in opposition to one another." (Galatians 5:16,17 NASB) The 'desires' of the Spirit are for the things of God, not for the things of the world.

Jesus used the word '*epithumia*' to describe His own 'fervent or eager desire' to eat the final Passover meal with His disciples. "I have *eagerly desired* to eat this Passover with you before I suffer." (Luke 22:15 NIV) Another translation renders this verse as, "I have looked forward to this hour with *deep longing*." (NLT) The fact that Jesus also experienced these intense desires suggests that '*epithumia*' is intrinsic to the image of God. Larry Crabb argues that these deep longings within the human personality reflect the very image of God within us. "Something within mankind is capable of longing for satisfaction in the deepest part of the personality. Both God and man have the capacity to long deeply."[35] Crabb points to the deep longing expressed by God for His people in the book of Hosea. "How can I give you up? My heart is turned over within Me." (Hosea 11:8 NASB) According to Crabb, "The rich, passionate language [of Hosea] suggests the existence within His personality of a subjective reality not easily defined as an emotion. It is deeper than that. With all the intensity of His being, God is longing for the restoration of relationship with His children."[36] We also find these deep longings with ourselves. The critical question is; what is the object of our affections and longings? We can set our affections on things above or upon things on the earth. (Colossians 3:2)

The problem lies in the fact that when man fell away from God his desires were directed toward sin and worldly pleasure instead of toward God. Defiled by sin, all of man's desires became corrupt. Paul said, "Sin...produced in me all manner of *evil* desire." (Romans 7:8) "You were taught, with regard to your former way of life, to put off your old self, which is being corrupted by its deceitful desires." (Ephesians 4:22 NIV) Because we are sexual beings and the drive for sex is a fundamental characteristic of what it means to be human, sexual desire becomes one of the most dominant expressions of the deep longings within us. Perverted sexual desire is most commonly described as lust. Paul said, "It is God's will that you should be sanctified: that you should avoid sexual immorality; that each of you should learn to control his own body in a way that is holy and honorable, not in *passionate lust* like the heathen, who do not know God." (1 Thessalonians 4:3-5 NIV)

If we would understand the nature of the fallen human heart we must wrestle with this concept of lust. Solomon said, "Do not lust in your heart..." (Proverbs 6:25 NIV) Jesus warned men that to look upon a woman to lust after her is to commit adultery in the heart. "For everything in the world – the *cravings* of sinful man, the *lust* of his eyes and the boasting of what he has and does – comes not from the Father but from the world." (1 John 2:16 NIV) Peter spoke of escaping "the corruption that is in the world through lust." (2 Peter 1:4) He identified lust as the root cause of societal and personal corruption. Lust is a deep and insatiable desire that cannot be satisfied outside of God. Paul said, "So put to death the sinful, earthly things lurking within you. Have nothing to do with sexual sin, impurity, lust, and shameful desires." (Colossians 3:5 NLT)

Another fundamental drive in human beings is the desire for food. When this natural desire is corrupted by sin it leads to gluttony and eating disorders. In the book of Isaiah the Lord likened a specific judgment that was about to come upon certain nations to that feeling of emptiness that each of us are so familiar with. "It shall even be as when a hungry man dreams, and look; he eats; but he awakes, and his soul is still empty; or as when a thirsty man dreams, and look; he drinks; but he awakes, and indeed he is faint, and his soul still craves..." (Isaiah 29:8). Solomon was a student of human nature and as such he was deeply familiar with this unsatisfied yearning of the human soul. Everywhere he looked he saw unfulfilled people vainly seeking satisfaction in the fleeting things of this present world.

In the book of Proverbs Solomon wrote; "Just as death and destruction are never satisfied, so human desire is never satisfied." (Proverbs 27:20) In Ecclesiastes, a book that epitomizes the vanity of man seeking to satisfy his wandering desires apart from God, he wrote; "Whoever loves money never has money enough; whoever loves wealth is never satisfied with his income." (Ecclesiastes 5:10) "The eye is not satisfied with seeing, nor the ear filled with hearing." (Ecclesiastes 1:8) "Their eyes are never satisfied with riches." (Ecclesiastes 4:8) "All man's efforts are for his mouth, yet his appetite is never satisfied." (Ecclesiastes 6:7)

These lusts of the flesh are the yearnings and cravings of a selfish man or woman who has purposed to satisfy these deep cravings by setting their affections upon the world and everything in it. The remedy is not in seeking to put to death the desires themselves but to recognize that the desires need to be re-directed toward God. Desire, in its original expression, is a vital part of the image of God in the human heart. We will never be able to extinguish desire in the heart any more than we are able to remove the image and likeness of God from our being. Many devout Buddhists have sought to extinguish desire but from a biblical perspective it is simply not possible.

Paul taught that the Spirit Himself stirs deep desires and groanings for God within our heart and this is where all of our deepest desires ought to be directed if we are to find true fulfilment in this life. Buddhism is a non-theistic religion and it has no concept of a personal God. It must be a difficult path indeed to attempt to snuff out the candle of desire if there is not even a concept of God to redirect our desires toward. The New Testament continually points us toward a purified expression of desire that is fixed upon the person of Christ. "Delight yourself in the Lord and He will give you the desires of your heart." (Psalm 37:4 NIV) We must always ask; what is governing our heart; our selfish desires or our pure desire directed toward God? Whenever we walk in the flesh the desires or lusts of the flesh will always take us away from God by setting our affections upon the world. But when we walk in the Spirit our desires will be satisfied in God and they will bring forth life and peace. Solomon said, "A longing fulfilled is a tree of *life!*" (Proverbs 13:12 NIV)

From heaven's perspective, all fallen expressions of lust and sensuality are the perversion of a misdirected hunger and desire for God. It was C.S. Lewis who famously said that when a man visits a brothel he is really searching for God. But the 'desires' of a selfish man or woman will immediately lead them into the arms of the demonic. James was discussing what he called 'self-seeking in your hearts' and in the next verse he revealed that all such selfish desire is "earthly, sensual, and demonic." (James 3:14,15) "For jealousy and selfishness are not God's kind of wisdom. Such things are earthly, unspiritual, and motivated by the devil. For wherever there is jealousy and selfish ambition, there you will find disorder and every kind of evil." (James 3:15,16 NLT) Wherever you of I turn in the Scriptures we will find the same revelation. It is our worldly lust and sensual desires that open people to the demonic influences of this present evil world.

Our Warfare with Worldliness

Paul revealed that we are all in a relentless wrestling match with this 'dark world.' Whenever he spoke about this present world he always inextricably linked it to the devil and the powers of darkness. "For our struggle is not against flesh and blood, but against the rulers, against the authorities, against *the powers of this dark world* and against the spiritual forces of evil in the heavenly realms." (Ephesians 6:12 NIV) As long as we are in this world we will be engaged in hand to hand combat with evil spiritual beings. These dark spirits have one great agenda: to drag Christians who have been delivered from the world back under the elementary spirits that are present in the world. "We were slaves to the spiritual powers of this world." (Galatians 4:3 NLT) "Now that you have found God (or should I say, now that God has found you), why do you want to go back again and become slaves once more to the weak and useless spiritual powers of this world?" (Galatians 4:9 NLT)

Peter warned Christians who had been delivered from the powers of this world through the new birth of the clear and present danger of being re-entangled in the defilement of the world. "For if, after they have escaped the defilements of the world by the knowledge of the Lord and Savior Jesus Christ, they are again entangled in them and are overcome, the last state has become worse for them than the first." (2 Peter 2:20 NASB) Paul lamented the loss of a good friend and fellow worker in the gospel who had been dragged back into the world by the seductive power of the evil one. "For Demas has forsaken me, having loved this present world, and has departed for Thessalonica." (2 Timothy 4:10) Demas was a man who walked with God and became a close companion of a great apostolic leader. Back in the good old days Paul could write to the Colossians and say, "Luke the beloved physician and Demas greet you." (Colossians 4:14) What went wrong with Demas? He yielded to worldly lusts and found himself entangled once again in the world and its demonic and seductive power.

All of us, as we seek to embrace the heart journey of wholehearted devotion to Christ, will be faced with a relentless pressure to capitulate to the temptations of the world. Living in the midst of this world even Jesus was tempted in every way just like us yet He never sinned. Paul held forth only two options for every Christian. He revealed the heart of the Father to conform us to the image of His Son (Romans 8:29) and the heart of the evil one to conform us to this present evil world. "Do not be conformed to this world but be transformed by the renewing of your mind." (Romans 12:2) J. B. Phillips wrote a wonderful translation of the New Testament and said something I have found unforgettable: "Do not let the world squeeze you into its mold." The only way to escape the pressure of conformity to the world is by embracing the heart journey of being conformed into the image of true sonship. The world produces spiritual orphans but the Father forms within us the heart of authentic sonship.

Do you remember Paul's powerful exhortation? "Therefore, 'come out from among them and be separate,' says the Lord. 'Do not touch what is unclean and I will receive you. I will be a Father to you and you shall be My sons and daughters, says the Lord Almighty." (2 Corinthians 6:17) We escape the corruption of the world through setting our affections upon our Father in heaven and by recognizing that through the new birth we are no longer of the world but we are of the Father. John revealed the pathway to a deep and comprehensive freedom from the world when he said, "Do not love the world or the things in the world. If anyone loves the world, the love of the Father is not in him." (1 John 2:15) The only reason a Christian is perpetually tantalized and seduced by all the world has to offer is because of their deficiency in experiencing the love of their Heavenly Father. The next time you find the world or the things in the world irresistible ask yourself how your spiritual love tank is going. Are you running on empty and in need of a fresh Father encounter?

Demas traded the love of the Father for the love of the world. He set his desires on earthly things instead of things above and he fell away from his loving Father. Had he ever really experienced the transforming love of his Father in the very core of his being? Perhaps he never did. There was a season when he had a heart for God and he travelled and ministered with Paul, but because he still felt like an orphan in the core of his being he harbored a secret love of the world. This love and attraction for the world still burned like a fire in his being and eventually, unable to break free of the carnal desires of his old orphan heart, he returned to the world like a dog returning to its vomit or a pig to the mud from which it was once washed. (2 Peter 2:22)

The Idolatry of Pleasure

Much of our love for the world revolves around our idolatry of pleasure. Ever since the fall in Eden when humanity broke relationship with God there has been a replacement of God with the pleasures of this present world. God ought to be the object of our greatest desire and the source of our greatest pleasure but if God is not at the very center of our hearts the next step down from that elevated place of drawing our pleasure from God is to descend into the love of pleasure. David said, "In Your presence is fullness of joy; at Your right hand are pleasures forevermore." (Psalms 16:11) Before the fall, Adam and Eve walked with God and derived their greatest pleasure from their uninterrupted fellowship with Him. God streamed the pleasure of His presence straight into their heart and they were deeply contented with His Fatherly love.

As we reflect upon our entanglement in the world we need to recognize that the greatest issue is the idolatry of our hearts. What is going on inside our heart when we exalt the pleasures of this world above the pleasure of God's intimate fellowship? James introduced a powerful concept when he spoke about "Your *desires for pleasure* that war in your members." (James 4:1) We automatically set our desires upon pleasure whenever we lose connection with God in our heart. People become "lovers of pleasure rather than lovers of God" (2 Timothy 3:4) whenever they turn away from God in their heart and set their affections on the things of the world instead of upon things above.

Many of the pleasures of this world are not necessarily wrong in themselves. God created man to enjoy the pleasures of the world that He created. We are told in Genesis that, "The Lord God placed the man in the **Garden of Eden** to tend and care for it." (Genesis 2:15) Eden in Hebrew means *'pleasure.'* The Septuagint translated Genesis 2:15 as "the Paradise of Pleasure." In the Douay-Rheims Catholic Bible (1610) we read, "And the Lord God took man, and put him into *the Paradise of Pleasure*, to dress it, and to keep it." The English word *'paradise'* is a transliteration of the Greek word *'paradeisos.'* The Greek word *'paradeisos'* is derived from an ancient Persian word; *'pardes'* which means *'a royal park, a king's garden or pleasure-park.'* The modern equivalent would be a pristine botanical garden. *'Pardes'* was adopted from Persian into the Hebrew language and it appears just three times in the Old Testament.

King Artaxerxes appointed a man to be "The keeper of the King's park [*pardes*]." (Nehemiah 2:8) There is a rich tradition in the Ancient Near East of kings building beautiful gardens. Solomon said, "I made gardens and parks [*pardes*] and planted all kinds of fruit trees in them. I made reservoirs to water groves of flourishing trees." (Ecclesiastes 2:5,6 NIV) The Assyrian King Sennacherib built a beautiful garden in the city of Nineveh on the Tigris River. Nebuchadnezzar, the King of Babylon also built a glorious garden for his wife: the famous 'Hanging Gardens of Babylon' that became one of the seven wonders of the ancient world. The 'Paradise of Pleasure' that we read about in Genesis 3 was built by the King of glory as a fit habitation for His bride. God established Adam and Eve as a king and a queen and gave them authority and dominion over Eden to cultivate, maintain and protect it.

'Paradise' is a place of infinite pleasure fit for a King. It is actually a powerful metaphor for the kingdom of heaven. "For He rescued us from the domain of darkness and transferred us to **the kingdom of His beloved Son**." (NASB) Eden was originally the kingdom of the Father's beloved son, Adam. The Father's glory had descended upon the earth and Adam and Eve were clothed in unfathomable glory. God bestowed the kingdom upon Adam and Eve and they lived in the ecstasy and bliss of heaven. They were surrounded by the infinite love and pleasure of their heavenly Father. In Eden there was a perfect synergy between heaven and earth. Adam and Eve and the Father were one! These two dimensions; the heavenly and the earthly had merged in a harmonious expression of supernatural oneness and divine union.

The glory of mystical union between God the Father and Adam and Eve, His beloved son and daughter is what made Eden a true paradise garden. The garden was not so much the physical Garden of Eden but **Adam and Eve** as a dearly beloved son and daughter. They were the Father's garden. "The vineyard of the Lord Almighty is the house of Israel and the men of Judah are the **garden of His delight**." (Isaiah 5:7 NIV) Of course, the church is now God's glorious garden paradise. It is noteworthy that Solomon also used this word '*pardes*' in reference to his bride.

> For you have ravished My heart. You have inflamed My being. My beloved one, My equal, My bride. I am undone by your love. Merely a glance from your worshipping eyes and you have stolen My heart. Just gazing into your heart, joined to Mine, and I am overcome! Conquered! Ravished! Held hostage by your love! How satisfying to Me, My equal, My beautiful bride. Your love is my finest wine; intoxicating and thrilling – and your sweet praise perfume so exotic, so pleasing! My darling, My bride, you are *My private paradise*, fastened to my heart. You are a secret spring that no-one else can have – My bubbling fountain, hidden from the public. What a perfect partner to Me! Your inward life is now sprouting, bringing forth fruit! *What a beautiful paradise* [*pardes*] unfolds within you! (Song of Songs 4:9,10,12,13 TPT)

The bride replies to the Bridegroom:

> Spare nothing as you make me your fruit filled garden. Hold nothing back until I release Your fragrance. Come walk with me as you walked with Adam in *Your paradise garden*. Come taste the fruits of Your life in me." (Song of Songs 4:16 TPT)

The Bridegroom replies to the bride:

> Here I am within you My bride – *My Eden paradise*, My darling! I have tasted and enjoyed My wine within you. I delight in gathering My sacred spice; all the fruits of my life I have gathered from within you, *My paradise garden*!" (Song of Songs 5:1 TPT)

The fall of man caused paradise to be lost. When Adam and Eve sinned they were immediately expelled from the glorious Kingdom of the Father. "For all have sinned and fallen short of the glory of God." (Romans 3:23) The 'fall' was an instantaneous expulsion from the glory realm.

So the Lord God banished Adam and his wife from the Garden of Eden, and he sent Adam out to cultivate the ground from which he had been made. After banishing them from the garden, the Lord God stationed mighty angelic beings to the east of Eden. And a flaming sword flashed back and forth, guarding the way to the tree of life. (Genesis 3:23,24 NLT)

As an immediate consequence of the fall, the supernatural dimension of God's paradise ascended back to heaven, finding no place to rest upon the earth. The early church fathers believed and taught that this supernatural 'Paradise' realm merely ascended above the earth but that it still exists as a spiritual, heavenly dimension called the realm (or kingdom) of heaven. This idea is supported by three verses in the New Testament. Jesus said to the thief on the cross, "Assuredly, I say to you, today you will be with Me in *Paradise*." (Luke 23:43) Paul said, "I was *caught up into Paradise* and heard things so astounding that they cannot be told." (2 Corinthians 12:4 NLT) Jesus said, "He who has an ear, let him hear what the Spirit says to the churches. To him who overcomes I will give to eat from the tree of life, which is in the midst of *the Paradise of God*." (Revelation 2:7) 'Paradise' is therefore a perfect biblical metaphor for the Kingdom of Heaven. It is the King's garden of infinite delights.

To experience the kingdom (or realm) of heaven is to experience the ultimate dimension of divine pleasure and delight. Paul said the kingdom of God was righteousness, peace and *joy* in the Holy Spirit. Remember the words we quoted from King David: "In Your presence is fullness of *joy*; at Your right hand are *pleasures* forevermore." (Psalms 16:11) David said, "How precious is Your unfailing love, O God! Therefore the children of men take refuge in the shadow of Your wings. They are abundantly satisfied [*ravah*] with the fullness of Your house and You give them drink from *the river of Your pleasures*. For with You is the fountain of life; In Your light we see light. Pour out your unfailing love on those who love you!" (Psalm 36:7-10) The Hebrew word for '*satisfied*' is '*ravah*' which means 'to be made drunk, or to be rendered completely intoxicated!' God has placed no limits on the extent to which we may immerse ourselves in the rivers of His pleasures and delights. Interestingly, the Hebrew word for '*pleasures*' in this passage is the Hebrew word: '*Eden*.'

Through Christ's redemption we have been restored to Eden; the royal kingdom, or garden of His pleasure. The infinite joy of divine pleasure is restored to those who believe in Christ. John Piper teaches that there is a legitimate Christian hedonism; a dimension of extreme pleasure that is found exclusively in the presence of the King of Glory. Before the fall, Adam and Eve lived in this dimension of extreme pleasure and bliss. The recovery of this divine ecstasy and bliss is central to the recovery of the Paradise of Eden.

> The Lord will surely comfort Zion and will look with compassion on all her ruins; he will make her wilderness like *Eden*, her wastelands like the garden of the Lord. *Joy and gladness* will be found in her, thanksgiving and the sound of singing. (Isaiah 51:3 NIV)

In Christ we again taste of this realm of infinite pleasure but our brain chemistry is still tragically wired to finding our pleasure in the world. Every single message sent to our brain from the world tells us that our greatest pleasures are found exclusively in this world. Think of the sensuality of chocolate advertisements! The world knows nothing of the pleasure of the Father which is why the world has created a false Eden of carnal, sinful pleasures. Babylon is the world's *pleasure garden.* "The kings of the earth have committed fornication with her, and the merchants of the earth have become rich through the abundance of her *luxury*." (Revelation 18:3) "She has lived in *luxury and pleasure*." (Revelation 18:7 NLT) "The kings of the world took part in her immoral acts and enjoyed *her great luxury*." (Revelation 18:9 NLT)

Thinking Biblically About Pleasure

Paul described fallen humanity as "lovers of pleasure rather than lovers of God." (2 Timothy 3:4 NIV) But all pleasure is clearly not evil in itself! There are good pleasures and there are evil pleasures. There are sinful pleasures and holy pleasures. God actually placed Adam and Eve in a garden paradise of luxurious pleasures that tantalized the senses. Undoubtedly God wants us to enjoy the immense pleasures of His creation. Paul said, "Once, we too, were foolish and disobedient. We were misled by others and became slaves to many wicked desires and *evil pleasures*." (Titus 3:2 NLT) While there certainly are *evil pleasures* there are just as many glorious pleasures. Consider how much pleasure humanity derives from the following activities:

- The pleasure of human relationships; of companionship, fellowship and sexual intimacy within marriage.

- The pleasure of creativity; tending the garden, developing technology, mining the earth for riches; gold, silver and precious jewels.

- The pleasure of creating and constructing objects of immense beauty: architecture, working with wood and metal, all forms of art and craft.

- The pleasure of food in abundance: fruits, vegetables, herbs, spices, the pleasure of the culinary arts and cuisine.

- The pleasure of sensual overload! Fragrances, tastes, sounds, sights, the warmth of sunlight, the cool of a breeze etc.

- The pleasure of immense aesthetic beauty; the expanse of the stars, forests, wildlife, mountains, rivers and streams.

- The pleasure of the sounds of creation: bird songs, waterfalls, babbling brooks.

- The pleasure of creating harmonious and beautiful music and singing.

- The pleasure of creating entertainment, comedy, laughter.

- Most of all; the pleasure of intimacy with God.

Intimacy with God is the ultimate pleasure of eating from the Tree of Life! In Eden, Adam and Eve could freely partake of all of the pleasures we have just considered. This is an important point in developing a biblical understanding of pleasure. Not all pleasures are evil.

God regarded Adam and Eve as the object of His supreme pleasure and enjoyment. "You are worthy, O Lord our God, to receive glory and honor and power. For you created everything, and *it is for Your pleasure* that they exist and were created." (Revelation 4:11 NLT) As a result, Adam and Eve luxuriated in the pleasure of God's divine pleasure. But pleasure becomes corrupted whenever God is taken out of the equation. Pleasure becomes *sinful* when the pleasure is idolized and exalted above God. Sinful pleasure is the pursuit of pleasure as a source of *comfort* instead of pursuing God as our source of comfort. Pleasure is the world's greatest idolatry because it replaces the pleasure of loving God and loving His creation. "They exchanged the truth of God for a lie and worshiped and served *created things rather than the Creator* – who is forever praised." (Romans 1:25 NIV)

Idolatry exalts *'created things'* above God. The pleasure of created things are a great blessing from God but they are not a blessing when they replace God. The Lord said, "You shall have no other gods before me!" (Exodus 20:3) God is grieved by the idolatry of humanity "because you have forgotten Me and trusted in false gods." (Jeremiah 13:25 NIV) "I have seen your adultery and lust and your disgusting idol worship out in the fields and on the hills." (Jeremiah 13:27 NLT) Using the pleasure of created things in an idolatrous and unlawful way brings God great displeasure. Consider these sinful and idolatrous pleasures:

- The idolatry of the pleasure of sexuality as a source of comfort.
- The idolatry of the pleasure of food as a source of comfort.
- The idolatry of the pleasure of nature as a source of comfort.
- The idolatry of entertainment as a source of comfort.
- The idolatry of the pleasure of substances as a source of comfort.
- The idolatry of self-worship (narcissism).

The world is comprehensively structured around the pursuit of pleasure apart from God. If you want to understand the world from heaven's eyes; it is a pleasure park for narcissists! God calls it supreme foolishness. "The heart of the wise is in the house of mourning, but the heart of fools is in the house of pleasure." (Ecclesiastes 7:4 (NIV) The fool seeks exclusive comfort in pleasure. The wise understand that mourning the state of our broken and idolatrous hearts is the doorway to divine comfort. Jesus said, "Blessed are those who mourn for they shall be comforted!" (Matthew 5:4) Only those who mourn their idolatry experience the comfort of the father. 'Mourning' requires us to *break* under the weight of idolatry. We mourn and grieve because we have set earthly pleasures above God as our source of comfort. We have forsaken God and turned to worthless idols.

True godly sorrow produces repentance. We ought to be grieving the idolatry of our hearts. The wise learn how to mourn in order to engage with the God of all comfort. Whenever we take our grief and pain to God there is always a divine transaction. "For I will turn their mourning into joy and will comfort them and give them joy for their sorrow." (Jeremiah 31:13 NASB) This is the divine exchange of "the oil of joy for mourning!" (Isaiah 61:3) You can go into the house of worldly pleasure to find your comfort or you can enter the house of mourning to find the only doorway into the house of the Father's deepest comfort. And there is a glorious secret: the house of the Father's comfort is the doorway into the house of wine; the ultimate joy and pleasure of intimacy with God. The only way to navigate the pleasure garden of Babylon is to mourn our sin and engage with the comforting heart of the Father. Only then we can enjoy the good pleasures of this world without descending into idolatry. The challenge is to not exalt earthly pleasures above God.

The way back to paradise in the heart is the path of true repentance and mourning. Jesus said, "Repent, for the kingdom of heaven is at hand!" (Matthew 3:2) This could be paraphrased as: "Repent for the realm of heavenly paradise is now entirely within your reach!" The descent of the kingdom (or realm) of heaven upon the human heart ushers us back into paradise in the Spirit. Jesus is continually commanding us to repent of our idolatry of pleasure so that we can freely partake of the tree of life that is in the midst of the Paradise of God. The repentant thief on the cross entered straight into paradise in the Spirit.

> One of the criminals hanging beside him scoffed, "So you're the Messiah, are you? Prove it by saving yourself and us, too, while you're at it!" But the other criminal protested, "Don't you fear God even when you have been sentenced to die? We deserve to die for our crimes, but this man hasn't done anything wrong." Then he said, "Jesus, remember me when you come into your Kingdom." And Jesus replied, "I assure you, *today you will be with me in paradise*." (Luke 23:39-43 NLT)

God's will is for His kingdom to come on earth as it is in heaven. The glory of His kingdom comes upon the hearts of men. This is Eden restored in the heart.

"Here I am within you My bride – *My Eden paradise*, My darling! I have tasted and enjoyed My wine within you. I delight in gathering My sacred spice; all the fruits of My life I have gathered from within you; *My paradise garden!*" (Song of Songs 5:1 TPT) When we are praying for God's kingdom to come on earth as it is in heaven we are praying for the intimacy of the *Paradise of Pleasure* to be restored to the human heart. Only then can we partake of the good pleasures of this world without descending into the blackness of idolatry.

Every Christian lives in the midst of this epic battle between the love of worldly pleasure and the love of the Father. It is our address here on earth. Each day we must choose between receiving the love of the Father in order to satisfy the deepest longings and desires of the human heart or turning to the world to attempt to satisfy that desire. All over the world there are countless millions of Christians deeply entangled in worldly lusts and worldly temptations because they have not learnt how to come to the Father to receive the supernatural transformation of our Papa's love.

How do we escape the entanglement of the world? We must intentionally come out from the world and separate ourselves to our loving Heavenly Father. We must open our hearts wide to receive the experiential love of the Father and He will literally take away our love for the world with all of its vanity and empty pleasures. Jesus wants us to discover the hidden feast of His Papa's love that satisfied His own soul in the midst of a world of temptations. We must switch our source of pleasure away from the world and toward our Father. "You will show me the path of life; in Your presence is fullness of joy; at Your right hand are pleasures forevermore." (Psalms 16:11) Discovering the pleasure of an intimate love relationship with the Father is the only pathway to the fullness of life that Jesus offers and the only path to escape the entanglement of this present evil world.

Chapter Ten

Entangled in the Tree of the Knowledge of Good and Evil

"Stand fast therefore in the liberty by which Christ has made us free, and *do not be entangled again* with a yoke of bondage."
(Galatians 5:1)

In this verse in Galatians Paul described the very real danger of Christians being entangled in a form of dead religion through being yoked to the Old Testament law. This is a condition of the heart that is bound in legalism and the law. Paul recognized the danger of those who had come to Christ out of Judaism remaining entangled in the law but he also recognized a danger of those who had been saved into a grace paradigm being seduced back into an entanglement with the law. This was the primary issue he was addressing in his epistle to the Galatians.

The concept of entanglement in the law is expressed through a mindset that obligates believers to adhere to an external code of rules and regulations. The law revolves around an external knowledge of good versus evil and whenever a Christian interacts with the law it always arouses a sense of striving to please God through outward performance. This is expressed by compelling a Christian to try very hard to do *good* in order to overcome the internal presence of *evil*. This chapter explores the theme of the tree of the knowledge of good and evil that runs implicitly through Paul's theology and his mission to disentangle every believer from this tree in order to live and to minister exclusively from the tree of life.

It always struck me as being quite odd the way some New Testament writers described the cross of Christ as a 'tree.' Peter wrote, "He Himself bore our sins in His own body *on the tree*, that we, having died to sins, might live for righteousness; by whose stripes you were healed." (1 Peter 2:24) It was also Peter who said in Acts, "The God of our fathers raised up Jesus whom you murdered by hanging *on a tree*." (Acts 5:30) Similarly, it was Peter who said, "God anointed Jesus of Nazareth with the Holy Spirit and with power, who went about doing good and healing all who were oppressed by the devil, for God was with Him. And we are witnesses of all things which He did both in the land of the Jews and in Jerusalem, whom they killed by hanging *on a tree*." (Acts 10:38,39)

Paul also used this language to describe the cross. "Though they found no proper ground for a death sentence, they asked Pilate to have him executed. When they had carried out all that was written about him, they took him down *from the tree* and laid him in a tomb." (Acts 13:228,29 NIV) "Christ has redeemed us from the curse of the law, having become a curse for us (for it is written, "Cursed is everyone who hangs *on a tree*.") (Galatians 3:13) Both Peter and Paul deliberately called the cross "a tree." The cross was a brutal instrument of death! Jesus "humbled Himself and became obedient to the point of death, even the death of the cross." (Philippians 2:8) The cross was a tree of death but through the atonement of Christ, God miraculously transformed it into a tree of life!

"He Himself bore our sins in His own body on the tree, that we, *having died* to sins, *might live*." (1 Peter 2:24) This concept of life coming from death runs through the entire New Testament. The invocation of the language of the death of Christ on the 'tree' deliberately recalls the language of the tree of the knowledge of good and evil and the tree of life in the early chapters of Genesis. In the Garden of Eden, God placed two trees: the tree of life and the tree of the knowledge of good and evil. "The tree of life was also in the midst of the garden, and the tree of the knowledge of good and evil." (Genesis 2:9) God explicitly warned Adam and Eve; "You must not eat from the tree of the knowledge of good and evil, for when you eat of it you will surely die." (Genesis 2:1 NIV) The fruit of this tree was death. "Through one man sin entered the world, and death through sin, and thus death spread to all men." (Romans 5:12) But the Father had a genius plan of redemption. "He made Him who knew no sin to be sin for us." (2 Corinthians 5:21) "Jesus tasted death for everyone." (Hebrews 2:9 NLT) "God demonstrates His own love toward us, in that while we were still sinners, Christ died for us." (Romans 5:8)

Jesus bore the penalty of death for us and He died in our place so that we should not suffer the penalty of death for our participation in the tree of the knowledge of good and evil. The Prince of Life suffered death and transformed a tree of death into a tree of life. This is why both Peter and Paul adopted the language of the cross as a tree. He bore our sins in His own body on the tree that we might live. Now, as we look at the cross in history we see, not an instrument of death but God's instrument of life in all of its fullness. Paul never once mentioned the tree of the knowledge of good and evil or the tree of life but the theology of these two trees runs all through his theology.

Ever since the fall the way to the Tree of Life has been inaccessible to humanity. "So He drove out the man and He placed cherubim at the east of the Garden of Eden and a flaming sword which turned every way, to guard the way to the Tree of Life." (Genesis 3:24) Of course, Jesus is the true Tree of Life. He is the only source of spiritual life. He is the life! That is why He could say; "I am the way, the truth, and *the life*." (John 14:6) The way to the Tree of Life was deliberately guarded after the fall because it was only through Christ's atonement on the tree that a way could be made back to the Tree of Life. We now have unfettered access to feed from the Tree of Life because of the blood of Jesus. John said, "Blessed are those who wash their robes, that they may have *the right* to the Tree of Life and may go through the gates into the city." (Revelation 22:14)

Every blood bought son and daughter now has the right to eat of this tree that is planted in the midst of the New Jerusalem. "The angel showed me the river of the water of life, as clear as crystal, flowing from the throne of God and of the Lamb down the middle of the great street of the city. On each side of the river stood the Tree of Life, bearing twelve crops of fruit, yielding its fruit every month. And the leaves of the tree are for the healing of the nations." (Revelation 22:1,2 NIV) But it is interesting that John revealed that even though everyone who receives Christ has the 'right' to eat of this tree, it was only the overcomers who were given to experientially eat of this tree. Jesus said via John the revelator; "He who has an ear, let him hear what the Spirit says to the churches. To him who overcomes I will give to eat from the Tree of Life which is in the midst of the Paradise of God." (Revelation 2:7)

Every Christian has the right to partake of this tree but only those who 'overcome' get to experientially eat of this tree. This strongly suggests that there are things we must overcome if we want to be fully restored to the river of life that now flows from heaven. Traditionally, it is widely understood that the enemies of the believer's soul are the world, the flesh and the devil. In biblical language we are challenged to overcome all three of these spiritual enemies. Jesus spoke about overcoming the world. John spoke about overcoming the evil one and Paul spoke about overcoming the flesh. However, there is another enemy that we must overcome and that is the deadly snare of religion. As long as a Christian still rallies around the law he or she is enticed back under the yoke of bondage and is entangled in the law. It is only as we overcome the world, the flesh, the devil and legalism that we learn to eat *exclusively* from the Tree of Life. It is one thing to have legal access to the Tree of Life but it is another thing entirely to experientially eat of this tree. The Tree of Life is the exclusive source of food and nutrition for the soul.

Jesus drew exclusively from the Father and He taught us how to draw exclusively from Him. "My food," said Jesus, "is to do the will of Him who sent Me." (John 4:34 NIV) Jesus taught His disciples to live and feed exclusively from the Tree of Life by living and abiding in Him. Whenever a believer is enticed back under the law he or she is drawn back to the tree of the knowledge of good and evil. This is not to suggest that the law of Moses was the tree of the knowledge of good and evil. Rather, it suggests that whenever a Christian engages with the law as an external body of rules and regulations they are drawn back into a way of living that compels them to work hard to be very good in order to overcome the presence of evil in their heart. The law was only ever given as a temporary schoolmaster to lead people to the Messiah in order to receive the free gift of eternal life.

The Law of Moses and the Knowledge of Good and Evil

Paul painstakingly sought to extricate believers from feeding from the tree of the knowledge of evil by learning to live exclusively from the Spirit with no further reference or dialogue with the law. He opens the 7th chapter of Romans by boldly proclaiming that Christians are now dead to the law. In this chapter Paul addresses those Roman Christians who had come to Christ out of Judaism.

> Do you not know, brethren (*for I speak to those who know the law*), that the law has dominion over a man as long as he lives? For the woman who has a husband is bound by the law to her husband as long as he lives. But if the husband dies, she is released from the law of her

husband. So then if, while her husband lives, she marries another man, she will be called an adulteress; but if her husband dies, she is free from that law, so that she is no adulteress, though she has married another man. Therefore, my brethren, *you also have become dead to the law* through the body of Christ, that you may be married to another; to Him who was raised from the dead, that we should bear fruit to God. (Romans 7:1-4)

The law always intensifies our knowledge of good and evil but it does not enable us to eat from the Tree of Life. In calling believers out from under the tyranny of the law of Moses Paul was calling them to be separated exclusively to the life that flows from Christ without any reference whatsoever to the law. Paul was very clear that we cannot be married to Christ and still remain 'under the law.' "Now we know that whatever the law says, it says to those who are *under the law*." (Romans 3:19) Paul's great headline is "For you are not under law but under grace." (Romans 6:14) The Christian is no longer married to the law but to Christ. But in Romans 7 Paul specifically addresses those Christians who were still in dialogue with the law in their minds and thus still living at the foot of the tree of knowledge of good and evil. As you read the following excerpt from Romans 7 pay careful attention to Paul's use of the language of *good* and *evil*. Also note the fact that living from the wrong tree results in *death* because in the day we eat from this deadly tree we surely *die*.

I was alive once without the law, but when the commandment came, sin revived and *I died*. And the commandment, which was to *bring life*, I found to *bring death*. For sin, taking occasion by the commandment, deceived me, and by it *killed me*. Therefore the law is holy, and the commandment holy and just and *good*. Has then what is *good* become *death* to me? Certainly not! But sin, that it might appear sin, was producing *death* in me through what is *good*, so that sin through the commandment might become exceedingly sinful. For we know that the law is spiritual, but I am carnal, sold under sin. For what I am doing, I do not understand. For what I will to do, that I do not practice; but what I hate, that I do. If, then, I do what I will not to do, I agree with the law that it is *good*. But now, it is no longer I who do it, but sin that dwells in me. For I know that in me (that is, in my flesh) nothing *good* dwells; for to will is present with me, but how to perform what is *good* I do not find. For the *good* that I will to do, I do not do; but the *evil* I will not to do, that I practice. Now if I do what I

will not to do, it is no longer I who do it, but sin that dwells in me. I
find then a law, that *evil* is present with me, the one who wills to do
good. (Romans 7:9-21)

Every Christian still entangled in the yoke of bondage would powerfully
resonate with this internal struggle to conform to the demands of the external
law. However, the law, which brings a comprehensive knowledge of good to
humanity, only produces death! Paul taught that the law kills because it
exacerbates the internal crisis of attempting to conform to an outward code of
righteousness without the power to overcome evil. God has "made us
sufficient as ministers of the New Covenant, not of the letter but of the Spirit;
for *the letter kills*, but the Spirit gives life." (2 Corinthians 3:6) Christians
continue to eat of the tree of the knowledge of good and evil by seeking to live
according to the letter of the law of Moses. As long as they continue to live
'under the law' they exclude themselves from eating from the Tree of Life!
That is why religion and legalism must be overcome in the heart of the
believer if we really desire to be separated exclusively to the free gift of the
life that is in Christ.

By the law comes the knowledge of good and the knowledge of evil and all the
law ever accomplishes is to exacerbate the struggle between good and evil
within us! This is why Paul described the law as a 'schoolmaster' to bring us
to Christ. Paul knew exactly what it felt like to live under the tyranny of the
law so he wrote Romans 7 to deliberately resonate with the hearts of his
brethren who still lived in perpetual dialogue with the law of Moses. Paul's
self-confessed attempts to do good and not evil (in Romans 7) represent his
own attempts to redeem himself through obeying God's law, which he agreed
was 'good.' All those who still choose to live 'under the law' end up trying to
be very good in order to overcome the presence of evil in their hearts.

But God has made a new way of living in Christ without reference to the
struggle between good and evil characterized by Romans 7. Paul's theology of
life in the Spirit is the gateway to the Tree of Life. As soon as Paul concluded
his anguished narrative of living in dialogue with the law in Romans 7 he takes
the believer into the glory of Romans 8, which is all about *life*. "For the law of
the Spirit of *life in Christ Jesus* has made me free from the law of sin and
death." (Romans 8:2) "For to be carnally minded is death, but to be spiritually
minded is *life* and peace." (Romans 8:6) "But if Christ is in you... your spirit
is *alive* because of righteousness." (Romans 8:10 NIV) "If you *live* according

to the sinful nature, you will die; but if by the Spirit you put to death the misdeeds of the body, you will *live*." (Romans 8:13 NIV)

Paul taught us to live in and through Christ without reference to the old carnal struggle between good and evil. Paul did not teach us to be 'good' people in order to overcome evil in our own strength. As soon as law enters the equation we are back under the tree of the knowledge of good and evil. Paul's primary goal was to teach believers to eat only from the Tree of Life. The genius of Paul is that he did all of this in the book of Romans without even mentioning the tree of the knowledge of good and evil or the Tree of Life. As a Jew, steeped in the theology of the Old Testament, Paul had a deep knowledge of the two trees of Genesis and he wove his theology around this revelation in such a way that his Jewish audience could not escape the power of his logic. The theology of the two trees runs like a river through all of Paul's theology. It is a sub-text that Paul was continually dialoguing with in his own mind. The evidence of this is only deepened in his dispute with the Judaizers in his 2nd epistle to the Corinthians.

Life giving churches and life-giving preachers are those who have discovered the secret of living exclusively from the Tree of Life. Paul called this the "simplicity of devotion to Christ." He said to the Corinthian believers whom he had consigned to life; "For I am jealous for you with a godly jealousy; for I betrothed you to one husband, so that to Christ I might present you as a pure virgin. But I am afraid that, as the serpent deceived Eve by his craftiness, your minds will be led astray from the simplicity and purity of devotion to Christ." (2 Corinthians 11:2-3) In betrothing them to one husband, Christ, Paul handed them their certificate of divorce from being married to the law of Moses. They were now comprehensively dead to the law through their spiritual union with Christ in the fullness of His life. But Paul deliberately invokes the imagery of the serpent in the Garden of Eden to remind the Corinthians that they have been set free from living under the knowledge of good and evil.

Paul reveals that every born again believer, living in newness of life, is now just like Adam and Eve in the Garden of Eden before the fall. We have been re-introduced to Jesus, the Tree of Life. But the Serpent seeks to entice believers back under the tree of the knowledge of good and evil and he does this by seducing believers back under the law. The Tree of Life represents a place of child-like innocence before the fall. Paul said, "I want you to be wise about what is good, and innocent about what is evil." (Romans 16:19 NIV)

The tree of the knowledge of good and evil is actually the tree of death. The moment Adam and Eve ate of this tree they died spiritually! "Of the tree of the knowledge of good and evil you shall not eat, for in the day that you eat of it you shall surely die." (Genesis 2:17) If the serpent can beguile believers to resume dialogue with the law they are immediately enticed back into the arena of spiritual death through their participation in the tree of the knowledge of good and evil.

The temptation in the garden was to be more like God. The serpent said to Adam and Eve, "For God knows that in the day you eat of it your eyes will be opened, and you will be like God." (Genesis 3:5) The serpent appealed to humanity's desire to be spiritual and wise. We must never forget that the tree of the knowledge of good and evil is also the tree of 'good!' Its subtle appeal is in its apparent goodness. Satan seeks to entice the believer away from Christ (the Tree of Life) to an expression of religion that denies the free gift of life offered to us in Christ. The enticement is always to a *good* spiritual life outside of Christ. "You will be (more) like God." "Your eyes will be opened!" The Pharisees were focused on obtaining life through the law and outside of Christ. Jesus said, "You search the Scriptures, for in them you think you have eternal life; and these are they which testify of Me. But you are not willing to come to Me that you may *have life*." (John 5:39,40)

The battle is between life and death. "The thief does not come except to steal, and to kill, and to destroy. I have come that they may have life, and that they may have it more abundantly." (John 10:10) The devil understands that if he can entice a Christian to re-enter into a dialogue with the law that he could bring him back under a yoke of bondage that will only produce death in his or her soul. "The good law, which was supposed to show me the way of life, instead gave me the death penalty." (Romans 7:10 NLT) This strategy has been a masterstroke of the evil one. Whenever the devil can subtly entice a Christian back under the 'good' law he experientially cuts them off from their enjoyment of the free gift of life in Christ Jesus. The Tree of Life is a life of joy in the empowering grace of God in which we are clothed in the strength of Christ from above. The grace paradigm gloriously frees us from our bondage to the law.

The tree of the knowledge of good and evil is death because it places the focus on our own strength to fulfil our duty and our obligations to God. "I must try to serve God; I must be diligent to read the Scriptures; I must regularly go to church; I must pay my tithes; I must pray harder, I must be a good Christian!" Many Christians still try to live their Christian life under the tree of the knowledge of good and evil by trying harder and harder every day to be 'good' and to please God. Religion is the attempt of man to be good independently of the life God offers us in Christ! Religion is always an earth to heaven paradigm of man building his tower to the heavens. Grace is a heaven to earth paradigm in which God lavishes the free gift of eternal life on everyone who simply puts his or her faith in Christ.

A significant part of our heart journey is in learning how to live in the glorious freedom of authentic sonship. God offers us life in all of its fullness as a free gift in Christ but the serpent is relentlessly seeking to entice believers back under the yoke of religion. If we desire to partake exclusively of the Tree of Life in the midst of the Paradise of God we have to learn how to overcome this masterstroke of the evil one that has brought millions of Christians back under the tree of the knowledge of good and evil. And it can be as easy as enticing a preacher to preach his or her message in such a way as to convince Christians that they are still obligated to an external set of rules and regulations instead of living a gloriously exchanged life. If a preacher stands in the pulpit and brings believers into dialogue with the law he has unintentionally come into agreement with the powers of darkness to use the 'good' law to entangle the saints in a yoke of bondage, which, according to Paul, consistently produces death in the soul of the believer.

Penetrating the Veil of Religion

Before Jesus can proceed to the real work of supernaturally transforming the human heart He must penetrate the veil of religion that enshrouds the heart of every single person. We are mistaken if we think that only adherents to a particular form of religion are 'religious.' Religiosity is one of the defining characteristics of the entire human race; we are all religious in one way or another, if we define religion as the fleshly commitment to an outward appearance of righteousness. Although Jesus never used the word 'religion' He was continually coming up against the phenomenon of religion, not only in the Pharisees but also in His own disciples.

People, by nature, consistently seek to gloss over the actual condition of their own hearts by creating an outward impression of righteousness, goodness or spirituality. The Pharisees were an extreme caricature of this phenomenon but the truth is that every person engages in the quest to appear to be something that they are not. We don't want other people to see just how broken we really are and sometimes *we* don't want to see how broken we really are either! Religion and denial go hand in hand. Whenever we are unwilling to face the truth about ourselves we readily embrace denial as a safe refuge from reality. A person in denial does not have to face their personal problems or seek a solution. No solution is needed if there is no problem to resolve and God can't help a person who doesn't think that he or she has a problem.

One of the central themes in the theology of Jesus was His dialectic between the revelation of the true condition of the heart and mere outward appearance. Jesus taught that one of the defining characteristics of humanity was their fundamental commitment to outward appearance. Everything that people do they do to be seen by men. The primary motive in the heart of the religionist is to appear to be righteous before others. No one wants to be seen as wrong! Jesus exposed the fact that everything the Pharisees did, they did in order to be highly esteemed in the eyes of their peers and those under their religious control. The Pharisees loved to pray in public places so that they would be perceived as deeply spiritual. This is the very heart of religion. But it doesn't always come under the guise of spirituality. Even unspiritual secularists generally desire to be attractive and appealing to others. Jesus spoke directly to this bizarre condition of the heart that clamors to be seen and accepted by others.

> Therefore, when you do a charitable deed, do not sound a trumpet before you as the hypocrites do in the synagogues and in the streets, that they may have glory from men. Assuredly, I say to you, they have their reward.... And when you pray, you shall not be like the hypocrites. For they love to pray standing in the synagogues and on the corners of the streets, that they may be seen by men. When you fast, do not look somber as the hypocrites do, for they disfigure their faces to show men they are fasting. (Matthew 6:2,5,16)

The Pharisees surrounded all of their religious activities with much pomp and pageantry in order to receive the praise and recognition of their peers. They had mastered the art of appearing righteous before men.

> Everything they do is done for men to see: they make their phylacteries wide and the tassels on their garments long; they love the

place of honor at banquets and the most important seats in the synagogues; they love to be greeted in the marketplaces and to have men call them 'Rabbi.' (Matthew 23:5-7)

This tenacious commitment to outward appearance is the very core of religion and it highlights the nature of living from the tree of the knowledge of good and evil. Penetrating the universal lie and exposing this interior motive to be seen by men was one of the goals of the ministry of Jesus. Unless this motive was brought into the light people would persist in their tenacious pursuit to appear righteous because the pursuit of outward appearance represents the very basis of their acceptance and their religious standing before both God and man. It would not be an overstatement to say that this paradigm of outward appearance versus the true hidden condition of the heart lies at the very center of Jesus' teaching.

Jesus intentionally trained His disciples to look beyond mere outward appearance. "Do not judge according to appearance, but judge with righteous judgment." (John 7:24) To judge with righteous judgment was to make a decisive evaluation in the light of the Word of God. A good illustration was the presence of false prophets. Jesus said, "Beware of false prophets, who come to you in *sheep's clothing*, but inwardly they are ravenous wolves." (Matthew 7:15) A false prophet could potentially be one of the nicest people you could ever meet but in their hearts they could be fully deceived. Because they are deceived they actually become a spiritual menace to humanity. "They will go on deceiving others, and they themselves will be deceived." (2 Timothy 3:13 NLT) Deceived people inadvertently deceive others but they often appear as innocent little lambs.

As part of their religious observances the Pharisees were dedicated to ritual cleanliness but they had neglected the cleansing of the heart as the following story reveals.

When Jesus had finished speaking, a Pharisee invited him to eat with him; so he went in and reclined at the table. But the Pharisee, noticing that Jesus did not first wash before the meal, was surprised. Then the Lord said to him, "Now then, you Pharisees clean the outside of the cup and dish, but inside you are full of greed and wickedness. You foolish people! Did not the one who made the outside make the inside also?" (Luke 11:37-40 NIV)

The point of this statement was that the Pharisees had become so obsessed with the appearance of holiness and spirituality that they had forgotten that true spirituality issues from the heart. Jesus had to remind them that God had also created them with a heart and that the condition of their hearts was the real problem. The Pharisees were preoccupied with outward defilement but had overlooked the fact that defilement came from within.

> "Are you so dull?" Jesus asked. "Don't you see that nothing that enters a man from the outside can make him 'unclean?' For it doesn't go into his heart but into his stomach, and then out of his body." (In saying this, Jesus declared all foods "clean.") He went on: "What comes out of a man is what makes him 'unclean.' For from within, out of men's hearts, come evil thoughts, sexual immorality, theft, murder, adultery, greed, malice, deceit, lewdness, envy, slander, arrogance and folly. All these evils come from inside and make a man 'unclean.'" (Mark 7:18-22 NIV)

Jesus appeared particularly fond of the metaphor of the cup that was outwardly polished and shiny but inside was still coated in filth. He used this same metaphor in his scathing denunciation of the hypocrisy of the Pharisees in Matthew 23.

> Woe to you, teachers of the law and Pharisees, you hypocrites! You clean the outside of the cup and dish, but inside they are full of greed and self-indulgence. Blind Pharisee! First clean the inside of the cup and dish, and then the outside also will be clean. Woe to you, teachers of the law and Pharisees, you hypocrites! You are like whitewashed tombs, which look beautiful on the outside but on the inside are full of dead men's bones and everything unclean. In the same way, on the outside you appear to people as righteous but on the inside you are full of hypocrisy and wickedness." (Matthew 23:25-28)

Jesus solemnly warned his disciples against the leaven of hypocrisy, which had a way of permeating and blinding anyone who did not tenaciously guard against it. As long as Jesus was around He was committed to exposing this deadly poison and freeing people from its insidious influence. After His fiery confrontation with the Pharisees Jesus began to say to His disciples; "Beware of the leaven of the Pharisees, which is hypocrisy. For there is nothing covered that will not be revealed, nor hidden that will not be known." (Luke 12:1,2) The Message Bible sets forth a fascinating paraphrase of this verse.

> Watch yourselves carefully so you don't get contaminated with Pharisee yeast, Pharisee phoniness. You can't keep your true self hidden forever; before long you'll be exposed. You can't hide behind a religious mask forever; sooner or later the mask will slip and your true face will be known. (Luke 12:1,2 MSG)

This inside/outside paradigm runs like a golden thread through the theology of the entire New Testament. Paul was also at pains to delineate between the true condition of the heart and mere outward appearance. He emphasized that "God does not judge by external appearance." (Galatians 2:6 NIV) On one occasion he wrote to the Corinthians; "The trouble with you is that you make your decisions on the basis of appearance." (2 Corinthians 10:7 NLT) Like Jesus, Paul sought to expose "those who take pride in what is seen rather than in what is in the heart." (2 Corinthians 5:12 NIV) Paul's entire theology of salvation by faith alone hinged upon this issue of the inward versus the outward. He said;

> A man is not a Jew if he is only one outwardly, nor is circumcision merely outward and physical. No, a man is a Jew if he is one inwardly; and circumcision is circumcision of the heart, by the Spirit, not by the written code. (Romans 2:28,29 NIV)

Paul spent his lifetime campaigning against outward religion. He taught that the principle of the free gift of righteousness through faith in Christ overthrew the necessity to establish an outward righteousness through the works of the law. The gift of Christ's righteousness made all self-righteousness appear as filthy rags. Self-righteousness was a vain attempt to justify ourselves before a holy God when God had already given us the free gift of justification through faith. Paul's entire theology of justification by faith in Christ exposed the folly of outward religion. Paul systematically developed and expanded upon Jesus' criticism of the Pharisees when He said to them, "You are those who justify yourselves before men, but God knows your hearts." (Luke 16:15) Paul ruthlessly stripped away every avenue of self-justification by exposing every outward religious work that people engaged in, in order to create a sense of self-righteousness.

Paul specifically targeted circumcision because it had become a symbol of outward Jewish righteousness before God. "Those who want to make a good impression outwardly are trying to compel you to be circumcised." (Galatians 6:12 NIV) Like Jesus, Paul also campaigned against every form of outward ceremonialism. He stripped away all ceremonial rules and laws such as "do not touch, do not taste, do not handle," (Colossians 2:21) arguing that these rules were not the basis of our justification. "These things indeed have an appearance of wisdom in self-imposed religion, false humility, and neglect of the body, but are of no value against the indulgence of the flesh." (Colossians 2:23)

Paul insisted that there was nothing that we could do to establish any sense of righteousness before God. "Therefore do not let anyone judge you by what you eat or drink, or with regard to a religious festival, a New Moon celebration or a Sabbath day." (Colossians 2:16 NLT) Paul's theology, properly understood, represented the death-knell of outward religion. We see this same internal/external paradigm in the writings of Peter who contrasted outward physical beauty with the interior condition of the heart.

> Your adornment must not be merely external – braiding the hair, and wearing gold jewelry, or putting on dresses; but let it be the hidden person of the heart, with the imperishable quality of a gentle and quiet spirit, which is precious in the sight of God. (1 Peter 3:3,4 NASB)

Because God looks upon the heart He is not concerned with outward appearance. There is no place for outward religious performance in the sight of God. His eyes are continually on the hidden motives and purposes of the heart and if any of His children are still focused upon external religion God calls them to repentance, to turn from externalism to embrace an expression of spirituality that springs from the free gift of righteousness. This principle of sincere heart devotion is ruthlessly applied to every aspect of the Christian life, even to slaves in the 1st century.

> Slaves, in all things obey those who are your masters on earth, *not with external service, as those who merely please men*, but with sincerity of heart, fearing the Lord. Whatever you do, do your work heartily, as for the Lord rather than for men, knowing that from the Lord you will receive the reward of the inheritance. It is the Lord Christ whom you serve. (Colossians 3:2 NASB)

As Christians, we are faced with a simple choice between religious externalism and true heart devotion to Christ. But if we are unwilling to allow the Lord to break up the fallow ground of our hearts, all we are left with is a mere shell of religious activities and 'dead works' with which to create the appearance of genuine Christian devotion. The heart of religion is learning to act out a particular role in the eyes of others. At the core of all religion is the pursuit to imitate the righteousness of Christ in the power of the flesh. The pure and holy life of Christ is the benchmark of goodness and true spirituality and it is the standard that religion seeks to attain in the strength of human flesh. Christians who have not received a clear revelation of God's free gift of righteousness are extremely vulnerable to the snare of outward religion.

Even outside of Christian circles most people seek to be 'good' because they intuitively understand that acceptance is based upon performance. Anyone in search of his or her partner understands the imperative to present as well as is humanly possible. The same is true for someone searching for good employment. That is why the concept of 'religion' extends considerably beyond the parameters of those who adhere to a particular spiritual path or creed. It is an interesting fact that the vast majority of people almost always seek to be good, righteous and upright. It is the rare exception when people take pleasure in being openly evil. Most people understand that to live in society and to succeed in life we must impress one another as being people of good moral character.

This pursuit of the appearance of human goodness is the very essence of religion whether it is expressed in a secular or spiritual form. In order to avoid rejection, castigation and ostracism we must be 'good.' This message is drummed into us from early childhood and is reinforced throughout our entire life. We are rewarded if we are good but there are penalties if we misbehave. The problem, of course, is that by nature we are not good. In the story of the rich young ruler's encounter with Jesus, Jesus highlighted the fact that no one is 'good' except God alone. "Now a man came up to Jesus and asked, "Teacher, what good thing must I do to get eternal life?" "Why do you ask me about what is good?" Jesus replied. "There is only One who is good." (Matthew 19:16,17 NIV) From cover to cover God makes it clear through the pages of Scripture that no one is essentially 'good' by nature.

As it is written: "There is no one righteous, not even one; there is no one who understands, no one who seeks God. All have turned away, they have together become worthless; there is no one who does good, not even one." (Romans 3:10-12 NIV)

Jesus had no illusions about human nature. He taught that the whole of humanity (apart from the redeemed) were fundamentally evil by nature. He says it in such a matter of fact way because from the perspective of heaven it is an indisputable fact. "Brood of vipers! How can you, *being evil*, speak good things? For out of the abundance of the heart the mouth speaks." (Matthew 12:34) "If you then, *being evil*, know how to give good gifts to your children, how much more will your Father who is in heaven give good things to those who ask Him!" (Matthew 7:11) From an earthly perspective we relativize good and evil. People who do good are generally regarded as good even though they still actually have an evil selfish nature that is masked by good deeds. It is not as though fallen human beings are incapable of doing extraordinarily good things but these good deeds have no capacity to change basic their fallen human nature.

If, in the eyes of God unredeemed humanity is *evil* by nature why do so many people appear to be so nice? The answer lies in our capacity to appear nice even though we are not nice by nature. Because so much is at stake people spend their entire lives cultivating 'niceness.' We all know how to behave in certain situations. Even people who swear like troopers know how to dial down the swearing in appropriate situations. People can even restrain themselves from blaspheming in certain religious company or may quickly apologize if they allow blasphemy to accidentally slip out in the wrong company. Beyond merely restraining ourselves from inappropriate public behavior there is the capacity of the soul to attempt to counterfeit the fruits of the Holy Spirit. Our attempts to be nice are essentially an attempt to imitate the goodness of Jesus in our own strength.

If we train ourselves through diligent self-effort we can pretend to be loving, peaceful, joyful, patient, kind, compassionate and merciful. Often we will encounter people who appear to have cultivated a deep sense of personal goodness. We would not hesitate to describe these people as fundamentally 'good.' Often devout 'spiritual' people, be they Buddhists, New-Agers or whatever, will appear to be so loving and caring that people are deeply impressed and attracted to their aura of spirituality. Similarly we are impressed by the charisma, charm and personal magnetism of great secular figures who dazzle us with the apparent largeness of their souls. But all of this, according to Jesus, is the result of self-effort. Jesus taught that evil people know how to do good and to give good gifts. He observed that even sinners know how to show love and kindness to their friends.

> But if you love those who love you, what credit is that to you? For even sinners love those who love them. And if you do good to those who do good to you, what credit is that to you? For even sinners do the same. (Luke 6:32,33)

Paul described this innate capacity to be nice as 'natural affection.' (2 Timothy 3:3) If people are indeed capable of cultivating the life of their soul to create the impression of goodness, charm or spirituality we must understand, from a biblical perspective, that it is all a great pretense. If we are trained in the Scriptures we must exercise true spiritual discernment and realize that things are not always as they appear. In one of the Messianic prophecies in the book of Isaiah it was foretold of Jesus that, "He will never judge by appearance or hearsay." (Isaiah 11:3 NLT) We too must look beyond appearances and live in the light of divine revelation. Solomon was a keen student of human nature. He observed that although people "pretend to be kind, their hearts are full of all kinds of evil." (Proverbs 26:25 NLT)

From God's perspective the whole human race is steeped in deep selfishness and moral evil but this fact is so abhorrent to humanity that the notion is completely rejected. The only alternative to accepting the truth about our own hearts is to immerse ourselves in a life of *play-acting*. We may be shocked to learn that Jesus taught that the whole human race, in their quest for an appearance of personal goodness, has resorted to play-acting. Jesus consistently confronted this play-acting in the Pharisees who had perfected the art of hypocrisy.

Hypocrisy and Pretense

Jesus used the word 'hypocrites' to describe the Pharisees. The Greek word, *'hupocrites'* is a very interesting and insightful word, not only in reference to the lives of the Pharisees but also in reference to fallen human nature in general. Kenneth West, in his *'Expanded Translation of the New Testament'* renders Jesus' eight-fold denunciation of the Pharisees in Matthew 23 in this way; "Woe to you, men learned in the Scriptures, Pharisees, actors on the stage of life, playing the role of that which you are not..." The Greek word *'hypocrites'* actually means 'a play-actor, or an actor under an assumed character.' Jesus exposed the Pharisees as mere actors who were playing out a role in the eyes of the public that was thoroughly inconsistent with the true condition of their hearts.

In ancient Greek theatre the play-actors would wear masks that represented the particular role that they were playing. An actor would hold up to his or her face a 'happy' mask or an 'angry' mask or a 'melancholy' mask depending on the role they were playing at the time. Jesus regarded the Pharisees as mere actors who were acting out a role of super-spirituality in order to be recognized and esteemed by men. Jesus was not restrained in exposing this religious hypocrisy because it stood as the primary wall of defense between the heart of the Pharisee and God. At the heart of religious hypocrisy is the deception that an appearance of human goodness and righteousness will be accepted by God as righteousness! Jesus deliberately exposed the inconsistency between the words and the deeds of those who took refuge in religious hypocrisy.

> The teachers of religious law and the Pharisees are the official interpreters of the Scriptures. So practice and obey whatever they say to you, but don't follow their example. For they don't practice what they teach! They crush you with impossible religious demands and never lift a finger to help ease the burden. But all their works they do to be seen by men. (Matthew 23:2-5 NIV)

The tragedy deepens when we begin to passionately believe in the role that we are playing. The greatest tragedy of all was that the Pharisees had become so deeply enmeshed in this web of deceit that they had come to believe in the role themselves. In fact they were more convinced than anybody! The Pharisees had immersed themselves so deeply in self-deception that they literally imagined that they were better than other men. Jesus exposed this foolish heart of self-righteousness when He said: "The Pharisee stood and prayed thus with himself, "God, I thank You that I am *not like other men*; extortioners, unjust, adulterers, or even as this tax collector." (Luke 18:11)

People who pursue religious hypocrisy end up believing that they actually are the person they are pretending to be! The Pharisee not only believed in his heart that he was better than other people; he also boasted that his religious performance outstripped that of his neighbor. "I fast twice a week; I give tithes of all that I possess." (Luke 18:12) Like the best Hollywood actors, the Pharisees had so perfected the role they played that they ended up believing it themselves! They had literally reinvented a new self-image that was rooted in self-deception, thus deepening the vice-like grip that denial held over their hearts. But this is not just the heart condition of the Pharisees; it is a caricature of the heart of fallen humanity. All human beings have been in some sense tainted by this quest to appear righteous and good both before God and their friends.

The Pharisees arrogantly strutted about parading their spirituality in the sight of men, but Jesus could see right through their foolish pretense: "On the outside you appear to people as righteous but on the inside you are full of hypocrisy and wickedness." (Matthew 23:28) The deeds that they did and the words that they spoke were merely an outgrowth of the deceitfulness of their own hearts. Paul described the thoughts of fallen man as *'futile.'* (Romans 1:21) Man's thoughts are vain, ineffectual and incapable of producing any spiritual fruit. The best that fallen man can achieve is to merely *pretend* to be righteous. Like the Pharisees all human beings pretend to be something they are not. The Pharisees were merely an exaggerated caricature of fallen human nature. Perhaps Jesus came at a time in human history when the cultish behavior of the Pharisees had reached its zenith in order to juxtapose the extremes of human religiosity and pretense with the righteousness that comes from above?

Until Christians address this stronghold of religion in their own lives they will never learn to live out of the free gift of righteousness that Christ has already established in their spirit. Paul said to Christians: "Don't just pretend that you love others. Really love them." (Romans 12:9 NLT) Paul had to continually confront this downward slide toward hypocrisy and pretense in the churches: "These teachers are hypocrites and liars. They pretend to be religious." (1 Timothy 4:2 NLT) Likewise Peter warned the disciples: "Get rid of all malicious behavior and deceit. Don't just pretend to be good! Be done with hypocrisy!" (1 Peter 2:1 NLT) This deeply ingrained self-righteousness and religious pretense parades in the church as true righteousness.

Christians are just as vulnerable to religious hypocrisy as the Pharisees. In fact, Christians are in the highest risk category on the face of the earth because the powers of darkness love to lock Christians into the religion of self-effort and pretense. This is a trap set by the devil himself and far too many believers have come to Christ and fallen straight into this trap. Some get stuck there for life; others struggle to get free and some barely manage to escape. Those who truly overcome get to enjoy the heavenly privilege of eating exclusively from the Tree of Life.

The Pharisees were adept at pretending. On one occasion the Chief Priests deceitfully sent a handful of men to observe Jesus in the hope of catching Him out. "So they watched Him, and sent spies who *pretended to be righteous* that they might seize on His words in order to deliver Him to the power and the authority of the governor." (Luke 20:20) These deceitful men posed the thorny question to Jesus; "Is it right for us to pay taxes to Caesar or not?" Luke tells us that Jesus immediately "saw through their duplicity." (Luke 20:22,23 NIV) Duplicity is one of the uglier aspects of fallen human nature. It means to be 'two-faced.' The Greek word for duplicity used by Luke is *'panourgia'* and it means 'subtlety, trickery or cunning craftiness.' When we pretend to be something we are not we are really using deception to conceal our real motives and intents.

 God hates religious pretense, whether it is the deliberate pretense of religion or the pretense of those who do not even consider themselves religious or spiritual. Fallen men and women are all by nature great pretenders. "One man pretends to be rich, yet has nothing; another pretends to be poor, yet has great wealth." (Proverbs 13:7 NIV) But without doubt, those who are most susceptible to pretense are people who have high moral values and a strong desire to be considered as good, respectable citizens or church-goers. Twenty centuries of church history attests to the fact that it is much, much easier to 'talk the talk' than it is to 'walk the walk.'

Throughout the Scriptures the Lord repeatedly lifted the lid on the superficiality of His people in their constant tendency toward outward religion. Jesus exposed the hypocrisy of the Pharisees, "who devour widows' houses, and *for a pretense* make long prayers." (Luke 20:47) Inwardly their hearts were still full of greed. They did not hesitate to swindle old ladies of their life's savings if they thought they could get away with it. Nevertheless, they perpetuated their impressive public prayers in order to be esteemed by men as the spiritual giants of their day! Jesus called this pure *pretense.*

The people of God fell into religious pretense time and time again under the Old Covenant: "And yet for all this her treacherous sister Judah has not turned to Me with her whole heart, *but in pretense*," says the Lord." (Jeremiah 3:10) "The Lord says: 'These people come near to me with their mouth and honor me with their lips, but their hearts are far from me." (Isaiah 29:13 NIV) Heaven is unimaginably grieved by the hypocrisy of religious lip service. On one occasion the Lord actually highlighted this phenomenon in His private dialogue with the prophet Ezekiel whom He had sent to call the children of Israel back to Him.

> As for you, son of man, the children of your people are talking about you beside the walls and in the doors of the houses, and they speak to one another, everyone saying to his brother, "Please come and hear what the word is that comes from the Lord." So they come to you as people do, they sit before you as My people, and they hear your words, but they do not do them; for with their mouth they show much love, but their hearts pursue their own gain. (Ezekiel 33:30,31)

Note how this passage is translated in the New Living Translation:

> So they come ***pretending*** to be sincere and sit before you listening. But they have no intention of doing what I tell them. They express love with their mouths, but their hearts seek only after money. (Ezekiel 33:31 NLT)

Rather than incur the disapproval of their neighbor, it was much easier for the Israelites to merely fake submission to God. Religious pretense was elevated to a national pastime but it didn't fool God or His prophets for a moment. The truth was that the children of Israel hated God and regarded His laws as the primary obstacle to their freedom. This passage in Ezekiel is quite revealing. From God's perspective His people were engaged in a giant corporate charade. There was a great chasm between their words and their outward religious appearance and the actual condition of their hearts. "With their mouth they show much love, but their hearts pursue their own gain!" They did not love God and they did not love the prophet Ezekiel but they covered up their hatred of God with words of kindness and love.

As the Psalmist wrote, "The haters of the Lord would ***pretend*** submission to Him." (Psalms 81:15) It is so easy to say that we love somebody or that we love God but words are cheap. So much is said about love and the word is always on everybody's lips but the truth is that sincere love for God and our neighbor is often the furthest thing from the human heart. Even deeply selfish people sing songs about love! That is why John said, "Let us not love in word or in tongue, but in deed and in truth." (1 John 3:16) The real test of love is in our deeds not in our words. Solomon highlighted this trait of fallen human nature in the book of Proverbs;

> Fervent lips with a wicked heart are like earthenware covered with silver dross. He who hates disguises himself with his lips, but in his heart he harbors deceit. Though his speech is charming, do not believe him, for seven abominations fill his heart. His malice may be concealed by deception, but his wickedness will be exposed in the assembly. (Proverbs 26:23-26)

The New Living Translation exposes this religious pretense with even greater clarity;

> Smooth words may hide a wicked heart, just as a pretty glaze covers a common clay pot. People with hate in their hearts may sound pleasant enough, but don't believe them. Though they pretend to be kind, their hearts are full of all kinds of evil. While their hatred may be concealed by trickery, it will finally come to light for all to see. (Proverbs 26:23-26)

Words, words, words! The world is full of words, especially words and songs about love. But in the end fallen men and women are all just 'great pretenders.' They pretend to be loving and kind and they pretend to be righteous but all their righteousness is as filthy rags. If we harbor sin in our hearts we cannot walk in love because sin is the very antithesis of love. Sin destroys love. Sin and love cannot co-exist. The Scriptures reveal that sin is the transgression of the law whilst love is the fulfilment of the law. God seeks to deliver our hearts from sin in order to fill the vacuum with His love but the love of God cannot abide in a heart that is thoroughly yielded to sin and selfishness. John systematically chipped away at this religious state of mind in the New Testament people of God. "If anyone says, "I love God," yet hates his brother, he is a liar. For anyone who does not love his brother, whom he has seen, cannot love God, whom he has not seen." (1 John 4:20 NIV)

If the love of God does not truly fill our hearts our only recourse is to *pretend* to be loving and kind. Similarly, if the righteousness of God does not fill our hearts then all we can do is pretend to be righteous and hope that people cannot see through the charade. Selfishness runs deep in the human heart but God is committed to delivering us from ourselves so that we can truly walk in love as Christ has loved us. The prophets relentlessly sought to penetrate the veil of religion in order to get to the true condition of the heart. "If anyone has material possessions and sees his brother in need but has no pity on him, how can the love of God be in him?" (1 John 3:17 NIV)

Our deepest fear is that people will find out what we are really like and that if they find out they will reject us. In our fallen state, cut off from, and ignorant of the unconditional love of God, we live in constant fear of being rejected by our peers. So we dare not let people see us as we really are. We must maintain the pretense at all costs and hope that no one ever sees through the mask and discovers that we are really just a fake. How many hearts are gripped by this mortal fear of being exposed as a fraud?

Truly coming to Christ means stripping away all religious pretense so that we really live from the heart. I sometimes wonder what it must be like to be God in heaven listening to all of our worship songs when half the time the entire congregation can potentially be drawing near with their lips when their hearts are actually far from God. How many times have you been singing a congregational love song to Jesus and you suddenly realize your heart is totally disengaged from fellowshipping with God and you are merely giving lip service to the Lord?

Practicing Falsehood

Religious pretense is described in the Scriptures as *'falsehood.'* Whenever we seek to cover up our selfishness with a mask of spirituality or merely with the appearance of moral uprightness we are perpetrating a lie. In the book of Revelation Jesus placed *"everyone who loves and practices falsehood"* in the same camp with "the sorcerers, the sexually immoral, the murderers and the idolaters." (Revelation 22:15 NIV) This is clearly not a nice crowd but it sheds light upon God's perception of those who live a life of deceit. God has a really big problem with deceit. He says, "He who works deceit shall not dwell within My house; He who tells lies shall not continue in My presence." (Psalms 101:7)

The Greek word used for 'falsehood' in Revelation 22:15 is *'pseudos.'* It describes the person who makes a deceitful pretense. It describes someone who is not genuine but who has the appearance of being genuine. Even the Mafia boss knows how to come home from work and be nice to his own kids! Isaiah recognized that falsehood had come to characterize the people of God in his day and in solidarity with God's people he confessed the sin of falsehood before the Lord.

> Our sins testify against us; for our transgressions are with us. And as for our iniquities, we know them: in transgressing and lying against the Lord, and departing from our God, speaking oppression and revolt, *conceiving and uttering from the heart words of falsehood.* (Isaiah 59:12,13)

According to Jeremiah, all those who take refuge in falsehood are speaking out of the deception of their own hearts. "Is there anything in the hearts of the prophets who prophesy falsehood; even these prophets of the deception of their own heart?" (Jeremiah 23:26 NASB) Most people prefer to live in falsehood rather than endure the pain of coming out of denial. It is the rare exception to discover the man or woman who practices sincerity and integrity. Solomon said, "Most men will proclaim each his own goodness." (Proverbs 20:6) Not many people actually desire to appear to be evil. Paul spoke of "those who want to make a good impression outwardly," (Galatians 6:12 NIV) and of "those who boast in outward appearance rather than in what is in the heart." (2 Corinthians 5:12 NRSV/NIV) Let's face it; falsehood is a widespread human phenomenon.

Sometimes King David felt like he was drowning in a sea of falsehood. Everywhere he turned he encountered false lips. "They delight in falsehood; they bless with their mouth, but inwardly they curse." (Psalms 62:4 NASB) "They speak falsehood to one another; with flattering lips and with a double heart they speak." (Psalms 12:2 NASB) "Your tongue plots destruction; it is like a sharpened razor, you who practice deceit. You love evil rather than good, falsehood rather than speaking the truth." (Psalms 52:3) "Behold, the wicked brings forth iniquity; yes, he conceives mischief and brings forth falsehood." (Psalms 7:14) From heaven's perspective humanity is awash with deceit and falsehood. "Run up and down every street in Jerusalem," says the Lord. "Look high and low; search throughout the city! If you can find even one person who is just and honest, I will not destroy the city. Even when they are under oath, saying, "As surely as the Lord lives," they all tell lies!" (Jeremiah 5:1,2 NLT)

David's personal quest for integrity and uprightness caused him to be a man set apart from the multitude. He understood that most men lived out of the deceitfulness of their own hearts and had no care for the true condition of their heart before God. But David had experienced the glory of the Lord and had cultivated an intimate relationship with God. He understood that only those who turned from darkness to light and from falsehood to the truth could abide in the house of the Lord. "Who may ascend into the hill of the Lord? And who may stand in His holy place? He who has clean hands and a pure heart, who has *not lifted up his soul to falsehood* and has not sworn deceitfully." (Psalms 24:4 NASB) But even David, a man after God's own heart experienced a very dark season of living in falsehood until Nathan the prophet called him back into the light.

To depart from falsehood means to come out of denial about the stronghold of religious pretense and to acknowledge the propensity of the old selfish nature to create an impression of goodness and righteousness. The stronghold of denial can only be demolished when we humbly embrace the truth about our old nature. A stronghold is a house of thoughts that stands in agreement with the devil. In order to be completely free of religion Christians need to break every agreement with the evil one and come into full agreement with the Word of God. Only then will we stop believing the lies that we have projected about ourselves for our entire life. When the human race fell into sin we "exchanged the truth of God for a lie." In the process of redemption we must "exchange the lie for the truth of God!" The stronghold of religious pretense holds many of God's people in bondage to the old selfish nature because pretense is a work of the flesh.

The old King James Version listed '*emulation*' as one of the fruits of the flesh. (Galatians 5:20) To 'emulate' means to imitate or copy someone for the purpose of appearing to be just like someone else. It also means to 'strive to equal another.' The New King James Version uses the term 'selfish ambition,' which indicates an ambition to be just like someone else that is rooted in self-effort. Ambition is always about comparison. The flesh compares itself with others in an attempt to be like others in order to avoid being rejected. Wherever we look in the Bible we are confronted with the loving voice of God spoken through anointed heart prophets calling the people of God out of the shadows of hypocrisy and religious pretense and into the light of Christ who has come to heal the human heart.

Shame and Religion

This edifice of falsehood begins in childhood when we first become aware of our failings and our deep sense of inadequacy. The constant reminders of our shortcomings from our parents, our teachers and our peers reinforce the sense of shame that hovers over each of us like a dark cloud. Shame forces us to retreat into a false reality in order to silence the voices of accusation. In his insightful book, '*The Secret Life of The Soul,*' J. Keith Miller describes how this process "happens gradually in consequence of several painful experiments in lying, in which the child wrestles with his or her soul but in the end ignores its entreaties and tells lies again and again. This struggle is also influenced if the child knows that a parent is lying and uses the parent's dishonesty to justify his or her own falsehood."[37] Falsehood can be a generational stronghold.

It was shame in the Garden of Eden that caused Adam and Eve to sew fig leaves to cover their nakedness and it is shame that causes each of us to create our modern day fig leaves to cover up our sin. "He who covers his sins will not prosper, but whoever confesses and forsakes them will have mercy." (Proverbs 28:13) Shame causes us to go into hiding, to avoid the light at all costs lest our deeds should be exposed. Jeff Van Vonderen gives us an excellent definition of shame. "Shame is the painful sense that you lack value as a person. It is the belief that you are defective, worthless and unlovable. It is not that something is wrong with your behavior, it is that something is wrong with *you* as a person."[38] J. Keith Miller continues to describe the construction of this edifice of falsehood.

> In order to avoid the shame of the condemning voices that continually bombard the child with the message that he or she is inadequate and not worth much, the child begins to look for a more permanent way out and does a very strange and ingenious thing: The child begins secretly to construct another personality, one that is false but appears to be more adequate, intelligent and/or honest than the child actually is. The child has laid the cornerstone for the construction of the larger, "more-righteous-than-life" but false, "constructed personality" that he or she hopes will perform adequately enough to quiet the shaming voices. And the habit of denial has been established. The purpose of the constructed personality is twofold. The first is to quiet the shaming voices. After all, in our constructed person we are now looking and acting more intelligent, cool, tough, sexy – whatever the shaming voices have told

us we are not. The second purpose of the constructed personality is to represent to the world inflated, constructed characteristics in order to succeed "out there."[39]

In a world where image is everything people will go to any length to prove that they are cool. As children progress from childhood into adolescence and ultimately into adulthood, peer group pressure and the fear of rejection squeeze them into a pre-ordained mold that is in step with fashion and the mass media culture. Like lemmings we dance to the beat of the same drum fearing that any expression of non-conformity will cost us our popularity. Whether it is the rules and regulations of religion or the rules of social engagement we quickly learn that falsehood pays good dividends.

This world is characterized by falsehood and the quest for the ultimate cool, sexy outward appearance. Paul said in Romans 12:3, "Do not be conformed to this world." J. B. Phillips translates this verse in this way: "Don't let the world around you squeeze you into its own mold."[40] If we would live in the light we must renounce falsehood. "Therefore each of you must put off falsehood and speak truthfully to his neighbor." (Ephesians 4:25) "A righteous man hates falsehood, but a wicked man acts disgustingly and shamefully." (Proverbs 13:5 NASB) True righteous living has no place for the falsehood of play-acting. The righteous man or woman hates falsehood because it is a form of deception.

The Imagination of the Heart

If we are honest we will admit that the forthright language of Scripture shocks us. God doesn't play around with words. He cuts right to the heart and says it as it is! That is the nature of prophetic ministry! From His perspective the whole human race is enmeshed in a tangled web of falsehood, self-deception and denial. The role that we seek to act out in the sight of man is nothing more than the product of the imagination of a deceitful heart. We bring our old deceitful ways into the Christian life and the Spirit is at work to expose these old ways in order to set us free from the power of religion that grips the entire human race. God is attempting to dismantle and deconstruct everything that constitutes our old selfish lives. The unrenewed parts of our heart have taken refuge in an alternative reality; a parallel universe created by our own imagination and our stubborn refusal to accept the truth about the depths of our fallen and broken condition.

Because fallen people are hell-bent on proclaiming their own goodness and denying the presence of evil in their hearts they readily embrace the re-created self-image of their proud imagination. This is the way of the flesh! The power of the human imagination is in its ability to form a mental image of something that is actually not real. The newly imagined 'self' is nothing more than a figment of the human imagination! But because people passionately want to believe the lie about themselves they are quick to exonerate themselves of all blame whilst pointing the finger at everyone else. "Others are wrong, but I am not!" This kind of thinking is so illogical that it should cause us to blush yet it is typical of almost every human being on the face of the earth! "A fool has no delight in understanding, but in expressing his own heart." (Proverbs 18:2) If foolishness is bound up in our heart we can convince ourselves of anything! That is why Paul exhorts believers to ruthlessly uproot all self-deception by "casting down *imaginations*." (2 Corinthians 10:5 KJV)

God clearly warns against giving heed to those who speak out of the context of their own imaginations. In Jeremiah's time there were false prophets who prophesied to the people of God out of their own imaginations. "They are leading you into futility; they speak a vision of their own imagination, not from the mouth of the Lord." (Jeremiah 23:16 NASB) "Say to those who prophesy out of their own imagination: 'Hear the word of the Lord!'" (Ezekiel 13:2 NIV) But it was not just a trait of the false prophets to walk in the imagination of their own hearts. In the book of Isaiah the Lord confronted the deceitful imagination of the entire nation of Israel. "All day long I have held out my hands to an obstinate people, who walk in ways not good, *pursuing their own imaginations* – a people who continually provoke Me to My very face.... who say, 'keep away; don't come near me, for I am holier than you!" (Isaiah 65:2,3,5 NIV)

The product of their proud imagination was the delusion that they were in fact holier than other people were. Our natural tendency is always toward self-canonization. Remember the Pharisee who flattered himself with the thought that he was not like other men? Because of this universal tendency to flatter ourselves by down-playing our fallen status, Paul wrote: "For I say, through the grace given to me, to everyone who is among you, not to think of himself more highly than he ought to think, but to think soberly...." (Romans 12:3)

This brings us to the root cause of the vain imaginings of the flesh. Proud man struts around as if he has no sin. The deluded state of mankind has its roots firmly in pride and conceit. The Psalmist was contemplating the state of the wicked and wrote these words; "They wear pride like a jeweled necklace...from their callous hearts comes iniquity; the evil *conceits* of their minds know no limits." (Psalms 73:7 NIV) The NASB renders this verse as "the imaginations of their heart run riot." Unless our minds are firmly anchored in the Word of God we are susceptible to all kinds of gross delusions about ourselves. In Psalm 2 we read: "Why do the heathen rage, and the people *imagine* a vain thing?" (Psalms 2:1 KJV)

We must always remember that Jesus came as a prophet to expose the proud and stubbornly resistant heart of man and to call him to genuine repentance. When Mary, the mother of Jesus encountered Elizabeth the Spirit of prophecy fell upon her and she cried out: "He has shown strength with His arm; He has *scattered the proud in the imagination of their hearts.* He has put down the mighty from their thrones and exalted the lowly." (Luke 1:51,52) Jesus challenges us, just as He challenged the Pharisees, to step down from our thrones and humbly embrace the truth about the deceptive nature of fallen man. We have to see it in all its ugliness before we will truly repent and forsake our carnal ways.

From a biblical perspective, the boastful pride of the heart of fallen man is regarded as the source of his deep self-delusion. Man's estimation of himself is such that he convinces himself within his own heart that he is sufficiently wise to solve every challenge that life may bring. Through his boastful arrogance he flatters himself to the point that he becomes blind to the true condition of his own heart. David wrote: "An oracle is within my heart concerning the sinfulness of the wicked: there is no fear of God before his eyes. *For in his own eyes he flatters himself too much to detect or hate his sin.* The words of his mouth are wicked and deceitful; he has ceased to be wise and to do good." (Psalms 36:1-3 NIV) The NLT renders this verse as: "In their blind conceit, they cannot see how wicked they really are!" This verse is the key to understanding fallen man's inability to detect the depth of his sinful condition. Self-flattery; the tendency to think more highly of ourselves than we ought, is the root cause of spiritual blindness.

It is a universal trait of fallen man to exalt himself and to consider himself wise in his own eyes but the Scriptures declare from cover to cover that the man who considers himself to be wise in this world is considered by God to be a fool. "Do you see a man wise in his own eyes? There is more hope for a fool than for him." (Proverbs 26:12 NIV) Paul explained to the church in Corinth that, "the wisdom of this world is foolishness in God's sight." (1 Corinthians 3:19 NIV) Man's wisdom is foolishness because it rejects the light of God's wisdom. Without the foundation of the Word of God upon which to build our thought life we are left to drift in an ocean of irrational futility. Immediately after Paul declared that the best of man's wisdom was actually foolishness in the sight of God he quoted from Psalm 94: "The Lord knows the thoughts of man, that they are futile." (Psalms 94:11)

Because fallen man is so intractably unwilling to contemplate the depths of his sinfulness he must find an alternative explanation for his oftentimes-bizarre behavior. But because he is so deeply committed to independence and the myth of self-sufficiency he is doomed to live in a state of perpetual falsehood. "Every way of a man is right in his own eyes, but the Lord weighs the hearts." (Proverbs 2:2) Is it not a universal tendency for people to put a positive spin on their own actions, no matter how wrong they might be? No matter how wicked our deeds may be, we are all extremely vulnerable to seek to convince others and ourselves that we were actually justified in our actions! Pride is the root cause of self-deception and it is the only adequate explanation for man's misguided thinking. David specifically linked this condition of falsehood with pride: "How blessed is the man who has made the Lord his trust, and has not turned to the proud, nor to those who lapse into falsehood." (Psalms 40:4 NASB)

This is the graphic nature of the flesh. As we trace back the roots of religious performance we come all the way back to the pride of the old nature. While this is no longer the core identity of the New Covenant people of God it is nevertheless the universal nature of the flesh and a new Christian has absolutely no understanding of the depths of their own carnality. Paul anticipated the carnality of new believers but he worked hard to extricate them from the edifice of carnality and religion in order to usher them into the true life of the Spirit. He said, "And I, brethren, could not speak to you as to spiritual people but as to carnal, as to babes in Christ. For you are still carnal." (1 Corinthians 3:1,3) Paul used the Greek word; '*sarkikos*' which means 'fleshly.' The new Corinthian believers were still living under the sway of the old fleshly nature but Paul was working to set them free to become people of the Spirit.

A new believer comes into the kingdom of God with the old nature still intact. He is given a new nature in his spirit and his spirit is now alive to God and dead to sin but he is so accustomed to living out of the old proud and selfish nature that the enemy immediately gets a hook into the 'old man' in order to hijack him into dead religion. The harsh reality is that many new believers don't make it! There are so many religious churches filled with born again but deeply religious people and they are still largely living under the power of sin and self-righteousness.

Religion has a way of locking new believers into the flesh and many simply do not escape. We have to face the reality that there is a universal tendency amongst Christians to fall victim to the danger of actually building a stronghold of religion that progressively deepens rather than diminishes over the years. The devil is hell bent on hijacking every new believer into a successful life of religion in order to paralyze them and keep them from living from their regenerated spirit. The ultimate purpose of the evil one is to cripple Christians to render them ineffective in advancing the kingdom of God for their entire lives.

Sincerity of Heart

The concepts of religion, hypocrisy and falsehood are all significant themes in the Bible. Religion is not just a matter of outward appearance, it is a condition of the heart that acts as a buffer or a wall of protection from the truth of Scripture. Tragically, even after a person has turned to Christ he is at risk of following in the footsteps of the religious hypocrites if he is not yet awakened to the truth that Christ is pre-eminently concerned with the issues of the heart. God opposes the proud but gives grace to the humble. All He is looking for is a humble and sincere heart that trembles at His word and allows the sword of the Spirit to cut through this religious veneer. There was a word that was used in the New Testament that described the very opposite of hypocrisy (*hupokritos*). That word was '*anupokritos*' and it has been translated as 'sincere, genuine or unfeigned.' The word essentially means 'without hypocrisy' and it is used in the context of both faith and love. It is a quality of the heart of Christ and of our new nature in Christ and it can become a quality of our personal lives if we are willing to turn away from every form of prideful hypocrisy.

Paul said, "Love must be sincere (*anupokritos*)." (Romans 12:9 NIV) The NKJV translates it as "Let love be without hypocrisy," whilst the NLT renders it as, "Don't just pretend that you love others. Really love them." Paul had to write this because of our propensity to fake our love for others, which lies at the core of religious flesh. Remember what the Lord said to Ezekiel; "For with their mouth they show much love, but their hearts pursue their own gain." (Ezekiel 33:31) Peter also used the word '*anupokritos*' in reference to love. "Since you have purified your souls in obeying the truth through the Spirit in **sincere** love of the brethren, love one another fervently with a pure heart." (1 Peter 1:22) The point is that we cannot love one another in sincerity unless the Holy Spirit has purified our hearts of our old religious flesh!

Paul also used the word '*anupokritos*' in the context of faith. "Now the purpose of the commandment is love from a pure heart, from a good conscience, and *from sincere faith* from which some, having strayed, have turned aside to idle talk." (1 Timothy 1:5) The KJV used the term "faith unfeigned," implying that the 'faith' of some people is a mere pretense that consisted of idle talk instead of a heart that trusted unswervingly in God. This is a life of merely talking the talk rather than walking the walk. Joshua said to the Israelites, "Now therefore, fear the Lord, serve Him **in sincerity and in truth**, and put away the gods which your fathers served on the other side of the River and in Egypt." (Joshua 24:14) God could see right through the lack of sincerity in the hearts of His people, even though His name was continually on their lips. "They do not cry out to me with sincere hearts. Instead, they sit on their couches and wail. They cut themselves, begging foreign gods for crops and prosperity." (Hosea 7:14 NLT)

The Scriptures confront us with the choice between a life of hypocrisy or a life of sincerity. Everything we do as Christians must be done with 'sincerity of heart.' "Bondservants, obey in all things your masters according to the flesh, not with eye-service, as men-pleasers, but in **sincerity of heart**, fearing God." (Colossians 3:22) "Let us draw near to God with **a sincere heart** in full assurance of faith, having our hearts sprinkled to cleanse us from a guilty conscience." (Hebrews 10:22 NIV) True sincerity before God does not take into consideration the opinions and the esteem of men. John talked about those who "loved the praise of men more than the praise of God." (John 12:43) Sincerity of heart is lived out before an audience of One. Paul talked about "those who brag about having a spectacular ministry rather than having **a sincere heart** before God." (2 Corinthians 5:12 NLT) As long as believers are focused upon 'their spectacular ministry' they still have their eyes on the opinions of man. Jesus said they have their reward: the praise of man!

Those who have a sincere heart before God are not concerned about their reputation. Respectability and the praises of men should be the furthest thing from our minds. Paul taught that, "Jesus made himself of no reputation." (Philippians 2:7) "He had no beauty or majesty to attract us to Him, nothing in His appearance that we should desire Him." (Isaiah 53:2 NIV) Jesus was so focused upon the heart that he was unconcerned with the need to cultivate an appearance of spirituality. If we would follow after Him we should not be concerned with outward appearance. "You should be known for the beauty that comes from within, the unfading beauty of a gentle and quiet spirit, which is so precious to God." (1 Peter 3:4 NLT)

Jesus was completely sincere and without any trace of hypocrisy. Peter quotes from Isaiah 53:9 when he tells us that Jesus "did no sin, neither was guile found in his mouth." (1 Peter 2:22 KJV) The Greek word used for guile was '*dolos*,' which means 'a bait, a snare, a deception or a decoy.' '*Dolos*' describes the use of words to create a smoke screen in order to cover something up. Peter's point was that Jesus was completely free of subterfuge. He had nothing to conceal because He had no sin. Peter counsels us to lay aside "all *guile* and hypocrisies." (1 Peter 2:1 KJV) These two things go hand in hand because play-acting necessitates the use of decoys and subterfuge to convince the audience that we really are the person we are pretending to be.

Peter's purpose in quoting Isaiah 53:9 was to present Christ as an example "that you should follow in His steps." (1 Peter 2:21 NIV) Guile describes a particular skill and cleverness in tricking people. It is a cunning, deceitful form of behavior. To be free of guile is not an unattainable goal. Jesus commended Nathanael, saying, "Behold, an Israelite indeed, in whom is no guile (*dolos*)!" (John 1:47 KJV) Sincerity of heart simply describes the absence of guile, deceit and hypocrisy. It is a quality of heart that humbly embraces the truth about ourselves and does not attempt to cover up our brokenness and our sin.

Paul urged believers to celebrate "Christ, our Passover," with "the unleavened bread of *sincerity* and truth." (1 Corinthians 5:8) If we would renounce the leaven of guile and hypocrisy and embrace the truth with a sincere heart, God will begin to truly transform our hearts. Paul concluded his letter to the

Ephesians by saying; "Grace be with all those who love our Lord Jesus Christ *in sincerity*." (Ephesians 6:24) Sincerity of heart is the gateway to the outpouring of the grace of God in our lives. "God resists the proud but gives grace to the humble." (James 4:6) In the Word of God, pride is the root of hypocrisy whilst humility is the root of sincerity. It was in the context of His eight-fold denunciation of the Scribes and Pharisees in Matthew 23 that Jesus said,

> Whoever exalts himself will be humbled, and he who humbles himself will be exalted. But woe to you, scribes and Pharisees, hypocrites! For you shut up the kingdom of heaven against men; for you neither go in yourselves, nor do you allow those who are entering to go in. (Matthew 23:12,13)

It is only the pride of our old nature and its obsession with outward appearance that prevents us from entering into true life in the kingdom. The Scriptures make it clear that God actively resists those who are proud in their hearts. In contrast, God promises throughout His Word to bless and enlarge the hearts of the humble. "For the Lord takes pleasure in His people; He will beautify the humble with salvation." (Psalms 149:4) "I will bless those who have humble and contrite hearts; who tremble at My word." (Isaiah 66:2 NLT) Jesus befriends the humble but keeps His distance from the proud. "Though the Lord is on high, yet He regards the lowly; but the proud He knows from afar." (Psalms 138:6) The proud hearted never taste true spiritual intimacy with Christ!

> For thus says the High and Lofty One who inhabits eternity, whose name is Holy: "I dwell in the high and holy place, with him who has a contrite and humble spirit, to revive the spirit of the humble, and to revive the heart of the contrite ones." (Isaiah 57:15)

Every attempt to proudly establish our own righteousness brings us under a powerful yoke of bondage. Graham Cooke nailed it when he said; "We are all Pharisees being healed." The pursuit of true humility and sincerity of heart is the only way to disentangle ourselves from religion and the tree of the knowledge of good and evil. This is one of the greatest strongholds that keeps the church in bondage to the flesh. God has to penetrate the veil of religion in order to usher us into a life of authenticity and of living humbly from the heart. This is a journey that every believer in Christ must travel if they truly want to be free. The stronghold of religion is stronger in some Christians than in others but it is a stronghold that has to be demolished in the life of every true follower of Christ regardless of the degree to which it has influenced our lives.

I want to commend the contents of this chapter to every reader with the prayer that they will take this word to heart and actively pursue the dismantling of this pernicious stronghold that holds so many believers back from a true life of radical freedom and joy. This is fundamental to the heart journey that Jesus calls us to. Orphans live out of religion but sons live a life of sincerity and authenticity before their Father. I have been on a long journey out of the bondage of religion and after all these years I still feel my own propensity to lapse back into falsehood and hypocrisy. This is a huge stronghold for many Christians but God is able to comprehensively disentangle us from religion and every attempt of the flesh to be good in order to overcome evil. Those who overcome the entanglement of the tree of the knowledge of good and evil will get to enjoy the supreme privilege of feasting from the Tree of Life in the midst of the Paradise of God.

There is hope for every believer, no matter how entangled in religion they have become. God will show us the path to freedom if we will humble ourselves and deal ruthlessly with the stronghold of religion. Jesus came to set the captives free and to disentangle us from everything that would hold us back from the new life He has implanted in our regenerated spirit. God is tenaciously committed to bringing us into a life of tremendous fruitfulness as we learn how to abide in His finished work.

Chapter Eleven

Entangled in Emotional Brokenness

"The cords of death entangled me; the anguish of the grave came upon me; I was overcome by trouble and sorrow." (Psalms 116:3 NIV)

If all of the pain in the entire world resulting from the brokenness of the human condition could somehow be quantified, I think we would all be utterly astonished. Oceans of tears have been wept because of the pain and suffering felt by billions who have suffered terribly on account of humanity's deep descent into sin. We live in a world of sorrow and deep emotional pain and God has witnessed all of the suffering that humanity has collectively endured as a consequence of our inhumanity toward one another.

For decades the Lord observed the sufferings of Israel at the hand of Pharaoh's harsh oppression. "I have surely seen the affliction of My people who are in Egypt and have given heed to their cry because of their taskmasters, for I am aware of their sufferings." (Exodus 3:7 NASB) Israel was collectively, God's adoptive son, and more than being aware of their suffering, He felt the pain of His people. He said of His chosen people; "He who touches you touches the apple or pupil of His eye." (Zechariah 2:8 AMP) "For the Lord's portion is His people; Jacob is the allotment of His inheritance. He found him in a desert land, and in the howling waste of a wilderness; He encircled him, He cared for him, He guarded him as the pupil of His eye." (Deuteronomy 32:9,10 NASB)

Just as the Lord witnessed and felt the horrors of Israel's harsh oppression so He looks down on a 21st century world filled with the same kind of suffering and oppression. "The Lord looked down from His sanctuary on high; from heaven He viewed the earth to hear the groans of the prisoners." (Psalm 102:19 NIV) Not a tear falls without God seeing it and feeling it. Our Father in heaven is intimately acquainted with all of our suffering and grief. He weeps with those who weep. David prayed; "You keep track of all my sorrows. You have collected all my tears in your bottle. You have recorded each one in your book." (Psalm 56:8 NLT)

The day will finally come when "God will wipe away every tear from their eyes; there shall be no more death, nor sorrow, nor crying. *There shall be no more pain*, for the former things have passed away." (Revelation 21:4) But until that day comes there shall be pain and indeed, that pain is one of the defining characteristics of the human race in its descent into sin and the subsequent deep emotional brokenness that always accompanies the presence of sin. The cry of the broken and the oppressed ascends to our loving Father from the four corners of the earth and He is filled with compassion for those who suffer under the tyranny of sin.

It was for this reason that Jesus came into the world with a specific mandate from the Father to heal broken hearts. From heaven's perspective, the condition of 'brokenheartedness' is a form of spiritual bondage because it locks people into a prison of negative and destructive emotions. This spiritual condition can exercise considerable power over the soul from which many find no escape or relief. Our ongoing entanglement in these negative and destructive emotions systematically erodes our spiritual wellbeing and it yields a harvest of spiritual death within the soul. Intense feelings of heightened emotional pain and distress drag people downward, imprisoning them in a dark place where they can feel completely overwhelmed.

Jesus came to impart the fullness of His life to every part of our being, especially to our emotional life. But to the extent that we are overcome by negative and destructive emotions such as fear, shame, rejection, depression or bitterness, to that extent we are held fast by what David called the 'cords of death.' Only the power of the Father's healing love can deliver us from the power of everything that locks us into a state of spiritual death within our souls. Broken emotions are never life-giving.

David was no stranger to deep emotional pain and heartache. He wrote in his prayer journal; "I am afflicted and in pain!" (Psalm 69:29 NASB) "I am worn out from groaning; all night long I flood my bed with weeping and drench my couch with tears." (Psalm 6:6 NIV) Before he became king, David had been relentlessly pursued by King Saul who was intent on murdering him. The fear of death gripped David's soul and he was completely overwhelmed by the terror of impending doom. Each morning he awoke wondering if it would be his last. In his mortal fear he said, "The cords of death *entangled me* and the torrents of ungodliness terrified me." (Psalms 18:4 NIV/NASB)

In a parallel passage David said, "The cords of death *entangled me*; the anguish of the grave came upon me; I was *overcome by trouble and sorrow.*" (Psalms 116:3 NIV) Understandably, David found himself deeply entangled in emotions over which he felt he had no control. He recognized that he was entangled in fear and deep anguish of soul and that the Lord was His only hope. His solution was to call upon the Lord. "In my distress I called to the Lord; I cried to my God for help. He reached down from on high and took hold of me; He drew me out of deep waters." (Psalm 18:6,16 NIV)

Whenever negative emotions dominate our soul we are entangled in the cords of death. God's plan of redemption is for the life of Jesus to permeate and govern our emotions but when negative and destructive emotions rule in our heart it brings forth a harvest of death. Our entanglement in emotional brokenness is just as much an entanglement as our entanglement in sin, selfishness, worldliness or religion. If emotional pain serves any useful purpose in this life it is to drive us into the arms of our loving heavenly Father. Paul revealed that there are two ways to endure pain on this planet; either we process our pain in the context on an intimate relationship with our loving Father or we seek to overcome it in our own strength and in a state of independence from God. "For *godly sorrow* produces repentance leading to salvation, not to be regretted; but *the sorrow of the world* produces death." (2 Corinthians 7:10) Paul identified two kinds of sorrow: a godly sorrow and a worldly sorrow. This represents two fundamentally different approaches of dealing with emotional pain. The Amplified Bible really explains the mechanism of godly sorrow and of worldly sorrow.

> For *godly grief* and *the pain God is permitted to direct*, produces a repentance that leads and contributes to salvation and deliverance from evil, and it never brings regret; but *worldly grief* (the hopeless sorrow that is characteristic of the pagan world) is deadly [breeding and ending in death]." (2 Cor. 7:6-10 AMP)

Worldly sorrow leaves us wallowing in self-pity, which results in an entanglement in the cords of death. There is no life in an entanglement in negative and destructive emotions. But consider this profound statement: *'the pain God is permitted to direct!'* Which way will God direct our pain when we submit to Him in the midst of our pain? As beloved sons and daughters we ought to yield to the Holy Spirit and allow Him to lead us to the Father with our pain. When we come to the Father with our pain and process it with Him we practice the art of casting all our cares and burdens upon Him. But if we resist the leading of the Spirit we are at risk of falling into the temptation of seeking to resolve our inner pain through our own misguided wisdom. Those who fail to bring their pain to the Father will always seek to soothe their pain by seeking comfort in the world. If we are feeling overwhelmed by the entangling cords of death we should follow David's example in the Psalms. "In my distress I called to the Lord; I cried to my God for help." (Psalm 18:6) "When my heart is overwhelmed; lead me to the rock that is higher than I." (Ps. 61:2) The Message Bible is even clearer in its explanation of these two contrasting modes of resolving the distress of deep emotional pain.

> Let the distress **bring you to God, not drive you from Him**. Distress that drives us to God does that. It turns us around. It gets us back in the way of salvation. **We never regret that kind of pain**. But those who let distress **drive them away from God** are full of regrets, and end up on a deathbed of regrets." (2 Corinthians 7:9,10 MSG)

God wants to shower deep spiritual comfort upon the hearts of His beloved sons and daughters whenever they are in pain.

> Now may our Lord Jesus Christ Himself and God our Father, who loved us and by His grace gave us eternal **comfort** and a wonderful hope, **comfort you** and strengthen you in every good thing you do and say. (2 Thessalonians 2:16,17 NLT)

The Father's answer to the pain and suffering of this world is His deep comfort. The Father, the Son and the Holy Spirit are in a divine conspiracy to comfort every heart that suffers. The Father sent Jesus into the world with an explicit mandate to comfort all who mourn.

> The Spirit of the Lord God is upon Me because the Lord has anointed Me to preach good tidings to the poor; He has sent Me to **heal the brokenhearted** to proclaim liberty to the captives and the opening of the prison to those who are bound; to proclaim the year of the Lord's favor and the day of vengeance of our God; **to comfort all who mourn, to console those who mourn in Zion, to give them beauty**

for ashes, the oil of joy for mourning, the garment of praise for the spirit of heaviness; that they may be called trees of righteousness; the planting of the Lord, that He may be glorified. (Isaiah 61:1-3)

One of the great signs of the coming of the kingdom was the appearance of the Messiah who came to love the outcasts and to heal all of their wounds. "The Lord builds up Jerusalem; He gathers together the **outcasts** of Israel. He heals the brokenhearted and binds up their wounds." (Psalms 147:2,3) The Beatitudes are pronouncements of great blessings for those who receive the Kingdom of Heaven.

Blessed are the poor in spirit for theirs is the kingdom of heaven. ***Blessed are those who mourn for they shall be comforted.*** Blessed are the meek for they shall inherit the earth. Blessed are those who hunger and thirst for righteousness for they shall be filled. Blessed are the merciful for they shall obtain mercy. Blessed are the pure in heart for they shall see God. (Matthew 5:3-8)

Jesus specifically promised that those who were in the grip of deep emotional pain would experience the comfort of the Father if they were willing to come to Him with their pain. The Father who continually observes the deep suffering of humanity sent His Son with a mandate to comfort every single person who was suffering deep pain and anguish of heart. Did you know that one of Jesus' divine titles is the 'Comforter?' Luke wrote: "And behold, there was a man in Jerusalem whose name was Simeon, and this man was just and devout, waiting for the **Consolation of Israel**." (Luke 2:25) The Greek word for 'consolation' is *'paraklesis'* which means 'comfort' or 'Comforter.' This would explain why the Holy Spirit is called *'another'* comforter. "And I will ask the Father and He shall give you *another* Comforter, to be with you forever; the Spirit of truth." (John 14:16) The Father gave His Son a glorious mandate: "Comfort, yes, comfort My people!" (Isaiah 40:1) Ten verses later we read; "He will feed His flock like a shepherd. He will carry the lambs in His arms, holding them close to His heart." (Isaiah 40:11 NLT)

"When Jesus saw the multitudes He was moved with compassion for them, because they were weary [***distressed and ready to faint***] and scattered [***cast out***], like sheep having no shepherd." (Matthew 9:36) God's love is powerfully expressed in the heart of the Good Shepherd who was sent to gently nurse and heal the lost sheep of the house of Israel. One of the great signs of the coming of the kingdom was that God sent Jesus to comfort all who mourn. But He can only comfort those who turn to Him to receive His comfort in all of their pain. After Jesus pronounced the beatitudes He pronounced a series of 'woes' for those who chose to reject the coming kingdom. "Woe to you who are rich, for you are receiving your **comfort** [*paraklesis*] in full. Woe to you who are well fed now, for you shall be hungry. Woe to you who laugh now, for you shall **mourn** and weep." (Luke 6:24,25 NASB) These woes are juxtaposed against the beatitudes. Those who reject the kingdom seek their comfort in the world but their celebration of affluence which they used to insulate themselves against the suffering of this world will ultimately end in mourning because they refused the comfort of the Father.

The Suffering Messiah

One of the great mysteries of the incarnation of Christ was His willingness to be immersed into the full suffering of humanity. To become fully man meant that He had to be subjected to the pain that humanity carries as a consequence of the fall. The writer of Hebrews observed that;

> In all things He had to be made like His brethren that He might be a merciful and faithful High Priest in things pertaining to God, to make propitiation for the sins of the people. For in that He Himself has suffered, being tempted, He is able to aid those who are tempted. (Hebrews 2:17,18)

Jesus was the suffering Messiah! *The Message* says that Jesus entered into "every detail of human life. He would have experienced it all Himself – **all the pain**, all the testing!" (Hebrews 2:17,18) Isaiah declared prophetically that Jesus was a "man of sorrows" who suffered great emotional pain.

> He was **despised** and **rejected** – **a man of sorrows**, acquainted with the **bitterest grief**. We turned our backs on Him and looked the other way when He went by. He was **despised**, and we did not care. (Isaiah 53:3 NLT)

Again, *The Message* says, "He was a man who suffered, **who knew pain firsthand**. One look at Him and people turned away." (Isaiah 53:3 MSG) The Father sent His Beloved Son into a world full of intense pain knowing that He would endure great emotional agony. "He came to His own, and those who were His own did not receive Him." (John 1:11) "The stone which the builders *rejected* has become the chief cornerstone." (Psalms 118:22) Jesus was intensely hated, violently persecuted and ultimately murdered. He was the object of numerous assassination plots. Throughout His entire ministry Jesus endured deep hatred at the hands of people who were under the grip of demonic power.

> Anyone who hates Me hates My Father, too. They saw all that I did and yet hated both of us; Me and My Father. This has fulfilled what the Scriptures said: "They hated Me without cause." (John 15:23-25 NLT)

When He finally fell into the hands of His enemies he was viciously beaten, scourged, flogged, spat upon, sexually abused, mocked and brutally slain by being nailed to a cross. Did you know that Jesus was sexually abused by being hung naked as a public spectacle? How did Jesus endure such intense suffering throughout His three years of ministry? The only way He could keep pouring out the comfort of the Father was because He Himself was living in the comfort of the Father. Jesus walked through this world in intimate fellowship with His Father; continually sharing His pain with His loving Father. His pain became His Father's pain because they were 'one!' The Father weeps with those who weep. He grieves with those who grieve. The Father willingly entered into Jesus' pain and they willingly enter into our pain. Jesus endured excruciating agony and pain but He endured it *inside the heart of His Father* who continuously ministered deep comfort to His heart. Jesus was never cut off from the comfort of the Father except in that final hour when He died upon the cross. "And about the ninth hour Jesus cried out with a loud voice, saying, "Eli, Eli, lama sabachthani?" that is, "My God, My God, why have You forsaken Me?" (Matthew 27:46)

Remarkably, Jesus was a profoundly joyful person even in the midst of the intense pain of persecution that characterized the three years of His ministry. Luke tells us that, "Jesus was filled with the joy of the Holy Spirit!" (Luke 10:21 NLT) How is it that the man of sorrows could be simultaneously filled with joy in the midst of His pain? It was because He knew the deepest source of comfort and love in the universe! It is as though He said, "My Father loves Me and He is always present to comfort all who mourn. He pours out upon Me the oil of joy for mourning!" The writer of Hebrews says concerning Jesus: "You love justice and hate evil. Therefore, O God, your God has anointed you, pouring out the oil of joy on You more than on anyone else." (Hebrews 1:9 NLT)

Pain is a fact of life in this world. Jesus warned us; "In the world you will have tribulation." (John 16:33) Tribulation is 'suffering, sorrow, troubles or anguish of heart.' Because we are human beings living in a deeply fallen world we will always be in a level of pain and anguish of heart in this life. We experience pain in this world from a myriad of sources. It is as though pain keeps coming at us from the outer world and rises up within our interior world. All of us at various times experience:

- The pain of broken or difficult relationships.
- The pain of wounding or abuse.
- The pain that comes from deep unmet needs.
- The pain of persecution or rejection.
- The pain of our own sinful choices and personal brokenness.
- The pain of loneliness.
- The pain of the loss of a loved one.
- The pain of financial hardship.

In this world God has called us to live in the place of Christ: in the intersection of the extremes of the Father's love and the extremes of human brokenness. The cross is the ultimate picture of the pain of living in the intersection of ultimate love and ultimate human brokenness! Ultimate pain and ultimate love collide at the cross! There is a unique pain experienced by every believer who has come to know the heart of the heavenly Father; he or she has come to experientially know the intensity of the love of God in a world full of loneliness, heartbreak and pain. A song by Bruce Cockburn captures this sense of pain endured by those who have come to know the God of all hope. "I've seen the flame of hope among the hopeless; and that was truly the biggest heartbreak of all. That was the straw that broke me open!"[41] As we have seen, pain and suffering that is experienced outside of the Father's love produces deeper and deeper despair and ultimately spiritual death, but pain that is shared with our Father produces spiritual life and leads us into a participation in the supernatural joy of Jesus. "These things I have spoken to you, that My joy may remain in you, and that your joy may be full." (John 15:11)

As faithful followers of Jesus we will surely suffer in this life. Jesus said, "If they persecuted Me, they will also persecute you." (John 15:20) Peter said, "If you suffer for doing good and you endure it, this is commendable before God.

This suffering is all part of what God has called you to. Christ, who suffered for you, is your example, that you should follow in His steps." (1 Peter 2:20,21 NIV/NLT) Paul said, "For you have been given not only the privilege of trusting in Christ but also the privilege of suffering for Him. We are in this struggle together. You have seen my struggle in the past, and you know that I am still in the midst of it." (Philippians 1:29,30 NLT) The Greek word Paul used for 'struggle' was '*agon*' from which we derive the word 'agony.' It is a deep inner struggle or agony of soul as we live in the intersection of the intensity of divine love and the intensity of earthly sorrow and pain. Jesus said, "If the world hates you, you know that it hated Me before it hated you. If you were of the world, the world would love its own. Yet because you are not of the world, but I chose you out of the world, therefore the world hates you." (John 15:18-19)

Christians are called to view the extremes of human brokenness through the lens of the Father's love and to view the extremes of the Father's love through the lens of deep human brokenness. The cross brings these two realities together. When we behold Jesus dying on the cross we gaze upon the greatest evil and the greatest love in history expressed in the ultimate collision of the powers of heaven and of hell. We are called to live at the foot of the cross and this will inevitably lead us to live in the ultimate pain of the extremes of love and evil, of goodness and human brokenness and of heaven in direct collision with hell. This is right where Jesus lives as He continues to endure the rejection of an ungodly world. And this is where we are called to live; in the intersection of the agony and the ecstasy. But there is a place God is calling us to where we walk through the valley of the shadow of death as Jesus walked; where we experience pain and suffering but we are not overcome by negative and destructive emotions that lead us into the cords of death. Jesus suffered but He was never overcome by dark and destructive feelings. We can only walk this spiritual tightrope if our hearts are continually being healed by the experiential love of the Father.

Negative and Destructive Emotions

Having feelings or emotions is a significant part of being made in the image of God. God has emotions and so do we, but our emotions can be deeply damaged and when they are damaged they can become quite destructive. Larry Crabb discusses the concept of constructive and destructive emotions.

Exactly what makes an emotion constructive or destructive? Constructive or destructive of what? The place to begin is to recognize that some emotions seem to interfere with what people should do – namely, love God and others – and may on that basis be labeled destructive. Other emotions encourage our loving movement toward God and others and are therefore constructive. They facilitate our functioning in the way our Maker intended. Feelings, whether pleasant or unpleasant, should be evaluated to determine whether they are constructive or destructive.   Whether an emotion is constructive or destructive depends not on what happens to us but on how we internally respond to whatever happens. Events determine whether we feel pleasant or unpleasant emotions, but we determine whether our feelings are constructive or destructive. The presence of destructive emotions indicates that there is a problem within us. [42]

Jesus suffered great emotional pain but He never descended into negative or destructive emotions. As a consequence of living in a fallen world all of us inevitably become entangled in negative and destructive emotions that have the potential to overwhelm us. But Jesus came as the only one who could truly heal our hearts and deliver us from the power of these destructive emotions. Only our first-hand engagement with the love of the Father can comprehensively break our entanglement in negative and toxic emotions. At the commencement of His ministry Jesus returned to His hometown of Nazareth and entered the local Synagogue. In His first public sermon Jesus read the following words from the scroll of the prophet Isaiah;

> The Spirit of the Lord is upon me, because He has anointed me to preach the gospel to the poor.   He has sent me to *heal the brokenhearted*, to preach deliverance to the captives and recovery of sight to the blind, to set at liberty *those who are bruised* and to proclaim the year of the Lord's favor. (Luke 4:18,19)

Immediately after Jesus finished reading this passage of Scripture Luke tells us that, "the eyes of all who were in the synagogue were fixed on Him and He began to say to them, "Today this Scripture is fulfilled in your hearing." (Luke 4:20,21) This was a defining moment in human history because with the reading of this ancient prophecy, Jesus proclaimed that the time of its fulfilment had finally arrived and that He was the One who had come to fulfil it. This verse, more than any other in the gospel narratives, defines the very essence of the kingdom ministry of Jesus. In this heavenly 'kingdom ministry mandate' we discover that healing the brokenhearted is as much a part of the ministry of the kingdom as preaching the gospel and praying for the sick. Healing a "broken heart" is a form of *inner healing* in contrast to the outer healing of the body. Historically there has been a tremendous lack of revelation concerning this extraordinary aspect of the kingdom ministry of Jesus. Up until the late 20th Century virtually nothing had been written on this theme and to this day only a handful of authors have written any kind of in-depth treatment on this subject.

Evangelicals have traditionally viewed the entire concept of inner healing with a great deal of suspicion. It is widely believed amongst many conservative Evangelicals that inner healing is just one of a number of troublesome expressions of the infiltration of New Age or secular psychotherapeutic ideas or practices into the church. A number of popular books were written in the 1980's that denounced this type of ministry, which served only to consolidate the perception that the practice was unbiblical and perhaps even dangerous. One of the chief reasons that so many Christians have rejected the entire concept of inner healing is because a number of concepts that reflect certain New Age practices or secular psychotherapeutic models have indeed crept into the church under the banner of inner healing. Subsequently the entire concept of inner healing has been widely rejected or viewed with suspicion. But as we explore the Scriptures that relate to this theme it will become quite apparent that by and large the church has 'thrown the baby out with the bath water.' The idea of healing the brokenhearted is a significant theological theme in the tapestry of radical kingdom ministry.

This widespread rejection of the concept of inner healing has been a great disaster for the church because, as we have seen from the above quote from Luke chapter 4, the ministry of healing the brokenhearted is one of the centerpieces of kingdom ministry. Not only has this lack of spiritual revelation into the nature of Christ's ministry deprived the church of this ministry to their own hearts, it has also prevented the church from learning to work with Jesus in extending this aspect of His kingdom ministry throughout the earth. This is a deep vein of divine revelation designed to lead us into a rich experience of the healing love of the Father to transform us from emotional orphans into contented sons and daughters.

The church's widespread ignorance of the fullness of the ministry of Christ is reminiscent of the religious men in Jesus' day who were the custodians of divine truth. "How terrible it will be for you experts in religious law! For you hide the key to knowledge from the people. You don't enter the Kingdom yourselves, and you prevent others from entering." (Luke 11:52 NLT) According to Paul the nation of Israel had been "entrusted with the whole revelation of God," (Romans 3:2 NLT) but they themselves did not have eyes to see what God was offering them. Satan works feverishly to blind our eyes to the ministry of Christ in order to hinder our reception of the fullness of His ministry into our hearts. Jesus Christ is a wellspring of spiritual healing for all the nations and Satan rubs his hands together in glee to see the widespread blindness of the church to this single biblical revelation. There is still so much that we do not see or understand about the supernatural kingdom ministry of Christ. Jesus said,

> Seeing they do not see, and hearing they do not hear, nor do they understand. And in them the prophecy of Isaiah is fulfilled, which says: 'Hearing you will hear and shall not understand and seeing you will see and not perceive; for the hearts of this people have grown dull. Their ears are hard of hearing, and their eyes they have closed, lest they should see with their eyes and hear with their ears, lest they should understand with their hearts and turn, so that I should *heal* them. (Matthew 13:13-15)

Because of the deep emotional brokenness within the church there is an urgent need to develop a purely biblical theology of inner healing that does not step outside of the parameters of biblical orthodoxy. If we can see this ministry in the Word of God we will feel safe to receive the fullness of this glorious ministry of Jesus as He seeks to reach into our hearts to heal all of the broken places. The essence of this supernatural ministry of Jesus is the systematic demolition of every stronghold of negative and destructive emotions that wrap themselves around our hearts like the cords of death. There is simply no way that we can walk as Jesus walked through the valley of the shadow of death without being overcome by negative and destructive emotions unless we receive the comforting love of our Heavenly Father. Only as we receive His healing love can we come to a place of emotional health so that we can truly walk in love as Jesus walked. Destructive emotions are absolute killers of the life of love because they push us into a place of fear and emotional self-protection and this is the very antithesis of love.

As I have grown in an understanding and appreciation of Pauline theology over the past three decades I have come to see that Paul moved powerfully in an inner healing anointing. He established a familial framework of the Father and His family of beloved sons and daughters and he pioneered an apostolic paradigm of deep heart transformation in unveiling our journey from being orphans to becoming true sons and daughters of a loving Father. Paul placed an extraordinary emphasis upon growing in love with God and with our brothers and sisters in community. He left us to figure out how to walk out this journey in relationship with one another but he very deliberately laced his teachings with a rich language of the heart.

In the body of his extant written material Paul used the term 'heart' more than all of the references to the heart in the four gospels combined. He spoke of the 'heart' or 'hearts' a total of 59 times. As an author of Scripture Paul was second only to Solomon who used the term 'heart' 130 times. Paul's choice of words often centered around themes of inner healing. I was so fascinated by Paul's use of words that I did an analysis of the words he used. In each case, when I list a word I am also including all of the cognates of that word. For example Paul spoke of love and its cognates (loved, beloved, loves etc.) a total of 144 times. He referenced forgiveness (12x), hope (47x), joy and rejoicing (57x), peace (46x), gentleness (8x), patience (13x), kindness (9x), fear (21x), shame (27x), jealousy, (6x), anger (4x), bitterness (3x), lust (17x), pride (5x), comfort (25x), distress (5x), despair (2x), downcast (1x) grief (5x), mourning (2x) and sorrow (20x). These are all powerful components in the discussion of our emotional transformation. Paul had really taken to heart Jesus' call to heal the brokenhearted!

In writing this chapter I have chosen not to import concepts or terminology from secular psychotherapeutic paradigms of emotional healing. As a non-integrationist I am committed to opening up the Scriptures in order to build a sound theological framework that invites people into the safety of Jesus' kingdom ministry. Conservative Evangelicals may be surprised by the degree to which a sound biblical theology of inner healing may be constructed exclusively from the Scriptures. For centuries the church has not had a clear revelation of the nature of this aspect of Christ's ministry and as a result most Christians have not sought to minister in this arena at all. But we are living in a time when God is unveiling the fullness of the glorious ministry of Jesus Christ and many in the church are subsequently beginning to do the same works that Jesus Himself did.

The ministry of Christ in healing the brokenhearted needs to be understood as an aspect of the restoration of our souls and of our conformity to the image of Christ. The concept of restoration means to bring something back to its original state either by repairing or rebuilding. Central to this whole project of restoring our souls is the issue of the broken condition of the human heart and the quest for personal wholeness. Scripture and indeed all of human experience make it painfully clear that the heart of humanity is seriously and 'incurably' broken. Jeremiah reminds us that the heart of fallen humanity is "deceitful above all things and *incurably* sick." (Jeremiah 17:9) Jeremiah had encounter the healing love of God and said, "For the brokenness of the daughter of my people I am broken; I mourn, dismay has taken hold of me!" (Jeremiah 8:21 NASB) Jeremiah lamented that even the prophets and priests had failed to deliver the mandate of the Father to heal the brokenness of the hearts of God's people. "They have healed the brokenness of My people superficially, saying, 'Peace, peace,' but there is no peace." (Jeremiah 6:14 NASB)

Apart from significant divine intervention we have no more hope of cleansing and healing the brokenness of our hearts than the leopard has of changing its spots! (Jeremiah 13:23) But Jesus came, not only to make us holy but also to make us *whole*. Paul wrote to the Ephesians, "Long before He laid down earth's foundations, He had us in mind, [He] had settled on us as the focus of His love, to be made *whole and holy* by His love." (Ephesians 1:4 MSG) If we will allow Jesus to do in our hearts all that He desires to do we will experience a gradual process of being made whole in our emotions. Jesus longs to make the broken heart whole again. He desires to deliver us from the power of every negative and destructive emotion that threatens to overcome our soul.

The Broken Heart

It is vital that we understand the language of Scripture as it reveals the heart of our Father toward us. The term 'brokenhearted' in Luke 4:18 is derived from a combination of two Greek words; *'suntribo'* and *'kardia.'* Interestingly, *'suntribo'* is also used in Luke 9:39 to describe physical 'bruising.'[43] In light of this, a 'broken' heart may also be described as a 'bruised' heart. In contrast to physical bruising *'suntribo'* is also used in a spiritual sense in Matthew 12:20 where we read, "a *bruised* reed He [Christ] will nor break." Jesus ministers gently to those who have been bruised and hurt by the harsh experiences of life. *'Suntribo'* is also the word used by Paul in Romans 16:20

where he said; "And the God of peace will *crush* Satan under your feet shortly." Thayer, in his Greek Lexicon, tells us that the term 'brokenhearted' in Luke 4:18 means 'to suffer extreme sorrow and to be, as it were, crushed.' The term is descriptive of a heart that has been bruised, wounded or crushed by the harsh and oppressive treatment of others. David said, "For I am afflicted and needy, and my heart is wounded within me." (Psalm 109:22 NASB) Anyone who has endured deep emotional pain knows exactly what it means to be brokenhearted.

Jesus' kingdom mandate in Luke 4:18,19 is a quote directly from Isaiah 61:1,2 where Isaiah prophesied about the Messiah's future ministry. Isaiah also revealed that the Messiah would minister specifically to the "bruised reeds." (Isaiah 42:3) These are the people whose hearts have been bruised, crushed and broken by the sins of others. Healing the brokenhearted is an aspect of the pastoral ministry of Jesus whom Peter described as the "Shepherd and Overseer of our souls." (1 Peter 2:25) The reference to the ministry of healing the brokenhearted in Luke 4 and Isaiah 61 follows immediately after the reference to preaching "the gospel to the poor." This suggests that healing the brokenhearted is a ministry of Christ that is reserved for those who have responded to the gospel. In order of priority, Jesus' ministry to the brokenhearted is secondary to the ministry of the gospel. We can get into heaven with a broken heart but we cannot get into heaven with an unrepentant heart. But once we are saved Jesus then seeks to heal the broken places to make us emotionally whole.

Not only did Jesus Himself heal the brokenhearted but He sought to extend this ministry through those who had received this ministry into their own lives. It is a principle of ministry that we can only give away what God has already given to us. "Freely you have received, freely give." (Matthew 10:8) God rebuked the spiritual shepherds in the Old Testament because of their neglect of this ministry. The shepherds did not minister to the brokenhearted because they had not received this ministry themselves. They were still blind to the true ministry of the Lord. "Woe to the shepherds of Israel who feed themselves! Should not the shepherds feed the flocks? The weak you have not strengthened, nor have you healed those who were sick, nor *bound up the broken*, nor brought back what was driven away, nor sought what was lost." (Ezekiel 34:2-4) The *Message* says they failed to "doctor the injured."

True pastoral ministry ministers love and healing to the hurt and the wounded. "The hurt and crippled you have not bandaged...but with force and hardhearted harshness you have ruled them." (Ezekiel 34:4 AMP) Not only did the shepherds of Israel fail to heal those who were hurting, they contributed to their pain even further by harshly oppressing and abusing them. I have seen churches where the pastors were wounding the sheep with a spirit of control instead of healing their hearts with love. This resembles what Ezekiel prophesied when he indicted the leaders for failing to heal the brokenhearted.

The Hebrew word for 'broken' in this passage in Ezekiel is 'shabar.' It is the same Hebrew word that is used in Isaiah 61:1 where we read that Jesus had come "to bind up the *brokenhearted*." The Hebrew lexicon defines 'shabar' as 'a crushed or shattered heart or emotion.' The pastoral ministry of Jesus, "the great Shepherd of the sheep," (Hebrews 13:20) extends to every sphere of human need; He lovingly ministers to physical, spiritual, mental and emotional needs. Perhaps a better term to describe this aspect of the ministry of Jesus would be 'emotional healing' instead of inner healing. It is a glorious deliverance from every emotional stronghold of negative and destructive emotions.

There are a number of references in the Old Testament to brokenheartedness. In the Psalms we read, "The Lord gathers together the outcasts of Israel. He *heals the brokenhearted* and binds up their *wounds*." (Psalm 147:2,3) The Hebrew word for "*wounds*" is 'assebet' and it means "a pain, a wound or a sorrow." A broken heart is synonymous with a wounded heart. It is the same word that is used in Proverbs 15:13 to describe "sorrow (*assebet*) of the heart." The NIV uses the term; "heartache." In Psalm 34:18 we read, "The Lord is near to those who have a *broken heart*." God is near to those whose hearts have been deeply hurt and wounded. He is moved with compassion for the hurting and troubled heart. David said, "I am afflicted and in pain!" (Psalm 69:29 NASB) *Assebet* is really a synonym for deep emotional pain.

Frequently the words that are employed to describe the broken condition of the human heart are those that are also used to describe physical injuries. In the Scriptures we repeatedly find terms such as "pain, hurt, bruised, afflicted, wounded and crushed" to describe the 'beaten up' condition of the heart. The idea is that just as our physical bodies may be damaged and abused, so too our heart may be damaged by invisible injuries inflicted upon us by Satan, by calamity or by those living under the power of sin. In the Bible these emotional wounds are called 'afflictions.' In the first book of Kings, Solomon stressed the need for each of those who trusted in God to be "aware of" what he called "the *afflictions* of his own heart." (1 Kings 8:38 NIV) A parallel passage in the second book of Chronicles reads;

> When famine or plague comes to the land, or when enemies besiege them in any of their cities, whatever disaster or disease may come and when a prayer or plea is made by any of your people Israel – *each one aware of his afflictions and pains*, and spreading out his hands toward this temple; then hear from heaven, your dwelling place. Forgive, and deal with each man according to all he does, since you know his heart (for you alone know the hearts of men). (2 Chronicles 6:28-30 NIV)

God sees every single wound and affliction inside of every human heart because He sees right into our hearts. But Solomon urged the people of Israel to be personally aware of the afflictions and emotional pain caused by calamity, oppression or disaster. God never wants us to bury the pain. Instead He wants us to bring our pain to Him and share it with Him. The prophet Isaiah described the spiritual condition of the nation of Israel. "Why do you persist in rebellion? Your whole head is sick, *your whole heart afflicted.* From the sole of your foot to the top of your head there is no soundness – only wounds and welts and open sores, not cleansed or bandaged or soothed with oil." (Isaiah 1:5,6 NIV) A broken heart, therefore, is a heart that has been *afflicted* by sin, rebellion or other *external causes* that have crushed the heart.

In Psalm 69:20 David complained that, "Reproach has *broken my heart* and I am full of heaviness." David endured many afflictions in his life but on this occasion he realized that it was the harsh words that were continuously spoken against him by his enemies that had broken his heart. "My heart is stricken and withered like grass...my enemies reproach me all day long." (Psalm 102:4,8). The writers of the Old Testament understood that cruel words have the power to inflict wounds upon the human heart. According to the book of Proverbs, "The tongue has the power of life and death," (Proverbs 18:21 NIV) and "the *words* of a talebearer are as *wounds*." (18:8 KJV) "A lying tongue hates those who are *crushed* by it." (26:28) "There is one who speaks like the piercing of a sword, but the tongue of the wise promotes health." (12:18) David's heart had been crushed and wounded by the reproachful words of his enemies. The tongue can be extremely destructive but in contrast, "Pleasant words are like a honeycomb, sweetness to the soul and health to the bones." (Proverbs 16:24)

Psychologists emphasize the fact that people develop a perception of themselves on the basis of what others say about them. This idea is presented as though it was a 21st century discovery. Yet the book of Proverbs taught nearly 3,000 years ago; "a man is valued by what others say of him." (Proverbs 27:21). One of the primary biblical causes of a wounded heart is the damage that people inflict upon one another through their constant barrage of harsh and critical words. The lack of honor in our culture produces a harvest of deep level emotional brokenness. A child who is raised in an environment of constant reproach and negative criticism will inevitably grow up with a *crushed and wounded heart.* Until the Lord heals his or her heart a wounded child will limp through life with an enormous gaping wound that is invisible to the naked eye but highly visible to our Father who understands and sees the afflictions of the heart.

Unlike Jesus we simply don't know how to deal with these invisible wounds without them becoming infected by negative, destructive feelings. Jesus had a pre-determined plan to release forgiveness to His adversaries straight away and to receive the immediate loving comfort of His Father. That is why He could be the 'Man of sorrows' without descending into an emotional prison of dark and brooding feelings toward His persecutors. He had mastered the art of keeping His heart comprehensively disentangled from negative and destructive feelings of vengefulness, hatred and bitterness because He kept His heart with all diligence. Remarkably, he never crossed that line! "When He was reviled, [He] did not revile in return; when He suffered, He did not threaten, but committed Himself to Him who judges righteously." (1 Peter 2:23)

The Scriptures make it clear that it is within the power of evil people to emotionally and psychologically crush another person. David said "For the enemy has persecuted my soul; he has *crushed* my life to the ground; he has made me dwell in darkness like those who have long been dead. My heart within me is distressed!" (Psalm 143:3,4). The Hebrew word for 'crushed' is '*dakka*' and it means 'bruised or crushed to powder.' The Old Testament writers were deeply aware of the reality of broken heartedness and the language of the wounded heart permeates their writings. David said to the Lord; "Look on my affliction and my pain and forgive all my sins." (Psalms 25:18)

Often when the writers of the Old Testament attempted to describe the stabbing pain of human brokenness they spoke in terms of their *'bones.'* David said, "There is no health in my *bones* because of my sin." (Psalm 38:3) "When I kept silent [about my sin] *my bones* grew old through my groaning all the day long." (Psalm 32:3) The Hebrew word for bones is *'esem.'* In most instances *'esem'* is used in its literal sense to describe physical bones, but according to the *International Standard Bible Encyclopedia*, "very often we find these words used in *metaphorical phrases*, in which a disease or a discomfort of the body denotes certain emotional or mental attitudes."[44] *Vine's Expository Dictionary of Old and New Testament Words* says that the bones, [*esem*] sometimes represent *"the seat of pain."*[45] Proverbs 12:4 says, "An excellent wife is the crown of her husband, but she who causes *shame* is like *rottenness in his bones."* In other words that shame produces deep heartache and emotional pain. The Psalms employ metaphorical language to convey the intense emotional pain associated with a broken heart.

What did David do with his stricken and afflicted heart? He cried out to God to come and *heal it!* "Heal me for my bones are troubled!" (Psalm 6:2) In the midst of intense emotional brokenness he cried out to the Lord and the Lord came and ministered to him. But what if David didn't know the Lord? What would he do with his pain? Millions of unbelievers throughout history have been subjected to even greater abuse and trauma than David. What can they do with their pain? In most instances the invisible unhealed wounds of their hearts inevitably fester into gangrenous sores, as they are swept into a deepening vortex of their wounding and pain.

Many people become so completely overwhelmed by these destructive emotions that they commit suicide in an attempt to find some relief from the anguish and inner torment of their soul. But David experienced genuine healing for his emotional pain through his experience of the love of God. He confidently proclaimed that the Good Shepherd 'restores my soul.' (Psalm 23:3)

Oppression and Abuse

A parallel idea to being crushed and afflicted is that of being 'oppressed.' In Jesus' kingdom mandate He also said that part of His ministry was to "set at liberty them that are *bruised."* (Luke 4:18) The NIV translates this as "releasing the oppressed." The Greek word for 'bruised' is *'thrauo'* and it means to be "broken in pieces, to be shattered or to be broken down." The Amplified Bible specifically says that it is part of the ministry of Jesus to "set at liberty those who are downtrodden, bruised, crushed and broken down by calamity." Again 'bruised' describes the heart condition of the person who has suffered calamity as a result of someone else's sin. As we have already seen, it was prophesied of Jesus that, "a *bruised* reed He will not break," (Isaiah 42:3) suggesting that it was His heart to set free those who have been bruised through their exposure to living in the midst of sin. The best word in our contemporary language to describe this kind of oppression is the word 'abused.' Jesus came to release people from the pain of having been abused!

In Isaiah 58:6 we read, "Is this not the fast that I have chosen; to loose the chains of injustice; to undo the heavy burdens and to let the *oppressed* go free." The Hebrew word used here for 'oppressed' is *'rasas'* and it means, "broken, crushed, bruised or smashed to pieces." It is not surprising that the Greek version of the Old Testament, the Septuagint, used the Greek word *'thrauo'* [i.e. 'bruised' Luke 4:18] to translate the Hebrew word *'rasas'* as it corresponded perfectly. *'Rasas'* occurs 19 times in the Old Testament. For example it occurs in 2 Kings 23:12 where we read about the altars of foreign gods that had been "broken down and pulverized" during King Josiah's sweeping reforms.

When *'rasas'* is used in reference to the heart it describes the consequence of living under harsh and oppressive circumstances. When a person endures spiritual oppression of any kind, their heart literally becomes bruised and pulverized to pieces. This violation of fundamental human rights comes in all shapes and sizes. There is the harsh military and political oppression of the deranged dictator who tortures his own citizens. There is the personal oppression of domestic violence where the drunken husband beats his wife and children. There is the oppression of the schoolyard where one child endures a continuous pattern of bullying, ridicule and victimization and there is the oppression of the dominating housewife who controls and intimidates her insipid husband. Throughout the Bible we see countless instances of the harsh oppression that sinful people inflicted upon one another. Solomon wrote in Ecclesiastes,

> I looked again at all the acts of oppression that were being done under the sun. And behold I saw the tears of the oppressed and that they had no one to comfort them; and on the side of their oppressors

was power, but they had no one to comfort them! (Ecclesiastes 4:1 NASB)

Throughout their history the people of God suffered many periods of harsh oppression at the hands of their enemies. In Judges chapter 4 we read of Jabin, the King of Canaan. "For twenty years he harshly *oppressed* the children of Israel." (Judges 4:3) In Judges 6:9 the Lord reminded His people that, "I snatched you from the power of Egypt and from the hand of all your *oppressors*." Whenever the children of Israel turned back to the Lord He faithfully delivered them from their oppressors. "The Lord had compassion on them as they groaned under those who *oppressed and afflicted* them." (Judges 2:18 NIV) The book of Judges records the detailed history of Israel's oppression under their hostile neighbors. We read of how the Philistines and the Amorites "*shattered and crushed* them. For eighteen years they *oppressed* all the Israelites on the east side of the Jordan." (Judges 10:8 NIV) There were even periods when their own Kings oppressed Israel. We read of Asa, King of Judah who imprisoned the prophet Hanani because he did not like the prophetic word that he gave the King. "Asa was angry with the seer because of this; he was so enraged that he put him in prison. At the same time Asa *brutally oppressed* some of the people." (2 Chronicles 16:10 NIV)

Human history is characterized by brutal oppression, sometimes on a massive scale such as in the Jewish Holocaust under Hitler and in Cambodia under Pol Pot and sometimes simply on a personal scale. All of us were undoubtedly mortified by the stories of evil men who had enslaved and imprisoned women in the basement of their house, using them as sex slaves to satisfy their perverse desires. Isaiah prophesied that, "People will oppress each other – man against man, neighbor against neighbor. The young will rise up against the old, the base against the honorable." (Isaiah 3:5 NIV) Whenever one person seeks to dominate and control another for whatever reason, whether it is in the form of physical abuse, sexual abuse, spiritual abuse or psychological abuse there is oppression and the fruit of that oppression is a broken and wounded heart.

In all of this history of human violence and oppression we read of the heart of the Father toward His children. God is deeply moved by the tears of the oppressed. He is not a God who is stoically removed from human suffering and pain. The Lord said: "I have surely seen the oppression of My people who are in Egypt, and have heard their cry because of their taskmasters, *for I know their sorrows*." (Exodus 3:7) The Scriptures depict the Father as the One who weeps with those who weep and who suffers with those who suffer. God's response to the cry of the oppressed and brokenhearted was to deliver His people from oppression and to reveal His healing heart of love. The story of the Israelites' deliverance from Egyptian oppression was the foundation of their history as a nation. "The Egyptians treated us harshly and afflicted us, and imposed hard labor on us. Then we cried to the Lord, the God of our fathers, and the Lord heard our voice and saw our affliction and our toil and our oppression." (Deuteronomy 26:6,7 NASB)

This deliverance formed the benchmark of their revelation of the kindness and mercy of God to those who are afflicted. Their deliverance was a revelatory act. The children of Israel understood the heart of God toward the afflicted and this redemptive event was rehearsed again and again throughout their history as a reminder of the unfailing love of God. "Because of the oppression of the weak and the groaning of the needy, I will now arise," says the Lord. "I will protect them from those who malign them." (Psalm 12:5 NIV) Throughout the Old Testament we are presented with a revelation of God's heart toward the wounded hearts of men and women.

Whenever the people of God are "brought low through oppression, affliction and sorrow," (Psalm 107:39) God responds. "The Lord is a refuge for the oppressed, a stronghold in times of trouble." (Psalm 9:9 NIV) "He upholds the cause of the oppressed and gives food to the hungry. The Lord sets prisoners free, the Lord gives sight to the blind, the Lord lifts up those who are bowed down." (Psalm 146:7,8 NIV) "The Lord builds up Jerusalem; He gathers together the outcasts of Israel. He heals the brokenhearted and binds up their wounds. The Lord supports the afflicted; He brings down the wicked to the ground." (Psalm 147:2,3,6)

As God looks down from heaven upon the human race He sees man oppressing his fellow man, women oppressed by men, children oppressed and abused both physically and sexually by adults and entire nations oppressed by cruel dictators and His heart is deeply moved. Jesus came to "release the oppressed" but this does not always entail the removal of the oppressor. In the midst of a harsh and oppressive world Jesus heals the brokenhearted. The freedom from oppression does not always necessitate a change in our outward circumstances but it does necessitate a change inside the heart. When Christ heals the broken heart He restores a sense of dignity so that people can walk in the midst of oppression without being crushed. This was the story of the

African American community when they were oppressed as slaves. Many called on the Lord and they walked in a personal sense of dignity in spite of their harsh oppression.

Just as the physical body can be 'sick' so too the human heart can be *sick*. In Proverbs we are told that, "hope deferred makes the heart sick." (Proverbs 13:12) Jeremiah described the human heart as "*incurably sick*." (Jeremiah 17:9) The word he used for 'incurably sick' was '*anash*' which according to the *Gesenius Lexicon*, "is used of a disease or wound such as is scarcely curable."[46] '*Anash*' was used repeatedly by Jeremiah and was usually translated 'incurable' or 'beyond cure.' "Why is my pain perpetual and my wound *incurable*, which refuses to be healed?" (Jeremiah 15:18) In chapter 30 Jeremiah prophesied that the spiritual condition of the nation of Israel was so bad that, humanly speaking, it was beyond the point of healing.

> This is what the Lord says: "Your wound is incurable, your injury beyond healing. There is no one to plead your cause, no remedy for your sore, no healing for you. Why do you cry out over your wound, your pain that has no cure? But I will restore you to health and heal your wounds," declares the Lord, "because you are called an outcast, Zion for whom no one cares." (Jeremiah 30:12,13,15,17)

Israel had suffered such extreme rejection and hatred at the hands of the surrounding nations that the Lord described them as 'outcasts.' Israel may have been 'cast out' and rejected by other nations but "The Lord builds up Jerusalem; He gathers the outcasts of Israel. He heals the brokenhearted and binds up their wounds." (Psalm 147:2,3) The idea in all of these references is that the condition of the wound is so severe that without God it is indeed incurable! Our hearts can take such a beating in this life and we can become so wounded and broken that without God there is absolutely no hope of healing. This is the condition of the human heart and God seeks to unveil the broken state of our hearts in order to bring the healing that only He can bring. Only God can heal a wounded heart.

Is it any wonder that a significant part of Jesus' ministry is to heal the brokenhearted when millions of souls languish under emotional burdens too heavy to bear? "And seeing the multitudes He felt compassion for them because they were *distressed and downcast* like sheep without a shepherd." (Matthew 9:36) Being 'distressed' and 'downcast' describes the inner condition of the heart that is languishing under the overwhelming effects of sin and death. Jesus' heart of compassion was extended to the brokenhearted multitudes when he said, "Come to me all you who labor and are *heavy laden* and I will give you rest. Take my yoke upon you and learn from me, for I am gentle and lowly in heart, and you will find rest for your souls." (Matthew 11:28,29). When we are heavily laden with both our sin and our emotional brokenness our souls find no rest. At the height of his personal apocalypse, Job said, "And now my heart is broken. Depression haunts my days. At night it pierces my bones within me, and my gnawing pains take *no rest*." (Job 30:16,17)[47] Jesus fully entered into the pain of humanity. He participated in it and He sought to ease the burden of our souls by showing us the path to life and emotional wholeness. He releases us from the cords of death!

Wounded by Words

One of the greatest and most common sources of human oppression is the tongue. In describing the wicked, David said, "His mouth is full of cursing and deceit and oppression; under his tongue is trouble and iniquity." (Psalms 10:7) The Scriptures liken the tongue of the wicked to a sharp sword or an arrow. Sharp words lodge in the heart and need to be surgically removed by the Great Physician. Solomon said, "There is one who speaks like the piercing of a sword." (Proverbs 12:18) "A man who bears false witness against his neighbor is like a club, a sword and a sharp arrow." (Proverbs 25:18) The NLT makes this verse even clearer. "Telling lies about others is as harmful as hitting them with an axe, wounding them with a sword, or shooting them with a sharp arrow!" David knew exactly what this felt like. "My soul is among lions; I lie among the sons of men who are set on fire, whose teeth are spears and arrows, and their tongue a sharp sword." (Psalm 57:4) In one of David's prayers for protection from his adversaries he said;

> Hide me from the secret counsel of the wicked, from the insurrection of the workers of iniquity, who sharpen their tongue like a sword, and bend their bows to shoot their arrows – bitter words, that they may shoot in secret at the blameless; suddenly they shoot at him and do not fear. (Psalm 64:2-4)

Jeremiah also likened hurtful words to sharp arrows. "Like their bow they have bent their tongues for lies...their tongue is an arrow shot out; it speaks deceit." (Jeremiah 9:3,8) When an arrow hits its appointed target it goes in deep and it needs to be skillfully removed. People who have been 'pierced' by the tongue of the wicked and who have never received healing are like the walking wounded with arrows lodged deep in their soul. Some Christians who minister healing in this area have testified that in the process of ministering to those who have been deeply wounded they have received a prophetic picture from the Lord revealing arrows or spears lodged deep in the heart. As they have ministered emotional healing through prayer the arrows were visibly dislodged.

James described the tongue of the wicked as "a restless evil, full of deadly poison." (James 3:8 NIV) David prayed, "Deliver me, O Lord, from evil men...They sharpen their tongues like a serpent; the poison of asps is under their lips." (Psalm 140:1,3) Life and death are in the power of the tongue and the person who uses their tongue to destroy is capable of completely crushing the heart of their victim. Just as with verbal abuse, physical abuse also crushes and wounds the heart. The physical wounds of a violent attack may heal with time but the damage inflicted upon the human heart still pierces like a sword. The little girl who is repeatedly abused sexually by a perverted pedophile is literally crushed in her heart by a deep sense of worthlessness.

The world is full of children who have been treated like pieces of trash with no thought whatsoever for their emotional wellbeing. The child sex trade leaves unimaginable emotional scarring in the hearts of defenseless children. Childhood victims of sexual abuse have been deeply pierced with an invisible sword and that spiritual sword needs to be delicately removed and the wounds healed up. Because Jesus can see into our hearts He has the ability to discern the presence of inner wounds and He longs for the opportunity to delicately remove the sharp arrows that have pierced and wounded the heart. If God were to open our eyes in the realm of the spirit, we too would be able to see people walking around with arrows and swords lodged deeply in their hearts. Jesus waits patiently for His body on earth to awaken to the full revelation of His ministry so that we will join Him in His glorious ministry of healing wounded hearts.

A person with a broken heart has suffered such emotional brokenness that they begin to find themselves locked into certain patterns of destructive emotional responses. No matter how hard they try to break out of these patterns of responding they simply cannot. The negative responses become automatic and they spring spontaneously from a heart that has been emotionally scarred.

These seemingly programmed responses are often disproportionate to the issue that triggers them because the pain of a small offence is tapping into a deeper reservoir of emotional pain. Let's use the illustration of a person who has been subjected to a history of negative and destructive parental criticism. In later life as an adult someone comes along and makes a small, well-meaning comment about how a certain task could be done more efficiently and the wounded person literally explodes in a tirade of defensive rhetoric and anger. Someone has just touched a button of deep emotional wounding and pain. The emotional response was entirely inappropriate to the comment that triggered it. Because of the presence of wounding the person who responded in anger has completely misinterpreted the good intentions of the person offering the helpful advice.

Let's consider another example of a woman who has been sexually abused as a child. When she became an adult she met the man of her dreams and they married. She was deeply in love with this man but every time he touched her and they attempted to make love she literally froze up on the inside. Any sexual advances were interpreted as a threat to her wellbeing. Her responses made no sense. She loved her new spouse but their love life was in tatters and the verbal conflicts just seemed to escalate. Her programmed emotional responses indicated the presence of deep emotional pain that had never been resolved.

The problem with a wounded heart is that there is no way out apart from the intervention of Christ. Once a deep spiritual wound has been incurred it simply does not go away until Jesus heals it. The best we can do to overcome the debilitating effects of the wound is to bury the problem so deeply that for all intents and purposes it appears to be gone. But the problem is that when we are faced once again with circumstances in life that replicate the circumstances that induced the initial wounding we act in ways that are beyond our control. Our relentless quest to protect ourselves from being hurt again can cause us to have certain emotional responses that seem to come out of nowhere. We are shocked by our emotional responses because we had convinced ourselves that we had overcome the problem. All of this occurs in the depths of our heart and it defies any logical explanation. Our responses are automatic because our hearts have been programmed through the wounding experiences of life to respond in certain ways to avoid further emotional pain. We will explore this dynamic further in the chapter on *Entangled in Physical Biochemistry*.

Emotional Overwhelm

So much energy is expended in seeking to manage negative and destructive emotions. In order to function adequately in our world, oftentimes we need to keep our emotional brokenness buried and suppressed, otherwise we will not be able to hold down a job or maintain relationships with friends and family members. Keeping a lid on emotional pain can become a full time occupation and for many it becomes a losing battle. Many people who are chronically fatigued are actually exhausted from what feels like a futile attempt to suppress strong emotions that are bubbling just beneath the surface. Emotional volatility is a key indicator of our failed attempts to keep a lid on our fear, our anger and depression.

Depression has become a major mental health issue in our culture. There are two primary causes of depression. Clinical depression can be caused by biological factors in our brain chemistry but the more common cause of depression is a state of emotional overwhelm. If biological factors are not the cause of depression then it is most probable that there are negative and destructive emotions that have gotten on top of us. Joyce Meyer wrote an important book titled *Manage Your Emotions*. The subtitle is: '*Instead of Your Emotions Managing You.*' This is such an important lesson for every Christian to learn. Emotional management is vital to our spiritual growth and wellbeing. It is an essential element of the heart journey. If we can't manage our emotions they can send a cascade of problems rippling though every part of our life.

Out of control emotions are like a runaway train. Depression is a highly destructive emotional state that can progress into a deeper and deeper dark hole of negativity. Suicidal ideation is most often triggered by a sense of deep depression where there seems to be no way out of the blackness other than death. Depression often emerges when the pain of our life circumstances **overwhelms us** and we fail to bring our pain to the Father. Unresolved grief can also lead to depression. Solomon noted that one primary emotional factor that can lead to depression is an anxious heart. "Anxiety in the heart of man causes depression but a good word makes it glad." (Proverbs 12:25)

There are many factors in life that can cause heightened anxiety such as the fear of financial failure, the fear of relationships breaking down and the fear of death just to name a few. When our anxiety levels start peaking our hearts becomes overwhelmed and burdened by the pressures of life. A person who is prone to heightened anxiety who is not living in close relationship with God can become completely swamped by feelings of being overwhelmed. David said, "When my heart is overwhelmed; lead me to the rock that is higher than I." (Psalm 61:2) If we don't learn how to cast all our cares upon Jesus we will internalize them and carry them ourselves.

Peter understood the importance of casting our cares and anxious thoughts upon the Lord. "Cast all your anxiety on Him because He cares for you." (1Peter 5:7 NIV) Paul said, "Do not be anxious about anything, but in everything, by prayer and petition, with thanksgiving, present your requests to God. And the peace of God, which transcends all understanding, will guard your hearts and your minds in Christ Jesus." (Philippians 4:6,7 NIV) If we don't learn how to cast our anxieties upon the Lord and exchange it daily for His supernatural peace, our heart will be overwhelmed by the extreme pressures of life and we will begin the descent into the valley of depression and despair. Another word for anxiety is stress. We live in a fast paced society that is filled with countless stressors. A stressor is any factor in our life that induces a sense of stress. We don't have to search very hard to identify numerous factors in our life that contribute to our stress levels. These stresses are usually external pressures that burden our heart and unless we allow the Lord to relieve the stresses in our lives by exchanging them for His peace they will ultimately produce heightened anxiety. David said, "Search me, O God and know my heart; try me, and know my anxieties." (Psalms 139:23)

God wants to comfort our hearts in all the pain that we will endure in this life. He comforts the depressed in a way that lifts the hearts of the weary and the heavy burdened and imparts life to our emotions. He exchanges the cords of death for the bonds of peace and He imparts life to our emotions. Paul said, "God who comforts the downcast, comforted us." (2 Corinthians 7:6) The Amplified Bible translates this verse as: "But God, who comforts and encourages and refreshes and cheers the depressed and the sinking, comforted and encouraged and refreshed and cheered us." In all of the pressures that Paul endured he was sometimes overwhelmed with feelings of depression. The Bible has excellent counsel for the depressed and the overwhelmed. We were never meant to walk through the pressures of this life without God. He wants us to bring all our pain, all our fears, all our anxiety and worries to Him so that He can comfort and impart His life to our hearts.

Escaping the Void

When faced with the overwhelming pressures of life we can descend into the abyss of depression and a state of overwhelm or we can disengage from our actual emotional state in a way that leads us into deeper brokenness. Our propensity to emotionally dissociate is yet another aspect of our emotional brokenness. When we are faced with deep emotional pain there is a perennial temptation to disengage from our true feelings because we don't know how to cope with the pain that life inevitably brings. The sensation of unprocessed pain can bring a sense of disempowerment, leaving us feeling confused and robbing us of a sense of being in control of our own life. For those of us who come from emotionally shut down families it is extremely easy to slip into the same culture that our parents have modelled to us. It is the responsibility of parents to emotionally awaken their children by expressing strong emotions of love, affection and a sense of belonging to them; by drawing out their emotions and by training their children how to also express their love and their true feelings. But because many children grow up in homes where their parents are themselves deeply disengaged from their true emotional state and where love and pain are never expressed, their children are literally being trained to shut down emotionally. This condition is most clearly typified by parents always telling their children to stop crying and by teaching them to suppress their true feelings.

When these dissociative threads in the human personality are permitted to develop into a full-scale stronghold the person who has this propensity can ultimately become a fully dissociated person. Dissociative Identity Disorder, as a full-blown condition, involves a much higher degree of fragmentation of the personality into multiple personalities or a cluster of false identities built around strategic satanic lies that have taken firm root in someone's heart. To use the word 'dissociation' in relation to a propensity to emotionally disengage from our own feelings (or, for that matter, the feelings of others) can conjure for some professional psychologists a concept of the full-blown condition. I tend to use this word in a far looser sense so I find the concept of 'dissociative threads' an appropriate term because dissociation really describes a state where someone has lost an appropriate degree of association or connection with their actual emotional state.

Empathy is the ability to engage with and feel the emotional state of another human being. An empathetic person is capable of feeling where someone else is at emotionally and is therefore able to express appropriate love and concern toward them in their pain or in their joy. It is the ability to commiserate; to weep with those who weep and to rejoice with those who rejoice. People with dissociative threads also suffer a lack of empathy because they are not comfortable with their own emotions, let alone with the emotions of others. Such people find emotions extremely scary. The opposite of empathy is apathy. Apathy, by definition is a lack of emotional feeling or an indifference to one's own emotional state or the emotional state of others. An apathetic person is deeply desensitized to pain, whether it is their own pain or the pain of those they are in relationship with. An apathetic person has shut down emotionally and doesn't care at all about the emotional well being of others. This reminds me of the old adage: "Apathy is on the increase but who cares!"

I have personally suffered from a mild expression of emotional dissociation and I come from a long lineage of emotionally dissociated family members who were not at all comfortable with expressing any kind of feeling. Growing up I was not permitted to feel because my parents had never been given permission to feel by their own parents. They were clearly victims of their own family of origin. I have seen this trait in so many men of my generation, yet I found it strangely comforting because it didn't make me feel so alone in my spiritual journey as I have sought to break out of this generational pattern of brokenness. So many men that I have counselled and dialogued with have also testified to growing up in families that had these dissociative threads and who were seemingly traumatized by growing up during Word War II. Peter called this "the *empty way of life* handed down to you from your forefathers." (1 Peter 1:18 NIV)

My own incapacity to feel as I knew I should has left me sometimes wondering if there were any of my forefathers at all who were emotionally whole and who were deeply expressive of their love or even their pain. Shame is the archenemy of vulnerability and I had never been taught or encouraged to be vulnerable at all in my upbringing. A cloak of shame covered my entire family on both my father and mother's side. No one ever showed any vulnerability by expressing what was really going on inside their hearts or by drawing out what was really going on in the hearts of those around them. It was as thought they were vainly trying to live in a world without pain!

The Bible is not at all silent on this subject. King David had a term he used to describe this emotional condition. He was speaking about the ungodly when he said; "They have closed their *unfeeling heart*; with their mouth they speak proudly." (Psalms 17:10 NASB) An unfeeling heart is an apathetic heart that cannot feel personal pain or the pain of others. The NLT says, "They are without pity." People who lack empathy for others always lack connection to their own pain. David said, "Their hearts are callous and unfeeling." (Psalms 119:70 NIV) Paul described this condition perfectly in his epistle to the Ephesians.

> This I say, therefore, and testify in the Lord, that you should no longer walk as the rest of the Gentiles walk, in the futility of their mind, having their understanding darkened, being alienated from the life of God, because of the ignorance that is in them, because of the blindness of their heart; who, **being past feeling**, have given themselves over to lewdness, to work all uncleanness with greediness. (Ephesians 4:19)

Paul used a Greek world, '*apalgeo*,' to describe a unique emotional condition that can develop in people who live under the weight of sin and the hardness it inevitably brings to their heart. *Apalgeo* means an inability to grieve, to mourn or to feel emotional pain. It describes a callous, hardened heart that has become deeply insensitive to emotional pain, resulting in chronic apathy. It is interesting to explore how various Bible translators have handled this powerful concept. The NIV says; "Having lost all sensitivity...." The Amplified Bible says; "In their spiritual apathy they have become callous and past feeling and reckless..." (AMP)

The Message Bible says; "Feeling no pain, they let themselves go in sexual obsession, addicted to every sort of perversion." It is worth noting that this emotionally dissociated state is identified as the root cause of sexual immorality and perversion. In a deeply emotionally disengaged state a person can readily give themselves over to highly destructive practices such as an addiction to pornography or even pedophilia. These sorts of evil practices feed and strengthen extremely damaging strongholds of shame and hiddenness. The statistics for pornography addicted Christian men are terrifying. Perhaps their real problem is that they are so deeply disengaged from their own true feelings and the feelings of others, (especially their wives if they are married) that they have lost any awareness of the damage and the pain they are inflicting upon themselves and others in building up such a stronghold of shame. Vulnerability is the last thing on a porn addict's mind. The entire stronghold is built around secrecy and the cultivated art of staying well hidden.

The unfeeling heart has been incapacitated to feel either pain or love. The orphan heart is a heart that cannot or has not felt the loving heart of the Father. There is a giant void in the heart of a spiritual orphan and that void is hard to locate or detect because it is an emotional void. Through years of being emotionally shut down and cauterized to any sense of pain, the heart becomes hopelessly numb. Feeling no pain the orphan can immerse him or herself into sin and immorality without a sense of deepening pain because their 'painometer' has been severely impaired. Paul talked about those who have seared their conscience as with a hot iron. (1 Timothy 4:2) Such a person has so given him or herself over to sin that they have lost their moral compass and have destroyed their own capacity to discern good from evil. Unchecked emotional dissociation inevitably leads to moral problems. The concept of 'searing something with a hot branding iron' could be appropriately used to describe someone who has cauterized their own ability to feel pain because they have dissociated to such an extent from the actual pain in their heart. The pain is certainly there but they have trained themselves not to feel it any longer. That is an emotional condition rather than a moral condition but the effect is the same: a spiritual mechanism designed by God to be part of the necessary equipment to navigate life has been destroyed, impaired or rendered inoperative.

When someone cannot locate or articulate the 'void' they enter a zone where they are numbed to their true condition. If you asked them if they felt a sense of emotional void they might look at you blankly. If you asked them how they felt about certain upsetting situations that would cause other people immense pain they might also stare at you blankly. The void becomes an unlocatable abyss. Some people call it their 'nothing box.' They go to their nothing box because in this counterfeit secret place they feel absolutely nothing and it becomes their safe hiding place. It is a private world where there seemingly is no pain. It is a man-made state of blissful ignorance from which they navigate life in a deeply unfeeling way. They look upon others in pain with a detached amusement as if they were clinically examining a weaker human being who has somehow failed to transcend the common sensation of human pain.

Such a person who lives from the void is almost completely detached from their own emotional state of being so that it is as though they are a passive observer of their own suffering and anguish; almost as though they were physically removed from their own body. They watch themselves move through life in such an emotionally disconnected manner that they can walk through the pain of deep personal loss, such as the death of a loved one or a divorce or family breakdown with a detached smile on their face. When this condition develops into a major stronghold they can even calmly discuss their own hardship and misfortune with a chuckle in their voice and perhaps even with a sense of laughter. David said, "Even in laughter the heart may sorrow and the end of mirth may be grief." (Proverbs 14:13) The NLT says; "Laughter can conceal a heavy heart but when the laughter ends, the grief remains." Dissociated people simply cannot connect with their own pain. They have become the apathetic theatergoer of their own Shakespearean tragedy.

If a person is deeply empty at the core of their being how do they locate the void when there is nothing there to find? Some people, especially those who have experienced abandonment, who have been orphaned, rejected or cast away have lived with the void their entire life. In some people's hearts there can be such an ocean of unmet need, such a condition of profound inner emptiness, such a lack of being loved and a sense of not belonging that the soul can become traumatized by the depth of the emotional void. It is as though the person is living in a prison of the pain of their isolation and loneliness but the condition is so abhorrent they have constructed a fantasy world where everything is really OK. Some call it blissful ignorance, some call it denial, some call it living in 'la la land.'

In this strange twilight world the person living from the void convinces themselves that no matter how badly or abusively they have been treated by others they are impervious to pain because they don't have a painometer. It just doesn't register anything anymore because they have transcended the ordinary pain and suffering of humanity. Feeling no pain they give themselves over to lifestyle choices that would inflict deep pain on the average person but it causes them no pain because they have convinced themselves they have transcended pain. To quote Pink Floyd, they have become 'comfortably numb.' Such is the heart of the orphan.

But Jesus promised not to leave us as orphans. He promised to come to us, to lead us to our adoptive Father and so fill our heart with the Father's love that we come alive again on the inside. Song of Songs calls this 'awakened love.' The beloved said, "Promise me, O women of Jerusalem, by the gazelles and wild deer, not to *awaken love* until the time is right." (Song of Songs 2:7 NLT) The Father and the Bridegroom long to awaken our heart to feel again and to bring us out of the shadows of emotional dissociation. Only the experience of the overwhelming love of God can awaken such a broken heart and fill the deep void on the inside of our hearts. The void cannot be filled by anything except the adoptive love of the Father. John identified the root cause of the Christian's enduring love of the world: it is because the [experience of] the love of the Father is not in them. Jesus prayed specifically to His Heavenly Father that the love with which the Father loved Him would also be in us. Only an encounter with the Father's love can begin to fill and displace the horrible empty void that torments the heart of the orphan.

What is the genesis of the void? In an enlightening book titled *The Life Model: Living From the Heart Jesus Gave You*, the authors distinguish between what they call 'Type A' traumas and 'Type B' traumas. "Type A traumas come from the absence of good things we should all receive, things that give us emotional stability."[48] "Type B traumas come from bad things. A Type B trauma is harmful by its presence."[49] Type B traumas come from acts of sin and abuse perpetrated against us in life's journey. "Many people find it hard to see that Type A traumas are the cause of their pain, depression or isolation. Their importance is denied, leaving the persons puzzled about why they feel so awful about themselves, why they are so afraid to trust or why they feel the continual need to prove their worth. With the significance of the traumas denied, people are at a loss to understand where the disturbing feelings come from."[50]

The authors of *The Life Model* are the pioneers of *Shepherd's House*; an inner healing ministry. They identify a set of indicators of the absences that contribute to the emotional void that emerge from Type A traumas.

1. Not being cherished and celebrated by one's parents simply by virtue of one's existence.

2. Not having the experience of being a delight.

3. Not having a parent take the time to understand who you are – encouraging you to share who you are, what you think and what you feel.

4. Not receiving large amounts of non-sexual physical nurturing: laps to sit on; arms to hold you.[51]

I would call this the orphan wound that comes from not being loved or given a deep sense of belonging. David said, "Although my father and my mother have forsaken me, yet the Lord will take me up [adopt me as His child]." (Psalms 27:10 AMP) The remedy is a glorious combination of experiencing the Father's love but also in being integrated into community and healthy relationships where we are loved. "God places the solitary in families and gives the desolate a home in which to dwell." (Psalms 68:6 AMP) However, the full healing of our broken hearts will not come exclusively through being reintegrated into healthy earthly relationships but through encountering the experiential love of our Heavenly Father who has come to heal the deep orphan wound and to bring many sons and daughters to glory.

Brokenheartedness and Sin

It is vital that we understand the complex relationship between brokenheartedness and sin. Brokenheartedness is *not* in itself a sinful condition; it is the *effect* of living in the *presence of sin and death*, and as such, every human being experiences a degree of brokenheartedness. Some however experience more than their fair share, especially those who have been the victims of wicked and criminally minded people, such as the perpetrators of violent crimes, assault, rape, sexual or physical abuse or other extreme forms of wickedness. We live continuously in the presence of sin and we are surrounded by people who have given themselves over to the sinful nature.

"The wicked in his proud countenance does not seek God; God is in none of his thoughts. His mouth is full of curses and deceit and oppression; under his tongue is mischief and wickedness." (Psalm 10:4,7) Throughout the Bible and all of human history we see the rich oppressing the poor and the strong oppressing the weak. Solomon observed something that has always characterized fallen humanity. "I observed all the oppression that takes place in our world. I saw the tears of the oppressed, with no one to comfort them. The oppressors have great power, and the victims are helpless." (Ecclesiastes 4:1 NLT) Oppression is in the heart of man. Jeremiah said to an apostate nation; "Your eyes and your heart are set only on dishonest gain, on shedding innocent blood and on oppression and extortion." (Jeremiah 22:17 NIV) The Psalmist said, "For I see violence and strife in the city. Day and night they prowl about on its walls; malice and abuse are within it. Destructive forces are at work in the city; oppression and deceit do not depart from its streets." (Psalm 55:9-11 NIV) It sounds like the cities of ancient times were not too dissimilar to our modern cities.

Because we have become so accustomed to the presence of sin we tend to overlook the fact that it is both unnatural and extremely destructive to our souls. Paul said, "He who sows to the flesh will of the flesh reap *corruption*." (Galatians 6:8) The Greek word for 'corruption' is *'phthora'* and it literally means *'ruin'* or *'destruction.'* Paul warned believers against the destructive consequences of falling into the temptation to sin. "People who want to get rich fall into temptation and a trap and into many foolish and harmful desires that plunge men into ruin and destruction." (1 Timothy 6:9 NIV) When we yield to sin it literally destroys our own souls, but when sinful people sin against us it also exercises a powerful destructive force upon us. Unless we are discipled by Christ in how to effectively and promptly deal with the sins that have been committed against us they too have the potential to destroy us. Remember that the devil, who is the archetypal 'sinner,' has come to "*rob, kill and destroy*" (John 10:10) and he never seems to lack those who are willing to lend him some assistance! No wonder the Psalmist said, "Destructive forces are at work in the city." Sin will ultimately destroy our lives either from within or from without unless we truly repent!

Have you ever noticed that whenever you suffer rejection, oppression or abuse it automatically causes your old sin nature to rise up as a default reaction? If we are still controlled by wounded and broken emotions we find ourselves reacting out of our brokenness. This is why it is so important to understand the relationship between sin and a wounded heart. But before we explore this theme we need to consider Jesus. The sinless and spotless Lamb of God was subjected to the harshest treatment that any human being could possibly endure. Right from the beginning of His ministry His own people rejected Him. "Even in His own land and among His own people, He was not accepted." (John 1:11 NLT) "He was despised and rejected by men, a man of sorrows, and familiar with suffering. He was wounded…He was crushed… He was oppressed and He was afflicted yet He did not open His mouth; He was led like a lamb to the slaughter, and as a sheep before her shearers is silent, so He did not open his mouth." (Isaiah 53:3,5,7 NIV) "The stone which the builders **rejected** has become the chief cornerstone." (Psalms 118:22)

Jesus suffered betrayal even by His closest friends. "If someone asks Him, "What are these wounds on your body?" He will answer, "The wounds I was given at the house of my friends." (Zechariah 13:6 NIV) He suffered betrayal and abandonment. "All the disciples deserted Him and fled." (Matthew 226:56) He was continually reviled and insulted throughout His ministry, however, "when they hurled their insults at him, He did not retaliate; when He suffered He made no threats." (1 Peter 2:23 NIV) Three years of abusive treatment culminated in his betrayal, His arrest, His torture and ultimately His brutal murder. Jesus was intensely hated and violently persecuted by the religious leaders. But even before His crucifixion He was the object of numerous assassination plots. Jesus was systematically hated by evil men who hated the light. "Anyone who hates Me hates My Father, too. They saw all that I did and yet hated both of us; Me and my Father. This has fulfilled what the Scriptures said: 'They hated Me without cause.'" (John 15:23-25)

The crucifixion of Jesus was described as His 'humiliation.' "He was humiliated and received no justice." (Acts 8:33 NLT) Jesus was humiliated because, in effect, He was sexually abused when He was stripped naked and hung on a cross in the public gaze. Even on the cross He was mocked and ridiculed. "The people passing by shouted abuse, shaking their heads in mockery." (Matthew 27:39 NLT) "In the same way the robbers who were crucified with Him also heaped insults on Him." (Matthew 27:44 NIV) Jesus suffered rejection on an unparalleled scale. But in all of this the sinless Lamb of God did not curse or retaliate, instead He said, "Father, forgive them, for they do not know what they do." (Luke 23:34) At His final end, as He hung upon the cross, He even endured the deepest agony of being forsaken by His Father as He took upon Himself the sin and the sorrow of the entire world. "My God, My God, why have You forsaken Me?" (Matthew 27:46)

Jesus was rejected, wounded and abused but remarkably He did not sin! If we were subjected even to a small proportion of this level of rejection and wounding we would probably fly off into a rage and our hearts would overflow with thoughts of retaliation and revenge. Unforgiveness would flood our hearts and we would wrestle with deep feelings of anger, resentment, bitterness and even hatred. We might even be tempted to consider murder! The entanglement of deep emotional wounds combined with an entanglement in our old sinful nature is a deadly combination. It is like mixing nitrogen and glycerin. When we are emotionally wounded, even the slightest provocation can cause all of our unresolved sin issues to kick in with surprising ferocity. The problem with wounding and abuse for those who are also deeply defiled and corrupted by sin is that a wounded heart causes people to get locked into sinful patterns of thoughts and actions. We are not wounded in a vacuum, we are often wounded in the context of our own sinful attitudes and responses. The brokenness in our hearts literally hold us in bondage to the sin nature and when we are oppressed or rejected by others our circumstances become significantly compounded.

This is why Jesus came to heal the brokenhearted. An emotionally unhealed heart can render the blood of Jesus inoperative. It is not that the blood of Christ is not efficacious in and of itself to cleanse us of all of our sins. One drop of His precious blood is sufficient to wash away all our sins. The problem is that when we are wounded by the sins of others we inevitably become ensnared in sinful attitudes of unforgiveness, vengefulness, judgment and bitterness. Until we experience the tender love of the Father that melts away all the bitterness in our hearts we find ourselves locked into bondage to sin. As long as the church seeks to apply a one-dimensional cure to a two-dimensional problem we will remain a broken and defeated people. Why is the church still so damaged and broken when the blood of Christ is so powerful? Our hearts have been so deeply wounded by living in the presence of sin that we need to experience the transforming love of God to heal the broken places in our hearts. Only as Christ ministers this supernatural healing to our wounded hearts can we fully escape the complex entanglement of sin and brokenness.

There are different levels of sin. In the initial stages following conversion the Holy Spirit convicts and cleanses us of many of the overtly sinful practices that once characterized our lives. One of the evidences of conversion is that people usually experience a sudden change of lifestyle. Things like drug abuse, heavy drinking, blaspheming, swearing, fornication etc. usually disappear fairly quickly because of their overt and obvious nature. But there are deeper level sins that take much longer to get free from. These are often in the realm of sinful attitudes and motives and the selfish strategies of the heart that govern the way we behave.

It is in this realm that the relationship between sin and deep level wounding comes into focus. Deep level freedom from sin goes hand in hand with deep level emotional healing. The deep spiritual wounds and hurts from the past entomb the sinful attitudes and intents of the heart and hold us in bondage to sinful strategies that continue to dictate our behavior. Jesus' ministry of healing the brokenhearted is the key that unlocks these doorways of the heart. It is not until the Lord unveils the deep brokenness in our hearts and begins the healing process that these deeper strongholds of sin and selfishness begin to shift. This is where the one-dimensional solution to the human condition really fails miserably!

All the evidence points in the direction that the healing and restoration of the soul takes place on two primary levels. On the one hand we need to repent of patterns of sinful thoughts, motives and actions so that we may be personally cleansed from the power of sin, but on the other hand we need to be healed of the *damaging consequences of sin* in our own lives. Wherever there is sin there is heartache and brokenness! The power of the gospel deals effectively with our sin through God's forgiveness and the sanctifying power of the blood of Jesus, but the ministry of healing the brokenhearted is intended to take away the *painful effects* of sin upon our souls. It is the ministry of the Father's love that heals the wounds in our emotional life. The cross and the new creation open up the doorway for us to experience the healing love of the Father but it is only as we tangibly experience His love poured into our hearts through the ministry of the Holy Spirit that we transition into the full freedom of our sonship.

The Effects of the Past

Some Christians stumble over the idea that experiences in our past can still exercise a measure of control over us in the present. There are some who believe that simply through turning to Christ all their past problems are now behind them. Denial of the effects of the past can be a universal problem but some Christian traditions, in their quest to promote rapid spiritual growth, are uniquely vulnerable to a particular theological rationale that insists we are dead to all our past pain and emotional brokenness. Rather than attempting to uncover the hidden sources of pain and wounding from the past and exploring their effect upon us in the present they simply deny the reality of the past. Some Christians are even taught by well meaning Bible teachers to completely ignore the past. Charles Kraft, in the opening chapter of his book, *Deep Wounds, Deep Healing*, describes an incident in which he heard a Christian teacher proposing this very method of dealing with issues from the past.

> The preacher was expounding on Philippians 3:13b, "Forgetting those things that are behind..." He had connected that verse with 2 Corinthians 5:17, "If anyone is in Christ, he is a new creature. Old things are passed away, behold, all things have become new." With enthusiasm, as if debating with someone who disagreed, he

emphasized his main point, that once a person has accepted Christ as personal Savior, the past is gone, all things have become new. So, he contended, we are not to look back but to forge ahead in our new life in Christ, just as if the past hadn't happened at all. Nothing from the past can affect our present lives, he said, for Jesus took care of it all at conversion. Though most of the audience listened without betraying what they were thinking, a few shifted in their seats after that last remark.[52]

This is fundamentalism at its worst. While on the surface the appeal to these two verses from the Bible may sound persuasive, the reality is that only an expert in the art of denial would suggest that our past does not exert some degree of influence over us. Emotionally dissociated Christians love this message. I met a man once who described to me the most broken past imaginable yet he insisted that he was fully healed in his emotions the day he received Jesus. Some people cannot distinguish between a smashed painometer and the healing of the heart.

Unprocessed pain always becomes toxic. In 2 Corinthians 5:17 Paul was stating the amazing reality of the regeneration of our spirit in Christ. Indeed in Christ we are glorious new creations! We are born again and the fullness of the divine nature dwells within us in the person of the Holy Spirit. Paul consistently stated the finished realities of the new creation to give believers a firm foundation upon which to begin the journey of sanctification and the renewing of their souls. We begin the journey of personal transformation on a foundation of victory and not defeat!

Even though Paul had not yet attained a state of sinless perfection, (Philippians 3:12) he could confidently affirm the reality of who he had become in Christ. "I have been crucified with Christ; it is no longer I who live, but Christ lives in me." (Galatians 2:20) When Paul said, "old things have passed away" this is factually true of what God has done within the human spirit of every human being who has put their faith in Christ! But no doubt many of Paul's ingrained habits of selfishness carried over into the present as he sought to wrestle with the residual effects of his former self-righteous life. In Christ "old things have passed away" but Paul himself still had to walk out the process of appropriating this new life in Christ through fighting the good fight of faith. He recognized that his inward man (his soul) was still being renewed day by day. (2 Corinthians 4:16)

By his own admission, Paul himself was greatly troubled by his own murderous past. Did he immediately recover from all of his anger, shame and hateful thoughts the moment he was converted? If Paul taught that Christians who idolized money had "pierced themselves through with many sorrows" (1 Timothy 6:10) how much more did Paul wound himself with his hateful attitudes and his calculated attempt to destroy the church of God? As we saw earlier in this chapter, Paul placed considerable emphasis upon the language of inner healing because, even from his own personal testimony, he knew how vitally important it is for Christians to walk out their healing journey. Even towards the end of his life Paul described himself as the "chief of sinners," suggesting that he was still somewhat haunted by his evil past.

> Even though I was once a blasphemer and a persecutor and a violent man, I was shown mercy because I acted in ignorance and unbelief. The grace of our Lord was poured out on me abundantly, along with the faith and love that are in Christ Jesus. Here is a trustworthy saying that deserves full acceptance: Christ Jesus came into the world to save sinners – of whom I am the worst. But for that very reason I was shown mercy so that in me, the worst of sinners, Christ Jesus might display His unlimited patience as an example for those who would believe on Him and receive eternal life." (1 Timothy 1:13-16 NIV)

Does anyone fully recover from all of the effects of their past simply because they have turned to Christ? The only people who would suggest such an absurdity are those with an overly shallow or simplistic understanding of sanctification. Conversion is only the beginning of the process of sanctification and we spend the rest of our lives becoming who we already are in Christ. Those who encourage Christians to believe that they are completely over their past once they are converted are actually applying a "hyper-faith" theology to the deep wounds of the heart. Proponents of extreme hyper-faith theology urge believers to deny the presence of sickness in their bodies because they believe that if we confess physical healing *we are healed* by our confession. Some even go as far as insisting that the persistent presence of the symptoms of disease are nothing more than a lie from the devil designed to challenge the truth that we are already healed in Christ.

In this strange religious culture people are told that if they are still sick it is because their faith is in some way defective. This theology is crushing for believers who still struggle with physical sickness because they are made to feel inferior and condemned. But this teaching is even more crushing when it is applied to the inner issues of the heart because it always ministers condemnation to the believer who is still struggling with fear, depression, rejection or any other emotional problem. Believers who become entangled in a culture of religious denial are compelled to put on a happy mask and bury their pain even deeper in order to find acceptance in a culture that cannot accept weakness and human brokenness.

I know this culture from first hand experience. In my early days in 1980's Pentecostalism these teachings were widespread. Faith teachers held out a false promise that new creations could effectively live outside of the realm of emotional pain and brokenness if only they believe what they teach. They claimed to be walking in a higher revelation that enables Christians to transcend much of what the average Christian suffers. But tragically, the best intentions of these neo-gnostic teachers always backfire, resulting in a deep sense of inner failure especially when their teachings are applied to the emotional life of the believer.

No amount of positive confession will substitute for the difficult and challenging process of exposing and healing the deep wounds of the heart. Our pain has to be processed with our Father. Joyce Meyer, in her book, *Managing Your Emotions*, uses the illustration of a ball of knots to describe our lives when we first come to Christ. When she teaches on the subject of emotional healing she holds up a set of colored shoestrings all knotted together and she says, "This is you when you first start the process of transformation with God. You're all knotted up. Each knot represents a different problem in your life. Untangling those knots and straightening out those problems is going to take a bit of time and effort, so don't get discouraged if it doesn't happen all at once."[53]

Rather than denying the past we need to face the hurtful experiences of the past and grasp their implications for our new life as followers of Christ. What does the reality of the new creation in Christ mean for the person who has suffered sexual abuse? What is the process involved in healing someone who has deep personal problems because of prolonged physical, sexual or psychological abuse? When the Lord recognizes that we are finally at a point in our heart journey that we are ready to face these issues He tenderly brings to light the wounds that we have suffered in our past and He gently leads us along the path of inner transformation and healing. Throughout the New Testament there is a consistent acknowledgement of the ongoing presence of such issues as bitterness, shame, depression, fear, anger, lust, rejection and brokenness of heart. Paul spent much of his time pastoring new creations through all of their brokenness. His epistles are evidence that once we are born again we begin a journey of healing.

But if Paul doesn't seem to have a problem with acknowledging the destructive effects of emotional brokenness from our past what then are we to make of his comment in Philippians where he said; "forgetting those things which are behind?" (Philippians 3:13) In order to understand this statement we must first examine it in its broader context. Paul had just finished cataloguing his former religious achievements as a Pharisee. His stately spiritual pedigree was the source of his self-righteous pride.

> If anyone else thinks he has reasons to put confidence in the flesh, I have more: circumcised on the eighth day, of the people of Israel, of the tribe of Benjamin, a Hebrew of Hebrews; in regard to the law, a Pharisee; as for zeal, persecuting the church; as for legalistic righteousness, faultless. But whatever was to my profit I now consider loss for the sake of Christ. (Philippians 3:4-7 NIV)

Paul had once boasted in his religious achievements and his high spiritual pedigree but he now considered them as rubbish. (Philippians 3:8) None of those things counted for anything in the sight of God once Paul discovered that righteousness only came through faith in Christ. This is what Paul determined to forget and put behind him! We always need to read the Bible in its context and understand the Scriptures in the context that they were written in. Good biblical exegesis always seeks to understand obscure statements in the light of the wider context. Bad exegesis takes individual statements out of context and builds a doctrine around obscure texts. Indeed Paul wanted to forget the folly of his religious past but only after he had evaluated it and dealt decisively with the roots of his own religious pride. His discovery of the free gift of righteousness through faith represented the climax of his journey out of self-righteousness and religious works. This was a journey of the heart in exchanging his own self-righteousness for the free gift of God and in the systematic dismantling of his well-constructed edifice of religious pride.

We are faced with two clear choices concerning our past. Either we completely forget and bury the past or we face it and deal with it. We must ask whether the path of completely forgetting our past is biblically responsible? If we have had involvement with the occult is it wise counsel to simply bury the past or should we process the things that we have exposed ourselves to? A repentant occultist, satanist or person who practiced witchcraft must deal with their past through prayers of renunciation, closing doors in the spirit realm and breaking the demonic strongholds that have come into their lives. Sometimes the deliverance may continue for a period of time as the Holy Spirit reveals the tentacles of darkness that have wrapped themselves around the person who gave themselves over to witchcraft or the occult. No one would dispute that there is a definite mopping up process that occurs in the life of the person who has opened him or herself up to the demonic realm. Why should we think it would be any different when it comes to the wounding and hurtful experiences of the past? The blanket denial of the past is both unwise and irresponsible and it always sets people up for failure!

Far from Paul counselling believers to slam the door shut on the past, he would have encouraged them to process and deal with the issues from their past that still haunt them in the present. If our hearts still condemn us we must find the root cause. Every fruit has its root and every wound has its origin. In the course of God's ministry to our heart He will not rest until He has uprooted all of the causes of our present brokenhearted condition. Jesus said, "Every plant that my Heavenly Father has not planted will be pulled up by the roots." (Matthew 15:13 NIV) The path to personal wholeness necessitates coming to terms with our past and understanding how it continues to affect us in the present. We all have our own unique personal baggage that needs to be systematically dealt with. Jesus has come to pour His life into the rooms of our hearts that are still under the dominion of past wounding and entangled in the cords of death.

God indeed wants to bring closure to our past but He wants us to do it His way. We may devise our own strategies to attempt to bring closure to the events of the past but unless it is the work of the Holy Spirit it will merely be a work of the flesh. Jesus said, "It is the Spirit who gives life; the flesh profits nothing." (John 6:63) Another translation says, "Human effort accomplishes nothing!" (NLT) All our vain attempts to bring closure will inevitably come to nothing. Jesus alone is the one who closes the doors on the past. "He opens doors, and no one can shut them; He shuts doors, and no one can open them."

(Revelation 3:7 NLT) When Jesus closes the door on our past the results are complete and the healing is deep and permanent. All of our human endeavors to distance ourselves from the effects of our past are nothing more than our own attempts to simply sweep our problems under the rug. This includes ridiculous theologies about immediately transcending all of our past problems simply by becoming a new creation.

Jesus has been revealed to humanity as the 'Healer of the Brokenhearted.' He has been sent by the Father into the world with a specific mandate to heal our damaged emotions. These spiritual wounds have their origin in our past, and these issues need to be processed in the present instead of being foolishly swept under the rug. The power of the new life in Christ reaches specifically to the issues we carry in our heart. Whether those issues are strongholds of sin or emotional wounding from the past they need to be acknowledged, healed and *then* finally put behind us. Only then can we truly say that these strongholds of the emotional life have truly passed away as a declaration of our *personal Christian experience*. We are all entangled in emotional brokenness until we have purposefully disentangled ourselves by walking out the heart journey of overcoming every single stronghold of the emotions under the loving guidance of the Good Shepherd.

Tribulation and Comfort

Jesus said, "These things I have spoken to you, that *in Me* you may have peace. In the world you will have tribulation; but be of good cheer, I have overcome the world." (John 16:33) Jesus warned us that; "in the world you will have tribulation!" The word 'tribulation' literally means 'suffering, sorrow, troubles and anguish of heart.' In this world we will all experience deep emotional pain but Jesus promised that in the midst of our pain we can find unlimited peace in Him. At the end of Romans 8 Paul had just finished saying that nothing could separate us from the love of God in Christ when he said: "At the same time, you need to know that I carry with me at all times a huge sorrow. It's an enormous pain deep within me, and I'm never free of it. I'm not exaggerating; Christ and the Holy Spirit are my witnesses. It's the Israelites...They're my family. I grew up with them." (Romans 9:1-4 MSG)

Paul lived in the love of the Father but he was simultaneously in agony over the spiritual blindness and the lost condition of his family of origin. Many of us live with the pain of loved ones who don't know Jesus. In the midst of all our pain we have to learn to walk as Jesus walked. Jesus continuously processed His pain with the Father. He endured pain on earth in the context of the love of the Father. The purpose of pain is to drive us into the arms of a loving heavenly Father.

As we draw this chapter to a close, I want to revisit what Paul revealed when he taught that there were two ways to endure pain; we can endure our pain in intimate relationship with God or on our own in independence from God.

> For *godly grief* and *the pain God is permitted to direct*, produces a repentance that leads and contributes to salvation and deliverance from evil, and it never brings regret; but *worldly grief* (the hopeless sorrow that is characteristic of the pagan world) is deadly [breeding and ending in death]. (2 Corinthians 7:6-10 AMP)

"The pain God is permitted to direct!" What a profound revelation. We must allow the Holy Spirit to lead us to the Father with our pain. "Let the distress *bring you to God, not drive you from Him*. Distress that drives us to God does that. It turns us around. It gets us back in the way of salvation. *We never regret that kind of pain*. But those who let distress *drive them away from God* are full of regrets, and end up on a deathbed of regrets." (2 Corinthians 7:9,10 MSG) God wants to shower deep spiritual comfort upon the hearts of His beloved. "Now may our Lord Jesus Christ Himself and God our Father, who loved us and by His grace gave us eternal *comfort* and a wonderful hope, *comfort you* and strengthen you in every good thing you do and say." (2 Thessalonians 2:16,17 NLT) The Father's comfort is *His love* in action. He expresses His love through His great comfort poured into our hearts. Comfort is a powerful experience! The devil always tempts us to blame God for our pain so we will turn away from God instead of running into His arms of love. But God is never the cause of our pain; He is the one who seeks to comfort us and relieve us of our pain. Satan's goal is to leave us comfortless in our pain so that we seek consolation in the world.

Paul experienced such intense emotional pain but he also knew what it meant to experience the comfort of the Father in all his pain. "Blessed be the God and Father of our Lord Jesus Christ, the Father of mercies and God of all comfort, *who comforts us in all our tribulation*, that we may be able to comfort those who are in any trouble, with the comfort with which we ourselves are comforted by God. For as the sufferings of Christ abound in us, so our *consolation* also abounds through Christ." (2 Cor. 1:3-5) In this world we will experience tribulation but God promises to comfort us in all our tribulation if we bring our pain to Him. "You can be sure that the more we suffer... the more God will shower us with His comfort through Christ." (2 Corinthians 1:5 NLT)

"Look how much strength and encouragement you've found in your relationship with Jesus. *You are filled with His comforting love!*" (Philippians 2:1 TPT) We are meant to be the most comforted people in the entire world, yet many Christians live in excruciating pain, suffering in their own private world of grief and sorrow; separated from the comfort of the Father. The peace of God is intended to substantially overcome all of the pain of our tribulations and sorrows! The world relentlessly hurls pain and suffering at us but Christ in us seeks to overcome with His peace and love.

The Glorious Exchange

There is a recurrent prophetic theme throughout the Old Testament of the divine exchange of our sorrows for God's joy.

> To comfort all who mourn, to console those who mourn in Zion, to give them beauty for ashes; the oil of joy for mourning, the garment of praise for the spirit of heaviness. (Isaiah 61:2,3)

> The ransomed of the Lord will return. They will enter Zion with singing; everlasting joy will crown their heads. Gladness and joy will overtake them and sorrow and sighing will flee away. "I, even I, am He who comforts you!" (Isaiah 51:11,12 NIV)

> They will come and shout for joy on the height of Zion and they will be radiant over the bounty of the Lord. And their life will be like a watered garden and they will never languish again. Then the virgin will rejoice in the dance and the young men and the old, together, for I will turn their mourning into joy and I will comfort them and give them joy for their sorrow. (Jeremiah 31:12,13 NASB)

The hope of the Christian is that the pain of this world will not overwhelm us. Pain was never meant to be experienced outside of the context of the glory of the Father's love, peace and joy. Pain outside of the Father's loving embrace always becomes *toxic*. The longer a person is left in unresolved sorrow and pain, the deeper the turmoil becomes within their soul. We must stop trying to escape pain or to resolve it through whatever kind of medication we reach for. In this world we will have pain and suffering. But instead of enduring grief as 'worldly sorrow' we have the opportunity to take our pain to God and receive an experiential impartation of His comfort and joy. The agony can only be adequately processed in the context of the ecstasy.

Solomon said, "The heart of the wise is in the house of mourning but the heart of fools is in the house of pleasure." (Ecclesiastes 7:4 NIV) Both the wise man and the fool experience pain but the wise man is blessed if he mourns in fellowship with Christ because he shall be comforted. When we suffer pain we can take that pain to the house of worldly pleasure to try to alleviate it or we can take it into the house of mourning where we refuse to hide from the pain. It is only through the house of mourning that we can find the doorway into the house of comfort! The house of pleasure has no exits. When we bring our pain to the Father *He absorbs our pain* and literally draws it out of our heart. "Surely He has borne our griefs and carried our sorrows." (Isaiah 53:4) Let the God of all comfort bear your grief and carry away your sorrows. "Give all your worries and cares to God, for He cares about what happens to you." (1 Peter 5:7 NLT) We can and should share all our pain with God because our life is now in Him! Joy and peace will ultimately prevail when we bring our pain to the Father as Jesus did to find the doorway into the comfort of the Father's house.

Pain makes us feel vulnerable. We don't like it so we run away from it. We hide from our pain because it makes us feel weak and powerless but we need to learn how to express our pain by being vulnerable in our core relationships. As we cultivate vulnerability we should be learning how to express our pain and our deepest innermost feelings. Western Christians tend to do everything in their power to avoid pain. Rolland Baker, a missionary to Mozambique, has both experienced and witnessed horrendous suffering. He said, "In the West we don't like the idea of suffering very much. We would prefer that no one has to suffer – especially those who are in Christ." Pentecostals in particular do not have a developed theology of suffering or enduring pain as part of the Christian life. The 'word of faith' community despises pain. As a movement, it doesn't give people permission to be in pain or to be weak.

The preoccupation with the cult of success in the church always marginalizes the weak and the broken. Triumphalist culture doesn't allow for people to be weak, vulnerable or in pain. But pain is a fact of life. Like Jesus, we can enter into the spirituality of enduring pain and suffering by embracing *the agony and the ecstasy*. Heaven invades earth with ecstatic joy and counteracts the pain. Jesus invades our hearts with peace that transcends human understanding and that peace eclipses all our pain. According to Paul, we can rejoice in the glory in such a way that we are equipped to also rejoice in the midst of our pain because the pain itself, experienced in fellowship with a loving and comforting God, becomes an opportunity to know God more intimately and to live as Jesus lived on earth in the fellowship of His sufferings.

> Therefore, since we have been justified through faith, we have peace with God through our Lord Jesus Christ, through whom we have gained access by faith into this grace in which we now stand. And *we rejoice in the hope of the glory of God*. Not only so, *but we also rejoice in our sufferings*, because we know that suffering produces perseverance; perseverance, character; and character, hope." (Romans 5:1-5)

There is a largely untapped dimension of spirituality enfolded within this mystery of being conformed to the heart of true sonship. As a Son, Jesus rejoiced continually in His Father's love even in the midst of His sufferings. Paul also learnt to live in this place. He could say "Rejoice in the Lord always. Again I will say, rejoice!" (Philippians 4:4) This includes rejoicing even in the midst of emotional pain. "We can be full of joy here and now even in our trials and troubles!" (Romans 5:3 J. B. Phillips) But all of this is unquestionably premised upon the cultivation of an intimate relationship with God. If we are not experientially engaging our hearts with the glory of heaven we will not experience either comfort or peace and we will end up suffering as the world suffers; deeply entangled in the cords of death.

There is a place in the Spirit that God is leading us to where we can learn how to navigate life and all the pain it throws at us in the context of fellowship with a loving God. It is only as we locate this dimension of extraordinary grace in which we can now stand that we will be able to overcome all of the negative and destructive emotions that daily threaten to make shipwreck of our lives. So many of us who follow Christ never learn to manage our emotions and we inevitably find ourselves being managed by our emotions; tossed to and fro by negative and destructive feelings that carry the potential to destroy our lives and our relationships.

There cannot be substantial emotional healing if our primary goal is to avoid pain. Part of the healing of our emotions is in being reconciled to the reality of pain and to learn how to navigate life as Jesus did. He had intentional mechanisms in place to deal with every relational crisis and He His initial strategy was to pray for the forgiveness of those who sinned against Him. He had the Father's heart for everyone who wounded and abused Him because the pain never cut Him off from the Father's love. Walking as Jesus walked means that we are fully reconciled to the fact that in this world we will endure pain and suffering but now we are empowered through grace to walk through life out of the context of His glorious love, peace and joy which God is establishing in the core of our heart. This is the pathway to escaping the entanglement of emotional brokenness.

Chapter Twelve

Entangled in Demonic Infiltration

There are explicit warnings in the New Testament of the danger of Christians living in such a way that they inadvertently open the door to an entanglement in the demonic. No intelligent Christian with knowledge of the existence of the devil and his demons would intentionally choose to open their life to the powers of darkness. But the devil sets subtle traps or snares for the believer to unwittingly stumble into through their disobedience to God. Whenever a Christian makes a choice to entertain or traffic in spiritual darkness they are placing themselves in enemy territory and are immediately vulnerable to demons infiltrating the unrenewed regions of their soul.

A careful reading of the New Testament reveals many warnings addressed specifically to God's children of the danger of being ensnared in one of the devils traps. The most conspicuous warnings urge us to be vigilant because the devil seeks to 'devour' Christians. "Be sober, be vigilant; because your adversary the devil walks about like a roaring lion, seeking whom he may devour. Resist him, steadfast in the faith." (1 Peter 5:8,9) Peter's warning of the devil's agenda to 'devour' Christians is by no means an idle threat. The Greek word for 'devour' (*katapino*) means 'to drink or gulp down.' An unguarded Christian can potentially be consumed by the evil one.

Similarly, Paul warns Christians about the danger of falling into "the snare of the devil." (1 Timothy 3:7) Given the widespread propensity toward disobedience amongst believers, Paul instructed the servant of the Lord to "gently instruct" those who stray into the darkness "in the hope that God will grant them repentance leading them to a knowledge of the truth, and that they will come to their senses and escape from the trap of the devil, who has taken them captive to do his will." (1 Timothy 2:25,26 NIV)

Peter urged believers to adopt a posture of continuous spiritual sobriety and vigilance lest they be devoured by the evil one. When Peter said 'be sober' he used the Greek word '*nepho*' which means to 'abstain from wine.' When a person is drunk they have lost control of themselves and they cannot think clearly. Such a person is at risk of being gulped down by the evil one. Interestingly, Paul described the remedy to this condition. He said that once a Christian had fallen prey to the evil one they needed to come to repentance and "come to their senses." This is the Greek word '*ananepho*' which means 'to become sober again' or to regain one's senses. This describes a restoration of spiritual sobriety and prophetic clarity.

Not only are Christians warned about being devoured by, or falling into the trap of the devil; they are also warned that they can potentially give the devil a foothold or an opportunity. Paul said, "Do not give the devil a foothold." (Ephesians 4:27 NIV) A foothold describes an entry point whereby the devil can violate or infiltrate the life of the believer. Paul urged believers to continuously walk in love and forgiveness, "lest Satan should take advantage of us; for we are not ignorant of his devices." (2 Corinthians 2:11)

The devil has deliberate schemes and strategies to attack and bring about the downfall of the saints. "The dragon was enraged with the woman, and he went to make war with the rest of her offspring." (Revelation 12:17) Jesus said, "The thief comes only to steal and kill and destroy." (John 10:10) If a Christian fails to be vigilant or watchful he or she can easily be taken advantage of by the evil one. Our vigilance is so "that Satan might not outwit us" or "so that Satan will not outsmart us." (2 Corinthians 2:11 NIV/NLT)

Whenever the enemy has a strategic advantage over us it means he has prevailed in his strategy to cause us to fall in a particular area of our life. Paul said we wrestle with principalities and powers and in a wrestling match our adversary can sometimes prevail and exercise an advantage over us. Peter said, "For by whom a person is overcome, by him also he is brought into bondage." (2 Peter 2:19) When a believer is overcome by the devil in an area of their life they have been brought into bondage and taken captive to do his will rather than God's will.

There is a biblical imperative for all true followers of Jesus to walk in radical obedience by coming fully under the Lordship of Christ. "Do you not know that to whom you present yourselves slaves to obey, you are that one's slaves whom you obey, whether of sin leading to death, or of obedience leading to righteousness?" (Romans 6:16) Because of the intense spiritual warfare surrounding the lives of all born again believers Paul urged the saints in Corinth to "cast down arguments and every high thing that exalts itself against the knowledge of God, bringing every thought into captivity to the obedience of Christ and being ready to punish all disobedience when your obedience is fulfilled." (2 Corinthians 10:5,6) In other words, live a life of radical obedience so that any pattern of disobedience becomes so conspicuous in your life that it is intolerable.

Full obedience to the Lordship of Christ is designed to protect us from the attack of the evil one. A Christian who is living a life of true obedience to God is gloriously clothed in the full armor of God and cannot be violated or penetrated by the enemy. But whenever a Christian winks at patterns of disobedience in his or her heart they lay themselves wide open to demonic infiltration because they are not availing themselves of the protection that God offers. Paul makes this quite clear in Ephesians 2.

> And you He made alive, who were dead in trespasses and sins, in which you once walked according to the course of this world, according to the prince of the power of the air, the spirit who now works in the sons of disobedience, among whom also we all once conducted ourselves in the lusts of our flesh, fulfilling the desires of the flesh and of the mind. (Ephesians 2:1-3)

This satanic spirit "now works [*energeo*] in the sons of disobedience." Whilst Paul is referring to unbelievers outside of Christ the principle still applies that chronic disobedience to the Lordship of Christ creates an open door for enemy infiltration. If we flirt with disobedience and consider a lifestyle of low-level rebellion against God and His Word a viable option for our lives, we open ourselves up to the realm of darkness and darkness will infiltrate our lives because the devil is continually scanning our hearts in search of a foothold.

Paul employs the Greek word '*energeo*' to describe the kind of demonic infiltration that can occur when a Christian chooses a lifestyle of disobedience. He revealed that the devil actually 'energizes' all those who walk in disobedience. That is, his demonic power or energy accesses the hearts of rebellious Christians. This explains why so many Christians are so messed up and lacking in personal victory. Wherever there is disobedience there is darkness and whenever a follower of Jesus traffics in darkness there will be a degree of demonic energization. Demons look for legal loopholes to violate the soul of the believer and patterns of disobedience are the legal basis for infiltration. I don't think Paul is suggesting that a momentary lapse into a state of disobedience will result in instant demonization. Rather, it is the Christian who engages in a lifestyle of chronic disobedience who is at risk of demonic entanglement. But, statistically, this is not at all uncommon in the contemporary church.

In the abovementioned passage in Ephesians 2 Paul unpacks the intimate nexus between the world, the flesh and the devil. We live in a fallen world that is comprehensively energized and ruled by the evil one. Whenever we walk according to the course of this world we are 'walking in the flesh' and the flesh is hostile toward God. If, through disobedience, a believer walks for a period of time in the flesh they are vulnerable to a form of demonic energization that descends upon a pre-existing stronghold of the flesh. What was once exclusively a stronghold of the old flesh life can be supernaturally transformed into a demonic stronghold because it can be energized by a demon.

John Wimber once wrote: "Our situation with demons is analogous to our situation with the flesh and the world. We are forgiven and born again in Christ, but if we choose to believe the lies of the world and yield to our flesh, we will live in sin. Demonization works the same way: we have been delivered from the power of demons, yet we can still be effected by them."[54] Many Christians erroneously believe that because they are born again they cannot be violated by a demon. This is true of our spirit but it is not true of the unrenewed areas of our soul. The evil one can readily attach himself to any stronghold of the mind, the will or the emotions.

Historically, the translators of the Bible have done a great disservice to the church by consistently translating the Greek word '*daimonizomai*' as 'demon possessed.' So many Christians have dismissed the idea of a Christian having a demon because, rightly, they argue that a blood bought saint cannot be the possession of a demon. We are now God's purchased possession so, as the argument goes, how can a believer be 'possessed' by a demon or by the devil? But a far more accurate translation of '*daimonizomai*' is the English transliteration; '*demonized*.' To be demonized means to be influenced by a demon and this can range from a slight degree of influence all the way through to high-level demonization. I personally like to think of a scale of 1 to 10 with a '1' being very low level energization to '10' being severe energization.

The other primary argument against the possibility of the demonization of believers is the promise of protection from the enemy. There are a number of Scriptures that would convey the impression that a follower of Jesus is protected from the evil one. Paul boasted, "the Lord will deliver me from every evil attack." (2 Timothy 4:18) "Thanks be to God, who gives us the victory through our Lord Jesus Christ." (1 Corinthians 15:57) Jesus Himself said to His disciples; "I have given you authority to trample on snakes and scorpions and to overcome all the power of the enemy; nothing will harm you." (Luke 10:19) God promised His people that, "No weapon formed against you shall prosper," says the Lord." (Isaiah 54:17) David proclaimed, "The Lord is my rock and my fortress and my deliverer; my God, my strength, in whom I will trust; my shield and the horn of my salvation, my stronghold." (Psalm 18:2) "For You have been a shelter for me, A strong tower from the enemy." (Psalms 61:3)

However, all of these promises are conditional and predicated upon a life of obedience to the Lordship of Christ. In fact, all of the promises of God to the believer are conditional. God has provided full armor to protect us but we must put on the full armor of God in order to be protected. There is full and comprehensive protection from the powers of darkness *if* we avail ourselves of all that God has provided through a life of obedience and faith. Notice the conditional nature of the word 'if' in the following verses:

- "If you abide in me..." (John 15:7)
- "If you obey my commands..." (John 15:10)
- "If you continue in my Word..." (John 8:31)
- "If you continue in his goodness..." (Romans 11:22)
- "If you continue in the faith..." (Colossians 1:23)

Psalm 91 beautifully captures the big picture of God's protection from the evil one for those who choose to obediently dwell in the secret place of the Most High God. This Psalm is set against the backdrop of extreme spiritual warfare but it is a wonderful promise for those who choose to make the Lord their fortress and their stronghold.

> He who dwells in the secret place of the Most High shall abide under the shadow of the Almighty. I will say of the Lord, "He is my refuge and my fortress; my God, in Him I will trust." Surely He shall deliver you from the snare of the fowler and from the perilous

pestilence. He shall cover you with His feathers and under His wings you shall take refuge; His truth shall be your shield and buckler. You shall not be afraid of the terror by night, nor of the arrow that flies by day, nor of the pestilence that walks in darkness, nor of the destruction that lays waste at noonday. A thousand may fall at your side and ten thousand at your right hand; but it shall not come near you. Only with your eyes shall you look and see the reward of the wicked. Because you have made the Lord, who is my refuge, even the Most High, your dwelling place, no evil shall befall you nor shall any plague come near your dwelling; For He shall give His angels charge over you to keep you in all your ways. In their hands they shall bear you up lest you dash your foot against a stone. You shall tread upon the lion and the cobra, the young lion and the serpent you shall trample underfoot. "Because he has set his love upon Me, therefore I will deliver him; I will set him on high, because he has known My name. He shall call upon Me, and I will answer him; I will be with him in trouble; I will deliver him and honor him. With long life I will satisfy him and show him My salvation." (Psalm 91)

Perhaps the clearest statement of the conditional nature of our spiritual protection is revealed in 1 John. "He who has been born of God keeps himself and the wicked one does not touch him." (1 John 5:18) Note that the wicked one not 'touching' the believer is *conditional* upon him "keeping himself." The grammar is a little clumsy but the meaning is clear. The born again believer who 'keeps himself' becomes untouchable. But this opens up a rich vein of revelation because there are many verses in the Bible that exhort us to keep ourselves. All of them imply a life of radical obedience in order to avail ourselves of the full protection that God provides from the powers of darkness.

- "Keep your heart with all diligence." (Proverbs 4:23)
- "Keep yourself pure." (I Timothy 5:22)
- "Keep yourself from sexual immorality." (Acts 21:25)
- "Keep yourself unspotted from the world." (James 1:27)
- "Keep yourself from idols." (I John 5:21)
- "Keep yourself in the love of God." (Jude 21)
- "Keep yourself from every wicked thing." (Deuteronomy 23:9)
- "Keep your garments on." (Revelation 16:15)
- "Keep your lives free from the love of money." (Hebrews 13:5)
- "Keep your spiritual fervor." (Romans 12:11)

This concept of 'keeping ourselves' or 'keeping our heart' is a prevalent theme in Scripture. "Thorns and snares are in the way of the perverse; but he who *keeps his soul* will be far from them." (Proverbs 22:5) Unfortunately, the hearts of many believers are like un-kept gardens; choked with weeds and overgrown with thorns and thistles. Jesus alluded to the weeds that choke the good seed in our hearts in the Parable of the Sower. "The one who received the seed that fell among the thorns is the man who hears the word, but the worries of this life and the deceitfulness of wealth choke it, making it unfruitful." (Matthew 13:22)

Similarly, Solomon used the metaphor of a garden full of weeds to describe the man who failed to keep his heart. "I went past the field of the sluggard, past the vineyard of the man who lacks judgment; thorns had come up everywhere, the ground was covered with weeds, and the stone wall was in ruins. I applied my heart to what I observed and learned a lesson from what I saw: a little sleep, a little slumber, a little folding of the hands to rest – and poverty will come on you like a bandit and scarcity like an armed man." (Proverbs 24:30-34) David said that the un-kept heart is "like a city broken down, without walls." (Proverbs 25:28)

The Scriptures give us no basis for assuming automatic unconditional protection from the enemy simply because we are Christians. There is only one human being who walked in perfect protection from the powers of darkness and that was Jesus. He boldly proclaimed that Satan *"has no hold on Me."* (John 14:30) The Amplified Bible expands upon this statement; "He has no claim on Me, he has nothing in common with Me, there is nothing in Me that belongs to him, he has no power over Me." Jesus was completely untouchable because He kept His heart perfectly. Our goal as disciples of Jesus ought to be to follow in His footsteps and to pursue a life of perfect obedience.

The extent to which we actively 'keep ourselves,' is the extent to which we walk in divine protection where the enemy of our souls cannot 'touch' us. Many Christians are not only 'touched' by the wicked one; they are comprehensively violated and infiltrated by the powers of darkness. As a pastor I am painfully aware that many believers have never broken through into freedom from a life of chronic disobedience. They have compromised their walk with God to such an extent that all they have ever known as believers has been the violation and harassment of the evil one. Obedience to

Christ has been elusive because they have chosen to wink at compromise and accept it as a viable option for their lives.

Paul said, "The reason I wrote you was to see if you would stand the test and be obedient in everything." (2 Corinthians 2:9 NIV) In the next verse he wrote; "What I have forgiven – If there was anything to forgive – I have forgiven in the sight of Christ for your sake, in order that Satan might not outwit us. For we are not unaware of his schemes." (v. 10,11) Satan only outwits the disobedient. Radical obedience is always the test. We often learn the hard way, discovering through our disobedience the consequences of our foolish choices. Paul spoke more about the consequences of disobedience to the Corinthians than any other Christian community because they were developing habits of chronic disobedience that were resulting in considerable devastation.

The key passage in the entire New Testament concerning the capabilities of the powers of darkness to wreak destruction in the lives of disobedient believers is unquestionably 1 Corinthians 10. In this chapter Paul explains, through a series of warnings to New Testament believers, the dangers of rebellion for the follower of Christ. We have already seen in an earlier chapter titled '*The Promised Land of the Heart*' that Paul gave two explicit warnings to the saints in Corinth about the devil's capability to destroy those who rebel against the Lordship of Christ. He drew from two instances of rebellion in the history of the Israelites and applied these two stories explicitly to New Testament believers. "We should not test the Lord, as some of them did and were destroyed [*apollumi*] by serpents." (1 Corinthians 10:9 NIV) "We should not complain, as some of them also complained, and were destroyed [*apollumi*] by the Destroyer." (1 Corinthians 10:10)

Jesus indicated that theft, murder and destruction were the hallmarks of the evil one. He has come to rob, to kill and destroy. Whenever a Christian strays into a consistent lifestyle of disobedience and rebellion to the known will of God they place themselves in the hands of the Destroyer. Tragically, this pattern of chronic disobedience has historically characterized the majority of believers down through the ages who have settled down into a lifestyle of disobedience and rebellion against the will of God and have rationalized their lifestyle in their own minds. Paul's primary point in writing 1 Corinthians 10 was that the Corinthian believers were themselves beginning to settle into a consistent lifestyle of rebellion and that this would inevitably lead to their destruction.

Paul sought to make it as plain as he possibly could that the consequence of chronic disobedience would be destruction. There are a number of New Testament passages that indicate the potential for Christians to be 'destroyed,' 'ruined,' 'defiled,' or 'corrupted' by the powers of darkness. Satan is the Destroyer who comes specifically to kill Christians. If he cannot kill them he will settle for robbing and destroying them. "His name in Hebrew is Abaddon, and in Greek, Apollyon; *the Destroyer.*" (Revelation 9:11 NLT) Paul warned that "The one who sows to please his sinful nature, from that nature will reap *destruction* [*phthora*]; the one who sows to please the Spirit, from the Spirit will reap eternal life." (Galatians 6:8 NIV) Carnal Christians who consistently walk in the flesh open up their lives to the Destroyer and they will certainly reap destruction. "Do not be deceived, God is not mocked; for whatever a man sows, that he will also reap." (Galatians 6:7)

The neo-gnostic believers of Corinth were claiming that their superior revelatory knowledge permitted them to eat food sacrificed to idols in the pagan temple of Aphrodite; the Greek goddess of love, beauty and pleasure. Their so-called 'liberty' gave license to their brethren to continue participating in the idolatrous and perverse practices of the local temple of Aphrodite. This rebellion was resulting in what Paul identified as the 'destruction' of the believers. "For if anyone with a weak conscience sees you who have this knowledge eating in an idol's temple, won't he be emboldened to eat what has been sacrificed to idols? So this weak brother, for whom Christ died, *is destroyed* [*apollumi*] by your knowledge. When you sin against your brothers in this way and wound their weak conscience, you sin against Christ." (1 Corinthians 8:10-12 NIV) Participation in pagan idolatry as a Christian results in destruction.

Apparently a similar problem had emerged in the church in Rome; the headquarters of pagan idolatry. "If your brother is distressed because of what you eat, you are no longer acting in love. Do not by your eating *destroy* [*apollumi*] your brother for whom Christ died." (Romans 14:15 NIV) "Do not *destroy* [*apollumi*] the work of God for the sake of food. All food is clean, but it is wrong for a man to eat anything that causes someone else to stumble. It is better not to eat meat or drink wine or to do anything else that will cause your brother to fall." (Romans 14:20,21 NIV) There is a principle embedded in this passage: enticing other believers to sin will result in spiritual destruction because their rebellion opens up their lives to the Destroyer who is searching for a way to destroy the followers of Christ.

There is one other place where we encounter the Greek word '*apollumi*' in the New Testament in reference to personal destruction. "Watch yourselves, that you do not *lose* [*apollumi*] what we have accomplished, but that you may receive a full reward." (2 John 1:8) Throughout the gospels, the Greek word '*apollumi*' frequently denotes loss. The 'destruction' a Christian reaps through disobedience is a loss where something has been robbed or stolen away by the evil one. There are a couple of other Greek words used in the epistles to describe the ruin and destruction that comes into the lives of disobedient Christians. Two of them are found in the following passage.

> People who want to get rich fall into temptation and a trap and into many foolish and harmful desires that plunge men into *ruin* [*olethros*] and *destruction*. [*apoleia*] For the love of money is a root of all kinds of evil. Some people, eager for money, have wandered from the faith and pierced themselves with many griefs. (1 Timothy 6:9,10 NIV)

The Greek word '*apoleia*' was used a number of times to describe the destruction that was wrought in the lives of Christians who strayed from the path of righteousness. '*Apoleia*' is a derivation of '*apollumi*' and is used in the following verses:

> "But my righteous one will live by faith. And if he shrinks back, I will not be pleased with him." But we are not of those who shrink back and are *destroyed*, but of those who believe and are saved. (Hebrews 10:38,39 NIV)

> But there were also false prophets among the people, just as there will be false teachers among you. They will secretly introduce destructive heresies, even denying the sovereign Lord who bought them – bringing swift *destruction* on themselves. (2 Peter 2:1)

> Bear in mind that our Lord's patience means salvation, just as our dear brother Paul also wrote you with the wisdom that God gave him. He writes the same way in all his letters, speaking in them of these matters. His letters contain some things that are hard to understand, which ignorant and unstable people distort, as they do the other Scriptures, *to their own destruction*. (2 Peter 3:15,16 NIV)

We can see from these passages that in each of these instances there was some kind of transgression that preceded the destruction. Those who "shrink back to destruction" (NASB) have put their hand to the plow but have gradually withdrawn from the front lines of battle through fear or intimidation regarding the cost of following God with all of their hearts. Those believers who strayed into theological error wrought destruction within themselves because they rejected the true doctrine of Christ, thereby opening themselves to what Paul calls "doctrines of demons."

Another Greek word used by Paul to describe the destruction or ruin that a disobedient Christian invites into his life is *'phtheiro'* which means, "to spoil, to ruin, to corrupt, defile or destroy." Paul attributes this corruption to poor choices and to the destruction that comes directly from the Destroyer. "But I fear, lest somehow, as the serpent deceived Eve by his craftiness, so your minds may be ***corrupted*** [*phtheiro*] from the simplicity that is in Christ." (2 Corinthians 11:3) "Do not be misled: "Bad company ***corrupts*** [*phtheiro*] good character." (1 Corinthians 15:33 NIV)

In the church of Corinth there was a major problem with believers who had been saved out of pagan idolatry still visiting the temple of Aphrodite and having sex with the temple prostitutes. Paul addressed these disobedient believers by saying; "Do you not know that he who is joined to a harlot is one body with her? For 'the two,' He says, 'shall become one flesh.' Do you not know that your body is a temple of the Holy Spirit, who is in you, whom you have received from God? You are not your own; you were bought at a price. Therefore honor God with your body." (1 Corinthians 6:16,19,20) "Do you not know that you are the temple of God and that the Spirit of God dwells in you? If anyone ***defiles*** [*phtheiro*] the temple of God, God will ***destroy*** [*phtheiro*] him. For the temple of God is holy, which temple you are." (1 Corinthians 3:16,17) The NLT says, "God will bring ruin upon anyone who ruins this temple. For God's temple is holy, and you Christians are that temple."

The rebellious Corinthian believers were destroying the temple of God on both a personal and corporate level. On a personal level they were reaping deep inward corruption and ruin from the evil one. Corporately they were bringing ruin upon the believing community by opening the door to the kingdom of darkness, thus empowering demons to wreak havoc within the church. As James observed; "Wherever there is selfish ambition, there you will find disorder and every kind of evil." (James 3:16 NLT) Paul taught that we are all members of the body of Christ and that our spiritual condition has a direct impact upon the wider body. "Now the body is not made up of one part but of many... If one part suffers, every part suffers with it; if one part is honored, every part rejoices with it." (1 Corinthians 12:14,26 NIV) Paul said, "Who is weak without my feeling that weakness? Who is led astray, and I do not burn with anger?" (2 Corinthians 11:29 NLT)

Paul spoke directly to this issue of idolatry and sexual perversion in 1 Corinthians 10 when he said; "Do not become idolaters as were some of them. As it is written, "The people sat down to eat and drink, and rose up to play." Nor let us commit sexual immorality, as some of them did, and in one day twenty-three thousand fell; nor let us tempt Christ, as some of them also tempted, and were **destroyed** by serpents." (1 Corinthians 10:7-9) The Corinthians were completely oblivious to the spiritual warfare dimension of their actions and were completely unaware that they were well down the path of being destroyed by demons.

"You were taught, with regard to your former way of life, to put off your old self, which is being **corrupted** [*phtheiro*] by its deceitful desires." (Ephesians 4:22 NIV) A Christian who consistently sows to the flesh will reap corruption within themselves and will sear their conscience with a hot iron. Instead of being on a healing journey a carnal believer who deliberately continues in sin is still accruing deep inward corruption. There were even more Greek words that the writers of the New Testament used to describe the destruction of the believer who fall into a pattern of regularly yielding to temptation and sin.

As Christians we usually tend to set our focus upon the possibility of living victoriously and we preach and emphasize the high ideals of a life in pursuit of the glory of God. But Paul and Peter also explored the consequences of chronic disobedience in the life of the believer in order to warn us of the grave danger of being swept along by the spirit of the world. In their description of the darker side of the life of the believer who comes to Christ but who refuses to turn from sin they used the word '*phthora*' which meant ruin, destruction and corruption. Paul said, "The one who sows to please his sinful nature, from that nature will reap destruction [*phthora*]." (Galatians 6:8 NIV) Peter urged believers to "Escape the **corruption** [*phthora*] in the world caused by evil desires." (2 Peter 1:4 NIV) He warned of false teachers who promised believers freedom but "they themselves are slaves of **corruption** [*phthora*]; for by whom a person is overcome, by him also he is brought into bondage." (2 Peter 2:19)

Another Greek word also meaning 'corruption' is '*miasma*.' Peter warned about the Christian who began well but who came back under the power of sin. "If they have escaped the **corruption** [*miasma*] of the world by knowing our Lord and Savior Jesus Christ and are again entangled in it and overcome, they are worse off at the end than they were at the beginning." (2 Peter 2:20) Paul described the catastrophic ruin of the believer who falls into the snare of the devil. "Keep reminding them of these things. Warn them before God against quarrelling about words; it is of no value, and only **ruins** those who listen." (2 Timothy 2:14) The Greek word for '*ruin*' in this passage is '*katastrophe*.' No explanation required.

Another theme in the epistles is that of spiritual defilement. "Therefore, having these promises, beloved, let us cleanse ourselves from all **defilement** of flesh and **spirit**, perfecting holiness in the fear of God." (2 Corinthians 7:1 NASB) Paul used the Greek word '*molusmos*' to describe this defilement. This verse cannot be describing the defilement of the human spirit because in Paul's theology the human spirit has been made perfectly righteousness; it has already been glorified and is now completely inviolable. Therefore, the only alternative interpretation is that Paul is describing a defilement that comes from unclean demonic spirits.

This would fit the context of 2 Corinthians because Paul emphatically warned the Corinthians of the spiritual corruption that would come from entertaining 'another Jesus' or 'another **spirit**.' (2 Corinthians 11:4) Satan masquerades as an angel of light and seeks to destroy believers by bringing them under a false gospel message. Paul also warned the Corinthians that the serpent exercises a corrupting influence upon the mind. "As the serpent deceived Eve by his craftiness, so your minds may be **corrupted** from the simplicity that is in Christ." (2 Corinthians 11:3) As we have previously noted, '*phtheiro*' means "to spoil, to ruin, to corrupt, defile or destroy."

Further support for the idea that Paul is warning about spiritual defilement that comes directly from the demonic realm is found in 2 Corinthians 10. In the context of spiritual warfare Paul urged the Corinthians to "cast down arguments and every **high thing** that exalts itself against the knowledge of God, bringing every thought into captivity to the obedience of Christ." (2

Corinthians 10:5) The Greek word for '*high things*' is '*hypsoma*' and Colin Brown observes, "The New Testament use of '*hypsoma*' probably reflects astrological ideas and hence denotes cosmic powers. 2 Corinthians 10:5 [is] concerned with powers directed against God, seeking to intervene between God and man. They are possibly related to the '*stoicheia tou kosmou*;' the 'elemental powers of this world.' (Colossians 2:8,20)."[55]

In Colossians Paul warns against these '*elemental powers*' defiling or corrupting the minds of believers. "Don't let anyone lead you astray with empty philosophy and high-sounding nonsense that come from human thinking and from **the evil powers of this world**, and not from Christ." Colossians 2:8 NLT) "You have died with Christ, and he has set you free from the evil powers of this world." (Colossians 2:20 NLT) Because the atonement of Christ has spoiled principalities and powers and delivered us from our bondage to these 'elemental powers' Paul urged the saints to avoid any entanglement is the defilement that comes from these spiritual hosts of wickedness in the heavenly places. Tying all of these themes together it is highly probable that Paul's exhortation to "cleanse ourselves from all **defilement** of flesh and **spirit**" (2 Corinthians 7:1 NASB) is a clear reference to the corrupting and destructive effects of the demonic realm.

The Greek word Paul used for 'defilement' was '*molusmos*.' Paul consistently warned of the danger of Christian's minds being corrupted or defiled by doctrines of demons. For example, in Titus Paul wrote, "To the pure all things are pure, but to those who are **defiled** and unbelieving nothing is pure; but even their mind and conscience are **defiled**." (Titus 1:15) In all likelihood this is a reference to demonic defilement. 'Those who are defiled' have placed their minds under the 'elemental powers' of darkness through submitting to false teachings and false prophets. The Greek word Paul used for '*defiled*' in Titus is '*miaino*' which means to be '*contaminated*.' The same Greek word is used in the following passage: "See to it that no one comes short of the grace of God; that no root of bitterness springing up causes trouble, and by it many be **defiled**." (Hebrews 12:15) The Amplified Bible renders this passage as: "In order that no root of resentment shoots forth and causes trouble and bitter torment, and the many **become contaminated** and defiled by it."

One of the greatest problems amongst 1st century Christians coming out of hard core pagan cultures was the temptation to compromise with the idolatry that pervaded the Greco-Roman world. In Athens, the epicenter of pagan idolatry, Paul's "spirit was provoked within him when he saw that the city was given over to idols." (Acts 17:16) At the council of Antioch the apostles released an edict that the disciples of Jesus should "abstain from things *contaminated by idols*." (Acts 15:20 NASB)

The problem of Christian entanglement in the worship of idols and in eating food offered to idols was so widespread in the early church that in 90 AD Jesus said, "You have a few names even in Sardis who have not *defiled* [*moluno*] their garments; and they shall walk with Me in white, for they are worthy. He who overcomes shall be clothed in white garments." (Revelation 3:4,5) The Greek word '*moluno*' came from the root word '*melas*' which meant 'black,' so this is clearly a play on words. Many had blackened their garments through the contamination of idols. But there were others who had kept themselves undefiled from idolatry. "For they are spiritually *undefiled* [*moluno*], pure as virgins, following the Lamb wherever He goes." (Revelation 14:4 NLT)

Any entanglement in sin, immorality, idolatry or false teaching opens the door to potential demonic infiltration. Throughout Paul's epistles he appears to consistently acknowledge the possibility for the believing saint to become entangled in demonic bondage. In 1 Corinthians 10, the chapter that I have suggested gives us the clearest New Testament warning of demonic infestation through willful disobedience, Paul explicitly warned the Corinthians that they could be destroyed [*apollumi*] by serpents and by the Destroyer, just as some of the children of Israel had been destroyed in their rebellion in the wilderness.

> These things became our examples, to the intent that we should not lust after evil things as they also lusted. And do not become idolaters as were some of them. As it is written, "The people sat down to eat and drink, and rose up to play." Nor let us commit sexual immorality, as some of them did, and in one day twenty-three thousand fell; nor let us tempt Christ, as some of them also tempted, and were destroyed by serpents; nor complain, as some of them also complained, and were destroyed by the destroyer. Now all these things happened to them as examples, and they were written for our admonition, upon whom the ends of the ages have come. (1 Corinthians 10:6-11)

A few verses later in the same chapter Paul explicitly confronted the issue of the temptation for the Corinthian Christians to join their unsaved family and friends in participating in the feasts dedicated to the goddess Aphrodite. He said "No temptation has overtaken you except such as is common to man; but God is faithful, who will not allow you to be tempted beyond what you are able, but with the temptation will also make the way of escape, that you may be able to bear it. Therefore, my beloved, *flee from idolatry*!" (1 Corinthians 10:13,14) Why does Paul command Christians to flee all association with pagan idolatry? He answers this question a few verses later: "The things which the Gentiles sacrifice they sacrifice to demons and not to God, and I do not want you to have *fellowship with demons*. You cannot drink the cup of the Lord and the cup of demons; you cannot partake of the Lord's table and of the table of demons. Or do we provoke the Lord to jealousy?" (1 Corinthians 10:20-22)

Participation in the food and wine dedicated to Aphrodite and joining themselves to the temple prostitutes brought the unstable Corinthian believers into direct fellowship with the demonic realm and back under the control of the devil. Paul used the Greek word '*koinonos;*' a word usually reserved for fellowship with the Father, the Son and the Holy Spirit, in reference to demons. '*Koinonos*' means 'companionship or communion or common union.' The NIV says, "I do not want you to be participants with demons." The NLT says, "I don't want any of you to be partners with demons." (NLT) Idolatry brings Christians into direct union with a demon; they become joined to the demon, which is another term for demonization.

Christians have been joined to the Lord through the new birth and brought into mystical union with Christ; spirit-to-spirit. We are now related to Christ through the new creation miracle and this is a permanent relationship that God has created. Because we are in relationship we can now choose to enter into fellowship with God or we can choose to have fellowship with demons. We can follow the example of the saints in Sardis who were commended by the Lord; "You have a few names even in Sardis who have not *defiled* their garments." "They shall walk [in fellowship] with me in white [garments] because they are worthy." (Revelation 3:4 Wuest Translation) The choice is literally between black or white; we can enjoy fellowship with Christ in pure light-soaked garments or we can fellowship with demons in the darkness.

If a Christian is overcome in any way by a demon he is brought into bondage to the demonic. "By what a man is overcome, by this he is enslaved." (2 Peter 2:19 NASB) Demonization is a form of demonic bondage in which a believer is brought under the influence of demonic powers. Christians cannot afford to flirt with the darkness in any way. The New Testament writers were very explicit about the grave danger of any kind of rebellion, subtle or overt. The potential for destruction is very real and millions of believers have strayed into the path of rebellion. Jude warned about Christians who had come under ruling spirits of rebellion. "Woe to them! They have taken the way of Cain; they have rushed for profit into Balaam's error; they have been *destroyed* [*apollumi*] in Korah's rebellion." (Jude 1:11 NIV)

Jesus asks us a straightforward question: "Why do you call Me 'Lord, Lord,' and do not do the things which I say?" (Luke 6:46) His name is the Lord Jesus Christ but if He is not Lord of all, then he is not our Lord at all! Why are there so many compromised Christians who settle into a lifestyle of lukewarmness and apathy? Paul said, "Who has bewitched you that you should not obey the truth?" (Galatians 3:1) "What magician has cast an evil spell on you?" (NLT) It is a spirit of witchcraft and confusion that bamboozles and traps Christians in a state of perpetual disobedience. There are so many Christians who have become entangled in fellowship with demons because they have been bewitched by the devil into believing that compromise and the tolerance of disobedience is an acceptable lifestyle.

My own experience as a pastor and counsellor has led me into the deliverance ministry. It was not something I chose for myself but through making myself available to do kingdom ministry with countless people in the past 20 years I have been engaged in casting hundreds of demons out of people whom I have personally known within my church and have been certain that they were genuine Christians who had faith in Christ for their salvation. My experience in doing deliverance with Christians coupled with the extensive experience of ministry colleagues with the same clinical experience has led me into a deeper study of the New Testament to seek to understand what the Bible really teaches about the vulnerability of unguarded believers to demonic infiltration.

On this fallen planet we are living in a spiritual environment that is energized by satanic and demonic power. God has provided a way for us to walk in complete spiritual protection from the powers of darkness but there needs to be a level of intentionality in availing ourselves of this divine protection.

Obedience to God is the only path in our heart journey that ensures our comprehensive protection from the ever-present danger of the entanglement of demonic infiltration. Experiencing deliverance from the infiltration of evil spirits is all a part of the heart journey into glorious freedom. God wants us to get free and to stay free from the influence of evil spirits and this has everything to do with living fully from the heart.

Chapter Thirteen

Entangled in Physical Biochemistry

God does not look upon our outward appearance but He looks upon the state of our heart. The biblical concept of the 'heart' encompasses our thoughts, our choices and our emotions. When we speak the language of the heart we all immediately think of the hidden thoughts and feelings that we think and feel inside. In recent decades there has been a scientific recognition of the fact that all of our thoughts and feelings within what we call our 'heart' are seamlessly integrated into the physical electrochemical processes of the human brain. Neuroscience reveals that no process of human thought or emotion can be distinguished from the electrochemical impulses within different regions of the brain. Brain mapping identifies the different regions of the brain that reflect the activity of rational thought, of emotions, of memory and of the five senses of hearing, sight, touch, taste and smell. This means that as physical beings there is a direct correlation between the actual condition of our heart and our physical brain chemistry. The implication is that these two realities of what we call our 'heart' and the brain are comprehensively and seamlessly integrated.

The human brain is an astonishing organ of divine design. For years, the standard estimate of the number of neurons in the average human brain has been 100 billion. But a recent clinical study has settled the issue once and for all by determining that the human brain contains an average of 86 billion neurons.[56] More impressive is the fact that the brain contains an estimated 1,000 trillion connections! This may still be a conservative figure as the actual number of synapses between neurons continues to elude neuroscientists. In the cerebral cortex alone, which is a thin layer of tissue on the outer surface of the brain, there are more than 125 trillion synapses, which is the equivalent of the number of stars in 1,500 Milky Way galaxies combined![57] That is just the cerebral cortex let alone the rest of the brain! The human brain is the most astonishing organ in the whole world of biology. Neuroscience is one of the fastest growing sciences and it is yielding astonishing discoveries that just keep on coming. Stephen Smith (Ph.D.) is a neuroscientist and professor of Molecular and Cellular Physiology at Stanford University, California. In a Stanford School of Medicine article published in 2010 we read:

> The brain's overall complexity is almost beyond belief, said Smith. "One synapse, by itself, is more like a microprocessor —with both memory-storage and information-processing elements — than a mere on/off switch. In fact, one synapse may contain on the order of 1,000 molecular-scale switches. A single human brain has more switches than all the computers and routers and Internet connections on Earth."[58]

All of our mental and emotional processes are carried out within the brain and alongside the physical heart; the brain is the most important organ in our body. From a biblical perspective the mind is greater than the brain because it has the capacity to exist as an expression of our spirit apart from our physical body in the same way that the mind of Christ exists independently of His physical, earthly body. Nevertheless, in this life, all of our thoughts and feelings are literally processed through our physical brain. For the duration of our earthly existence God has woven the human mind and the physical brain into a seamless whole.

The brain is still a mysterious organ! Medical researchers have now documented a two-way impact of our physiology upon our mind and emotions and of the processes of the mind and emotions upon our human physiology. Psychosomatic illness is a term that has been adopted to describe any physiological condition that has been directly caused by chronic unhealthy mental or emotional states. It is well known that sustained stress or anxiety has the capacity to trigger physical illness. But it is also well documented that certain biochemical conditions exercise a deleterious effect upon the mind and the emotions. For example, it has now been well established that chemical or hormonal imbalances can trigger clinical depression. Similarly, the deterioration of brain function can trigger a decline in our capacity to think rationally. Alzheimer's disease is an excellent example of this.

The deterioration of the physiology of the brain exercises a profoundly negative impact upon a person's ability to think clearly, to communicate or to access memories. Hormonal imbalances within the brain can cause mood swings or anxiety disorders. Our moods are often shaped by the release of certain hormones that can in turn be affected by something as simple as our diet. Chocolate, for example, boosts the production of serotonin and endorphins; the so called 'happy hormones.' A significant decline in serotonin production will cause depression.

Aberrant brain chemistry can also cause heightened emotional states and mental illnesses. All of these findings lead us to the conclusion that human beings are unquestionably biochemical machines that are mysteriously integrated with the spiritual dimension of our being; what we commonly call the soul. Therefore, we cannot discuss the 'heart journey' without recognizing and acknowledging our entanglement in our physical biochemistry and the affect the function of our brain exercises upon the condition of our 'heart.'

In human beings the spiritual and the physical are deeply interwoven with one another. "God is spirit," (John 4:24) and angels and demons are also spirit beings; all of whom have the capacity to think and feel without a physical dimension of existence. But, in contrast, human beings are spirit beings whose spirit and soul are interrelated to their physiology and their biochemistry. Our spirit is clothed in our body and the function of our spirit is inseparable from our physical existence. As tripartite beings we are a spirit that possesses a soul and a body. The soul; the mind, the will and the emotions are all designed to be an expression of our spirit.

Similarly, our physical body, along with our physical brain is also an expression of our spirit. Our spirit is housed within our body and the body without the spirit is dead. (James 2:26) But until our spirit is separated from our body at death there is a seamless integration between all of the functions of the spirit, the soul and the body. We are holistic beings that cannot function in this life apart from the integration of spirit, soul and body.

The Body and the Brain

When sin entered the human race everything dramatically changed within human beings. The brain, the most significant organ of our body, became immediately enslaved to sin. Before Adam fell into sin his spirit was alive to God and dead to sin. The moment Adam and Eve sinned their spirit became dead to God and alive to sin. "When Adam sinned, sin entered the world. Adam's sin brought death, so death spread to everyone, for everyone sinned." (Romans 5:12 NLT) As 'sinners' by nature our fallen 'dead' spirit, deeply defiled by the presence of sin, became the driver of our entire being and this includes every aspect of our soul and our body. Our fallen self became deeply compromised by sin and sin progressively defiled our physical body, our mind, our will and our emotions. Under the dominion of sin it is as thought the driver of the car is completely reckless, out of control and hell bent on self-destruction. The car is destined for destruction because the driver is in a deranged state. The presence of sin in the heart always distorts our perception of reality.

As followers of Christ we need to carefully consider the relationship between the brain and sin. What has been the effect of humanity's fall into sin upon the function of the brain? What happens when sin drives the brain? We also need to consider the new relationship between the brain and our new nature of the perfect righteousness of Christ that has been imparted to our spirit. As believers in Jesus we are glorious new creations. There is a new driver of the vehicle now. He or she has been gloriously re-created in righteousness and true holiness. Paul gave every believer clear instructions to "put on the new man which was created according to God, in true righteousness and holiness." (Ephesians 4:24) We can now 'put on' the new man because of the miracle of the new creation. This doesn't mean that we always do this as Christians but there is a new freedom to do this through the empowerment of the indwelling Spirit.

Paul stated as an historical fact that if you have put your faith in Christ, "You have taken off your old self with its practices and have put on the new self, which is being renewed in knowledge in the image of its Creator." (Colossians 3:9-10 NIV) God Himself did this for us as a miraculous act through the new birth. The human spirit has been supernaturally created in true righteousness and holiness and if we really believe the gospel message we will embrace the revelation that there is a now a new driver of the car. Through the new birth you were supernaturally transformed from being a sinner to instantaneously becoming a saint in your regenerated spirit. Under the control of the old driver our brain was habitually controlled and driven by sin but now our brain has entered into a brand new relationship to righteousness if we choose to put on the new man. But in the journey into freedom from sin and all of its destructive effects, there is still an ongoing entanglement in sin because our brains have become 'hardwired' through years of functioning under the power of sin.

New Software: Old Hardware

The physical body, including, of course, the brain has its own internal programming. This programming has been shaped through years of allowing sin to reign in our mortal bodies. The brain has been programmed to live in the presence of sin and under the dominion of sin. It has literally become hardwired to sin. As a result the brain itself has suffered a condition of spiritual 'death' because the wages of sin is death. Whatever is contaminated by sin instantaneously dies. The new nature and the new heart that God has given us is like a brand new software program installed inside our body. When activated, this new 'program' of righteousness is in direct conflict with the hardwiring of the physical body that has been programmed according to unrighteousness.

In the book of Romans, Paul deliberately developed a clear theology of the human body and its relationship to the old nature of sin and its relationship to the new nature of righteousness. Paul's theology of the body has direct implications for our understanding of the brain. In Romans 7 Paul explores the dynamics of indwelling sin and its relentless orientation toward sin and evil. He does this as an expression of solidarity with the unregenerate Jew who is struggling under the knowledge of the perfect law of God. Every God fearing Jew would comprehensively resonate with the struggle that Paul describes in this chapter.

> For we know that the law is spiritual, but I am carnal, sold under sin. For what I am doing, I do not understand. For what I will to do, that I do not practice; but what I hate, that I do. If, then, I do what I will not to do, I agree with the law that it is good. But now, it is no longer I who do it, but sin that dwells in me. For I know that in me (that is, in my flesh) nothing good dwells; for to will is present with me, but how to perform what is good I do not find. For the good that I will to do, I do not do; but the evil I will not to do, that I practice. Now if I do what I will not to do, it is no longer I who do it, but sin that dwells in me. I find then a law, that evil is present with me, the one who wills to do good. (Romans 7:14-21)

The exasperation of being bound by sin led Paul to cry out three verses later; "O wretched man that I am! Who will deliver me from this *body of death*?" (Romans 7:24) Paul introduces us to a powerful biblical concept that he calls the '*body of death.*' Kenneth Wuest, an authority on New Testament Greek writes; "The body here is the physical body, as that body in which the sinful nature dwells and through which, when it is in the ascendancy, it operates."[59] This 'body of death' describes the human body living under the dominion and tyranny of sin. Sin has defiled every part of our body because the body has become an instrument of unrighteousness, enslaved to sinful passions. Our bodies have directly suffered from the dire impact of the fall.

According to Paul, our bodies are now in a deeply humiliated state. But Paul assured the believer that in the resurrection God "will transform and fashion anew the ***body of our humiliation*** to conform to and be like the body of His glory and majesty." (Philippians 3:21 AMP) Kenneth Wuest observed that, "These physical bodies of ours have death in them, and sickness, and weakness. The body has been humiliated by the fall of Adam. The enswathement of glory, which proceeded out from within the inmost being of Adam before he sinned, and provided a covering of glory for his body, was taken away in the fall of man. The mind of Adam, functioning perfectly before the fall, was wrecked by sin."[60] Before the fall Adam and Eve had glorious bodies. They didn't have glorified bodies but their bodies were filled with the glory of the Lord. This included their brains that were once a repository of glory.

In this discussion it is worthwhile reflecting upon the body and the brain of Jesus when He walked upon the earth. Paul called Him the 'last Adam.' (1 Corinthians 15:45) Paul drew a direct comparison between the first Adam (prior to the fall) and the second Adam because both men walked in a sinless state. Just as Adam, before he fell, was clothed in glory, so Jesus, the only human being without sin, had a body that was not defiled by sin. This means the brain of Jesus was completely undefiled by sin and death. Every neuronal template and circuit in Jesus' brain functioned perfectly. His body was not humiliated by the presence of indwelling sin. In fact, His brain was full of the glory of God. His perfect spirit expressed itself through His soul and His physical brain. The miracle of the new birth restores the human spirit to a glorious state of righteousness so that we can begin to express the divine nature of Jesus through our body and our soul and this includes our brain that progressively becomes a powerful instrument of righteousness, just like the brain of Jesus.

Whenever we read about the 'body' in Scripture we need to remember that it includes the brain as part of our human anatomy. Paul indicated that the human body, in its humiliated state has been significantly compromised and impaired by the presence of sin. He wrote; "The body is sown in corruption, it is raised in incorruption. It is sown in dishonor, it is raised in glory. It is sown in weakness, it is raised in power. It is sown a natural body, it is raised a spiritual body." (1 Corinthians 15:42-43) Our bodies are as yet unredeemed. "We ourselves groan within ourselves, eagerly waiting for the adoption; the redemption of our body." (Romans 8:23) In the meantime the body is not only in a state of humiliation; it is also corrupted, dishonored and weakened. Paul described the human body as being in a state of 'corruption' which means it is in a state of decay, ruin, and impairment through the fall. He also described our bodies as existing in a state of 'dishonor' which means to be disgraced or in a state of shame. And finally he described the body as being in a condition of 'weakness' (*astheneia*) which describes a state of feebleness (of either the mind or the body) or of physical frailty and fragility.

Corruption, dishonor and weakness are the defining attributes of our body of humiliation that have endured years in exile from the glory realm of heaven and years of exposure to the debilitating nature of sin. Kenneth Wuest writes; "The mind of Adam, functioning perfectly before the fall, was wrecked by sin. The sense functions, operating perfectly before the fall, became debilitated after he sinned. As such, our present bodies are imperfect mediums through which the regenerated Spirit-filled inner life of the believer seeks unsuccessfully to express itself in the fullest measure. The Greek word [for 'humiliation'] speaks of the unfitness of our present bodies to fulfill the claims of the spiritual life."[61]

As part of our body, our brain has also suffered humiliation because of the intrusion of sin. It has been enfeebled and compromised so that it cannot reach its full potential because it has always operated outside of the realm of God's glory. But now, because our spirit is alive because of the free gift of righteousness there has been a restoration of the glory at the core of our being so that through faith we can activate the power of a glorified spirit. As we activate this power of the new creation within our regenerated spirit this will inevitably transform our physical brain, progressively delivering it from the power of sin and death. Paul said, "But, assuming that Christ is in you, on the one hand ***the body is dead on account of sin***, but on the other hand the [human] spirit is alive on account of righteousness." (Romans 8:10 Wuest) Paul's assertion that "the body is dead on account of sin" echoes his description of the 'body of death' just mentioned eleven verses prior in Romans 7:24. In 21st century language, the human spirit is an entirely new software package installed inside a body likened to old computer hardware and these two realities are powerfully conflicted.

Resurrection Life and the Body of Death

Nevertheless, Paul anticipated a significant physical impact of the presence of the resurrection life of Jesus upon our physical body (including our brain) as long as we are willing to embrace the power of the cross in putting to death the deeds of the body so that we forbid sin to reign in our mortal bodies. He said, "Do not let sin reign in your mortal body, that you should obey it in its lusts." (Romans 6:12) We must now let the resurrection life of Jesus reign in our body. "For if you live according to the flesh you will die; but if, by the Spirit, you put to death the deeds of the body, you will live." (Romans 8:13) "If the Spirit of Him who raised Jesus from the dead is living in you, He who raised Christ from the dead will also *give life to your mortal bodies* through His Spirit, who lives in you." (Romans 8:11 NIV) Eugene Petersen translated this verse in this way: "It stands to reason, doesn't it, that if the alive-and-present God who raised Jesus from the dead moves into your life, he'll do the same thing in you that he did in Jesus, bringing you alive to himself? When God lives and breathes in you (and He does, as surely as He did in Jesus), you are delivered from that dead life. With His Spirit living in you, your body will be as alive as Christ's!" (Romans 8:11 MSG)

So, while the body was initially 'dead' because of sin, God gives life to our mortal body but only as we put to death the sinful deeds of the body. This has clear implications for the condition of our physical brains. Every time Paul used the Greek word '*soma*' which is translated as 'body' we can effectively insert the word 'brain' because the brain is a significant part of the human body. Our body (and brain) comes alive because of the free gift of Christ's own perfect righteousness and hence our brain can again experience the presence of the glory of God through the indwelling life of Christ.

As we have already seen, Paul described the effect of the fall upon the human body by calling it the 'body of death.' But there is another technical term that Paul used in Romans that parallels this concept. In Romans 6 Paul used a term which he called the 'body of sin,' to describe the human body in its fallen and humiliated state. Paul envisioned the power of the new creation to deactivate the body of sin through the new power of the indwelling life and righteousness of Christ. Paul said, "Knowing this, that our old man was crucified with Him, that the body of sin might be done away with, that we should no longer be slaves of sin." (Romans 6:6) The phrase 'done away with' is a translation of a Greek word, '*katargeo*,' which is an interesting word filled with profound implications for the impact of righteousness upon our physical body, and by implication, upon our brain.

Kenneth Wuest tells us that, "The word 'body' is *soma*, the human body. The word 'sin' is in the genitive case, here, the genitive of possession. The reference is therefore to the believer's physical body before salvation, possessed by or dominated and controlled by the sinful nature. The person the believer was before he was saved was crucified with Christ in order that his physical body which before salvation was dominated by the evil nature, might be 'destroyed.' The word 'destroyed' is *katargeo*; "to render idle, inactive, inoperative, to cause to cease."[62] We have to think this through carefully but it is a powerful revelation once we get it. In light of this, Wuest translates this key passage as follows:

> For in view of the fact that we are those who have become permanently united with Him with respect to the likeness of His death, certainly also we shall be those who as a logical result have become permanently united with Him with respect to the likeness of His resurrection, knowing this experientially, that our old [unregenerate] self was crucified once for all with Him in order that the physical body [heretofore] dominated by the sinful nature might be rendered inoperative [in that respect], with the result that no longer are we rendering a slave's habitual obedience to the sinful nature, for the one who died once for all stands in the position of a permanent relationship of freedom from the sinful nature. (Romans 6:5-7 Wuest)

This means that our body can now become an instrument of righteousness instead of an instrument of sin. This interpretation of this passage is supported by the following translations. J. B. Phillips said, "Let us never forget that our old selves died with him on the cross that the tyranny of sin over us might be broken." (Romans 6:6 J. B. Phillips) The Amplified Bible says, "We know that our old (unrenewed) self was nailed to the cross with Him in order that [our] body [which is the instrument] of sin might be made ineffective and inactive for evil, that we might no longer be the slaves of sin." (Romans 6:6 AMP) The Holman Bible says, "For we know that our old self was crucified with Him in order that sin's dominion over the body may be abolished, so that we may no longer be enslaved to sin." (Romans 6:6 HCSB) What did Paul intend to communicate to us in Romans 6:6? The flow of Romans 6 is intended to convey in no uncertain terms that the physical body need no longer be enslaved to sin but that it can now be enslaved to righteousness. But the human body can only become the slave of righteousness as each Christian takes full responsibility for the sanctification of his or her body.

We are explicitly instructed to "put to death the deeds of the body." (Romans 8:13) The 'deeds of the body' are the passions and cravings of the physical body. These must be put to death by a choice to embrace the power of the cross so that God can impart the fullness of His resurrection life to our mortal bodies. Paul taught believers how to pursue the sanctification of their physical bodies. "Each of you should know how to possess his own vessel in sanctification and honor." (1 Thessalonians 4:4) The NIV says, "Each of you should learn to control his own body in a way that is holy and honorable, not in passionate lust like the heathen, who do not know God." (4:4,5 NIV) Paul exhorts us to pursue the complete sanctification of our body. "Now may the God of peace Himself sanctify you completely; and may your whole spirit, soul, and body be preserved blameless at the coming of our Lord Jesus Christ." (1 Thessalonians 5:23) Paul said, "I discipline my body and bring it into subjection." (1 Corinthians 9:27) Remember, whenever we see the word 'body' we can insert the word 'brain' because our brains are a major part of our body. This means that we must intentionally bring our brain into subjection to our regenerated spirit, just as the physical body of Jesus was entirely subjected to the spirit of Jesus. Jesus is our pattern of wholeness.

Our brain can be submitted to the dominion of sin so that it becomes an instrument of wickedness or we can present our brain to God as an instrument of righteousness. Paul said, "Do not present your members as instruments of unrighteousness to sin, but present yourselves to God as being alive from the dead, and your members as instruments of righteousness to God." (Romans 6:13) The NIV explains this more clearly. "Do not offer the parts of your body to sin, as instruments of wickedness, but rather offer yourselves to God, as those who have been brought from death to life; and offer the parts of your body to him as instruments of righteousness." (NIV) So we are now called to offer our brains to God so that they may become an instrument of righteousness!

The Greek word for 'instrument' in this passage is '*hopla*.' Kenneth Wuest reveals, "In classical Greek the word referred to the weapons of the Greek soldier. Paul thinks of the members of the Christian's body as weapons to be used in the Christian warfare against evil. The saint, counting upon the fact that he has been disengaged from the evil nature, does two things, he refuses to allow it to reign as king in his life, and he stops putting his members at its disposal to be used as weapons of unrighteousness."[63] Paul employed the metaphor of slavery as this was extremely familiar to the culture of Rome to whom he was writing. "I put this in human terms because you are weak in your natural selves. Just as you used to offer the parts of your body in slavery to impurity and to ever-increasing wickedness, so now offer them in slavery to righteousness leading to holiness." (Romans 6:19 NIV) This now includes our brain that is now intended to become a 'slave' of righteousness, meaning that it is now intended to be driven and controlled by the new nature.

The pathway to holiness involves the presentation of every part of our body and soul to God. We will either be a slave of sin or a slave of righteousness. When we intentionally choose to bring every part of our physical body and of our soul under the reign of righteousness we are exposing our body and soul to the glory of Christ who dwells in our regenerated human spirit. Paul taught that all have sinned and fallen short of the glory of God. Sin cut us off from the glory realm but the regeneration of our spirit through the free gift of righteousness restores our spirit to the glory realm. When we activate our glorified spirit through faith in the revelation of who we are in Christ we switch the radiance of God's glory on and it permeates our entire being with the outflow and shining effulgence of divine glory. This was the state of Christ's body and soul when He walked upon the earth. Our spirit has now been comprehensively restored to the state of Christ's glorified spirit when He lived on earth.

The Sanctification of the Body and the Brain

The good news is that we can learn how to sanctify our physical brain and employ it as a weapon of righteousness; filled with God's glory. Pornography addiction is a great example of the presentation of our physical brain as an instrument of sin and unrighteousness. The more a porn user indulges his senses in pornographic images the more physically addicted he will become.

His brain develops patterns that respond to the sexual gratification of porn. The same is true of a person who has developed an addiction to substances. The more they use drugs the more they are training their brain to respond to the gratification of those substances. These patterns of living establish strong neuronal networks of dependency, gratification and reward. In this way, the brain becomes hard wired to sin. A person who is still habitually gratifying their old sinful nature is still effectively allowing sin to drive the car instead of the new nature of righteousness.

Paul said, "Clothe yourselves with the Lord Jesus Christ, and do not think about how to *gratify* the desires of the sinful nature." (Romans 13:14 NIV) "So I say, live by the Spirit, and you will not *gratify* the desires of the sinful nature." (Galatians 5:16 NIV) "For all that is in the world—the lust of the flesh [craving for sensual *gratification*] and the lust of the eyes and the pride of life – these do not come from the Father but are from the world." (1 John 2:16 AMP) Paul said, "She who lives in pleasure and *self-gratification* [giving herself up to luxury and self-indulgence] is dead even while she lives." (1 Timothy 5:6 AMP) Whatever we give ourselves to in our reckless pursuit of carnal and temporal gratification imprisons us and makes us its slave. Jesus said, "Most assuredly, I say to you, whoever commits sin is a slave of sin." (John 8:34)

Presenting our members as instruments of righteousness means that we must turn away from all sensual, worldly forms of gratification to find our ultimate gratification in the presence of the glory of God. God and His glory becomes for the devout lover of Christ the ultimate form of spiritual gratification. "You will show me the path of life; in Your presence is fullness of joy; at Your right hand are pleasures forevermore." (Psalms 16:11) The path to life is found in setting our minds on things above where we find the ultimate gratification of the soul. "For to be carnally minded is death but to be spiritually minded is life and peace." (Romans 8:6) God pours out infinite ecstasy and bliss upon those who set their affections upon Him and who embrace the mystic path of union with Christ in the fullness of His divine glory and blessedness.

There is a part of the human brain that is designed as the 'reward center' of the brain. It is this part of the brain that responds to gratification. Martin Daubney is a British man who was previously the editor of a soft-core porn magazine called *Loaded* from 2003 to 2010. He is now the presenter of a documentary titled *Porn on the Brain,* which examines the effect of pornography upon the teenage brain. His discoveries were deeply disturbing.

> Having established that 'basically, porn is everywhere,' we set out to discover what all this porn was doing to their brains. Was it having any effect at all? Could it be addictive? We found Dr. Valerie Voon, a neuroscientist at Cambridge University and a global authority on addiction. Then, in the first study of its kind, we recruited 19 heavy porn users who felt their habit was out of control and had Dr. Voon examine their brain activity as they watched, among other things, hardcore porn. She showed them a variety of images, both stills and videos. These ranged from images known to excite all men, such as bundles of £50 notes and extreme sports in action, to mundane landscapes and wallpapers – all inter-spliced with hardcore porn videos, plus pictures of both clothed and naked women. The ways in which their brains responded to this diverse imagery were compared with the responses of a group of healthy volunteers. She was interested in a particular brain region called the *ventral striatum* – the 'reward center' – where our sense of pleasure is produced. This is one of the areas where an addict will show a heightened response to visual representations of their addiction - whether it's a syringe or a bottle of vodka. What we discovered was a revelation. When shown porn, the reward center of normal volunteers barely reacted, but that of the compulsive porn users lit up like a Christmas tree. The compulsive porn users' brains showed clear parallels with those with substance addictions. Everybody on the project was astounded, even Dr. Voon, who admitted she had been 'skeptical and ambivalent' about the study at the outset. If porn does have the insidious power to be addictive, then letting our children consume it freely via the internet is like leaving heroin lying around the house, or handing out vodka at the school gates.[64]

The pathway to the comprehensive disentanglement of our physical brains from the enslavement of sin comes through the renewing of our minds. "Do not be conformed to this world, but be transformed by the renewing of your mind, that you may prove what is that good and acceptable and perfect will of God." (Romans 12:2) The concept of the renewal of our mind is predicated upon everything that Paul unveiled in Romans chapter 6 to 8 where he reveals the glory of our mystical union with Christ and our deliverance from being orphans to becoming sons and daughters of the living God. Romans chapter 9 to 11 describes the place of natural Israel in God's redemptive plan in the light of the new creation and the redefining of what it means to be an Israelite.

I see these three chapters as something of a theological excursus and a diversion away from the major flow of Paul's argument. So, if we leap from the last verses of Romans 8 (where Paul proclaims that absolutely nothing can now separate us from the love of God in Christ) over to Romans 12:1 (where Paul proclaims that our supernatural transformation comes through the mechanism of the renewing of our minds) it is clear that Paul is really linking the transformation of our minds to the theological foundation that he painstakingly laid in Romans chapters 6 to 8.

As our minds are supernaturally transformed by the Holy Spirit this glorious transformation finds its expression in the virtual rewiring of the physical brain. God's glory inhabits a deeply renewed mind so that the mind is effectively disentangled from sin and gloriously entangled in righteousness just as Jesus' mind was entangled in the glory of His perichoresis with the Father. Paul said that we have the mind of Christ as part of the package of being partakers of His divine nature. When we learn how to activate the mind of Christ within us it actually transforms our mind, which in turn transforms our physical brain! We become partakers of an entirely new way of thinking and as we become established in these new patterns, new neuronal networks and templates are established and old pathways begin to atrophy through disuse.

Brain scientists now tell us that the 'neuroplasticity' of the brain enables the brain to completely rewire itself so that brand new neuronal pathways can be established within regions of the brain. I have a friend who was involved in a car crash at the hands of a drunk driver. One passenger was killed and my friend suffered serious brain damage. The entire speech center of his brain was surgically removed because it was so damaged. His parent's greatest fear was that he would become a vegetable but over time, through diligent speech pathology and loads of prayer, his brain comprehensively rewired itself! He can now speak just as well as he could before the accident. But for a time, because the entire speech center of his brain was removed he had no capacity to speak at all.

Norman Doidge, the author of *The Brain That Changes Itself,* says, "The idea that the brain can change its own structure and function through thought and activity is, I believe, the most important alteration in our view of the brain since we first sketched out its basic anatomy and the workings of its basic component, the neuron."[65] Doidge notes that scientists who are pioneering the field of neuroplasticity have proven that, "children are not always stuck with the mental abilities they are born with; that the damaged brain can often reorganize itself so that when one part fails, another can often substitute; that if brain cells die, they can at times be replaced; that many 'circuits' and even basic reflexes that we think are hardwired are not."[66]

The Dark Side of Neuroplasticity

Neuroplasticity has a distinctly dark side. The more a person engages in a particular sinful practice the more the brain adapts and establishes neuronal templates that lock people into habitual or addictive sin patterns. This is clearly true of people addicted to substances. Similarly with habitual pornography use, the porn addict is radically rewiring his brain, setting up a reward system built around stimulation and gratification. Norman Doidge writes,

> The addictiveness of Internet pornography is not a metaphor. Not all addictions are to drugs or alcohol. People can be seriously addicted to gambling, even to running. All addicts show a loss of control of the activity, compulsively seek it out despite negative consequences, develop tolerance so that they need higher and higher levels of stimulation for satisfaction, and experience withdrawal if they can't consummate the addictive act. All addiction involves long-term, sometimes lifelong, neuroplastic change in the brain. For addicts, moderation is impossible.[67]

Habitual porn users rarely consider that their secretive activities are systematically rewiring their brains, setting up a chemical reward system and new neuronal pathways that deepen the addiction. Doidge observes that,

> Cocaine, almost all other illegal drugs, and even nondrug addictions such as running make the pleasure-giving neurotransmitter dopamine more active in the brain. Dopamine is called the reward transmitter, because when we accomplish something—run a race and win—our brain triggers its release. Though exhausted, we get a surge of energy, exciting pleasure, and confidence and even raise our hands and run a victory lap."[68]

"The usual view is that an addict goes back for more of his fix because he likes the pleasure it gives and doesn't like the pain of withdrawal. But addicts take drugs when there is no prospect of pleasure, when they know they have an insufficient dose to make them high and will crave more even before they begin to withdraw. Wanting and liking are two different things. An addict experiences cravings because his plastic brain has become sensitized to the drug or the experience. Sensitization is different from tolerance. As tolerance develops, the addict needs more and more of a substance or porn to get a pleasant effect; as sensitization develops, he needs less and less of the substance to crave it intensely. So sensitization leads to increased wanting, though not necessarily liking. Pornography is more exciting than satisfying because we have two separate pleasure systems in our brains, one that has to do with exciting pleasure and one with satisfying pleasure. The exciting system relates to the 'appetitive' pleasure that we get imagining something we desire, such as sex or a good meal. Its neurochemistry is largely dopamine-related, and it raises our tension level. The second pleasure system has to do with the satisfaction, or consummatory pleasure, that attends actually having sex or having that meal, a calming, fulfilling pleasure. Its neurochemistry is based on the release of endorphins, which are related to opiates and give a peaceful, euphoric bliss. Pornography, by offering an endless harem of sexual objects, hyperactivates the appetitive system. Porn viewers develop new maps in their brains, based on the photos and videos they see. Because it is a use-it-or-lose-it brain, when we develop a map area, we long to keep it activated.[69]

Norman Doidge likens regular pornography use to drug addiction. The pornographer literally becomes addicted to the rush of dopamine and endorphins and the brain establishes strong neuronal connections that make overcoming the addiction extremely difficult.

In order to determine how addictive a street drug is, researchers at the National Institutes of Health (NIH) in Maryland train a rat to press a bar until it gets a shot of the drug. The harder the animal is willing to work to press the bar, the more addictive the drug.[70] The men at their computers looking at porn were uncannily like the rats in the cages of the NIH, pressing the bar to get a shot of dopamine or its equivalent. Though they didn't know it, they had been seduced into pornographic training sessions that met all the conditions required for plastic change of brain maps. Since neurons that fire together wire together, these men got massive amounts of practice wiring these images into the pleasure centers of the brain, with the rapt attention necessary for plastic change. They imagined these images when away from their computers, or while having sex with their girlfriends, reinforcing them. Each time they felt sexual excitement and had an orgasm when they masturbated, a 'spritz of dopamine,' the reward neurotransmitter, consolidated the connections made in the brain during the sessions.[71]

The biochemistry of drug or porn addiction is equally true of every other form of sin. Sin, by its very nature is addictive. We can become addicted to food just as readily as we can become addicted to rage or intense emotional states. People who become addicted to horror movies seek greater and greater spikes of fear to satisfy their ever-deepening quest for gratification. Sin is not only addictive; it is also progressive. In his book, Norman Doidge explores aspects of sexual perversion that reveal the progressive nature of sin. How does someone end up in bizarre sexual perversion? Their sensitization to sexual immorality demands greater stimuli in order to satisfy their quest for a greater dopamine hit.

The rewiring of our pleasure systems, and the extent to which our sexual tastes can be acquired, is seen most dramatically in such perversions as sexual masochism, which turns physical pain into sexual pleasure. To do this the brain must make pleasant that which is inherently unpleasant, and the impulses that normally trigger our pain system are plastically rewired into our pleasure system. People with perversions often organize their lives around activities that mix aggression and sexuality. Sexual sadism illustrates plasticity in that it fuses two familiar tendencies, the sexual and the aggressive.[72]

How can someone possibly get free of deeply established neuronal templates of reward and gratification? It is only through the replacement of old neuronal networks with entirely new neuronal networks that the old templates atrophy through disuse. If we go back to the old templates of addiction and fleshly gratification we can reignite them and those old patterns can be powerfully reactivated. But if we starve them through establishing entirely new neuronal networks and consistently exercising these new networks we can become completely free of our old templates. Paul juxtaposes the reprobate mind with the mind of Christ; the carnal mind with the spiritual mind. He asserted that carnal thought patterns produce death whereas spiritual thought patterns produce life. "For to be carnally minded is death, but to be spiritually minded is life and peace." (Romans 8:6) The same is true of negative and destructive emotions that equally produce death whereas positive and constructive emotions produce life and peace.

The brain, empowered by carnal thinking is rendered spiritually dead. This adds new meaning to the concept of being 'brain dead!' Paul's concept of the 'body of death' or the 'body of sin' includes our physical brain. But, as we have seen, "If the Spirit of Him who raised Jesus from the dead is living in you, He who raised Christ from the dead will also give life to your mortal bodies through His Spirit, who lives in you." (Romans 8:11 NIV) The presence of the resurrection life of Christ in our spirit actually imparts life to our brain!

It is through the process of the supernatural renewing of the mind that our brain is switched on and enlivened through the indwelling Spirit. When the mind of Christ is powerfully activated in our brains and new spiritually oriented neuronal templates that correspond to heavenly thinking are firmly established, our brain literally begins to reflect the brain of Jesus when He walked upon the earth. The physical brain of Jesus powerfully expressed the mind of Jesus, which, in turn, was an expression of the glorified spirit of Jesus. Jesus' brain was full of the glory of the Lord. Similarly, our brains can be transformed from glory to glory and can also reflect the glory of the new creation that God has established within our spirit.

The glory of heaven invades earth through the glorified spirit of the new creation in Christ. In the Old Testament the glory of the Lord came upon furniture. But in the New Testament the glory of the Lord comes upon human hearts and upon relationships that are established in the glory realm. Through the free gift of righteousness the kingdom comes secretly into the human heart. "Those who receive abundance of grace and of *the gift of righteousness* will reign [*basileuo*] in life through the One, Jesus Christ." (Romans 5:17) Jesus said, "For behold, the kingdom [*basileia*] of God is within you [in your hearts]." (Luke 17:21 AMP)

We now have the exact same potential as Jesus to release the glory of the kingdom of God through our hearts. As we activate our glorified spirit we can now impart glorious new life to our brain through the resurrection power of Jesus in us. We can train our brain to become like Jesus' brain when He lived upon the earth by releasing the river of the glory of the Lord out of our innermost being so that it floods the human brain, setting up neuronal pathways that powerfully reflect the glorious mind of Christ. We can actively participate in this process by intentionally renewing our minds day by day through washing our minds with the water of the Word of God until we begin to think just like Jesus.

Dr. Caroline Leaf, author of *Who Switched Off My Brain,* argues that the brain can be powerfully switched back on when a Christian takes charge of their brain processes and brings their brain into submission to the Spirit of Christ. She writes,

> As scientists, we now understand so much more about how our thoughts affect our emotions and bodies. Because we can see clearly how brain science lines up with Scripture, we can also start breaking the chains of toxic thinking in a dynamic way, proving that your mind can be renewed, toxic thoughts and emotions can be swept away, and your brain really can be 'switched on.' You really can overcome toxic thinking and its effects. You really can renew and refresh your mind. Not only does Scripture uphold this principle, but science proves when we work with how our brains are wired, lasting, life-giving change really is possible. [73]

The Bible tells us what we ought to fix our thoughts upon. "Finally, brothers, whatever is true, whatever is noble, whatever is right, whatever is pure, whatever is lovely, whatever is admirable – if anything is excellent or praiseworthy – think about such things." (Philippians 4:8 NIV) The Amplified Bible says, "Fix your minds on them." We can literally train our physical brain to think like Jesus thought. Because we are now partakers of the divine nature we can release the unlimited resources of the love, peace and joy of Christ to permeate our brains so that every old neuronal template is dismantled. Quantum physics teaches us that consciousness exercises a direct impact upon the quantum field through the observer effect.

In my book, *Quantum Glory*, I develop the idea that the quantum fabric of the cosmos has been designed by God to be supernaturally restructured through the directed invasion of the glory realm of heaven. This is the basis of heaven invading earth and affecting supernatural miracles in the physical realm. As we focus on biblical truth and it becomes revelation inside of us we can literally restructure our brains at a quantum level through the directed power of a renewed mind. A human brain that is radically alive to God through the indwelling glory of the Lord is capable of releasing the glory of the Lord everywhere we go because, as Bill Johnson teaches in his book, *The Supernatural Power of a Transformed Mind*, our minds are the gateway of heaven. He writes, "Our goal is to agree with heaven all the time; to let our minds be the gate of heaven."[74]

The Mind and the Brain

Biblical theology boldly asserts that the human mind transcends the physical brain. Although the mind is intimately associated with the intricate processes of the brain, the existence of the mind of God independent of matter reveals that the biblical concept of 'mind' is greater than a combination of mere physical processes. The fact that the soul exists independently of the physical body supports the idea that the mind transcends matter. In recent years some neuroscientists have broken away from the materialistic assumptions of the older neuroscience community, arguing that the mind is more than the firing of synapses within the brain. The dominant materialist view is that the mind is a product of the brain, which leads to a deterministic view that we become the tragic victims of our hardwiring. This view promotes the idea that our will is not free and that we are subject to a kind of biochemical predestination. Such a view doesn't offer a great deal of hope.

Jeffrey Schwartz, author of *The Mind and the Brain*, rejects this idea, arguing that our consciousness transcends our brain functions and that we have genuine freedom to choose in a way that can direct the capacity of the brain to rewire itself. "If we truly believe, when the day is done, that our mind and all that term entails—the choices we make, the reactions we have, the emotions we feel—are nothing but the expression of a machine governed by the rules of classical physics and chemistry, and that our behavior follows ineluctably from the workings of our neurons, then we're forced to conclude that the subjective sense of freedom is a "user illusion."[75] But we are not the victims of biological predeterminism!

Schwartz is joined in his conviction by Mario Beauregard, author of *The Spiritual Brain; A Neuroscientist's Case for the Existence of the Soul.* Beauregard writes;

> The discipline of neuroscience today is materialistic. That is, it assumes that the mind is quite simply the physical workings of the brain. Materialists think that the distinction you make between your mind as an immaterial entity and your brain as a bodily organ has no real basis. The mind is assumed to be a mere illusion generated by the workings of the brain. Some materialists even think you should not in fact use terminology that implies that your mind exists. We intend to show you that your mind does exist, that it is not merely your brain. Your thoughts and feelings cannot be dismissed or explained away by firing synapses and physical phenomena alone. In a solely material world, 'will power' or 'mind over matter' are illusions. The brain, however, is not the mind; it is an organ suitable for connecting a mind to the rest of the universe.[76]

Paul's exhortation to "be renewed in the spirit of your mind" (Ephesians 4:23) suggests that our consciousness transcends our physical brain and that we have the freedom in Christ to make choices that will result in what Jeffrey Schwartz calls "directed neuroplasticity." He says, "I propose that the time has come for science to confront the serious implications of the fact that directed willed mental activity can clearly and systematically alter brain function; that the exertion of willful effort generates a physical force that has the power to change how the brain works and even its physical structure. The result is directed neuroplasticity."[77] Paul would wholeheartedly agree by asserting that the power of the resurrection life of Christ in us can give life to our physical brain; switching it on in such a way that the brain of the person who is a new creation in Christ can be powerfully transformed to reflect the mind of Christ. Norman Doidge reveals that the entire human brain can be dramatically rewired!

> Research has shown that neuroplasticity is neither ghettoized within certain departments in the brain nor confined to the sensory, motor, and cognitive processing areas we have already explored. The brain structure that regulates instinctive behaviors, including sex, called the hypothalamus, is plastic, as is the amygdala, the structure that processes emotion and anxiety. While some parts of the brain, such

as the cortex, may have more plastic potential because there are more neurons and connections to be altered, even non-cortical areas display plasticity. It is a property of all brain tissue. Plasticity exists in the hippocampus (the area that turns our memories from short-term to long-term ones) as well as in areas that control our breathing, process primitive sensation, and process pain. If one brain system changes, those systems connected to it change as well. The same 'plastic rules'—use it or lose it, or neurons that fire together wire together—apply throughout. Different areas of the brain wouldn't be able to function together if that weren't the case.[78]

This is incredibly good news for people who have been comprehensively stuck in their old strongholds of the mind, will and emotions. Every part of our brain can be switched back on in a way that releases the life and the glory of Christ into our brain so that it becomes a powerful instrument or weapon of righteousness instead of a weapon of unrighteousness. Every negative and destructive emotion can be rewired to reflect the healthy emotional life of Jesus. Every stronghold of the mind can be systematically dismantled. Every stronghold of the will resulting in addictions and a sense of powerlessness can be overcome through the power of the resurrection life of Jesus who has come to transform our will into His will.

If Paul lived in the 21st century he would have been delighted by the cutting edge science of neuroplasticity. He wholeheartedly believed and taught that the body of sin could be rendered inoperative through the power of Christ. The brain could be powerfully switched back on and we can escape the entanglement of our old physical biochemistry through the supernatural transformation of a renewed mind. Doidge writes: "Because a new word is useful for those who do a new thing, I call the practitioners of this new science of changing brains "neuroplasticians.""[79]

Paul was a new creation neuroplastician who sought to raise up a generation of supernatural neuroplasticians who could walk in the Spirit in such a way that heaven could invade earth in their mind, will and emotions and the glory of Christ could be restored so that our brains, which were created to reflect the glory of God could be switched back on to facilitate the expression of the mind of Christ.

This is a glorious vision of what it practically means to be conformed to the image of the Son. Jesus promised, "If the Son sets you free, you shall be free indeed." (John 8:36) This freedom includes our emancipation from the dictates of our old neuronal templates through the establishment of heavenly templates that produce life instead of death. This concept of 'directed neuroplasticity' through Spirit empowered neuroplasticians is incredibly exciting and it offers extraordinary hope that has the potential to radically transform our physical brain into an unimaginably powerful weapon of righteousness that functions as the gateway of heaven in such a way that we can release the glory of the Lord everywhere we go on earth because our minds, and by implication, our brain have become energized by heaven, paving the way to bring heaven on earth.

God wants to fill us with a supernaturally energized hope that we can actually escape all of the constraints of our old physical neurological hardwiring. "Now may the God of hope fill you with all joy and peace in believing, that you may abound in hope by the power of the Holy Spirit." (Romans 15:13) We may have a brand new operating system installed into a body that has old hardwired circuits but the hope of heaven is that the old hardware can now be upgraded so that it is comprehensively rebuilt to function in a divine synergy with the new operating system that is encoded in our new nature. There is nothing like a state-of-the-art computer hardware system that is designed specifically to work perfectly and seamlessly with an operating system. This is one feature that has given Apple an edge over Windows. Seamless integration of hardware and software creates a much smoother computer experience.

Jesus was the divine pattern of sonship and His life on earth exemplified the perfect synergy of a heavenly operating system and a body that was undefiled by sin which provided the perfect vehicle for His glorified spirit. It takes time to rewire the brain and set up new networks that serve heaven but the more we invest ourselves into rewiring our brains the more ease there will be in our thought life and the more natural heavenly thinking will become. Until our brains are rewired by the indwelling glory there will be great internal conflict. But our hope is that the glory of God will usher us into greater ease in our thought life as we disentangle ourselves from our old brain chemistry that operated in slavery to sin.

Chapter Fourteen

The Triumph of Divine Entanglement

"Thanks be to God, who made us His captives and leads us along in Christ's triumphal procession." (2 Corinthians 2:14 NLT)

In light of the broad spectrum of unique heart entanglements that we have explored in the previous seven chapters we really should not be surprised by the grip that the old nature continues to exercise upon the hearts of so many believers. Church leaders and Bible teachers faithfully preach the promise of breakthrough and victory in the church because that is unquestionably the purpose and plan of God and the desire of all who have ever aspired to live in the freedom that the Scriptures promise. We dare not lose sight of the glorious hope of freedom held out to us by God. To let go of this hope is to embrace a slippery downward slide into a state of gloom, despair and defeat.

However, the experience of the average Christian appears to be at odds with the glorious promises of Scripture. Looking back over two thousand years of church experience, surveying the landscape of contemporary church life and the common experience of the average Christian it would appear that in so many seasons of church history human brokenness has sadly triumphed over the powerful new creation realities described in the pages of the New Testament. In most periods of the history of the church it was the rare exception to find a remnant of true believers who broke through into a dimension of supernatural freedom. The vast company of defeated believers confirms the difficulty that so many have experienced in attaining the life of the overcomer. Given the complexity of our deep entanglements it is really quite amazing that any Christians break through into freedom at all!

To appreciate the challenge that the heart journey represents we need only consider the multiplication effect that occurs when one deep entanglement of the heart is combined with another. Take for example the combinational effect of sin and brokenheartedness that we explored in the chapter on the entanglement of emotional brokenness. Entanglement in sin is one thing but when it is intertwined with strongholds of emotional brokenness the two entanglements feed into one another creating an unhealthy feedback loop. Unforgiveness (which is considered a sin by Jesus) combined with an attitude of harsh judgment toward those who have wounded or offended us can result in bitter root judgments that have the potential to hold us in bondage for decades without any breakthrough. Add to that a set of strategically placed lies from the evil one subtly inserted into the believer's mind and it becomes clear that a combinational effect is in operation.

If demonic infiltration enters the equation so that a spirit of bitterness locks itself on to a believer's unrenewed soul it exponentially increases the degree of bondage, not to mention the deep discouragement that accompanies such a state. I can personally think of countless Christians I have ministered to over the past few decades that perfectly fit this description. Is freedom possible for such a person? Absolutely! But circumstances such as these require a combination of different kingdom ministry skills to extricate such a person from the labyrinth of deep combinational entanglements. Such circumstances also require a supportive community environment saturated in a Spirit of prophetic encouragement to keep people's eyes on the prize and to keep their hope levels high as they journey through the processes of the heart necessary to obtain complete breakthrough.

The same is true for a Christian who has spent a few decades in bondage to pornography. Instead of experiencing deeper freedom, the experience of a person with deep sexual addictions tends to drag them deeper and deeper into brokenness and despair. What would it take to extricate such a person from this prison? For a Christian, years of willful rebellion to the clear revelation of the will of God always results in a deep corruption of the will that in turn creates an opportunity for the devil to gain a significant foothold that will lead to deep strongholds. Can such a person get free of their bondage to lust and demonic infiltration? Once again; absolutely! With God all things are possible. However a whole set of factors need to line up in this person's life in order for freedom to come, and for many, the supportive environment, the dedication of fellow believers and the keys for freedom often fail to materialize when the prevailing church culture isn't one of radical spiritual breakthrough.

When we also consider the state that many people come to the Lord in, we really shouldn't be surprised when we don't see the kind of breakthroughs that we might hope to see. Many come to Jesus out of extremely broken backgrounds with decades of deep entanglements in sin, selfishness, emotional brokenness, satanic lies, demonic infiltration and neuronal templates characterized by deep negativity and multiple addictions. The path to freedom is fraught with considerable challenges and it really is the rare exception when people with decades of deep brokenness come into glorious freedom. Subsequently, many Christians stay locked down in brokenness and defeat and hope merely for the grace of God to survive and to endure beneath crushing circumstances. Entanglement in unhealthy dysfunctional relationships also creates a worsening environment where the ongoing pain of broken relationships creates toxic circumstances that further hinder any hope of spiritual breakthrough. Regrettably the odds are stacked against Christians who are deeply broken and who are locked into dysfunctional relationships breaking through into a life of freedom and kingdom fruitfulness.

This assessment may sound rather negative and some might be critical about such a gloomy reality check. But the evidence supports the realization that there are multiple factors stacked against our personal transformation. But surely the resurrection life of Jesus living on the inside of our heart offers a much better prognosis. The revelation of the glory of New Testament grace calls us to a supernatural life of overcoming because the writers of the New Testament were singularly focused upon the prophetic destiny of every New Covenant believer. To pitch the vision lower that God's perfect will for the believer would be fatalistic because it would make concessions to sin and darkness and that is something that falls way below God's glorious plan. Prophecy always calls us to God's perfect will. It is inconceivable to preach anything less than spiritual breakthrough and personal victory. But the recognition of the numerous entanglements of the heart exhibited in the writings of the New Testament highlight the strongholds that have to be overcome. The writer of Hebrews tells us about the sin that so easily entangles us. Religion is a yoke of bondage that also entangles us. The seduction of the world, which appeals to our old selfish nature, also easily entangles us if we are not getting the deepest needs of our heart met by our heavenly Father.

The Missing Ingredients

The revelation of Scripture compels us toward the conclusion that there must be a unique set of life skills for the Christian that are needed to break through into the life of radical obedience and holiness that God is continually beckoning us to. Every command in Scripture is really a promise because God always provides us with everything we need to do His will. The widespread malaise of the church supports the idea that it is this unique set of life skills that are the missing ingredients in the equation of supernatural transformation. There is nothing lacking on God's part. He has made a way through the cross and the glorious new creation miracle to set us up for incredible glory and freedom. So what are these missing ingredients?

The first is a lack of revelation into our glorious destiny. God has predestined us to be conformed to the image of Jesus, His Son. Where there is no vision the people of God dwell carelessly. But this vision is not a scarce commodity. Whenever we read the New Testament, which we ought to be immersing ourselves in daily, we are freshly envisioned for a life of victory and breakthrough. No one could claim ignorance concerning God's will to bring us into glorious freedom. Nevertheless, many Christians readily lose their vision because of the lies of the enemy that minister despair and hopelessness to those who have never experienced personal freedom. The devil always seeks to rob us of vision by convincing us that the life of the overcomer is completely unattainable. So many Christians settle for a life of disobedience and chronic failure. But this is one of the devil's greatest lies!

The Vision of the New Heart

Our destiny is to live in the freedom of the glorious new creation! God has given us the ultimate free gift of a brand-new heart and a standing of perfect righteousness before the Father. He has equipped us with all of the tools we could possibly need to overcome. The new creation gives us the best head start we could ever ask for. Through this miracle we can live from God rather than toward God. Clearly, one of the great keys to getting significantly greater traction in our heart journey is the deepening revelation of the new heart that Jesus has already given us. The clearer our vision of the glory of the new creation the greater the empowerment to live *'from* God.' The Holy Spirit continually magnifies the miracle of the new birth and the free gift of righteousness, relentlessly testifying with our spirit that we are now glory filled children of God. All of us are responsible to discover that we have a brand new glory filled core identity.

The Father continuously calls out the treasure of our new identity of sonship and the new heart of Jesus that God has planted inside of our heart. The Christian life has been designed to elevate us "from glory to glory." We cannot ascend "from glory" unless we have first been established in glory. The new creation miracle furnishes every single believer with the glory filled life of Jesus who has come to live His powerful resurrection life through us. Every believer who breaks through into a strong revelation of the power of the resurrected life of Christ in us is well positioned to become an overcomer. Overcomers live '*from* God' instead of '*for* God' because of the discovery of the glory of Christ in the center of their hearts.

Saying 'Yes' to the reality of the indwelling resurrected Christ inside of us is infinitely more powerful than saying a thousand 'No's' to the issues inside of our heart. All of our attempts to overcome the seven entanglements of the heart that we have explored in the previous seven chapters are doomed to failure if we seek to overcome these things independently of a life of deep devotion to Christ. Many Christians seek to overcome the world, the flesh and the devil but they often fail to do it from a proper new creation foundation. Paul established a profound revelatory principle when he said, "Do not be overcome by evil, but overcome evil with good." (Romans 12:21) All of our attempts to overcome evil (or any other entanglement for that matter) are destined to be an exercise in futility unless they are approached from a radical new creation paradigm. Walking in the glory of the new creation is the key to every breakthrough in the heart journey. If this foundation is destroyed the righteous stumble and spend their lives going around the same mountain over and over again. The 'heaven invading earth' paradigm is all about the displacement of evil through the revelation of the glory of Christ in us.

Paul expanded upon and demonstrated the application of this principle when he said, "Put on the Lord Jesus Christ and make no provision for the flesh, to fulfil its lusts." (Romans 13:14) In other words, our supernatural entanglement with Jesus in our participation in His life and divine nature is the key to activating the reality of who we really are in the core of our being. Belief in the glory of the new creation unlocks the treasures and the riches of heaven inside of our heart. Instead of battling strongholds on their own terms we search for the treasure hidden in the dung. The glory of our new creation identity is literally like a pearl buried in a pile of pig manure. The evil one always seeks to get our eyes fixed upon the stronghold itself in order to depress us and entice us into aligning ourselves with his assignments of accusation and self-condemnation.

John said, "If our heart condemns us, God is greater than our heart, and knows all things. Beloved, if our heart does not condemn us, we have confidence toward God." (1 John 3:20,21) Living under either demonic condemnation or self-condemnation is a tried and true method of robbing us of any confidence before God. The revelation of the free gift of righteousness is the key to breaking the power of condemnation and accusation. "Who dares accuse us whom God has chosen for His own? No one—for God Himself has given us right standing with Himself. Who then will condemn us? No one—for Christ Jesus died for us and was raised to life for us, and He is sitting in the place of honor at God's right hand, pleading for us." (Romans 8:33,34 NLT) The revelation of our perfect right standing before the Father is strategically designed to set us free from every demonic assignment of accusation and condemnation. "So now there is no condemnation for those who belong to Christ Jesus." (Romans 8:1 NLT)

Paul said, "Therefore from now on we recognize no one according to the flesh!" (2 Corinthians 5:16 NASB) The powers of darkness relentlessly seek to trick us into believing that we are still who we once were before we came to Christ. But Paul strenuously emphasized that we are no longer defined in any way by who we were when we were still in the flesh. "Those who are in the flesh cannot please God. However, you are not in the flesh but in the Spirit, if indeed the Spirit of God dwells in you." (Romans 8:8,9 NASB) We began our Christian life in the Spirit because we were supernaturally baptized into Christ and into the Holy Spirit. "Are you so foolish? Having begun in the Spirit, are you now being made perfect by the flesh?" (Galatians 3:3) It is a witchcraft spell that bewitches us into identifying ourselves according to the flesh. The devil works overtime to disorient us so that we always see ourselves from an earthly perspective. Paul said, "Oh, foolish Galatians! Who has cast an evil spell on you?" (Galatians 3:1 NLT)

Our new focus must be relentlessly upon Christ and His resurrection power over sin and death. We are commanded to "Fix our eyes on Jesus, the author and perfecter of our faith." (Hebrews 12:2) By fixing our eyes on Him we keep our focus upon the infinite supply of His Spirit and the limitless resources of the riches of His glory. Paul's permanent affirmation was: "My God shall supply all your need according to His riches in glory by Christ Jesus." (Philippians 4:19) The more we train ourselves to keep our eyes on Christ the more we will see who Christ is to us, who Christ is in us and who Christ is for us in every single situation. This is heaven's perspective! Part of sharing in the mind of Christ means that we get to see every problem we face as an opportunity for God to reveal His glory and His response to the problem, which is always Christ in you, the confident expectation of glory.

The heart journey is always built upon the foundation of learning to live from the new heart that God has already given us. Everything flows out of our glorified spirit and our capacity to activate and release our spirit through faith in the finished work of Christ. This is how we activate the flow of rivers of living water out of our innermost being. Christians who seek to embrace the heart journey without a strong revelation of the new creation miracle will go around and around in circles and will never fully learn how to live from the new heart that God has given them. A diminished revelation of Christ in us will significantly compromise the true heart journey. In contrast, a powerful, vibrant revelation of Christ in us and of our new nature in Christ sets us up for a glorious life lived from the foundation of new creation revelation.

Paul confidently proclaimed, "It's no longer I who lives; but Christ who lives in me!" (Galatians 2:20) He said, "For me to live is Christ!" (Philippians 1:21) Paul endlessly prophesied about "Christ, who is our life!" (Colossians 3:4) This is unquestionably how we ought to now live our lives as true followers of Christ. We are never permitted to take our eyes off Christ even when He addresses issues of hardness of heart, rebellion, stubbornness and deep emotional brokenness. Jesus doesn't highlight our strongholds to get us to fix our eyes on our strongholds. We need to be mindful of the actual condition of our heart at every point along the journey but we are to keep both eyes fixed squarely on Jesus and His unlimited resources. Our brokenness is merely the background noise that sets the stage and the context for God to display His glory in our life.

We escape the entanglements of the world, the flesh, the lies of the devil, our emotional brokenness, of demons and of religion through remaining resolutely focused upon our glorious new entanglement with Christ and with the Father through the Holy Spirit. Do not be entangled in anything that constitutes your old life but continually stay filled with the revelation of your entanglement with the triune Godhead and make it your quest to experientially live out the glory of your entanglement in the power and the divine nature of Christ. As you experientially step into the exceeding greatness of His resurrection power you significantly marginalize and displace everything that would seek to pull your heart out from the reality of your supernatural entanglement with the life of Christ. Our life is truly "hidden with Christ in God." (Colossians 3:3) We have a glorious identity.

Paul held in perfect tension the reality of these two spheres of entanglement, never denying or disputing the harsh and painful reality of the believer's entanglement with what he identified as 'old' but never denying the glory of our new entanglement in Christ. In many ways the concept of entanglement becomes the perfect metaphor for the heart journey. Are you increasingly being immersed in the ever-deepening revelation of your divine entanglement in the divine nature of Christ? Are you fully cognizant of your ongoing experiential heart entanglements in what Paul identified as old? I am personally fascinated by the way both Paul and John held these two realities in a careful theological tension. This was not accidental but powerfully intentional. If we can also walk in this divine tension we will be one step closer to walking in the victory of the life of the apostles.

As a mature son, Paul was so resolutely focused upon the glory of Christ in us that every obstacle and hindrance could only be legitimately viewed through the lens of the new creation. At the crescendo of his new creation revelation, as Romans 8 reached its glorious pinnacle, Paul asks; "Who shall separate us from the love of Christ? Shall trouble or hardship or persecution or famine or nakedness or danger or sword? No, in all these things we are more than conquerors through Him who loved us." (Romans 8:35,37 NIV) Paul never took his eyes off who Christ was or who Christ wanted to be to us in every single situation that life could bring. Whatever situation we face, no matter how strong the entanglement might appear, Christ is always greater and able to lead us into personal triumph. In every situation on life's challenging journey we can ask the question: who is Christ to me in this situation and what is His glorious solution for me. His glory powerfully corresponds to every valley, every mountain, every giant and every stronghold.

The spirit/soul paradigm serves as the perfect template to understand the different dynamics that are present in the journey of the heart as we walk out of everything that is old and into everything that is new. Old things have fully passed away in your spirit but they are still passing away in the life of your soul. Christ is both the author and the perfecter of our faith. The more our faith is perfected by Christ the more we will live from a deep consciousness of the pre-eminence of Christ in us and His glorious triumph over everything that would exalt itself above the knowledge of God in our lives. Perfect faith is centered upon the glory of Christ in us in the fullness of His resurrection power. This has to become the heartbeat of the true believer.

Unwavering Intentionality

Apart from a glorious vision of the new heart that Jesus has already given us, perhaps the greatest life skill of all is in embracing the call to the heart journey and in not allowing ourselves to be turned aside from this journey for the rest of our life here on earth. The Bible beckons us from cover to cover to keep our heart with all diligence! So many Christians appear to lack the necessary degree of intentionality to overcome. My own journey has so often been characterized by a lack of personal resolve to overcome. So often my intentionality has been the missing ingredient. God wants us to become so focused on activating the glory of the new creation that it borders on obsession. It really takes that level of intentionality and devotion because without such singleness of purpose we are easily diverted into setting our focus upon our brokenness and our strongholds and this is a recipe for a life of condemnation and shame. We need to find the place of balance where we never go into a state of denial about the actual condition of our heart but neither do we focus exclusively upon the brokenness because that always leads to identity problems. Far too many followers of Jesus build their identity around their brokenness and their pain instead of building it around the glory of their sonship and that is always the devil's plan. Our identity has to be built upon the solid rock of who we are in Christ and who Christ is in us. Anything short of this destabilizes our lives and gets our eyes off Jesus and onto our brokenness.

Each of us must lay hold of a high level of intentionality if we are going to see the glory of Christ in us overcome all of the entanglements of the soul. These entanglements are strong; that is why Paul calls them strongholds! They are so strong that they have held the vast majority of Christians throughout church history in bondage to one or all of the seven major entanglements that we have previously outlined. Take a look around you at the state of the church and recognize that the path of the overcomer is unquestionably the road less travelled. Look within your own heart and recognize that the same things that have held your brothers and sisters in a state of uninterrupted entanglement in their old life are the very same things that have held you in spiritual bondage. None of us are in a position to judge our brethren. The challenges all of us face in overcoming the enemies of our soul reveal that there are a number of indispensable virtues that a believer must seriously contend for if they are going to join the ranks of the overcomers.

Apart from the revelation of the new heart, the greatest need of every Christian in this crucial hour of history is a supernatural infusion of divine intentionality. Jesus set His face like flint to go up to Jerusalem. (Luke 9:51) He must have experienced considerable temptation to turn aside from the destiny of the cross. But when Jesus purposed something in His heart He fixed His heart in such a manner that nothing in all of hell could deter Him from fulfilling the intentions of His heart. There is a dimension of divine intentionality that God wants to impart to each of us out of the limitless resources of the nature of Christ in us. The combinational effect of the revelation of the glory of the new creation combined with an impartation of divine intentionality is sufficient to equip us for a life of overcoming every conceivable entanglement that could potentially hinder us from fulfilling God's perfect will for our life. There is no such thing as a true heart journey apart from these two factors being powerfully yoked together inside of our heart. If we have a new heart, how can we tolerate living our life from the old heart of sin and selfishness?

Bringing Many Sons to Glory

The heart journey is not just about your personal freedom and transformation as an end in itself. God requires us to wholeheartedly embrace the heart journey so that He ultimately gets what He paid for with His own blood. Paul sets the journey of our personal transformation in a much broader context in the latter half of Romans chapter 8. He sets your journey from the bondage of the orphan heart to the freedom of the heart of authentic sonship in cosmic terms. He proclaims that the entire creation is groaning in travail in eager anticipation of the 'unveiling' or the 'manifestation' of the sons of God. We are sons because we are in the Beloved Son. The Father now regards us as sons who are fully entitled to participate in the same inheritance as Jesus the Son. We are joint heirs with Christ.

> For His Holy Spirit speaks to us deep in our hearts and tells us that
> we are God's children. And since we are His children, we will share
> His treasures – for everything God gives to His Son, Christ, is ours,
> too. But if we are to share His glory, we must also share His
> suffering. (Romans 8:16,17 NLT)

There is a future glory of the saints that will not be revealed in its fullness until
we receive our glorified bodies at the resurrection of the dead. Nevertheless,
there is a dimension of glory that God is unveiling in us in this present age in
proportion to our willingness to be conformed to the image of the Son in all
His glory. Paul proclaimed that the creation is in travail for the sons of God to
be revealed in glory.

> For I consider that the sufferings of this present time are not worthy
> to be compared with the glory which shall be revealed in us. For the
> earnest expectation of the creation eagerly waits for the revealing of
> the sons of God. For the creation was subjected to futility, not
> willingly, but because of Him who subjected it in hope; because the
> creation itself also will be delivered from the bondage of corruption
> into the glorious liberty of the children of God. For we know that the
> whole creation groans and labors with birth pangs together until now.
> (Romans 8:18-22)

There are clear indications in the New Testament that there is a present
glorification of the souls of those who are allowing the Father to transform
their hearts into the likeness of the heart of Jesus. "It was only right that God –
who made everything and for whom everything was made – should bring His
many children into glory." (Hebrews 2:10 NLT) Jesus has imparted His glory
to our regenerated spirit and now He is imparting His glory to every part of our
soul as we submit to this process of supernatural transformation. During His
incarnation the soul of Jesus was filled with a heavenly glory and this becomes
the template for our glorious destiny in Him. "But we all, with unveiled face,
beholding as in a mirror the glory of the Lord, are being transformed into the
same image from glory to glory, just as by the Spirit of the Lord." (2
Corinthians 3:18) To the extent that the resurrection life of Jesus is made
manifest through our mind, will and emotions, to that same extent we are
entering into a participation in the divine nature of Jesus that is resplendent
with the radiant glory of God.

A human being under the government of the Holy Spirit, whose spirit has been supernaturally united with the very Spirit of Jesus, has the capacity through the cultivation of self-governance to powerfully express the glory of God in their mind, in their will and in their emotions. In the New Covenant God's glory comes upon human hearts instead of upon furniture. That is why the New Covenant is much more glorious than the Old Covenant. Transformed sons and daughters are infinitely more effective in revealing the glory of God upon the earth. The Father is bringing His many sons and daughters to glory so that His glory may be powerfully revealed to all of humanity. Jesus said, "The glory which You gave Me I have given them, that they may be one just as We are one: I in them, and You in Me; that they may be made perfect in one, and that the world may know that You have sent Me, and have loved them as You have loved Me." (John 17:22,23)

Paul taught that sons and daughters who have been made holy and pure in their soul as well as in their spirit are of infinitely greater usefulness to the Father. "In a large house there are articles not only of gold and silver, but also of wood and clay; some are for noble purposes and some for ignoble. If a man cleanses himself from the latter, he will be an instrument for noble purposes, made holy, useful to the Master and prepared to do any good work." (2 Timothy 2:20,21 NIV) The implication is that Christians who refuse to yield to the Refiner's fire effectively remain useless when it comes to God's glorious kingdom purposes. This means that our heart journey of supernatural transformation is of great prophetic significance in the highest purposes of God.

The King of Glory is utterly intentional about His glory covering the earth as the waters cover the sea but He cannot accomplish His ultimate intention without a company of sons and daughters who also intentionally embrace the heart journey of transitioning from glory to glory. Only the most intentional followers of Jesus who devote themselves to the heart journey of genuine supernatural transformation break through into the glorious liberty of those whom Jesus identifies as 'overcomers.' To give the Father what He desires we must passionately embrace the heart journey with wholehearted devotion.

The Scroll of Your Prophetic Destiny

No believer has ever fulfilled God's ultimate prophetic purpose for his or her life without embracing the fullness of the heart journey revealed in the

Scriptures. Embracing the heart journey is the key to fulfilling your prophetic destiny. Did you know that God has a glorious prophetic destiny for you to fulfil on the earth? As Jesus is in this world, so are we, because we are now His brethren and His joint heirs. Our life is now gloriously entangled in His life and in His continuing prophetic destiny. The Father gloriously predestined the entire life of His beloved Son. Jesus had a pre-determined prophetic destiny. There was literally a prophetic script written for Jesus to walk in. "Then I said, "Behold, I have come; in the volume of the book it is written of Me; to do Your will, O God." (Hebrews 10:7) The NIV says: "Here I am: it is written about Me in the scroll: I have come to do your will, O God." This was a Messianic prophecy originally written by David in the Psalms. "Sacrifice and offering You did not desire; My ears You have opened. Burnt offering and sin offering You did not require. Then I said, "Behold, I come; in the scroll of the book it is written of me. I delight to do Your will, O my God." (Psalm 40:6-8)

The entire life of Jesus was foreknown before the creation of the world. "He indeed was foreordained before the foundation of the world, but was manifest in these last times for you." (1 Peter 1:20) Jesus was "the Lamb that was slain from the creation of the world." (Revelation 13:8 NIV) His life was powerfully foretold from the beginning. Even in the Garden of Eden, God revealed that the 'seed' of Eve would 'crush' the head of the serpent even though the seed of the serpent would bruise His heel. "I will put enmity between you and the woman, and between your offspring and hers; he will crush your head, and you will strike his heel." (Genesis 3:15 NIV) This ancient prophecy foretold the glorious victory of the crucifixion of Christ that destroyed the works of the evil one.

The life, ministry, death and resurrection of Jesus were all powerfully detailed throughout the Old Testament. David and Isaiah in particular were taken into prophetic encounters where they saw detailed aspects of the life of Jesus. The Old Testament contains the prophecies of the coming Messiah of Israel and of the entire world. The Messiah would be born in Bethlehem of the Tribe of Judah. He would become "the Lion of the Tribe of Judah!"

> Judah, your brothers will praise you; your hand will be on the neck of your enemies; your father's sons will bow down to you. You are a lion's cub, O Judah; you return from the prey, my son. Like a lion he crouches and lies down, like a lioness; who dares to rouse him? The scepter will not depart from Judah, nor the ruler's staff from his

descendants, until the coming of the One to whom it belongs, the One whom all nations will obey. (Genesis 49:8-10 NIV/NLT)

Many of the details of the life of Jesus were prophetically foretold in the Old Testament. In fact, there are 61 major Messianic prophecies concerning the life of Jesus. Here are just a few. "But as for you, Bethlehem Ephrathah, too little to be among the clans of Judah; from you One will go forth for Me to be ruler in Israel. His goings forth are from long ago, from the days of eternity." (Micah 5:2 NASB) "Therefore the Lord Himself will give you a sign: behold, the virgin shall conceive and bear a Son and shall call His name Immanuel." [God with us!] (Isaiah 7:14) "For unto us a Child is born, unto us a Son is given; and the government will be upon His shoulders. And His name will be called Wonderful, Counsellor, Mighty God, Everlasting Father, Prince of Peace." (Isaiah 9:6) "Of the increase of His government and peace there will be no end. He will reign on David's throne and over his kingdom, establishing and upholding it with justice and righteousness from that time on and forever. The zeal of the Lord Almighty will accomplish this." (Isaiah 9:7 NIV)

Almost every significant aspect of the life of Messiah was foretold in the Old Testament. But beyond the ancient Scriptures, Jesus had a prophetic scroll written in heaven that foretold every single detail of His life. Jesus came and did the perfect will of His Father, fulfilling every single detail written in His prophetic scroll. "Then I said, "Behold, I come; in the scroll of the book it is written of me. I delight to do Your will, O my God." (Psalm 40:8) The scroll of the book was written in heaven as a prophetic decree. The prophets prophesied from the scroll of Christ's prophetic destiny. Every Messianic prophecy was effectively an extract from His heavenly scroll. Jesus did the will of God perfectly! He said, "For I have come down from heaven, not to do My own will, but the will of Him who sent Me." (John 6:38) "My food is to do the will of Him who sent Me and to finish His work." (John 4:34) Jesus walked in the perfect will and plan of the Father. Throughout His ministry on earth Jesus must have felt an uncanny sense of déjà vu as though He had seen it all from before the foundation of the world.

Just as Jesus was ordained before the foundation of the world, so we have been similarly ordained. We become part of God's redemptive story because we are in Christ. In fact, we are now swept up in Jesus' prophetic destiny!

He chose us in Him before the foundation of the world that we should be holy and without blame before Him in love, having predestined us to adoption as sons by Jesus Christ to Himself, according to the good pleasure of His will, to the praise of the glory of His grace, by which He has made us accepted in the Beloved. (Ephesians 1:4-6)

Listen to how beautifully The Passion Translation describes our glorious destiny.

He chose us to be His very own, joining us to Himself even before He laid the foundation of the Universe. Because of His great love He ordained us as one with Christ from the beginning so that we would be seen in His eyes with an unstained innocence. For it was always in His perfect plan to adopt us as His delightful children so that His tremendous grace that cascades over us would bring Him glory – for the same love He has for His Beloved Son, Jesus, He has for us! (TPT)

Paul luxuriated in the revelation of our glorious predestination from before the foundation of the Universe.

In Him also we have obtained an inheritance, being predestined according to the purpose of Him who works all things according to the counsel of His will that we who first trusted in Christ should be to the praise of His glory. (Ephesians 1:11,12)

Again, The Passion Translation explains our destiny as beloved sons and daughters.

This is why God selected and ordained us to be His own inheritance through our union with Christ! Before we were even born, **He gave us our destiny**, that we would fulfil the plan of God who always accomplished every purpose and plan in His heart. (Ephesians 1:11,12 TPT)

We have a glorious destiny because we are in mystical union with Christ. God's predestination is based entirely upon His foreknowledge. "For those whom He foreknew, He also predestined to be conformed to the image of His Son, that He might be the firstborn among many brethren." (Romans 8:29)

Predestination is a 'pre-determined destiny' that was previously ordained by the counsel of Almighty God. You have been gloriously predestined to be conformed to the image of the glorious Son of God. Paul taught that the wisdom of the cross was ordained for our glory!

> But we speak the wisdom of God in a mystery, the hidden wisdom which God ordained before the ages for our glory, which none of the rulers of this age knew; for had they known, they would not have crucified the Lord of glory. (1 Corinthians 2:7,8)

The Amplified Bible goes a step deeper in explaining the ultimate purpose of Christ's atonement upon the cross. It was for our glorification with Christ.

> But rather what we are setting forth is a wisdom of God once hidden from human understanding and now revealed to us by God — a wisdom which God devised and decreed before the ages for our glorification; to lift us into the glory of His presence. (1 Corinthians 2:7 AMP)

Paul revealed that our prophetic destiny in Christ is to be filled with God's glory. "That He might make known the riches of His glory on the vessels of mercy, whom He had prepared beforehand for glory." (Romans 9:23) You have been "prepared in advance for glory!" (NIV) Even from before the foundation of the world. David said, "You guide me with your counsel, leading me to a glorious destiny." (Psalms 73:24 NLT) Our glorious destiny is that Christ might be revealed in us and through us as we embrace the journey of the heart into the fullness of sonship. "Living within you is the Christ who floods you with the expectation of glory. This mystery of Christ, embedded within us, becomes a heavenly treasure chest filled with the riches of glory for His people." (Colossians 1:27 TPT) "He called you to this through our gospel, that you might share in the glory of our Lord Jesus Christ." (2 Thessalonians 2:14 NIV)

It is only in the context of God's glory that we discover our true prophetic destiny. Through the new birth we have been supernaturally restored to the glory realm of heaven. As new creations we now live from a glory filled center! God's glory is revealed as you and I step into our divine destiny. The prophetic destiny of Christ did not end at His ascension into heaven. There is a proceeding glory that extends beyond the life of Christ on earth. "Dear Theophilus: in my first book I told you about everything Jesus **began** to do and teach until the day He ascended to heaven after giving His chosen apostles further instructions from the Holy Spirit." (Acts 1:1,2 NLT) Christ's personal destiny has now gone corporate. Paul said, "For me to live is Christ!" Christ now lives His life and His unfolding prophetic destiny through us!!! "For as the body is one and has many members, but all the members of that one body, being many, are one body, *so also is Christ*." (1 Corinthians 12:12) Christ has now become a many membered body. This means that your destiny is now swept up in Christ fulfilling the entire scroll of His prophetic destiny.

> My old life was crucified with Christ and no longer lives; for I was fully united with Him in His death. And now the essence of this new life is no longer mine, for Christ lives His life through me! My real life is Christ – we live as one! My new life is empowered by the faith of the Son of God who loves me so much that He gave Himself for me, and dispenses His life into mine! (Galatians 2:20 TPT)

Christ now lives His life and destiny through us! All that is written in the volume of the scroll concerning Christ is now being outworked through those who are willing to fully step into their prophetic destiny. Each individual believer now has a personal prophetic destiny and plan for their life. Our personal destiny is the destiny of Christ expressed uniquely in us and through us. "For I know the plans I have for you," declares the Lord, "plans to prosper you and not to harm you, plans to give you hope and a future." (Jeremiah 29:11 NIV)

Just like Jesus, you have a glorious future destiny that is also written in a book. David said, "Your eyes saw my substance, being yet unformed. And in Your book they all were written, the days fashioned for me, when as yet there were none of them." (Psalms 139:16) "All the days ordained for me were written in your book before one of them came to be." (Psalms 139:16 NIV) "Your eyes have seen my unformed substance; and in Your book were written all the days that were ordained for me, when as yet there was not one of them." (Psalms 139:16 NASB) There is a book written in heaven for each of us who are in Christ. In fact, there is a whole library of books in heaven; each one telling the full prophetic destiny of every single Christian who will ever live. These prophetic books contain your perfect prophetic destiny. Part of our transformation is found in embracing the revelation that each of us now has a glorious personal destiny because we are in Christ and He is still fulfilling what has been written in His prophetic scroll from before the foundation of the world.

Your prophetic scroll exists in heaven and declares the perfect will of God for your life. "Be transformed by the renewing of your mind, that you may prove what is that good and acceptable and perfect will of God." (Romans 12:2) God wants to fill you with the knowledge of His will for your life. "For this reason we also, since the day we heard it, do not cease to pray for you, and to ask that you may be filled with the knowledge of His will in all wisdom and spiritual understanding." (Colossians 1:9) Part of being filled with the knowledge of His will includes a deepening understanding of our personal destiny. Jesus said, "When He, the Spirit of truth, has come, He will guide you into all truth; for He will not speak on His own authority, but whatever He hears He will speak; and He will tell you things to come." (John 16:13) The NLT says, "He will tell you about the future." Paul revealed that there is a perfect predestined plan for each and every Christian.

> For we are God's own handiwork; His workmanship, recreated in Christ Jesus, born anew that we may do those good works which God predestined or planned beforehand for us; taking paths which He prepared ahead of time, that we should walk in them. (Ephesians 2:10 AMP)

Again, The Passion Translation opens up the full intent of this passage.

> We have become His poetry; a recreated people that will fulfil the destiny He has given each of us, for we are joined to Jesus, the Anointed One. Even before we were born, God planned in advance our destiny and the good works we would do to fulfil it! (TPT)

Paul used the Greek word, '*poema.*' Each of you are poems being written by God as you step into a gloriously awakened state in Christ and as you walk out your prophetic destiny. Prophecy always invites you into God's perfect will. Prophecy never declares God's second best for your life. Prophecy always reveals God's highest calling. Paul said, "I press toward the goal for the prize of the high calling of God in Christ Jesus." (Philippians 3:14 J. B. Phillips) Prophecy is taking a page from your destiny scroll in heaven. It is always an invitation to embrace your prophetic destiny. We need to value our prophetic words because they are already written in heaven.

Paul Erdos was a brilliant Hungarian mathematician. He spoke of '*The Book*,' an imaginary book in which God had written down the best and most elegant proofs for mathematical theorems. Lecturing in 1985 he said, "You don't have to believe in God, but you should believe in 'The Book.' When he saw a particularly beautiful mathematical proof he would exclaim, "This one's from The Book!" When you hear a prophetic word spoken over you that powerfully resonates inside your heart you can exclaim: "This one is from the book!" We need to write our prophetic words down and revisit them regularly. We can use our prophetic words as weapons with which we contend in the spirit to lay hold of our highest prophetic destiny. "This charge I commit to you, son Timothy, according to the prophecies previously made concerning you, that by them you may wage the good warfare." (1 Timothy 1:18)

Satan is a destiny stealer and always seeks to rob our future hope. So many Christians fail to reach their prophetic destiny. There are a lot of scrolls flying around in heaven that are never read or even opened. Zechariah saw one of these flying scrolls. "I looked up again and saw a scroll flying through the air. "What do you see?" the angel asked. "I see a flying scroll," I replied. "It appears to be about thirty feet long and fifteen feet wide." (Zechariah 5:1,2 NLT) That's a big scroll! Similarly, Ezekiel saw a scroll and was instructed to eat it.

> Now when I looked, there was a hand stretched out to me; and behold, a scroll of a book was in it. Then He spread it before me. Moreover He said to me, "Son of man, eat what you find; eat this scroll, and go, speak to the house of Israel. So I opened my mouth, and He caused me to eat that scroll. And He said to me, "Son of man, feed your belly, and fill your stomach with this scroll that I give you." So I ate, and it was in my mouth like honey in sweetness. (Ezekiel 2:9-3:3)

When you eat the scroll you become the scroll and the scroll becomes a part of you. Perhaps this is what Paul meant when he described us as 'living epistles.'

> The only letter of recommendation we need is you yourselves. Your lives are a letter written in our hearts; everyone can read it and recognize our good work among you. Clearly, you are a letter from Christ showing the result of our ministry among you. This 'letter' is written not with pen and ink, but with the Spirit of the living God. It

is carved not on tablets of stone, but on human hearts. (2 Corinthians 3:2,3 NLT)

You and I are living scrolls! When you eat the scroll you and your future destiny become one! We are present-future people who are now powerfully overshadowed by our prophetic destiny. The poem of your life is still being written. As you step forth into your destiny the poetry of your life is being written. We all should want our lives on earth to be identical to the destiny scroll that has been written in heaven so the two books become one and the same. The history of Jesus' life on earth perfectly resembled what had been written in the volume of His book. I want my personal history to match my prophetic destiny. Like Zechariah and Ezekiel, we are urged to take the flying scroll of your destiny and eat it so that it becomes part of you! Jesus lived in the joy of perfectly walking on earth in the perfect will of the Father and so can we! But the only way we will fulfil the perfect will of God for each of our personal lives is if we are willing to embrace the heart journey of supernatural conformity to the Son in all of His glory.

Passing Through the Valley of Weeping

The language of the heart is often expressed through tears. A significant part of the heart journey is the recovery of a capacity to weep over our own brokenness to release the pain that gets locked inside of us. For David, there were seasons where tears were part of his daily experience. He wrote about this unlocking of his heart in his prayer journal. "Day and night, I have only tears for food, while my enemies continually taunt me, saying, "Where is this God of yours?" My heart is breaking as I remember how it used to be." (Psalm 42:3,4 NLT) He said, "I am worn out from sobbing. Every night tears drench my bed; my pillow is wet from weeping." (Psalm 6:6 NLT) "You keep track of all my sorrows. You have collected all my tears in your bottle." (Psalm 56:8 NLT) "Weeping may endure for a night but joy comes in the morning." (Psalms 30:5) "Those who sow in tears will reap with songs of joy. He who goes out weeping, carrying seed to sow, will return with songs of joy, carrying sheaves with him." (Psalm 126:5,6 NIV)

There is a day coming when all sorrow will finally cease. "God will wipe away every tear from their eyes; there shall be no more death, nor sorrow, nor crying. There shall be no more pain, for the former things have passed away." (Revelation 21:4) We long for the day when there shall be no more pain but until that final day we will have tribulation in this world. Jesus said, "Here on earth you will have many trials and sorrows. But take heart, because I have overcome the world." (John 16:33 NLT) The greater the pain, the more people need to have their heart unlocked to release that pain through weeping. I am envious of David's capacity to break before the Lord and to pour out his soul before God. David was an emotionally connected man. He wasn't a stranger to the language of tears because he kept his heart tender before the Lord. I have come out of such generational hardness that tears do not flow as readily. I feel as though I am more able to weep than some people. As a counsellor I have met with many people who simply cannot cry. But I have learnt that there is a relationship between tenderness and the capacity to release the pain inside of our heart. In seasons when I am tender, tears are not far away but in seasons when I am battling hardness I can feel like I am channeling the hardness that characterized by forefathers.

For David in his heart journey with God there were distinct seasons of deep emotional pain and weeping. "Blessed is the man whose strength is in You, whose heart is set on pilgrimage. As they pass through the Valley of Baca they make it a spring; the rain also covers it with pools. They go from strength to strength; each one appears before God in Zion." (Psalms 84:5-7) The Hebrew word 'Baca' means weeping. The valley of weeping was a significant place of transition is David's spiritual pilgrimage. In that place he unloaded his pain by pouring it out before the Lord. If we cannot cry there is a disorder of the heart.

God has to break the hearts of His children for the costly perfume of Christ to be released. Like the alabaster jar and Gideon's 300 clay jars, something has to be broken for the fullness of Christ to be released. Mark tells the story of a woman who approached Jesus with an alabaster jar full of very expensive perfume who, "broke the flask and poured it on His head." (Mark 14:3) Gideon commanded 300 warriors to break their clay pots to reveal light to the encircled enemy. Paul calls us earthen vessels or jars of clay and by implication; those vessels must be broken to reveal the excellency of God's great power in us. These prophetic pictures of broken vessels points to the necessity of breaking before the Lord in weeping for what is inside of us to fully shine forth.

In a vision the Lord took Ezekiel into the temple and showed him a series of scenes that spoke of His prophetic purposes. In one scene he saw the Lord instruct a man clothed in linen with a writer's kit on his side to "Walk through the streets of Jerusalem and put a mark on the foreheads of all those who weep and sigh because of the sins they see around them." (Ezekiel 9:4 NLT) Throughout the Bible weeping over sin and the brokenness of humanity is extolled as a great virtue of humility and intimacy with God. Tears are the language of the heart journey and if we want to do this journey well we need to recover the capacity to weep as we release our pain to God.

Wholehearted Lovers

The goal of the heart journey is to live our lives as wholehearted lovers of God. The first and second greatest commandments cited by Jesus both have wholehearted love at the center. Jesus said, "You shall love the Lord your God with all your heart, with all your soul, and with all your mind." This is the first and great commandment. And the second is like it: "You shall love your neighbor as yourself." On these two commandments hang all the Law and the Prophets." (Matthew 22:37-40) To love with our whole heart means we no longer live with a divided heart. In the book of Hosea, God's primary complaint against Israel was that, "Their heart is divided!" (Hosea 10:2) They believed in God but were not following Him with all their heart.

A wholehearted lover of God and of people is living from the new heart God has given them. They have discovered the inexhaustible, unlimited resource of the love of God flowing out of their innermost being and have learnt how to release it back to God and to every person they come in contact with. John said, "We love because He first loved us." (1 John 4:19 NIV) We cannot give away what we haven't received, so first we must receive and experience the love of God so that we can give it away. Beloved sons and daughters inevitably become lovers.

God wholeheartedly loves us and His ultimate goal in conforming us to the image of His Son is to make us wholehearted lovers. Jesus said that everyone will know we are His disciples by our love for one another. Our genuine love for one another proves our love for God because we cannot love God unless we love those whom God has placed in our lives. "If anyone says, "I love God," yet hates his brother, he is a liar. For anyone who does not love his brother, whom he has seen, cannot love God, whom he has not seen." (1 John 4:20 NIV) Biblically, our capacity to connect relationally with God is ultimately measured by our capacity to connect with people. This means that our heart journey isn't a privatized affair, worked out exclusively between God and me. It is a relational journey of interpersonal growth in love with the people God brings into my life.

Our human relationships are a remarkable litmus test of our real relationship with God. Our ability to connect with God is ultimately determined by our heart capacity to connect with the people we are in relationship with. Our human relationships are a stark reflection of our relationship with the Father and with Jesus as our brother. The critical heart issues that hinder our growth of wholehearted connection with people are the very same issues that hinder our wholehearted love for God. This means our human relationships become the mirror of our relationship with God. We cannot kid ourselves into thinking we have a great relationship with God when we have lousy human relationships. The touchstones of failure in our human relationships shine the light on our relational failures with the Father.

The old orphan heart is fundamentally non-relational. We are not just orphans in relation to God but also in relation to one another. A spiritual orphan is experientially disconnected from the Father but he or she is also experientially disconnected and dislocated from family. Restoration to wholeheartedness means a return both to the Father and to our core relationships. Love is the ultimate measure of spiritual maturity and growth. If we are not growing in love we are not really growing. God certainly has a way of keeping our heart journey simple and uncomplicated. There are clearly defined key indicators of genuine growth and these key indicators are all relational.

As we noted in the earlier chapter; *The Context of the Heart Journey*, we cannot walk out this heart journey with God in a vacuum. The context of the journey is our human relationships and doing life together in community. We are failing in our heart journey when we are failing in our relationships. A divided heart is not exclusively locked onto loving relationships. Our old self-centered existence is still active when our heart is divided. Sin and fear are the polar opposites of love. A fearful heart cannot love because fear is at the center instead of love.

If we find people scary and if we find certain people scarier than others we cannot walk in love because there is no fear in love. If our goal is to remain relationally safe through strategies of self-protection and keeping a safe distance from scary people we cannot grow in love because fear is the guiding principle. Danny Silk, author of *Keep Your Love On*, says "The truth is that every relationship has one of two goals: connection or disconnection." Orphans are fearful because they do not feel safe in relationship. But as we grow as beloved sons and daughters, confident of our Father's great love for us, we can break out of the fear cycle and step powerfully into other people's lives in pursuit of loving connections. We can begin to love others because we know that we are loved. God wants to uproot all fear from our lives so that we can become great lovers; husbands, wives, fathers, mothers, sons and daughters. Our journey of supernatural transformation is ultimately a journey into love.

Every entanglement we have outlined in this book hinders our capacity to wholeheartedly love God and to love one another. We have to conquer the mountain of 'me' if we want to be successful in our great calling to love. Paul said, "Live a life of love, just as Christ loved us and gave Himself up for us as a fragrant offering and sacrifice to God." (Ephesians 5:2 NIV) Entanglement in sin and selfishness is the very antithesis of a life of love. We cannot love God and love the world at the same time. Entanglement in the world distracts us from our spiritual journey of growth in love.

Entanglement in the tree of the knowledge of good and evil has nothing to do with a life of love because the focus is always upon religious performance as the basis of our acceptance with both God and people. Entanglement in emotional brokenness is a certain killer to walking in love. Whenever the destructive and toxic emotions of fear, rejection or shame rule our hearts we are comprehensively incapacitated to walk in love. Similarly, entanglement in demonic infiltration is not going to facilitate a life of love. Indwelling demons have a way of destroying all of our relationships. In the same way, when our neurological pathways are totally jammed up by biochemically programmed responses of fear; love becomes a complete impossibility! The management and conquest of the mountain of 'me' is crucial if we want to fulfil our prophetic destiny to be conformed to the image of love.

In the next and final book in this series; *The Glory of God and Supernatural Transformation*, we will explore the transformation of the human heart through the lens of our movement out of a life ruled by fear and brokenness into a life ruled by love and connection with God and one another. The focal point of our transformational journey is upon our relationships. The heart journey is a deep journey into community. At the center of our transformational journey of the heart is the glory of God to which we have been gloriously restored. All have sinned and fallen short of the glory of God but through the atonement of Christ we are restored to the glory of God by being planted in the garden of the Father's infinite and perfect love. The cross has made us one with divine love again. Atonement means at-one-ment.

The cross is God's supernatural means of making us 'at one' with the Father and the Son through the indwelling of the Holy Spirit. Our perichoresis [mutual indwelling], or divine entanglement in the love of the Father, Son and Holy Spirit is the supernatural key to unlock the fullness of the realm of heavenly love, ecstasy and bliss in our relationships. This miracle of being supernaturally planted in the garden of God's perfect love becomes the portal of a supernatural life of wholehearted love for God and for everyone we are in relationship with. Our supernatural transformation is exclusively defined by the experience of loving connection. This is the heart journey to which we are all invited.

Footnotes

[1] Graham Cooke: *A Divine Confrontation.* p. 214-218
[2] 168 = 24 x 7 NKJV Version
[3] A. W. Tozer:
[4] A. W. Tozer: The Knowledge of the Holy p.54-5
[5] ibid p. 2
[6] Larry Crabb: Understanding People   p.129 (Marshall Pickering London 1987)
[7] Richard Lovelace: Dynamics of the Spiritual Life p.86-7 (Downers Grove, Ill.: InterVarsity, 1979)
[8] John White: Changing On The Inside   p.58-59
[9] J.E. Colwell: 'Sin' in New Dictionary of Theology p.642
[10] Lovelace op.cit. p.88,89
[11] Crabb op.cit. p.123
[12] Watchman Nee quoted in the Women of Destiny Bible p.758
[13] 'Perisseuo' in Colin Brown: New International Dictionary of New Testament Theology.
[14] See Wayne Grudem's discussion on "The Definition of Sin" in Systematic Theology p.491
[15] See Titus 1:7, and 2 Peter 2:10
[16] Romans 2:8
[17] "And it's trouble ahead if you're satisfied with yourself. Your self will not satisfy you for long." Luke 6:31 The Message
[18] "Whoever exalts himself will be humbled." Matthew 23:12
[19] Romans 11:25 The Message
[20] Galatians 5:26 The Message
[21] "Obsession with self in these matters is a dead end; attention to God leads us out into the open, into a spacious, free life." Romans 8:12 The Message
[22] "Focusing on the self is the opposite of focusing on God. Anyone completely absorbed in self ignores God, ends up thinking more about self than God." Romans 8:13 The Message
[23] 2 Peter 2:10 The Message
[24] ibid
[25] "Fed up with their quarrelsome, self-centered ways, God blurred their eyes and dulled their ears." Romans 11:14 The Message
[26] "David was upset about the same thing: "I hope they get sick eating self-serving meals, break a leg walking their self-serving ways." Romans 11:16 The Message
[27] "Don't be so naive and self-confident. You're not exempt. You could fall flat on your face as easily as anyone else. Forget about self-confidence; it's useless. Cultivate God-confidence. 1 Corinthians 10:11 The Message
[28] "Don't be naive. There are difficult times ahead. As the end approaches, people are going to be self-absorbed, money-hungry, self-promoting, stuck-up, profane," 2Timothy 3:2 The Message
[29] Titus 1:10 The Message
[30] Matthew 23:25
[31] 1 Timothy 5:6 The Message
[32] James 3:14
[33] "But I also want you to think about how this keeps your significance from getting blown up into self-importance." 1 Corinthians 12:22 The Message

[34] Crabb op.cit. p.146-8.

[34] Matthew 23:25

[34] James 3:14

[34] "But I also want you to think about how this keeps your significance from getting blown up into self-importance." 1 Corinthians 12:22 The Message

[35] Crabb op.cit. p.94

[36] ibid

[37] J. Keith Miller: The Secret Life of The Soul p.63 (Broadman and Holman Publishers, Nashville 1997)

[38] Jeff Van Vonderen: Families Where Grace Is In Place p.28-29 (Bethany House Publishers, Mineapolis, 1992)

[39] Miller op. cit. p.64,66-67

[40] The New Testament In Modern English by J.B Phillips p.332 (Collins Fontana Books London 1972)

[41] Bruce Cockburn: Last Night of the World.

[42] Crabb op. cit. p.176-7

[43] "And behold, a spirit seizes him, and he suddenly cries out; it convulses him so that he foams at the mouth, and it departs from him with great difficulty, bruising him." (Luke 9:39)

[44] International Standard Bible Encyclopaedia Volume 1. 'Bones' p. 534

[45] Vine's Expository Dictionary of Old and New Testament Words p. 20

[46] William Gesenius: Hebrew – Chaldee Lexicon to the Old Testament. P.66

[47] NLT/NASB

[48] James G. Friesen: The Life Model: Living From the Heart Jesus Gave You p.69 (Shepherd's House Inc. Pasadena Ca. 9114 1999)

[49] ibid. p.73,75

[50] ibid. p.70-71

[51] ibid. p.72

[52] Charles Kraft: Deep Wounds, Deep Healing p.15 (Servant Publications Ann Arbor Michigan 1993)

[53] Joyce Meyer: Managing Your Emotions p.43 (Harrison House Tulsa OK. 1997)

[54] John Wimber: Power Healing p.129

[55] 'Hypsoma' in Colin Brown [Editor] The New International Dictionary of New Testament Theology

[56] http://www.theguardian.com/science/blog/2012/feb/28/how-many-neurons-human-brain

[57] http://med.stanford.edu/ism/2010/november/neuron-imaging.html

[58] ibid

[59] Kenneth Wuest: Commentary on the New Testament: Olive Tree Bible Software. Romans 7:24

[60] ibid. See Philippians 3:21

[61] ibid

[62] ibid Romans 6:6

[63] ibid Romans 6:13

[64] Experiment that convinced me online porn is the most pernicious threat facing children today: By ex-lads' mag editor Martin Daubney http://www.dailymail.co.uk/femail/article-2432591/Porn-pernicious-threat-facing-children-today-By-ex-lads-mag-editor-MARTIN-DAUBNEY.html

[65] Norman Doidge; The Brain That Changes Itself p. xix-xx

[66] ibid. p. xix

[67] ibid. p.106

[68] ibid.

[69] ibid. p.107-108

[70] ibid. p.106

[71] ibid. p.108-9

[72] ibid. p. 124-5

[73] Dr. Caroline Leaf; *Who Switched Off My Brain?*

[74] Bill Johnson: The Supernatural Power of a Transformed Mind p.62

[75] Jeffrey M. Schwartz; *The Mind and the Brain* Harper Collins, 2002

[76] Mario Beauregard & Denyse O'Leary: *The Spiritual Brain; A Neuroscientist's Case for the Existence of the Soul* p. x-xi

[77] Jeffrey M. Schwartz op. cit.

[78] Norman Doidge op. cit. p.97

[79] ibid. p. xx

Additional Information

Additional copies of this book can be easily purchased from Phil Mason's ministry website:

www.tribestore.org

Phil's website also contains a large selection of his unique teaching materials with downloadable mp3's and books. All resources can be obtained by ordering through our online store. PayPal, Master Card and Visa Card facilities are available for safe online transactions. We ship books anywhere in the southern hemisphere. Additional postage and shipping charges apply. To obtain quantities of this book for bookstores in Australia please contact: Phil Mason by writing to; Phil Mason, PO Box 1627, Byron Bay, New South Wales, Australia, 2481 or contact the author by email at philmason@tribebyronbay.com

To obtain copies of books by Phil Mason in the Northern hemisphere please visit www.amazon.com Phil's books are available on Kindle or in paperback.

Tribe Ministry School, Byron Bay, Australia

FOUNDED BY PHIL & MARIA MASON IN 2003, TRIBE MINISTRY SCHOOL IS A TRANSFORMATIVE, KINGDOM MINISTRY TRAINING SCHOOL

We are passionate about activating students of all ages and backgrounds into creative and prophetic expressions of heaven on earth. We offer short courses and two-day intensives, designed to train and equip you to build authentic community, grow in your creativity, walk in the supernatural and transform the culture around you. Our courses explore many different aspects of kingdom ministry and the establishment of New Testament culture including; intercession, worship, supernatural healing, creativity, the prophetic, personal heart transformation and the journey into deeper community.

TRIBE MINISTRY SCHOOL RUNS OUT OF THE TRIBE BYRON BAY MINISTRY CENTRE, LOCATED IN BYRON BAY, AUSTRALIA

To see our comprehensive list of courses visit us at:

www.tribeministryschool.com

All courses are available through attending live classes in Byron Bay that are streamed globally via 'Zoom.'

Other Books by Phil Mason

Quantum Glory: The Science of Heaven Invading Earth

Quantum Glory explores the intriguing intersection between the two realities of quantum mechanics and the glory of God. Part One of the book explores how the sub-atomic world is a revelation of exceptionally intricate divine design that unveils the mind of our Creator. In Part Two, the author explains exactly how the glory of God invades our physical universe to affect miracles of divine healing. This book is packed with revelation that is guaranteed to blow your mind! But more than that, it is designed to equip you in supernatural ministry so that you can also release the glory of God on earth as it is in Heaven!

"The real glory of this book is that it gives understanding of this wonderful world around us in a way that creates awe for what God has done. It also ignites praise in our hearts to the Creator of all, while at the same time giving us understanding of how things work. God left His message everywhere for anyone interested in truth. His fingerprints are everywhere: from the largest galaxies in existence, to the smallest thing known to man. I appreciate Phil's amazing insights and deep understanding of very difficult subjects addressed in **Quantum Glory**. I am especially thankful for his gift of taking big thoughts and breaking them down so that all of us can understand them. But I am also glad for how He values mystery. Anything that creates awe and wonder, all the while pointing to Jesus, to me is priceless. With that note, I highly recommend **Quantum Glory**. Enjoy. Be awed. Give God praise over and over again.

Bill Johnson

Senior Pastor, Bethel Church, Redding, California USA

God is still creating ways for His people to respond to His overtures. All creation speaks of Him and the language and principles of quantum physics are a vital part of His heavenly discourse with humanity. From quantum non-locality through sound waves, string theory, the mathematical order of nature, quantum geometry and the golden ratio, to the alignment between quantum physics and the supernatural, the glory of God and the key to miracles; you will understand more about the radiant nature of God in this book than in any other tome that is specifically non-specific. I heartily recommend Phil Mason to you as a leader in the field of modern day spirituality, the new sciences and the supernatural gospel of the Lord Jesus Christ.

Graham Cooke,

Author, Prophetic Speaker and Owner of Brilliant Book House.com

We are in the midst of a worldwide move of God with signs and wonders breaking out all over the world. In *'Quantum Glory,'* Phil Mason combines his passion for the science of quantum physics with his personal wealth of experience in supernatural ministry and sound Biblical theology. The result is an explosive mix of revelation that has the potential to powerfully envision and activate you to alter the very fabric of the physical world around you through the healing ministry of Christ. This book fills a vital gap in the literature that is emerging in this present wave of revival.

Dr. Che Ahn

President, Harvest International Ministry

International Chancellor, Wagner Leadership Institute

The Supernatural Transformation Series

If you have enjoyed reading this book Phil Mason has also written three additional volumes on the theme of the Supernatural Transformation of the Heart. This series outlines a supernatural Kingdom Ministry based model of personal transformation. God seeks to transform our hearts from the inside out as we embrace the call to a deep heart journey of intimacy with God and with one another in spiritual community. This profound theology of the heart puts in place all the conceptual building blocks for deep personal transformation. It begins with the miracle of the new creation and it unfolds the process of transformation from one degree of glory to another as we allow God to demolish every stronghold of the mind, the will and the emotions so that we can be gloriously transformed into the very image of Christ. The context of this transformation is spiritual community that values genuine supernatural encounter with Christ.

Volume 1: The Knowledge of the Heart

Volume 2: The New Creation Miracle

Volume 3: The Heart Journey

Volume 4: The Glory of God and Supernatural Transformation

To obtain these books visit Phil Mason's ministry website at:

www.tribestore.org

2000 years ago, Jesus came to pioneer a heart revolution that would catapult us into a dynamic, transformational journey of the heart. Jesus intended to supernaturally transition us from orphans to authentic sons and daughters who deeply know the heart of their Heavenly Father. This present-day apostolic reformation must be fueled by the healing journey that Jesus sought to initiate in our hearts, otherwise orphans will not become sons and sons will not become fathers! In the Old Testament God's glory came on furniture but in the New Testament God's glory comes on hearts.

It is time for the spiritual fathers and mothers of our nation to arise and to reveal the heart of the Father! It is time for an emotionally healthy community of beloved sons and daughters to arise. It is time to invest ourselves into the heart revolution! Tribe Byron Bay host Heart Revolution conferences in Australian capital cities. If you would like to find out more about these events please visit:

www.heartrevolution.com.au

The Glory Community: Volume 1 and 2

By Maria Mason

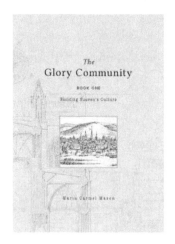 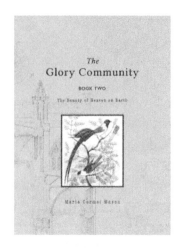

Intimate Community Has Always Been God's Dream!

How can we get back to an authentic expression of Christian community that is full of glory? In these two books, Maria Mason takes us on a journey, as she unpacks the reality that we are called to build the culture of heaven on earth within communities of faith.

Heaven's culture is built on a foundation of glory and presence filling our lives. It is a heart culture of care and expressed value, as we build upon the reality of Christ in us; the hope of glory.

The living temple of God is now built through heart connections in the context of true spiritual family that celebrates sonship. This is what cements the living stones of the temple together and attracts Heavenly glory.

Maria's writes from a deep well of experience as her community, Tribe-Byron Bay, has walked out an incredible journey for the last two decades. She paints a portrait of the radiant Bride; a church that overcomes, and is emerging as glorious and full of beauty, reflecting the Father's heart. A community of glory filled lovers! To obtain a copy of these books visit:

www.tribestore.org

Printed in Great Britain
by Amazon

46731314R00198